LAST CHANCE IN [illegible] *A*

by the same author

THE SONS OF NOAH

GOING FISHING

THE STORY OF A LAKE

BEHIND GOD'S BACK

BOMBER'S MOON
(*with Tom Purvis*)

TRANSGRESSOR IN THE TROPICS

THE WAY OF A TRANSGRESSOR

SEEING RED

SAILING ACROSS EUROPE

CAUCASIAN JOURNEY
(*in preparation*)

Negley Farson

LAST CHANCE IN AFRICA

I returned and saw under the sun that the race is not to the swift, nor the battle to the strong, neither yet bread to the wise, nor yet riches to men of understanding, nor yet favor to men of skill; but time and chance happeneth to them all.

—ECCLESIASTES

NEW YORK
HARCOURT, BRACE AND COMPANY

first American edition

Part of Chapter IX, "A Place to Fish," is printed by courtesy of *Country Life*.

PRINTED IN THE UNITED STATES OF AMERICA

to

KENYA

and the people there who have the vision of a new country, where white man, black man, Indian and Arab, can live together on terms of peace, co-operation, and something like equality of opportunity, I affectionately dedicate this book

CONTENTS

LAST CHANCE IN AFRICA

CHAPTER I

Return to Kenya

THE plane took off from Wadi Halfa in a cloudless desert dawn, and we flew eight hundred and fifty miles down over the heat haze of the Sudan, to find the Nile again where the stork-like Dinkas were standing on one leg in the delicious green marsh beside Malakal airstrip.

The black Dinkas wear no clothes, and a gorgeous display of swinging manhood met the startled eyes of some of our lady passengers; most of whom, indeed, had already had babies—and had them with us. This was when a truckload of us was driven off some distance from the plane, so that we could smoke and the babies have some fresh air, while we refuelled for the long flight over the emerald *sudd* and the elephant herds standing in the swamps of the upper Nile to Juba; then the bumpy flight over the mountains of Uganda, to come down on the shores of that great inland sea, Victoria Nyanza. For most of these women—those who were coming out to make their lives in Africa—this Dinka display was the first glimpse of one of its naked realities, the black man's breeding propensities, that was to be the major factor affecting their lives from then on. But I don't think many of them were troubled with such abstruse speculations. One of them asked me was the Sahara Desert larger than the British Isles?

But any African administrator staring at those Dinkas, living so contentedly in the marshes of the Nile, could not fail but have a lot of unhappy and uneasy thoughts come into his head: their *splendid* nakedness! Why couldn't we leave them alone? Provincial and District Commissioners become very fond of the people they are placed in charge of; it is an understanding that often develops into real love. The black man has done more to win us over than we ever have him. But we are not going to leave him alone: there is not the least chance of it. The black man is going to be forced, persuaded, cajoled into accepting our Western way of life. It is humiliating to call attention to what we think of that life ourselves. Or to state the real truth: that the white man's colonial life is parasitic upon the colored man's. Africa, still the backward continent, is the only place left (with the exception of the Indians in the Andes) where the indigenous natives are still helpless—that is, politically inarticulate; and where their side of the case—for it must always be remembered that we are also his problem—gets only the white man's interpretation placed upon it. In which, sadly enough, the would-be protectors of the African are often his worst enemies; they make such doctrinaire, unrealistic claims on his behalf. And even these intellectuals (who are seldom sufficiently intelligent) do not really love the African: they are in love with the picture of themselves, as being the "protector" of anybody. Africa is going to be "developed," whether it likes it or not. All depends, so far as the white man's morals are concerned, and the fate of the Africans, upon how it is done.

Kenya had asked me to come back largely on the strength of a book I had written about a long trip through Africa, made some ten years before. The book, *Behind God's Back*, had found favor there, though not with all Kenyans. I had given Kenya only a few pages, for one thing. This time they asked me to come back and do it again: make it all Kenya, and give as true a picture of that colony as I was able to. "Go where you like, see what you like, *say* what you like," said its Governor; then he had added a bit grimly: "I imagine you will want to be rude about many things." I have taken him at his word.

I begin this book at Wadi Halfa, because the minute I stepped out into the blinding sunlight there I wanted to walk up and shake hands with the first black man I saw. He was a huge Nubian camp guard, with slashed cheeks, looking like a scarecrow in his tattered suit of European khaki drill. He stood off at some distance, looking us over with his calm, ox-like eyes, looking worried, as if he was wondering what fresh portent, of good or bad luck, this new plane-load of Europeans could hold for him. Then our eyes met. We stared at each other, and I think he must have sensed something of what was going on in my mind; for his eyes opened widely, his thick lips gave a twitch, just the hint of a smile, and without moving another muscle he sent his message across to me—"You have been here before."

And so I had. Not at Wadi Halfa, but in the Valley of the Nile, with its strange sense of timelessness. And I had had a Nubian batman with cheeks slashed just like this man's. That was in the Egypt of 1917-18, when war was thought the supreme adventure which every completely-fulfilled man must have. I remembered Abdul, sitting on the sands out on Aboukir Point, trying to help me learn Arabic. The first sentence in *Hugo's Arabic* is not, as in all his other language books, "I love, you love, he or she loves." It was: "The Eunuch is in the Garden of the Merchant." Abdul could never understand my daily interest in eunuchs; he could hardly control his merriment. I got no further in Arabic. Abdul's one ambition was to be allowed to discard his turban and spotless white robe, to wear khaki shorts, a pith helmet, and silk purple stockings held up by pink garters, such as our miserable little crook of a camp headman delighted in—as odious a Cairo Arab as ever tried to sell you his sister. Abdul wanted to look like an *Englishman.* I opposed such progress.

But now, at Wadi Halfa, we walked across the sandy aerodrome, carrying the youngest of our plane's passengers in their delightful little pink and blue Moses-baskets, and came up against a round dozen Sudanese who had more than fulfilled Abdul's ambition. There they were in the Customs House, in shorts, khaki golf stockings, pith helmets, looking as languidly and officially bored as they could manage—looking more English than any but a dumb Englishman would dare to look. And to make us fully realise the ineffable importance of their position and their power to make trouble, they took as long as they could, making us fill out every form that a self-conscious, emerging nationalism could invent. My desire to shake hands with Africa ended with the camp guard.

You see, I still liked them primitive: that is the first thing to remember about the ordinary white man's feelings toward the colored man. *The* thing.

I begin this book at Wadi Halfa because in that quiet sunset (we had to lie there overnight) when I sat there below the Cataracts, watching the feluccas tacking up the Nile, coming about off the same spot they must have used for over a thousand years, I stared across to where the feluccas were seeking the slack water on the far side, and the bare, parched desert presses to within only a few yards of the brown river, and my mind was filled with the thoughts of all the gallant Englishmen who had passed by. Wolseley, in the ill-timed attempt to relieve Khartoum and save Gordon. Gordon, who knew that he was going to be murdered by Gladstone's bungling. Remember the last message he got out? "Now, mark this, if the expeditionary force—and I do not ask for more than two hundred men—does not come in ten days, the town may fall, and I have done my best for the honor of my country." ("Never have I known a man more like Jesus Christ," wrote Oliphant, who entertained Gordon in Jerusalem before his last return to the Sudan.) Kitchener taking Wadi Halfa on his way up to rout the Mahdi. Winston Churchill, pink-cheeked, charging with the 21st Lancers at Omdurman. A young British naval officer named Beattie pulling his gunboats up by cable through the splatter of grey rocks above me. What had it all been for? Theirs was the day of glory, ours the aftermath.

I recalled with a start that Nakroshy Pasha, the Premier of Egypt (since assassinated, and whose Chief Assassin, the head of the Moslem League, was then assassinated by his own followers—Nakroshy who, as everybody knew in Egypt at that time, had been the chief brain behind the murder of the Englishman Sirdar, Sir Lee Stack)—that Nakroshy Pasha had only recently returned from New York where, before an all-too-willing Committee of the United Nations, he had been skilfully arguing Egypt's petition to have the entire Anglo-Egyptian Sudan turned over into Egyptian hands. Such a U.N. decision would be only too easy to secure; not because the assorted Poles, White Russians and what have you—representatives of some of the most corrupt and brutal misgovernment extant—would give one damn about the fate of the poor Sudanese (not one in a hundred of whom can read a street sign), but because a recommendation for a plebiscite in the Sudan could be given as a bargain vote to Russia and her satellites, to obtain their support on other issues which might come up before the so-called statesmen at Lake Success. The main reason being, of course, that it would further embarrass hard-pressed

Britain, who seems to be everybody's whipping-boy these days. That sunset, as I sat there in what seemed the ageless peace of the Nile, the thought struck me that if England listened much more to what is commonly called world opinion, she would, in her good old way, lose every colony except the last.

I thought of those Sudanese, aping the Englishman as they officiated in the Customs House. I have often wondered as I have watched this process going on in various parts of the world—this imitation of the Englishman, wherever he has been, coupled with the increasing desire to drive him out—just what could be the cause of it all? The color bar? Yes; for the rudeness with which the second-rate white man overseas imposes that on the natives is enough to make even a worm want to get rid of him. More, the pomp and ceremony with which the Colonial Governor is invested, with a nimbus of A.D.C.'s deliberately appointed to increase his splendor (not that it always does; and it frequently has a bad effect upon His Excellency), has invariably given the leading members of any native community a soul-burning inferiority complex which nothing less than the complete evacuation of the whites can remove; whereupon the local liberators begin to get assassinated. Then, it may be, the laws regarding color relationships may have some fixed reactions—such as those governing an experiment in the chemical laboratory—in which case England would have had a date with History in the future's book. Just as have the thousands of splendidly altruistic administrators she has sent out overseas (and no nation has ever sent better), England would serve her time—and then go. No change of heart or of conduct; no attempt to get nearer the native (look at what is happening to the French and the Dutch); no willingness to be less the gentleman, less aloof, to mix with the native in his often wily and unpleasant ways—nothing could have changed it: England had to go. As she has gone, from India and Egypt.

But England will not go from Africa. That is, East and Central Africa. Kenya, Tanganyika and the two Rhodesias are *home* to thousands of good Englishmen. They are not time-serving there, intending to retire somewhere else. They *live* there. And most thinking people, those who really have the good of the African at heart, know that the English will only do good by remaining: depending upon how they do it, of course. Furthermore, as they know in their hearts that they do intend to stay in East and Central Africa, the best and the blunter among the British are saying so candidly:

> Up to a year or two ago the policy was "Africa for the Africans," which implied indirect rule and a consequent stagnation in progress, as has been emphasised lately by the Governor of Uganda. *Now the opposite course is being pursued.* In order to increase the world's production of raw materials, the word has gone out, "Full speed ahead," which means that the natives gradually must continue to come less and less under the rule of the chief and more and more to be part of *an active European organisation.* In order to carry out this new policy, tribal habits and customs have to go by the board.

How does that fit in with Tanganyika's former doctrine: "Native interests shall be paramount"?

> This is probably [*sic*] best for the African in the long run, but the Government [in Great Britain] must say so quite frankly and not wrap it up in pious hopes about Africans taking over the management or becoming the owners of great enterprises. . . .
>
> It must be made clear to the Africans of Northern Rhodesia [a British Protectorate, formerly supposed to be held in trust for the native; as was Tanganyika] and similar countries that it will be several generations before they will have sufficient experience honestly and capably to take a real part in the great enterprises or in the administration of the [their] country. . . . [All italics and brackets mine.]

That letter to *The Times* was written by Colonel Charles Ponsonby, Member of Parliament, Vice-President of the Royal African Society, Chairman of Sisal Estates, Ltd., which employs thousands of Africans on its vast plantations in East Africa.

It is an honest statement. It is the truth about the way Africa is going, as well as being true about the present, almost unbelievable, backwardness of the East Coast African. It makes you fear for the African. But—well, it is probably from such honest and open candor that the best hopes for a better Africa might come. These leading Englishmen, long versed in the handling of African problems, know better than some of their newer, more trusting colleagues that no big project can now be considered safe in the long run unless it is based upon more food, more education, and a much more intelligent understanding of the African. Long before the Labour Government found it out, these people knew that all grandiose schemes to make Africa produce food or fats, such as the gruesome £25,000,000 Groundnut Scheme in Tanganyika, cannot be morally justified, even economically sound, unless the greater part of the nourishment thus produced goes first and foremost into the half-starved black man's stomach. They know also that the black man has long since grown tired of promises. They know that, literally, Africa *has* reached a crisis: that a new *modus vivendi* must be found—something that will give real advance to the African, giving him his share of the country's development. That is, if they expect him to work for it.

I had left a Europe which was being driven almost mad by its warring ideologies; a machine-dominated civilisation, in which the white man has shown that he has learned how to run everything —except himself. The greatest danger to Africa at that time, as one saw it from London, was the frightened money trying to get out of England, to escape high taxation and nationalisation, willing to back any wildcat scheme overseas. And this, it may be said, was being amply supported by many highly placed white men in Africa: some for the money that they saw themselves making out of it, some for politics. Smuts, the most agile-minded of them all, trying to arouse the enthusiasms of one great Fleet Street editor, Frank Owen of the *Daily Mail*, later put it that "Africa is the great *reserve* [his italics] continent of the world, the last to be developed"—hoping, of course, to bring as many Europeans as he could into Africa, in order to bolster up the crisis-faced South African white population. Prominent businessmen in East Africa, going further, were informing London and New York (particularly the latter): "Africa will one day be the greatest continent in the world!"

Poor Africa. What idiotic expectations were being held out for it, that poorest of all continents on the earth's surface. What things were being said!

Sir Miles Thomas had just told what must have been a startled meeting of the Royal Empire Society that the entire sterling-dollar relationship could be altered by selling Wanki (Rhodesian) coal to the Argentine. Members of Parliament were orating about Southern Rhodesian Pittsburghs and Detroits. Listen to this one:

> I am a great enthusiast for the development of the vast resources in our territories in Africa. In the position in which we find ourselves in this country and in the developments that are going to take place in a few months from now, real salvation can be found in my view in the heart of our territories in Africa. . . . If we look at the map and see these various states, most of which are under our Colonial Office—territories like Kenya, Tanganyika, Northern Rhodesia, Nyasaland, and Bechuanaland, and the other great territory which comes under the Colonial Office, Southern Rhodesia—it becomes apparent that, with the resources already developed, each one of them can bear comparison with their own counterpart in the United States.
>
> For instance, in Southern Rhodesia there is every possibility of great development in the next few years and of places emerging like Pittsburgh and Detroit in Africa. . . .

This terrifying statement was made by Squadron-Leader Kinghorn, Labour M.P. for Yarmouth, in the House of Commons, March, 1948 (incidentally, Southern Rhodesia does not come under the Colonial Office; it is under the Commonwealth Relations Office), to which speech another M.P., Mr. Archer Baldwin, Conservative, replied:

> Because we in this country are getting a bit afraid we are going to starve, a great interest is shown in Africa. We are trying to make our people believe that there are great resources of food to come out of Africa to help this country. If the Natives of Africa are fed properly there will be no surplus to come out of Africa, and the sooner the Government let the people of this country know that fact the better. The Natives are increasing at a tremendous extent, and they are unable to provide food for themselves.

All too true. The natives of Africa have long since passed the point where they began to out-breed the productive capacity of their land. All but a minute proportion now spend some six months out of every year in a state of semi-starvation. And fear—the fear felt in London—was unquestionably behind the white man's wild claims for Africa in the winter of 1947-8. Things are better now; claims are being reduced; the British mind is settling down. But not altogether. Antrycide, the new drug, which, it is claimed, can cure cattle of the two most dangerous diseases carried by the tsetse-fly, and even proof them against such for six months, had not been discovered at that time: so Lieut.-Colonel Rees-Williams, Parliamentary Secretary to the Colonial Office, had not yet had the chance to make his world-startling announcement that

> four and a half million square miles of Africa—an area four times the size of the Argentine or seventy-five times the size of England and Wales—an area which has hitherto been dominated by the tsetse-fly, will be rendered safe for cattle raising by antrycide, a new drug discovered by Imperial Chemical Industries.

Any ecologist could have told him that Africa possesses the lowest-carrying capacity per square mile of any continent; that Africa is overstocked, not understocked, with cattle; that the pampas of the Argentine are covered by possibly the richest, most indestructible soil in the world. And the tsetse-fly, as it happens, if kept within bounds, is really a friend to the African man. It prevents just such large areas as above from being opened: vital areas of bushland, which hold the rains that replenish the water table, prevent floods, hold erosion at bay, etc. It is an obsolete idea to consider the tsetse-fly as Public Enemy No. 1. The deserts are already marching south in Africa. The water table is falling. There will be no Argentines. I was on a 20,000-acre dairy farm in Kenya this last trip—considered one of the two best in East Africa—and out of eighteen bore holes, nearly all drilled since the 1914-18 War, all very precious, ten have already dried up.

That is an African reality. And now, as this book is to be about Africa, what the people on the spot are saying and doing, I had better get on with it.

CHAPTER II

"Union" in Central Africa

I KNEW that Governor Sir Philip and Lady Mitchell, in the course of their long official life, had entertained many people at Government House whom they must have loathed. So it was with no false feelings that I walked up to him, and saw our bags sent upstairs. He was standing just as I had first seen him in Uganda, ten years before, in riding togs. At Entebbe, which is smack on the Equator, he had been wearing white whipcord breeks and a heavy blue sweater. Now he was in jodhpurs, standing before a log fire, but still less than 2 degrees off the Equator. With the same alert, tired, half-official smile. I don't think that anyone gets really close to him except his dog, Star, a solemn black Labrador. Some idea of his character may be gained from the following:

In Uganda, where he also was the Governor, and I had refused a cocktail, he smiled and said: "What else can I offer you?" I said that he could help me get a buffalo, as I had made a pact with myself that I would not leave Africa until I had faced the experience of killing one lion and one buffalo—on foot. But not more. (Poor old Simba; how remorseful I felt when I saw you stretched out on the ground.) I was headed for Fort Portal I told the Governor, where everyone said I would be "sure to get a buff."

Mitchell smiled:

"Why don't you shoot yourself now and save the petrol?"

I asked him what he meant.

"Because the buff will get you at Fort Portal, rather than you get the buff. The grass is too high. Wait a moment." He then got up, walked to the telephone, and called up someone hundreds of miles away. When he came back, he said: "That's all right.

Go up to the Ruizi River. Man named Kennedy. Tsetse-fly man. He'll put you on a buff; he's the salt of the earth." And so he was.

I thought then: this is the first Governor in Africa to whom I have not had to crawl up to on my belly through a horde of A.D.C.'s. There were no A.D.C.'s now: just Sir Philip and Lady Mitchell, she chain-smoking cigarettes and sipping a sherry. No couple could ever less "come the Governor" over you.

I shall always see Governor Mitchell against the background of his long service in Africa—thirty-three years to the night I stood there talking with him. I shall also always see him, and Africa, against the background of London. There is quite a difference, as I will show.

My wife and I woke up the next morning and stepped out on the balcony into what seemed a new world, after the smoke and the fogs and the gloomy forebodings of a December London. All that sunlight . . . the green lawns, the blue snow that had fallen during the night from the jacaranda trees. Beyond the scarlet blossoms of the Nandi-flames, our eyes feasted hungrily on the distant pastel blues, the freshness of the clear-cut Kenya mountains. It caught one's breath.

Another world? Well, it seemed like it. Two eggs for breakfast were one thing, when they were only one a month in London. But Government House has too many visitors from London these days ever to let that contrast be too sharp; the Mitchells live quietly. Enchanting William, who brought in our two trays—"Good morning, Master! You sleep well?" William's smile was indeed like the old days, which in all truth were in another world. I had shown him my dinner jacket the night before; it was old, its lapels were furred at the edges; I had not worn it during wartime London. In an hour William had returned it to me just as if it had come from the tailor. All that was fine. But—here are some other thoughts which had passed through my mind that night, now that I knew I had returned to an Africa which was fast being turned into a great factory to supply European requirements:

Ten years before, when I had first met Sir Philip Mitchell over in Uganda, that country was the most "African" country left in Africa. The kingdom of Buganda, its largest section, was ruled by its own Kabaka, with hereditary native chiefs (one, the seventeenth of his line) over the Toro, Ankole and Bunyoro territories.

Not *absolutely* independent rulers; but, when you know the arbitrary despotism of native chiefs, with just enough white control to ensure justice for the black inhabitants. The British were administering the Protectorate of Uganda in the full moral sense of that word. Entebbe was a colonial official's idea of heaven; a perfect little laboratory for the study of African administration, altruistic, where every conversation was held in an atmosphere of unhurried research; unworried by the grab of predatory big business interests or the rapacity of the average white settler. At that time there were 3,700,000 natives in Uganda, 17,300 Indians, 2,100 whites. The natives grew all the crops, chiefly cotton and bananas; the Indians did all the middle-man work in selling them; 76 per cent of the European community, the "whites," were Colonial Office officials, missionaries or their families. In a territory of 93,981 square miles, less than 500 were in non-native hands. Now, as I had learned even before leaving London, big British tea interests were seeking–practically demanding–the right to grow tea in Uganda; soap interests were putting up factories at Kampala; and the Aga Khan, so it was said, was heavily investing, buying up bus lines, etc. The post-war world was knocking insistently at the doors of Uganda; and if that Protectorate opened them, it would become rapidly less and less an "African" country.

Tanganyika, when I had passed through it ten years before, had been a mandate that was being administered almost too impeccably by the British. Its guiding principle was: *Native interests are paramount.* The country was truly being held in trust for the native. Dar-es-Salaam, against all the pressure of the settlers, was rigidly refusing to alienate any more land for white settlement. So jealously did the British guard the morality of their trust, refusing to let their own countrymen have any extra advantage, sometimes refusing to let them have what seemed even a fair deal on certain occasions, that the result was there were more German settlers in Tanganyika when this last war began than there were British. And the Indians swamped them both. Tanganyika was the Indian's Happy Hunting Ground. They were 90 per cent landlords in all the big towns, 100 per cent in the smaller ones. They conducted 70 to 80 per cent of all the retail business, 40 per cent of the wholesale. They controlled 70 per cent of the cotton output, exported 28 per cent of the sisal, Tanganyika's more important crop (the British exported 30 and the Germans and the Greeks 42 per cent); and the shopping center of every town in the territory was just a hive of homogeneous Indian traders. At that time Tanganyika was spoken of angrily by the European settlers there as the "Aga Khan Country!"—and nowhere in East Africa, which is an Indian paradise, was it more clearly demonstrated that the Indian stands across the black man's path on nearly every road along which he hopes to progress in life. Nevertheless, there were less than 8,000 Europeans in Tanganyika, men, women and children, in a country of over 5 million Africans (they are now 7,070,000!); and 1,640 of these whites were adult British officials on the Tanganyika staff list. Tanganyika was still a laboratory, and a scrupulously guarded one, for the indigenous development of the African, without pushing him too fast.

Today, the £25,000,000 Groundnut Scheme (which will now cost over £50,000,000) has been planted on that territory, ruthlessly establishing the principle that the white man's interests shall be first and paramount. Some 50,000 natives, it is estimated, will be taken away from their own homes and way of life, put to work for the Europeans. It would be a brash man who would say it is best for them. It requires no effort whatsoever to prove, despite claims made by the politicians, that these grandiose schemes will help the African—if at all—only in their stride. One thing is certain: the principle that "Native interests are paramount" is as dead as the dodo.

The Englishman prides himself on the liberality of his administration, wherever it may be. He gets excited, waves flags, and almost goes into tears when delegates from all the Commonwealth march down the aisle of Albert Hall on Empire Day. He would be shocked to be told how little he knows, or cares, about it. Look at the facts. Even as I write this, it is still possible to get honors in history at either Oxford or Cambridge without having to read one word of England's colonial story. When the Colonial Office (1948) asked 2,000 British citizens to give the names of *any* British colony, only one in every two could name any colony at all; one in four knew the difference between a dominion and a colony; only one in three could name any Colonial-produced raw material—this despite the fact that the Gold Coast annually exports 47 per cent of all the world's cocoa, and the tin and rubber of Malaya are more dollar-producing than all British Africa. Only one day a year used to be set aside in the House of Commons for the Debate on Colonial Affairs. The office of Secretary of State for the Colonies was a second-rate political plum, usually awarded to some faithful party hack, and not infrequently to a pompous ass; this despite the fact that Winston Churchill once held it, and such a brilliant man as L. S. Amery. In August, 1947—just when the most fantastic, even outrageous claims were being made for the possibilities of developing Africa, and the House of Commons should have been at least interested, if not on its guard—here was the interest shown in Africa by the House. More than one day was allowed for the Debate on Colonial Affairs, chiefly because of the excitement about Africa at that time; but the actual speeches, all told, covered only six hours—and the maximum number of M.P.'s present in the House at any one time was forty-six. For a large part of the time there were only thirty Members; and during some of the Colonial Debate only twelve members sat in their seats.

In short, "a House of 640 Members could hardly have demonstrated more forcibly its indifference to Colonial Affairs," said F. S. Joelson, owner and editor of that one and only periodical which faithfully gives a weekly, and unbiased, report of what is going on on the East Coast: I speak of that journal which has become almost a Bible for some of us, *East Africa and Rhodesia.* Some seventeen speakers, most of whom appeared not to have the faintest idea of what they were talking about, gave Africa the most un-understanding and materialistic treatment that perhaps ever went into *Hansard.* This, just when Africa has become the last continent left for British interest and enterprise.

It is against that background of apathy, even ignorance, that I wish to show Sir Philip Mitchell, and others like him, who really have to deal with Africa. And some of the things that are going on in Kenya and East Africa. Anyone who prides himself that British liberalism has been carried straight through, all the way to the native, had better read the report of the tribunal which sat on the 1947 Mombasa strike. He will find, instead of it being, as some people have written, a question of the British taxpayer helping to support an indolent native in a sylvan paradise, that the dock workers were being paid, and that not too much, *only* on the days that they worked—and the vast majority had to fend for themselves when ships were not in; that, instead of living in the few token modern dwellings which have recently been completed at Mombasa, practically all occupied by higher clerks, they were sleeping, like vagrants, four or five in a room, if they could find one, in some of the most overcrowded native slums left in Africa. The tribunal's decision was the award of considerably increased wages to all the Africans on Mombasa Island (except domestic servants and gardeners), and that decasualisation of dock labor should be immediately sought by the creation of a special pool (600-800 men) who are to be guaranteed a minimum monthly wage (40*s*.), "even if too few ships are in port to provide work for all of them."

> Some people will sharply criticise the grant of higher wages, [wrote F. S. Joelson, in *East Africa and Rhodesia*, who could hardly be called unsympathetic to big enterprise] on the ground that the Africans [the same old story!] will thus need to work fewer days in the month to acquire the money he needs. [The poll tax, it should be noted, is a means of forcing the African to work for the European.] To that we would reply that every businessman in or from Mombasa from whom we have heard on this subject in the past couple of years has expressed the opinion that the ruling rate of wages was too low, and that all had been severely critical of the Government for its failure to accept the advice of the successive commissioners who had reported conditions at the port. One warning after another had gone unheeded, and businessmen have therefore constantly expected Native discontent to express itself in a strike. . . . [My brackets.]

There is the picture of the conditions which caused the strike; with both businessmen and Provincial Commissioners repeatedly warning the Government it should take action. I was given a different version of this strike when I was in Nairobi (identical with one given in a recent book) which, having dealt with Government spokesmen for many years, I did not believe—even before I went to Mombasa. And how anybody could accept that Nairobi version who has been to Mombasa (and it is still being handed out: "That trouble in Mombasa was the work of native agitators; we have deported one of the worst of them") is beyond my comprehension. House boys, who had been with the same family for over fifteen years, just walked out without saying a word, and did not return for twelve days. Europeans in Mombasa (many of whom knew that the Africans had a just grievance) had to organise volunteer brigades to maintain some of the essential services. It was one of the most bitter, all-embracing, heart-felt protests that the African has ever staged against his low wage and working conditions. Go to Mombasa yourself, where you will see an immense social hall which has been built there for the Africans (far too grand, in my opinion); and you will notice that they can hardly persuade an African to go into it. It is a Symbol—but not of what it was meant to be. Welwyn City or any of the model towns of Britain would be enchanted to have such a hall; the Africans of Mombasa look upon it as one of the meanest things that has ever been done to them: it so hypocritically misrepresents their state. They want bread and not cakes. There are too many such officially grand buildings all over British Africa. They characterise both the most stupid and the most deluding aspect of British colonisation. They are still going up.

But any amount of good things are being done in Kenya. Per head of the European population (the annual income, for all colors, is about £2), there is more money being spent in Kenya for soil conservation, agricultural instruction and research and veterinary services than in perhaps any other country in the world, the United States not excepted. There are seven settlement schemes, for model farms, to put the African native on new land—one very big one—on not one of which the African has yet shown any willingness to co-operate. On the checker-board of Kenya it is always well to show both the black and white squares. Four Africans are appointed members of the Kenya Legislative Council, allowed to stand up and say just what they like; not that it always gets them very far. Still, they can have their say; and it goes down in the local *Hansard*. The British in Kenya are working, almost frantically, to get the African interested in becoming a skilled artisan, not just a white-collared clerk—which seems to be his extreme ambition. The repair shops of the Kenya and Uganda Railway and the artisan school out at Kabete offer opportunities to Africans that, because of their very practicability, will put the African in a good job the very day he leaves their course: give him a big boost in life. In Kenya the African is barred neither by color nor prejudice from any skilled trade; on the contrary, every inducement is given him to enter them. This is the very reverse of the South African policy. But the East Coast African is, aside from his suspicious, unco-operative attitude, exceedingly slow to learn: it is now generally accepted that it takes three generations (with, of course, some brilliant exceptions) to train an African skilled mechanic or to give him any education (read Julian Huxley's *Africa View*) that can be said to have taken. Meanwhile, as I have said, the ubiquitous Indian is filling, plugging up, every niche that he might have filled. This is a bad lookout, containing some of the most baffling problems concerned with how to raise the African's standard of life.

Good things are being done from London, where those connected with colonial development now have a Government fund of £120,000,000 to be spent in the next ten years in the colonies —to be used for education, research, and assistance to the colonies at key points in their development programs. If the doctrine that native interests shall be paramount has been dropped, so has the archaic idea that every non-self-governing colony must be self-supporting; which, believe it or not, was actually the case with the museum-minded British colonial system up to the outbreak of this last war. Britain seems to have awakened from a long sleep, so far as her colonies are concerned: and the condition of affairs that she has looked out on is enough to frighten anybody, even Whitehall.

This last war has changed the whole concept of Africa. The old, romantic one has gone; an Africa of ugly problems has now appeared. It will do no good to deny it. This means that many of the old shibboleths, even some of the good ones, must be got rid of; and that a new appraisement must be made. That morning as I stood on the balcony of Government House, looking out into all the freshness of a sun-filled Kenya, I knew that I had changed many of my own opinions which I had held so firmly (and I think correctly) ten years before; and that I was going to acquire several new ones.

Ten years before, I would have written with everything I had to oppose a political union of Kenya, Tanganyika and Uganda. Compared to Kenya, I had found Uganda a paradise for natives; I had seen the high civilisation they had developed for themselves; and I had spent a long, fruitful morning with the Cabinet Ministers and the *saza* and *gombola* chiefs, who, with almost desperation in their voices, repeated what their representative had said in London, that: "The Kabaka does not want to be a horse in Kenya stables!"

But now I had to revise my former feelings; I had to bring my opinions into line with present-day facts. And these tend to the belief that a political and economic federation of the three territories might be the best for all concerned, providing the present self-rule could be safeguarded for the natives of Uganda; and that Tanganyika should return to its former doctrine. I am afraid, though, that it is not going to happen that way. Similarly, if the Colonial Office still retains the final decisions concerning the welfare of the natives, the federation of the two Rhodesias with Nyasaland should be worked for. Strategically, in a defence policy, these two groups should then form a common unit for naval and air bases and an unbroken line of communications. Mombasa has already been made a permanent naval base, with its own warship; and some sixty miles behind it, at Mackinnon Road, is probably the greatest concentration of war material anywhere in the Empire.

Kenyans hope that some 70,000 * troops will be stationed and trained there; which, if it ever happens, would give the colony a sizeable increase of internal purchasing power, and thus provide some real reason for the establishment of secondary industries—which is always being preached in Kenya as the right way to absorb the excess native population; not that it possibly could. But here again comes the conflict. Southern Rhodesia taking the lead, a meeting was held at Victoria Falls on February 16th, 1949, of which a big right-wing London newspaper headlined: "12 MEN VOTE FOR UNITED AFRICA"—which has more truth in it than meets the eye. At that conference between the representatives of the two Rhodesias and Nyasaland, only the delegates of Southern Rhodesia, headed by Sir Godfrey Huggins, the Prime Min-

* The size of Mackinnon Road, and its strategic importance, will decrease or increase in proportion to bettering or worsening Anglo-Egyptian relations: i.e., the number and size of military establishments that the British are allowed to maintain in Egypt—and the future of the Anglo-Egyptian Sudan.

ister, had any Government backing; there was not a single African present; and the Africans constitute about 97 per cent of the populations concerned.

Partisans can play with those figures both ways. The British Colonial Office still retains the power of giving its assent or not, even (so I hope) against the British Parliament. It is still the best guardian of native interests in British Africa. And just because that is so, such a union in Central Africa might be safely formed. If so, it will do a lot to thwart the policy of South Africa; it will be large enough to withstand Cape Town's ambition one day to dominate the politics of Africa up to the Equator. The British Government has the final say, and the moral responsibility rests with Britain. That is why more than forty-six members should attend the Parliamentary Colonial Debates.

CHAPTER III

Beautiful, Perplexed Kenya

WHILE we were at Government House, Sir Philip Mitchell outlined some of the problems which face Kenya:

"We are faced here with about every kind of racial complication that you can imagine, together with a good many economic ones sufficient to turn people's hair grey. All I claim is that we do see the problems, or most of them, and that we are consciously devoting ourselves to trying to find a means of dealing with them. I do also claim that in the last five or six years there has been a very marked improvement between the various races, and a noticeably increased disposition to realise that it is only by leadership, friendship and co-operation that we are going to find our way through the intricacies which surround us."

Thus speaks the man on the spot, the governing man, who has to deal with the facts. It is somewhat different from the theorist, especially the political theorist, who after a short trip to East Africa returns to London and announces jubilantly, "Race relations are excellent"—when they can't be. The population figures in East Africa, the frightful discrepancies between the whites and the blacks, are appalling. But to anticipate the conclusions that one must draw from seeing them would be to rob the picture on the spot which I wish to give in this book. Mitchell's realism, his lack of false optimism, are latent in the above paragraph. What he and others of his thinking are trying to do to make Kenya a wise colony will become apparent as I go on. There can be some problems, of course, to which there are no answers. This population problem seems one of them. In 1933, the Kenya Land Commission (commonly known as the Carter Report) issued the first complete survey ever made of the lands of Kenya, with this grave warning:

> It is clear that no addition of territory (to the land now held by the Natives), *however large,* can itself solve problems caused by the density of population, if that population continues to increase. All that it can effect is *a certain saving of time* [my italics], and the value of that addition depends upon the use made of that time.

There in a nutshell—"the use made of that time"—is what is worrying the best brains in East Africa today. Men like Sir Philip Mitchell and Cavendish-Bentinck know that with every native hospital put up, every clinic, every veterinary station or school, every move that they make to prevent human starvation or death of the cattle from rinderpest or the formerly decimating East Coast fevers, they are *worsening* their problems. They are increasing the population's rate of increase. So, almost at the beginning of the picture I want to give of Kenya, you will see its most ironic truth: the Englishman administering Kenya today is being made to suffer because of his good, not his bad qualities. He is preventing Nature from adjusting the balance in her old, cruel way. This is also an African reality, frank discussion of which would shock the theorists: would it not be best, for the sake of establishing a civilisation which the land can bear, deliberately to let large numbers of people and cattle die? If that is not answered with a pitiless realism, then "the use made of that time" holds the questions of how long the inevitable can be staved off. Is this not a different picture from the ballyhoo which is being handed out about British Africa today?

Leaving Government House, we began a trip which took us from the shores of Lake Victoria to tea and coffee (both at the same sitting) with the Sultan of Zanzibar; from a long *safari* down on the great game plains running into Tanganyika, up through the lava rubble of the rainless Somali deserts to the frontier of Abyssinia. My wife picked up malaria over in Nyanza Province, and I had to leave her at Fort Hall (Eve ran a temperature of 105 for two days) while I went up into the camel country of the Somali nomads.

During these four months I endured some of the toughest travel (and talk) that I ever want to put up with. Rapid changes of elevation, both in people and of places, were sometimes disconcerting. I met some men I shall remember all my life—remarkable people; men made by the life they had made for themselves in raw places. And I met a few who still leave me wondering how they could exist in such grandeur as Kenya's, so totally unaware of the majesty of the scene they were living in. One of the most dismaying things about colonial life is that in scenes which hold you spellbound by their glory you should find such muttony materialism. And these are the materialists who will refuse to make Kenya wise. Any Governor has to deal with a chronic and powerful corps of them.

Kenya is a Crown Colony, yet its Government is carried on more by usage—and the personality of its Governor—than by any hard-and-fast rules. Theoretically, a Crown Colony cannot pass any important piece of legislation or pass its annual estimates without having first submitted them to the Secretary of State for the Colonies in London. All legislation is subject to the veto of the Crown. But with the right kind of Governor and a sensible Legislative Council matters should never come to a point where the veto would be used; and, to an amazing extent, a Crown Colony is a self-ruling territory. Kenya is uniquely so. The vociferous minority of whites in Kenya is so tough that it has taken the law into its own hands on several occasions. In 1923, Kenyans had a plan all worked out to kidnap their own Governor. This was when London, to please Mother India, tried to force ballot-box equality for the 46,000 Indians in Kenya, at that time, upon its 19,000 whites. Kenya was merely a helpless pawn in this game, so Whitehall thought. But when the British Cabinet learned that settlers were being armed—and there are more ex-officers in Kenya's population, in proportion, than there are in any other British possession—that people had been actually appointed who were to seize the railway and telegraph systems; and that the very farm itself had been provisioned on which the captive Governor was to be hidden, some sixty miles from Nairobi, then London backed down. When Kenyans are liable to do things like that, it is easy to understand why the *quality* of white leadership in that colony is of so much importance, and why it has given so much trouble.

Kenya has no political parties. It is just "Settlers *v.* Government," with both the Africans and the Indians fighting on the side-lines for what *they* want. There are 29,500 white people in

Kenya, about 100,000 Indians (24,000 Arabs down on the Coast; picturesque, many lovable, but only one or two individuals of whom play any part in the Colony's life) and over 5,000,000 Africans. The social implications of those figures are of first importance. This disproportion is so great that I refused to read Elspeth Huxley's book, *White Man's Country*, when I first passed through Kenya ten years ago; I disliked its title so much. Now I wish I had not been so finicky; it is a remarkable piece of work, and should be a "must" for anyone who wants to learn how Kenya came to be what it is. It will help you to understand why the Kenya legislature is a blissfully peaceful scene compared to any European parliament, and why it is usually such a fair one. There is a Legislative Council, renewed every four years, of which the Governor is President (although there is now an appointed President to sit for him). There are eleven *ex-officio* Official Members and nine Nominated Official Members (one especially to represent the Arabs). There are eleven elected European members, five elected Indians, four nominated Africans, and one Arab elected member. Two of these four African members have just been added. This gives the Kenya Legislative Council, for the first time, an unofficial majority. Great play is being made with this for propaganda purposes, but I think it will work out to be more the semblance of power than the substance: I cannot see any issue where European, Indian, African and Arab will unite to vote against the Official Members of Leg. Co., as it is called. On the contrary, short-sighted Europeans in Kenya now chortle that the Africans and the Indians will now cancel each other out with, of course, the expectation that this will further add to the power of white leadership.

The Africans (despite race riots in Durban) are psychologically closer to the Indians than they are to the whites, chiefly due to the color bar. The Indians work harder, perhaps with more guile, to enlist their sympathies. There have been times when the Indians in Kenya were working for what could be called a "colored front" against the whites. They said to the Africans: "This is your country. Why don't you tell the white man to get out?" But few of the Indians in East Africa could be dragged by wild horses back to India. And now that the communal dissension is spreading from India to Africa (and there is the possibility that one day India might leave the Empire), the Indians in Kenya are more inclined to play ball with the whites. They are afraid of the day when the African might say to them: "Why don't *you* get out?" The Aga Khan has told his people, the Khojas, the best organised Indians in Africa, to identify themselves with Africa: "You are Africans now."

Aside from the Leg. Co., there is an Executive Council. This is a sort of Cabinet of eight members appointed by the Governor, who advise him in private. There is also the Secretariat, drawn from officers of the British Colonial Service, as overworked a body as you will find in all Africa. And that splendid corps of Provincial and District Commissioners, through whom the Crown is still the arbiter of the daily affairs between black and white. Some idea of the actual mechanics of a Crown Colony may be given, when I say that some 41 per cent of the adult whites in Kenya are in Government service. And you won't think that Kenya Colony is top-heavy with officials when you realise that they have over 5,000,000 Africans to administer.

Of these Colonial Officers, practically all recruited from England, with the background of a strong training in character such as one can only get in the English public schools, and with some university training–many have been to Eton, Oxford or Cambridge–nearly all of them from upper middle-class families, there are today: 5 Provincial Commissioners, 4 Deputy P.C.'s, 2 Senior District Commissioners, and 129 District Officers (salaries ranging from £550 to £1,775). The upper posts are held by men with from eighteen to thirty years' service. Pensions are 1/600th on retirement for each month of service, i.e. an officer who is earning £1,000 when he retires after thirty years' service will get £600 a year for life. It is not a money-making walk of life; and most men enter it for much more praiseworthy reasons. They are the most professionally altruistic body of men I have ever encountered. All these salaries, and a proportionate pension based on the time a Colonial Officer has served in Kenya, are paid by Kenya Colony itself, and are not therefore a burden on the United Kingdom.

There are twenty-eight members on Kenya's Secretariat, whose salaries range from £970 to a Chief Secretary getting £2,600. In addition, there are 56 Medical Officers, 72 male Education

Officers, 35 female, 19 in the Engineering Service, 49 Police Superintendents, 118 Inspectors, and 35 Agricultural Officers. This list does not include Forestry, Veterinary, Pasture Research, Geological, Chemical and a variety of other specialist officers in branches of the Colonial Service in Kenya. Nor does it include officers in super-scale posts (e.g. Directors of Agricultural and Medical Services, Public Works and their Deputies, etc., whose salaries form an important item in the Colony's small budget). Nor does it include local European appointments on local pensionable or temporary terms. Many of these last—the non-career, non-pensionable officers—are among the best and most hard-working in Kenya.

This gives one some idea of the immense and varied teamwork necessary in a colony where there is a very small minority of white settlers and officials in comparison with the overwhelming number of backward native inhabitants. Among these people I have found some of the happiest I have ever known. I found many a man and woman in Kenya this time who seemed to have found just the job they were made for. Many of them—especially the Game Wardens—would like to refuse promotion if that meant office work instead of the gloriously open life they were enjoying. Kenya is a happy colony for the Indians and the Europeans.

It could be one for the Africans as well, if they could ever overcome their ingrained, almost cancerous suspicion of the white man and his every intention. The African natives do have a good life on most of the farms; the average white settler takes a far greater interest in their welfare than they could ever hope to get in the American southern states. Put on its very lowest basis, he knows that it is to his own best interests to look after them: they work better. But the big native reserves, which were originally established to keep the white man out, have now, because of their overworked land and bursting populations, come to be looked upon by the African as some place to keep him *in*. That makes all the difference. And some of the best-intentioned, hard-working agricultural teams in the world cannot change his opinion or give him any heart or confidence which would persuade him to make the best use of even his own land. The primary effort in Kenya today is this constant struggle to come to grips with the black man's mind.

In fairness to the African, it must be said that he meets enough woe in his daily life, trying to scratch a living from the eroded hillsides of his packed reserves—in one district of the Kavirondo Province they are 900 to the square mile—to make him think that it must be the white man and not the "will of God" which is responsible for his miserable condition. He will not be convinced that he is the greatest destroyer of the land in all Africa. The concept just can't be got through to him that the right to till any patch of land also brings with it responsibilities to that land. He regards it as an imposition to be asked to do contour terracing or to co-operate with another African to better or save their mutual land. By far the major problem facing Kenya today is the psychological problem. It is to make the African believe not so much in the capabilities of the European as in his good intentions. Even a partial success in the answering of that would at once make the African a happier man, and be the start of his co-operation in the Government's almost frantic efforts to arrest the erosion and exhaustion of the soil. Any idea that he should cut down on his birth-rate—use contraceptives, for instance—just strikes him as ludicrous. (They know plenty of secret contraceptives or methods of abortion, when they want to use them.) Fornication, the black man seems convinced, is about the only pleasure left to him.

The root trouble of the whole thing is, in my opinion, a woefully inadequate policy for education. In this, I may say, I have been confirmed by practically every Provincial or District Commissioner I have talked with. Until 1948 it could have been said truthfully that Kenya had no educational policy at all.

The Indians in Kenya are even more ubiquitous than they are in Tanganyika. The Indians do all the skilled artisan work (except the 4,000 Italians who are now being imported from Italy); they make all the clothes, boots and shoes, run practically all the food and retail shops, except for a few British chain-stores, such as chemists and hardware and agricultural machinery merchants; the Sikhs do practically all Kenya's carpenter work, as well as being station-masters, etc., on the railways; the Government employs Goanese clerks (even though they do have Portuguese passports) wherever it can get them, in preference to the African.

The Indians own 66 per cent of all plots in the townships, excluding Mombasa, and 90 per cent of the plots in the trading centers of the Native Areas, as well as in the shopping districts of the exclusive European Highlands. They own many of Kenya's best hotels, and are buying more. They come from an ancient civilisation, long skilled in the ways of trade; they subsidise their own countrymen; and no individual African, unless protected by restrictive laws, has the slightest chance against them. They work harder and longer than either white or black man; their stores are good–though most of the goods that they import from India cannot stand up against "Made in England" wares; but they are courteous, a pleasure to shop with. If the Indians ever left Kenya, that Crown Colony would come to a full stop within a few months.

There are about 2,500 European farms in Kenya, about 85 per cent of whose owners have to live on their land. Kenya has no coal, oil, or mines, no heavy industry–like the Rhodesias–and where the Indians are so self-sufficient and the 250,000 Africans working outside the reserves are paid an average of six pence a day, Kenya does not have an internal market to justify many secondary industries. None, that is, sufficiently large to be able to lift large numbers of natives off the land. Kenya, therefore, must solve its problems *on* the land, and *inside* Kenya. These are the main features of the outstanding characteristic of life in this very beautiful–but perplexed–colony.

CHAPTER IV

Animal Suburb

WILD animals are certainly Kenya's greatest attraction, and the Nairobi National Park provides a unique antidote to the town itself. I used it on several occasions. The best of them was when I dressed before daybreak in my comfortable room in the Norfolk Hotel (whose bar is a rendezvous for many of the old Kenyans) and drove out to see the sun rise. It was less than twenty minutes from my hotel to where I found Colonel Mervyn Cowie sitting in his Ford station-wagon at the gates of the reserve. The sun was just topping the horizon, the plains lay in pools of white mist, and a hundred miles away rose the snowy dome of Kilimanjaro. . . .

While we were signing the police-book which every motorist must sign before entering the park—you are not allowed in there on foot—a gang of dirty-nosed hyenas trotted impudently past.

"The Nairobi Dust-Bin Patrol," smiled Cowie, nodding back to the low roofs of the outskirts, where these unpleasant, slant-backed animals had been rummaging during the hours of darkness.

As the red ball of sun burned away the mists, we came on dappled giraffe, unable to tear themselves away from their curiosity as they stared at us over the twenty-foot flat-thorns, munching their mouthfuls sidewise, like an old American farmer chewing his tobacco plug. We soon came on herds of leaping, joyous russet impala—the most beautiful buck in all the world, found only in Africa. That afternoon we sat (still in the car, I may say) within seven paces of two bored, black-maned lions, who simply yawned at us. Then one of the big cats, annoyed by our presence, slowly arose and walked off to lie down behind a big rock, where he could sleep unobserved. The other majestic beast just closed his eyes and went to sleep where he was. I believe that were it not for the odd fool, who cannot be prevented from disturbing the peace of such a place, the wild game inside Nairobi's National Park might eventually become as unafraid of man as are those in some of the fabled valleys of Tibet.

Mervyn Cowie is the Executive Officer for Kenya's National Parks. And when I wrote of Kenyans who seem to have found just the very job that was made for them, I had this youthful ex-colonel, ex-chartered accountant in mind. I don't want to deal in superlatives, even though Kenya is a country of extremes, but I think he is one of the most quietly contented men I have ever come across. It is inspiring to see that such a job has been given to such a man. Under him an area of 7,700 square miles in the Voi district between Nairobi and the coast will be turned into a Chief National Park—if opposing claims for land-settlement do not block that project—and the large herds of elephant and rhino now in its dense brush will be given a good chance of survival. There is thorn-scrub there, with three-inch spikes, so thick and tangled that you would think that not even a snake could get through it. Similarly, in the sparsely settled Northern Frontier District, the land of the pagan Boran and the Somali nomadic camel tribes, another 9,000 square miles may be made into a game sanctuary. This would preserve some of the finest species of animals now alive.

In a two weeks' *safari* I took up there, to the border of Abyssinia and back to the elephant country of the Tana River, where there is the finest ivory in all Africa, I saw numbers of the deep liver-red reticulated giraffe; Grevy's zebra, which has narrow black stripes so close together that it looks grey; herds of the beautiful oryx, the long-horned antelope which, so it is said, gave the design of the heraldic Unicorn; and that strangest looking of all African buck, the gerenuk, which has the body of a deer and the neck of a giraffe. At the present moment, poaching Abyssinians, using Italian traps, selling to avaricious American fur buyers, are trapping the leopard to extinction in that district, and because of his beautiful spotted pelt this graceful beast looks like the first of the remaining African game animals which is doomed to disappear.

But on the green and golden thorn plains, less than half an hour from the heart of Nairobi itself, in a protected area of a little over forty square miles, you can see nearly every wild animal left in Africa. There are large numbers of giraffe, zebra, eland, wildebeest, hartebeest, waterbuck, impala, bushbuck, reedbuck, Grant's gazelle, Thomson's gazelle, steinbuck, hyena, jackal, bat-eared fox, ostrich, duiker, dikdik, pigmy antelope, monkeys, baboon, mongoose, smaller numbers of lion, leopard, hippo, a wealth of all the African birds, with the rhino, cheetah and wild dog as occasional visitors. You can see nearly all of them in any one day (except the rarely-seen leopard, of which there are supposed to be twelve living in the rock ravines of the reserve); and the fifty to sixty lions, who are known to Cowie and his rangers personally. This has never been elephant country; so unless they happen to stray that way in their majestic strolls across Africa, you will never meet old Tembo in the reserve. You will meet occasional Masai grazing their cattle in there, and see the huts of a few cattle-owning natives who, because of tribal rights, have been allowed to stay there for their own lifetimes. But otherwise you can spend day after day in the park and be in exactly the same atmosphere as you would in a part of unshot-over Africa. It is fenced only on the Nairobi side: to keep the wrong people out. Animals are free to enter or leave it as they will. It is a signal achievement to have kept it the way it is; and if Kenya, which is anxious to attract American tourists, was equally careful about preserving the game in the shootable areas, I think the colony, and the world, would greatly benefit in the long run. Though Kenya, it should be said here, has the most humane attitude towards protecting its wild animal life of any territory in British Africa. And is still the big game shooter's paradise.

It is a relief to get away from the human race for a time, and a day out on that range can be a tonic. To see the red-shanked plover rising and falling in the wind against the distant snows of Kilimanjaro, the great bustard standing sentinel, the blue sky flouting white luminous clouds, the secretary bird, with his quills erect, stalking across the plain like, as they call him in the Sudan, "the British Officer." To sit and watch a clan of monkeys playing in the green thorn tops of a *lugga*, until you can almost penetrate into their insolent little brains and know the fun they are making of you. To sit on the banks of a shady pool and watch a peacefully dozing hippo; to watch crocs sliding past. . . . It is all there. Even the black mamba, most deadly snake in Africa. Even if you have never seen any of these animals before, you soon get to notice their peculiarities. How the little Tommy gazelles always violently flick their black tails as they scamper off; how the joyous impala are so impetuous in their leaps that they often collide in mid-air; how a wildebeest can never trot or canter—he always has to go at a wild gallop, with his mane tossing in the wind; how the biscuit-colored rumps of the kongoni shine in the early morning dew, and their crescent horns and cupped ears always make them look as if they were wearing a crown; how giraffes always run, stiff-legged, like a rocking-horse; the way that circling vultures mark a lion's kill; the way that the francolin and guinea-fowl prefer to run on the ground rather than take to wing to get away from you—you certainly find that out if you try to shoot them without a dog!—how clean and chic the little silver-backed jackals always look; how like a handful of sapphires thrown in the sun a flock of blue starlings look as they shoot, iridescent, into the yellow-green fever thorn . . . and you learn that one glistening green tree, which looks strangely like a holly, has a leaf which, when boiled, provides the strychnine with which the local natives still poison their enemies. You notice, after a while, the way that the long necks of the giraffe, those "living towers of Africa," always lean in the same direction; you nearly always see a frieze of them, leaning, like masts at sea, somewhere on the plain's horizon. . . . The snake-bird, swimming across some shaded pool, with only his long head and kinked neck showing: he uses his head as a javelin to spear fish. The cormorants, "hanging out their wings to dry"—looking like the eagles on the Kaiser's old postage stamps.

And here, on the peace of these plains where the lives of the animals are left so undisturbed, you get a wonderful chance to study their protective coloring. The dazzle-striped zebra would be conspicuous against any background, you would think; but he begins to fade out completely at half a mile. A baby zebra, on the other hand, is much more brown and earth-like than its parents, and could fade into the plain at a hundred yards or so. I am speaking of complete camouflage, when you have no idea the animal is there at all. Thus I have almost stepped on a dappled, freshly-dropped fawn out in British Columbia.

And, of course, with birds this camouflage is unbelievable. Shooting sand grouse in what is known as the "brown country" between Nairobi and the coast, I have searched half an hour for a bird I knew I had dropped, only to find it lying beside my gun as I gave up the search. Lying on its stomach with its wings spread out in the brown grass, it was exactly the same color. It became almost invisible again when I replaced it in that position and stood up. I have had precisely the same experience, several times, shooting woodcock where I live in the West Country of England.

It was pleasant to sit there, idle, looking out on the plain from honeysuckled banks of the Athi River, with hundreds of doves, talking to each other, on the flat-top mimosa thorns. Sun . . . sky . . . and plain . . . you feel that you could go on this way for ever. . . .

The men looking after the park live in such intimacy with the daily life of the animals that they come to humanise them, as Kipling did in *The Jungle Book*. Warden K. deP. Beaton writes a weekly log of the park for the *East African Standard*, that well-edited and attractively brought out daily which always has the invidious task of choosing between news of England and of the world, opposed to what the Kenyans want to read about themselves (the settlers win!). One of the African rangers found a baby lion cub one dawn, sitting in the middle of the Magadi road and calling loudly for its mother. As it was obvious that it was lost and was in danger of being run over by some passing motorist in the reserve, the black African ranger took the cub to Beaton. Beaton wrote: "Knowing the locality, a patch of forest in the Kisembe valley, where the cub had been born, I took the cub in my car, and released it close to its home. For some ten minutes the cub could be heard calling in the forest, then all was still. . . ."

When Beaton came back in the afternoon he found the cub's mother close to where he had released the baby, and so, he thought, all was well. It wasn't, however, for when Beaton was on patrol in the afternoon he heard the cries of the cub in an entirely different part of the forest, so—

> imitating the mother's grunt, I called to the cub, which without hesitation came out of the forest to me.

The cub was taken back to the camp, and this time was fed with milk from a baby's bottle, and small pieces of meat. The little chap was ravenous. He was then put into a cosy box with straw in an outbuilding.

During the afternoon and evening he called again for his mother. Just after dark, as I was returning to the camp, I saw in the headlights of my car a lioness within fifteen yards of my house. Feeling certain that this was the cub's mother, I at once fetched the cub and returned to where I had seen the lioness. She was still there, and had now been joined by three other cubs of the same age.

Placing the cub on the ground, I retired a short distance. The mother at once came to her baby, and demonstrations of the greatest affection were displayed on both sides at the reunion. The lioness did not appear to resent the scent of human beings, which must have been strong about the cub, for she commenced licking it, and playing with it, with every expression of joy. The whole family then moved off.

On several occasions since then this lioness has been seen again, moving out on her night's hunting, in the company of other lions. She has evidently come to the conclusion that her family are safer at home.

In watching the communion and fellowship of the animals, and the sheer joy which they obviously get out of mere living, I have found more to restore my belief that life was really intended to be a joyous affair than in any sermons I have ever listened to. Sydney Downey, the white hunter, and I spent all one sunny afternoon years ago lying behind a knoll down in Southern Kenya watching a lioness playing with her cub; and as he rightly said as we stood up, "It makes you feel an absolute stinker to shoot 'em . . . after you've watched things like that." He recently refused to let an arrogant American oil millionaire put a bullet into one majestic old lion that he had become fond of. "He just wanted a skin to take home," smiled Downey. "He had no feeling for animals." And if you keep cats, as I do (two of them are lying by me as I write this), you know that animals are meant to be *understood*—not tacked on the wall. And what a delight it must have been to Warden Beaton to watch that licking performance, that joyous reunion of the lioness with her cub. The life of a game-ranger has a lot to be said for it.

The rhino, because of his tendency to charge any moving

object that comes within his short vision—they have even charged the Kenya and Uganda Railway coaches—can be said to be the only dangerous animal in the Nairobi National Park. A careful watch is kept on them by the Warden and his rangers to see that they do not move into the parts of the park where they might constitute a danger to visiting motorists.

One afternoon Cowie and I, after a long, zigzag search, came on a rhino and her cub. The mother was feeding on the bare, rock-studded plain and did not seem aware of us, except that once or twice she looked up and stared in our direction. The rhino cub was playing in a dust wallow. Seldom have I seen anything more attractive: whoof! it would go in a great slide; then it would chase the smoke-like wisps of dust. . . . Then it would dash back past its mother, and throw itself on its back . . . all four fat little legs kicking joyously at the sun. Then a silly scamper around, and—*up* she goes!—it would be off chasing the dust wisps again . . . and always, we could see, it was trying to make its mother look at it: "Look at *me!* Aren't I great! Whoof!—look at that one! I bet *you* can't turn a back somersault like that. . . ."

And so on; the huge, battleship-grey mother, bored, ambling, nosing, bumping the child about. Until finally its stare became fixed upon us and it moved nervously toward the Ford station-wagon. "I think this is where we came in?" I said to Cowie.

That sunset we passed rows of motor cars lined up along the banks of a green, thorn-filled *lugga,* waiting for some lions who were in there to come out. Most of the cars were filled with Indians. And when I say filled, I mean Indians, all ages, packed inside an asthmatic limousine as if in a basket of strawberries. The lions, for some strange reason, seem to hold a fascination for the Indians. And even if they only *think* they have seen a lion—say, having mistaken a hyena in the dusk—they drive back to their homes in Nairobi completely satisfied, all the little Abduls, etc., chirping like sparrows. I saw one Indian car broken down in the reserve, with about fifteen Indians pushing it. "Now I know why they have so many passengers," I declared to Cowie.

That particular evening, just as darkness came down, we sat on the edge of the forest at a place which Cowie knew was their customary exit, and watched five lions come out to begin their night's hunting. They strode past in single file—not fifty feet off the noses of about fifteen parked cars. With a disdain that must have made even the most thick-skinned among us feel conscious of the contrast—our own gaping vulgarity—they ignored us. Tawny, supple, great shoulder muscles rising and falling, one immense paw after another treading the earth as if it owned it, deliberate, purposeful, concentrated upon their night's kill, they disappeared into the darkness. . . .

"Some poor zebra's going to buy it tonight," sighed Cowie as he switched on the lights and turned for home. "But they gave us a pretty certain idea what they think of us, didn't they—we just have to be put up with!"

Half an hour later I was back in the Nairobi Club.

CHAPTER V

Prime Movers

THE Africans, as Lawrence said of the Arabs, believe in persons and not institutions. Therefore the character of the man on the spot is all important. These figures of Kenya should always be viewed against the background of Africa, the *décor* of their stage as it were; for perhaps nowhere in the world does environment have such a direct effect upon a man's character. You must see the people watching the heavens for rain as the grass begins to die on the great grazing plains; the settler fighting for his farm; the administrator and the missionary struggling with the African mind. You must never forget that European Kenya lies directly on the Equator, and that nearly all its white population live between the altitudes of 5,000 to 8,000 feet. Then you will understand what is meant by "Kenya nerves," and why tempers get a bit frayed towards the end of March, before the Long Rains come on.

There are four men in Kenya who are unquestionably the prime movers of the colony. They are as strangely different as any four men could be. They are the Governor, Sir Philip Mitchell; Sir Alfred Vincent, one of the biggest men in East Africa, and until recently the Leader of Opposition in the Kenya Legislative Council; Major Cavendish-Bentinck, who holds Kenya lovingly in the crook of his arm and is, very appropriately, Minister of Agriculture and Natural Resources; and Wyn Harris, the Chief Native Commissioner, an old Everest climber and the second man ever to have climbed Mount Kenya. The first two have one thing in common which may prove of great value to Kenya and the future of East Africa: they both have strong ties with the United States. Sir Alfred Vincent may play the major part in Anglo-American African developments, if Truman's

Fourth Point, to give U.S. aid to backward colonial territories, is carried out.

He is heavy-set, placid, prematurely grey, with a meteoric career (still rising) in Kenya politics and business that can only be compared to the spectacularly successful, self-made American men of affairs, to whom he has such a striking physical resemblance. He is as well known in the top business circles of New York, Chicago, Akron and Detroit as he is in most parts of East Africa, for his commercial activities there also cover Uganda and Tanganyika. For those territories he holds the agency for Chevrolet cars and trucks, Oldsmobile cars and trucks, Buick, General Motors—all divisions, frigidaires, diesels, and so on.

He handles these lines through his Motor Mart and Exchange, Ltd., with branches in all the larger towns of East Africa; and, I can speak from the heart, it was this splendidly efficient organisation which saved my skin on several occasions when, in 1938-9, I drove across Africa from the Indian Ocean to the Atlantic. In addition, he has the agency for twenty other big American concerns, among which are Bendix Corporation, Stewart Warner, American Bosch, Bosch Fuel Equipment, Zenith Radios, United States Asbestos, and American Steel Export Co.

Before the last war he made a trip to the United States every year, and is now resuming that good habit. When it comes to the conclusion of any big business deal, all I can say is, my own fellow countrymen must think they have met their match! His rise in politics is even more sensational than his commercial success, for he only entered that arena lately and, chiefly owing to his genius for mediation, the ability to guide strongly conflicting opinions to a usually successful compromise, he quickly became Leader of the Elected Members to the Legislative Council (no easy post to hold); and a racially-mixed Council of Europeans, Africans, Indians and Arabs recently elected him unanimously to represent Kenya on the East African Central Legislative Assembly (Kenya, Tanganyika, Uganda). Thus he represents all the mixed races of Kenya. Governor Mitchell intends to retire into private life up on his pleasant farm at Subakia in the Kenya Highlands in 1951, after his thirty-five years of official life in East Africa are over. (By a recent order, the terms of office of both Kenya and Uganda have been extended until December

19th, 1951: "Changes of governors at the present time may not be beneficial to either territory" runs the official pronouncement. This means that Sir Philip Mitchell, who is not at all a well man, will serve two more years than the usual five as Governor.) But Sir Alfred is a "permanent": he will indubitably play a major part in the future of East Africa.

He is a home man, devoted to his family and the superb aquatic garden which Lady Vincent has created in the green Ngong Hills, where the red-hot pokers grow in profusion around the shores of a wind-ruffled lake; and if he has any interests other than family, politics, and business—I put them in that order—I have yet to find them. He is a man very fond of getting on top of his facts, a thing he always emphasises:

"I always get them right, and if I feel that I haven't got them, I will send you to someone I think has the right dope. Come to me."

He is always present on the Nairobi Aerodrome to greet any distinguished visitor when he arrives. Sir Alfred Vincent is a happy man, and sometimes turns on the radio to play music while he dresses; at least, he did while I was staying with him. He was knighted in 1945. I did not see as much of him as I probably should have; my work took me farther afield, out of Nairobi, most of the time. In the first days, after we had left Government House, when I was staying with him at "Rhino Camp," as he has called his home, I was awakened by the roar of a shotgun shortly after midnight. In a few minutes Sir Alfred came stalking past my steel-grated window, in purple dressing gown, with a 12-bore over his arm. A booby-trap set by his son to catch motor-car thieves (the brazenly industrious black "spivs" of Nairobi) had just sounded the alarm as the thief had tried to lift the bonnet.

"Get him?" I asked.

"Nope. Just blazed away in the darkness to let him know we were on the job."

A few days before we came to stay with the Vincents these marauding black spivs of Nairobi (many of whom are ex-*askaris*, trained in stealth and Commando tactics in Burma) entered their one-story house while they were at dinner and stole £68 worth of laundry, including a household set of new sheets and the entire electric components of a new car. The Vincent watch-dog did not even bark. Sir Alfred claims he is the most useless, friendly dog in all Kenya. He is sort of a James Thurber dog.

Vincent is an outspoken defender of East Africa against all foreign institutions; a strong believer in closer ties with South Africa, where he was born; a great admirer of Smuts, who apparently recognises Sir Alfred as a powerful personality who will have an increasing influence in deciding the political direction which Kenya should take. Remember Smuts' dream (which has long been South Africa's "foreign policy")—Cape Town to dominate Africa up to the Equator. And this big Colonial businessman (with his American interests) probably is the outstanding representative of the imaginative and yet practical commercial side of the emerging Kenya. He is the senior of the eight members of the Executive Council who advise the Governor in private, unless he has resigned this office in order to give more time to his other important posts.

Governor Mitchell's tie-in with the Americans is of an entirely different nature. It began with a dispute; it ended with a wartime partnership of Britain and America in the Pacific which could well be a model for civilian life. Both Britain and the United States were mutually interested in a tiny strategic island called Canton in the Pacific. With the American Navy using it as a base, a British civilian wireless operator there kept sending out messages which, though innocent, threatened to endanger naval security. The Americans warned him twice to stop using his transmitter; the third time he ignored it they sent a detachment of Marines and closed it for him. This tiny incident snow-balled through diplomatic channels from the irate British High Commissioner in the Western Pacific standing on his dignity, through Washington, to London, where by that time it had reached a size which seriously endangered good Anglo-American co-operation in the entire western ocean. The British, acting quickly, withdrew their High Commissioner who had allowed this paltry affair to reach such a crisis and appointed Sir Philip Mitchell, K.C.M.G., M.C., etc., to be Governor of Fiji and High Commissioner for the Western Pacific.

Mitchell went to Washington, read the documents of the case that Lord Halifax gave him, and said: "It looks to me as if we are on a bad wicket. We were wrong here, and we've got to say so." He then flew to Pearl Harbor. There he paid his official call on Admiral Nimitz. "For about a quarter of an hour," he told me, "we exchanged the usual diplomatic nonsense, that falderal . . . with neither of us meaning a word of it, or speaking what was really on our minds. Then I thought it was time for me to go." As they stood up, Admiral Nimitz said: "Sir Philip, there was one little thing I wanted to take up with you—little place called Canton Island. Eh?"

"Canton Island? Oh," said Mitchell, hearing the one name he had been aching to bring into the conversation. "Well, sir, I am glad you brought that up. It gives me the chance to say that we think we were in the wrong there—that we are sorry, and that we undertake that it will not happen again."

"Oh—you do, do you? The *British?*"

Mitchell nodded and departed. He knew that he had planted the seed. That afternoon, when Admiral Nimitz turned up with his Aide to pay his official return call on the British High Commissioner for the Western Pacific, he looked around the hotel and asked Mitchell would he mind stepping out on the lawn. "Nobody can hear us there," he smiled. Then that bluff American Admiral stood there and stared at Mitchell: "Did you mean what you said this morning?"

"Admiral, when I talk to you I will always mean what I say. You are the Commander-in-Chief. I will do what you say. If you tell me to burn down Suva, I will do it . . . but I'd like to have that one in writing."

Nimitz began to grin. "Furthermore," said Mitchell, "I suggest that we take as our understanding between my people and yours: 'No politics west of Hawaii.' Suit you?"

"S-a-y!" Nimitz reached out and grabbed Mitchell's hand. " 'No politics west of Hawaii!' That's all right by me!"

That formula, "No politics west of Hawaii," solved many an awkward incident that came on. For more than two years Mitchell was with the American Forces. When they came to any disagreement, the answer in every case had to be: "What does the operational situation require, for *that* is what has got to be done." In this way the British Governor of the Fijis and High Commissioner lived continuously in American messes all over the

Pacific, and became fast friends with Nimitz, Halsey, Spruance, Fitch, "Popeye" McKain, etc., and was the host to the American Secretary of the Navy, of War, Mrs. Roosevelt and so on; he was with the Americans on Tarawa, Guadalcanal, Bougainville, etc., and was present at several of the operations.

"For all practical purposes," Sir Philip told me, "I found myself in the same relation to Admiral Nimitz as I had been to General Wavell." (He was a Major-General under Wavell in Egypt, taking over the Italian Empire—until Rommel drove them out of it.) "Nimitz was the C.-in-C., and what a great, brilliant commander and delightful personality he was! No better introduction could have been had to a great-hearted man like Nimitz than that Canton rumpus. I was lucky to begin my relations with him on such a foot."

Mitchell said to me: "It was in the Pacific, with the Americans, that I first fully realised that the distressing color conflict which disfigures so much of our life in Africa is totally unnecessary. There is no color bar and no color feeling in the Pacific. Each race respects the other and they get on very well together. It made a deep impression on me and has colored a great deal of my thinking ever since."

Kenya's hotels have the same color bar as those in the United States. When a distinguished Eastern scientist visited Kenya while I was there, Sir Philip invited him to stay at Government House so that he would not meet any unfortunate embarrassments. A young A.D.C., new to Africa, invited this Asiatic to dine at one of Kenya's most exclusive clubs. It took all his ingenuity and the appalled co-operation of the club members to extricate this innocent but ineligible guest from the awkward situation. It was managed so that he never once suspected he was the center of a scene. Mitchell was away at the time, on a tour of Western Kenya, but those at Government House made his stay particularly pleasant as a consequence. And a very pleasant place it can be!

That is one side of him. But Mitchell has an acrid personality; and thirty-three years of sweltering Africa have convinced him, I think, that the best thing to do is speak out and get it over with: being politic is just a waste of time. It is said of him, though the report may be apocryphal, that at a meeting of the War Cabinet where the arrangements he made for putting Haile Selassie back on his throne were being discussed (for he conducted those ticklish negotiations) and Mitchell was not agreeing to the "higher ups'" objections to some of them, that one angry war leader said: "Are you saying that you will not do what we tell you to do?"

Mitchell replied: "No, sir. I am merely saying that I will not think what you tell me to think." It would be just like him.

A man who was present at one of the secret meetings that Mitchell addressed in the House of Commons said to me: "He wasn't very polite about it. But I must say, what he had to say to us sounded very sensible." "Sensible" is unquestionably the operative word in Mitchell's character. People who don't like him—and it would be a poor Governor whom everyone likes—say that he is a careerist. So he is. But what a career! Look him up in *Who's Who*. Most people agree that he is the best Governor that East Africa ever had.

The character of its Governor can very nearly make or break a Crown Colony, as has been the case with Kenya on many a taut occasion. In fact, when you study the history of Kenya you begin to wonder how it ever survived Whitehall. The Governor is appointed by London, but very often, unless he is a rubber-stamp, he has to defy London. What is more, the acid test of a good Governor is that he must be able to make London take it and like it. In this Mitchell seems to have been peculiarly successful. His position was bound to be more difficult than usual, for he has to stand between a Conservative Kenya and a strongly Socialist British Labour Government which looked at the start as if it was going to sweep away many of the old traditions governing colonial life. But Africa is a great "converter" these days; it has undeniably made Creech Jones see the light—Kenyans appreciate his "realistic attitude"—and Governor Mitchell is a moderate man, not a fanatic. Perhaps the foremost duty of a Governor is to govern the *pace* that so-called progress is given to or forced upon a colony; and to one London directive that local government should be begun *at once* to provide Kenya's backward natives with political education and the channel for the expression of their opinions, Mitchell replied:

> It is not by any apologetic or defensive attitude, either before our own people at home or in Africa or in the international

> gatherings largely composed of representatives of the most corrupt and abominable misgovernment extant today, that we shall do what we have to do, but by a restored and reinforced belief in ourselves, our own strength and our own determination to persevere in the task to which we have set our hands, which I conceive to be no less than to civilise a great mass of human beings who are at present in a very primitive moral, cultural and social state, albeit most of them are eager to go further. How primitive the state of these people is and how deplorable the spiritual, moral and social chaos in which they are adrift at the present time are things which can perhaps only be fully realised by those who are in close personal touch with the realities of the situation . . .

The warning in the last sentence is unmistakable. Sir Philip massacres a cliché whenever he sees one. On the report of one official, who had warned that unless Kenya did such and such a thing she would be "hailed before the Bar of world opinion," Mitchell had noted: "There is no such Bar. There is no such thing as world opinion. I wish Mr. X would stop using these meaningless clichés. I am prepared to sign this Report, provided the project is begun at once. By that, I mean March 1st. . . ." In other words: Get cracking! But Mitchell, like most other Governors in Colonial Africa, finds it very hard to find men of the calibre he can delegate responsibility to.

I wish to make it clear that in this part of the book I am saying nothing about Governor Mitchell's other side: his relations with the Kenya settlers. He has, on more than one occasion, pressed for higher Income Tax, a thing they resent bitterly. But he has not pressed for the alienation of any large areas in the White Highlands for African settlement, nor, so far as I know, has he pressed any measure through which will make some Kenya big landowners sell sections of their vast estates which they are not developing. That this should be done, even in the interest of having more European settlers, is a truth that no Kenyan can deny: in fact, many of them are working for it; but not enough. And unless Kenya finds some amelioration of the population pressure of the bursting reserves, all, with the outstanding exception of the Masai and the Nandi, now straining at the seams, then the White Highlands cannot remain inviolate. Believe it or not, some of the settlers have even been agitating to take more land from the Africans. I speak of the Leroki Plateau.

It was recommended by a Land Commission in 1934 as morally belonging to the Samburu, a fine tribe, distant cousins of the warrior Masai. But the 7,000 Samburu natives have yet to be given legal title to this small area of good grazing ground. Psychologically, as I have learned from talks with other Africans, and some Provincial Commissioners, the apparent hesitancy of any Governor to bring that before the Legislative Council is giving the natives at least one good reason for doubting the white man's intentions. It is said—and it is probably true—that this land will never be taken away from the Samburu; the reason given for not bringing it up before the Legislative Council is: "Some of the settlers would raise such a fuss!"

Sir Philip Mitchell is a tired man. Shortly after the guests have gone, for there is hardly a night that Government House is not entertaining somebody, he rolls the *East African Standard* into a cylinder and speaks to his dog Star. Star takes it in his mouth. The two always leave the room together, and leave it early. It would be hard—very hard—to extract from Sir Philip just what impressions thirty-three years of African life have made on him. Scars, mostly. He will sometimes say to you, wearily: "I don't know. . . . I don't know . . ." and then not finish the sentence. He knows too much about Africa to be positive about anything.

The most likeable things about him are his sense of humor and love of sport. He is a great shot, great fisherman (as I can testify), and a top flight golfer. That is how he got Lady Mitchell: he always said that he would marry the first woman who could beat him at golf. Lady Mitchell, then the South African champion, did it. I fished with him up on the Thika River for three days, just before I left Kenya. I knew that he had long given up shooting big game, as most people do who live in Africa; but he had just come from shooting green pigeons, said to be the swiftest bird in the world. I asked him did he still get a thrill out of shooting birds. He smiled: "Do you know, I'm beginning to get the idea they don't enjoy it as much as I do. . . ."

Most members of the British Colonial Service shun publicity. Unlike politicians, they would rather not see their names in print. Of Wyn Harris, Kenya's Chief Native Commissioner, most people who know him well, black or white, seem to agree that he possesses the highest requisite for his post: a heart. Nothing is more needed than absolute sincerity when dealing with Africans. He has it. If Wyn Harris had his way, the color bar would go tomorrow: a black man would have as much right to enter any Kenya hotel, and with as much ease and assurance, as any white man. He is perhaps a little wiser than some of the hidebound whites in Kenya, for he knows that while such a decent state of affairs is unlikely, it can be greatly advanced by laws—and steady pressure. On the terrace of the Grand Hotel at Khartoum you will see Sudanese sitting every night, many as black as that camp headman I wanted to shake hands with, and it would never occur to them or their British colleagues to feel the least sense of awkwardness. This partly refutes the nonsense that you cannot abolish the color bar by any law. You can, when intelligent people begin to make that law a custom.

I think it is just as well to say here, with emphasis, that the more stupid the white man the less intelligent he thinks the black. And some of the white people in Africa who belong to this lower type get above themselves. The women are usually the worst. The story is that one white woman kicked the young Kabaka of Uganda as she climbed on to the train, yelling at him, "Out of my way, boy!" This handsome and sophisticated young hereditary ruler of a native kingdom was then on his way to be the house guest of Wyn Harris.

I need not say more about Wyn Harris, except to mention his existence—in that post. He can be tough with the Africans when he feels it necessary. The duels between himself and Mr. Eliud Mathu, senior African Member of the Kenya Legislative Council, must make even the oil painting of Lord Delamere, greatest Kenyan of them all, smile as he stares down at that session, so quizzically, from the wall of Assembly Hall. Mr. Mathu studied at Balliol. And he is no spring chicken when it comes to debating. He is only a Member nominated by the Governor, and in that invidious position, where he has more the semblance of power than its substance, the personal force of this witty, highly intelligent African (whose father was a witch doctor) often puts proposals he is speaking against in such an unpleasant light that the European members of Leg. Co. feel too embarrassed to go on with them. Mathu knows (as did Gandhi) that you can work wonders with the Englishman—if you make him feel ashamed of himself.*

Now I come to the most "Kenyan" of them all—Major Cavendish-Bentinck. Here is a public figure who will puzzle anybody. I have never met a more self-deprecating personality. But after a while, if your luck is with you, you will note something like summer heat lightning playing behind those half-amused eyes, and you will never know from then on whether he is laughing with you or at you. He takes a lot of knowing. Officially he bears the title of Minister for Agriculture, Animal Husbandry and Natural Resources. In practice, this has now placed him in the position of being the top man, together with the Governor, in putting into action, along a broad general front, all the trans-settlement and land-saving schemes which that hard-working colony now has in hand. In addition, he is in charge of the co-operative marketing schemes, such as the Maize and Produce Control. He is a sort of Sir Stafford Cripps of Kenya. As temperamentally indigenous as any native, I have never seen that bewildering tenderness which most Kenyans feel for their beautiful country better, if more silently, expressed than in the unobtrusive, unyielding resistance of this reticent man. I became aware of this the first time I met him, ten years ago.

At that time most of the big British Press lords (Beaverbrook especially) were trying to bullyrag the British Government into handing Tanganyika back to Germany; this, so as to buy peace in Europe. The Tanganyika British settlers said they would take up arms, fight even the British Army, before they would permit it. This promised civil war, something like Sir Edward Carson's threatened Ulster Rebellion on the eve of the 1914-18 War. Major Cavendish-Bentinck then founded the Tanganyika League. Its motto was: "For King and Tanganyika." It said nothing about England. They were patriots, they always ended their meetings by singing "God Save the King," but they began to train a military formation.

General Boyd Moss, the distinguished soldier who was to lead the Tanganyika rebels in the field, said to me on his beautiful

* Wyn Harris has recently been appointed Governor and Commander-in-Chief of the Gambia.

farm at Moshi: "I am an Englishman, but I am a Tanganyikan first. This is *our* country. We will fight, take up arms against our own people, before we will let any of those politicians in London trade it away from us. We will take to the bush. They'll have to kill a lot of us before they will get this country away from us. And I don't think that public opinion back home [he still called England "home"] will stand for it. However, I am only a simple soldier. The man you should see—the *brain* of the Tanganyika League—lives in Kenya. Nairobi. Cavendish-Bentinck."

It was thus that I met "C.-B.," as he is known all over East Africa, and his dozen or so dachshunds. I had eaten several breakfasts with him before I learned that this drooping, almost melancholic figure, who looks as haunted as De Valera and has much the same dignity, had really begun life as a "simple soldier": first in the Rifle Brigade, then service with Skinner's Horse out in India. Then it only came out accidentally. At one of these breakfasts, when I told him that I intended to meet Jomo Kenyatta, "that agitator!" whom the Kenya Government classes, not altogether justifiably in my opinion (I could name a few white men), as Public Enemy No. 1, C.-B. smiled: "Yes? Well, I've just dictated a letter to you, suggesting some of the people I think you ought to see. He's on the list. But I would go to him alone, if I were you. He won't talk before 'us.' "

I found as I went through Kenya that a signal had been sent out by the Governor instructing all Provincial and District Commissioners that they should feel free to say to me what they wanted. And, what was very much more to the point, it would be to the best interests of Kenya if they called my attention to what they considered to be the bad points of their territories as well as the good. And no man could ask fairer than that.

Sir Philip Mitchell is unconventional, a man of vision, who customarily thinks in terms that go beyond any colony. He is a good friend of the Mohammedan and Arab, a candid admirer of many things in their way of life. I believe that if he could get full understanding from London, enough money to carry out his plans, and the proper men to implement their details, he would do much to restore Britain's former prestige around the Indian Ocean.

CHAPTER VI

Valley of the Great Rift

NEARLY one-half of all the whites in Kenya live in Nairobi itself. But the real Kenya begins, so the old-timers will tell you, only after you have got forty miles out of Nairobi—on the Nakuru road. Although this is the main highway across Kenya the first twenty miles were, up until the end of 1948, incontestably the worst road built since the dawn of Creation. This was the last stretch, left unfinished, of the 100-mile macadam highway which the Italian prisoners of war built for the Kenyans before, much to most Kenyans' regret, they had hastily to be repatriated because of the increasing number of little *café au lait* bastards they were creating, in their spare time, with the otherwise unco-operative African population. Or it may have been only the prospect of that? Kenya wants to keep its blood-stream clean; there is astoundingly little miscegenation in that much misunderstood colony. There is also an astonishing absence of a foreman class or anybody, so it seems, who can build a road. However, the road is now finished. And it leads you to one of the most startling landscapes on earth.

Anyone's first stare out over the unbelievable space of the Great Rift is an emotional experience that he will never forget. You have left the town, passing through that rim of rotting Africans which you see, as the evidence of our civilising influence, on the edge of every European settlement in Africa; you have passed through the green hills, with their regimented rows of coffee bushes, on the European plantations; you have driven across the raw red waste of the worked-out land on the Kikuyu reservation, so reproachful in its barrenness; and then suddenly—at a height of 8,000 feet—the world just drops away from you.

There is a sheer drop here of 2,000 feet, like a wall, straight down from the Kikuyu Escarpment. It makes you gasp. It takes you several minutes to get both your brain and your eyes into focus, to realise that the dark islands moving so mysteriously across the tawny plain far below you are just the shadows of clouds. The Kenya sky in the dry season is a vividly luminous light blue, with a fleece of cream-puff clouds, all floating at the same level, to form a ceiling over you. The lion-colored plains and this light-filled white cloud ceiling form a perspective which pulls you mentally towards a row of bronze and blue volcanoes on the far horizon. A vulture, almost level with you, circles in his lonely space. It is a sight which must have staggered the first explorers, giving them such a thrill that they had to come back again and again to experience it, until, as so many of them did, they left their bones in Africa.

What lies beyond the volcanoes? You can imagine the mystery which must have drawn on the first white men. There is a Phoenician gold trail running straight through one of these bronze cones, showing that it must have erupted since they were there. But the Rift, this great drop, facing its opposite wall some thirty miles off, must have seemed almost ominous to the first white men who saw it. They could not know, of course, for it is only in modern times that it has been mapped and fully understood, that this great crack in the earth's surface was made by a colossal convulsion, which threw up snow-capped Kilimanjaro to the south and only ended by forming the Red Sea to the north. Even when you do understand it, it is a concept that almost scares you. Such is the effect of suddenly coming on the Great Rift. I and many a local Kenyan will always stop our cars there, to sit and eat lunch under the tall cedars, or just gaze with the ineffable freedom with which such space fills you, miles and miles out into nowhere. . . . When the first English settlers saw this country, they were dazzled. They wanted to go no further. And it was down here, in the Valley of the Great Rift, that that thing which we know as the Kenya way of life really began.

Some of the original settlers are still there today. After you have been with them for a time you can easily understand why a 50,000-acre sheep farm where the water-holes were ten miles apart—for that was what the first farms were like—could make a man feel fairly isolated from what was going on in the rest of the world. This is still an aspect of the Kenya mentality. But several of the great oak timbers of the colony, the most representative and travelled of Kenyans, often sent abroad to represent Kenya at the international agricultural conferences, live in this region around Nakuru. Mr. Will Evans and Lord Francis Scott had only recently returned from such a conference in Holland, as delegates from the Farmers' Union which Will Evans had started in the Rift. Will Evans is an ex-trooper from the Boer War, who, wounded, started to walk all the way up to Kenya from the Cape. He has a grand disregard for time or distance or most restrictive regulations. He took me out on his farm at Rongai and introduced me to the two black "boys" who had carried his blankets up from the Coast forty-three years before.

"There they are, the rascals!" he said, grinning at them affectionately. "Look at 'em!" They returned his grin, looking like toothless sharks who are about to bite. They had copper plugs through their dangling ear-flaps. Each wore an old Army service coat that he had given them, with nothing underneath. "Look at 'em! The rascals! I've pensioned them off. Don't know where they are, half the time. Do I, you old scallywags?"

The two black men knew that he was having a good joke. And there is no way better of winning an African's affection than of making him laugh with you. They watched his face, bowing their heads in solemn agreement when they saw that he was talking with me seriously, though neither could understand one word of what he said. "Eh! . . ." said Will, "if there were only more like this!"

Will Evans has a face which itself tells you he has borne "the heat of the day." High-cheek-boned, heavy-browed, with iron grey hair and about as kindly a smile as ever a man could show. It might tarnish the description if I said that he looked like a weather-beaten but much more thoughtful President Harding. "You ask me," he said, "what I think of the present progress of the natives?" He sighed. "All I can tell you is there must be something definitely wrong with the way we are handling them. Schools? All I can say is, we will have to build more jails to take the products of those schools. Just look at what is happening: it is the 'educated' native who is now organising all the stealing. *He* is the man who breaks down all the old, and good, tribal ways. The chiefs and the village headmen can't handle him, and we . . . we seem to be giving him something that isn't *good* for him. When you see a great mass of them going this way, well—you just must know that we are giving him something that is wrong. That stands to reason. I know what they say . . . all this business about the native being 'in transition.' But to what? That's the question that I would like to have answered. Where are we taking him? Breaking up his old life to make a white-collared clerk of him? That's not going to make him any good to anybody . . . himself included. Make a street-corner loafer out of him. Seems to me, all we're doing is making an unhappy man out of him. . . ."

You hear that everywhere from these old settlers, the sad story of the native African in transition from one civilisation to another. And frequently as you listen to them, you wonder if there really is not something fundamentally wrong that we are doing to his mind, with our ideas of what constitutes an education. And the wonder grows when you begin to realise how little we stop to analyse either the ethics or the efficacy of our imposition: our civilising mission, as we like to see it. Dr. Arnold's training in character seems to have done no good to the native African. He had it once; all we seem to be doing is take it away from him. It is but natural that a man who has lived cheek by jowl with the African for over forty years, borne the heat of the day with him, should be a little dubious about the value of a new Welfare Officer to supervise the way he should handle his black laborers. Will Evans has a good story to tell about that.

He had pensioned off these two old faithful retainers of his some years back, telling them that they had done enough hard work for him in their lives. He had a hard job to make them understand that. He gave each man a plot of land to build a hut on and to have him and his wife cultivate for themselves; he also gave them a pension of 7*s*. a month. "I just turned 'em loose—like a good horse that you want to have end his days in peace."

One day, one of these old natives was walking into Nakuru, when he was stopped by the new Welfare Officer who was making a tour of inspection in his motor-lorry. He was asked where he worked, and the native, with his chin, pointed in the direction of Will Evans' farm. How much did he get paid a month?

"Seven shillings."

"Seven shillings!" exclaimed the Welfare Officer, thinking he had caught some white settler underpaying his laborers (the average pay for a farm laborer is six pence a day). "How long have you worked for this *bwana?*"

"Eighty years."

"*What?*" The W.O. stared at the native, who might, or might not, be that old—natives age very quickly. "You jump in back," he ordered. "Show me where your *bwana* lives."

The frightened native was driven back to the farm. Will Evans came out, and this conversation took place: "Does this boy work for you?" "He does." "He—ah—says you only pay him seven shillings a month?" "That's right." "But—ah—he also says that he has worked for you *eighty* years?" "That's right also—according to his way of counting. You see," said old Will Evans patiently to the young officer, "this country here is a land of two seasons: we get two crops every year—that is, *if* the rains come, and the locusts *don't*. The natives don't keep any sort of calendar—they go by the *seasons*. . . . Well, when I pensioned these boys off some years back, I told them that they had worked eighty seasons for me. . . . So . . ."

"Oh. I *am* sorry!"

"Oh, that's all right, mister. Any time you want any help, just let me know. I've known most of these boys around here, this part of the world, since they were *totos* [babies]. Sent a lot of 'em to jail, in fact."

For seven years Mr. Will Evans had been the local magistrate. But his methods, it seems, had been rather unorthodox. I believe that when he discovered that the black thieves in the district were organising the young children to steal trek-chains, he organised counter-thieves to steal them back—and at the same time get the names of the men behind the thefts. He produced culprits from long distances, by unspecified methods, and made them face charges. Then he "slapped it to them." Effective, but not the precise juridical "niceness" that the legal purists of Nairobi are so insistent must be observed. He prefers farming.

He is ranching now 1,500 high-grade Ayrshires and Frisians

on 6,000 Kenya acres, only 4 acres to a beast—which is an achievement in that Colony. All of his land was once a great game country, full of lions, zebra, wildebeest—those three great inseparables—buck, rhino, with herds of elephants up in its neighboring forests. Today you will still see buck and giraffe and an occasional ostrich cantering across it. A volcano, Menengai, with a crater seven miles in diameter, lords it over this peaceful scene and seems to be trying to hold you in its spell. To get up to this part of the world, you drive over grassy plains, where the red-shanked plover and grey-hawks lift in the wind, on a straight strip of macadam (laid by these Italian prisoners of war), past three beautiful lakes: long and slender Elmenteita, with its thousands of pink flamingos looking like water-lilies on its edge; Naivasha, twelve by nine miles, with white yachts sailing and a hippo just as likely as not to stick its pink nose up and puff at you; and the white-shored soda lake of Nakuru, facing whose retreating edge lies the little cow-town which bears that name, still Kenya's third largest European settlement.

"When we first came here," said Will Evans placidly, "we didn't even know the seasons of the year; didn't know the rainfall; didn't know what to plant—nor when to plant it. By jingo! We didn't even know the right implements to use. Had to find out all that. Yes, and we had to find out also that a lot of the best-looking land around here was sheer poison. The Masai knew, but we didn't; we never stopped to think that we never saw a Masai graze his cattle on that land. That broke a lot of us! Killed cattle off fast as we put them on it. That's what nearly did for Lord Delamere, broke him a couple of times. . . ." He gave an unconscious sigh. "I thought I was done for myself once. Couldn't see any way out of it. Then old Grogs (E. S. Grogan) came to me. 'Stick it, Will,' he told me. 'You aren't done yet. Make the banks carry you.' So I stuck it and . . . well, here I am." He sighed again with contentment. "Old Grogs certainly knew how to handle the banks!"

E. S. Grogan is the famous Kenyan, still alive (and very much so) who, as a young Cambridge undergraduate, walked from Cape to Cairo in 1899-1900, fighting his way single-handed through the Kivu cannibals and up the marshes of the Nile through the terrible Dinka country. He is like a cat among the pigeons with some of the slower-witted Kenyans. Will Evans smiled: "This country will do for me, right where we're standing. This is 6,000 feet. As you get older, I suppose, you ought to go down a bit, ease the heart. But in this country every man can find his own altitude. Ha, ha. That's a joke, that is. And 6,000 feet suits me."

In the Rift Valley Club at Nakuru you will see these people. They may be a peer of the Realm, a relative of Royalty; they may be, like Will Evans, a trooper from the Boer War. They may be a unique personality, such as that astonishing woman, the mother of Elspeth Huxley, the Hon. Mrs. Nellie Grant—one of the most sensible, lovable, industrious women I have ever encountered; with her eight dachshunds and unorthodachshunds, her two boxers, her tame hornbill, household of black servants who just would not work for anyone else, her poultry, and the Angora rabbits she raises for their fur; that delightful little home on the slope of Njoro, with the Goya over its fireplace. But they are all members of the same clan. They all bear the mark of having been through adversity together; you can see it on their faces. New members will be admitted to the Rift Valley Club, but they will never "belong" to that original club. They will never have the experience which has united its charter members.

Hugh Coltart is another "character" in that district. He runs a 12,000-acre farm for Lord Egerton of Tatton and a 1,200-acre one for himself, on which he is running 500 head of cattle with 500 acres under cultivation, a remarkable example of good farming in this volcanic valley. The beauty of this huge volcanic plain with its miles of golden wheat rimmed by layers of blue mountains is enough to strike one dumb. So it is to listen to Hugh talk. He is slightly deaf; a red-faced, hearty man, who thinks he is whispering to you sometimes at cocktail parties (sundowners as they call them). And so one evening he told me how he had been back in London, where, much to his annoyance, he had to go into hospital to have an operation for piles:

"A mangy-looking sort of person came in to shave my backside in the morning. He had an old-fashioned razor. I said to him, 'Do you know how to use that thing?' He said: 'I've been shaving people, sir, for just your operation, for over twenty-five years.' I said: 'Shaving other people's bottoms for twenty-five years! My God! *What* a profession!' "

But get him to tell you about the locusts! In 1931-2 half the cereal crops in Kenya were destroyed by locusts, when they blackened the sky. "The first drove, I said: 'Well, we've got something left.' But then another . . . another. . . . Finally, there wasn't a *blawsted* sheaf left! By God! What a blow!"

Lord Delamere, the greatest Kenyan of them all, lost thousands and thousands of pounds in trying to ranch sheep and cattle on this very soil—land which today is rearing some of the finest cattle in Africa simply because of the addition of cobalt nitrate to the salt licks. (The effectiveness of this was discovered quite by accident in New Zealand—as a residue—when conducting experiments in soil treatment.) It was the absence of minerals which cobalt nitrate made up for which had made the grazing poisonous for the cattle. "The Masai knew!" as Will Evans said. As the red polls survived better than the Ayrshires and Frisians on the old mineral-deficient soil, Hugh Coltart has now gone in for red polls: "And—my God—they *blossom* on it!" Coltart has been on that spot for thirty-five years.

On the far side of blue Lake Naivasha you will see the white-turreted Moorish residence which used to belong to Lord Errol. It now belongs to Gilbert Colvile, who ranches more cattle than any man in Kenya—all native beasts. It is said (though I can't know with what truth) that if the warrior Masai ever had the chance to pick a delegate to represent them on the Kenya Legislative Council, it would be this quiet but very tough little man. He knows more about the Masai, and their cattle, than any European in the colony. He has some 30,000 acres around Naivasha, and much more than that elsewhere. He prefers native cattle to European because they are more or less immune to the tick fevers, and by skilful up-breeding he has produced a very good grade of beast. He has secured himself plenty of choice land to do it on. The average cattle ranch in that part of the world, the right-sized economic unit, is 20,000 acres. Lord Delamere had one sheep farm here of 100,000 acres. But those days are over.

Here is where the real Kenya way of life began. Not, as the world knew it, that sporting assortment of self-exiled aristocrats, known as the Happy Valley (they took that from *Rasselas*) lot up at Gilgil. That crowd which used to begin its drinking at sundown and not finish till sunrise, which shot various members of its own set when sexual adventures became too complicated; men who read Horace, lying under a tree with an iced champagne bottle handy—and who would go into the bush after a wounded lion as casually as if they were looking for their hat. Personally, I think that those decorative people did Kenya far more good than harm: they gave the Colony its exhilarating spirit of adventure. The Happy Valley lot defied all the laws of life (and retribution), and so has Kenya. If Kenya ever went by the accepted laws of economics, she would have been dead broke and gone into the receiver's hands long ago. If that spirit of adventure ever goes from Kenya, Kenya's backbone goes with it.

"What will maintain the prosperity and dignity of this Colony?" said one of its richest inhabitants to me. "Nothing! The prosperity is false—it is based on a false economy. And nothing but the feeling of adventure has enabled this colony to weather many a crisis. If you don't have that feeling of personal risk and the joy of adventure—but have a money-making philosophy—then this colony will be a flop. If a man comes here with a check for £20,000, *and expects a safe return*, he is a dangerous man to the country. If a man comes here with £2,000, and the determination that nothing in God's green earth is going to drive him out of Kenya, then that's the man we want. We want the plugger, the sticker. They're the men who made Kenya."

He ought to know. In November, 1903, this man landed at Mombasa with one bag of "Early Rose" potatoes, one bag of European peas, one bag of haricot beans, one bag of linseed for planting, two white Basuto ponies, and £23 10*s*. *od*.—all the money he had in the world. Today he owns the New Stanley and Norfolk Hotels (unless he has just sold them) and 40,000 acres of the best farm-land in Kenya.

The Happy Valley lot have gone. With them has gone much of the reckless "Kenya way of life." They were lions among men, and the lions are going with them; I think they understood each other; both were unafraid. If you want to know what they were like, read *Out of Africa*, by Baroness Blixen (Isak Dinesen), one of the finest books ever to come out of that continent. I have lunched in the home that she lost and loved so much, with its dark panelled walls of wood brought out from Denmark; and I have met her boy Ali—still talking about her! He is now Governor Mitchell's majordomo on private train or *safari* or at the Thika fishing camp. Sir Philip told me that when he engaged Ali, that smiling boy said to him: "But remember, *Bwana Makuba*, I am *Memsahib* Blixen's boy. If she come back, I go to her!" I rose peak high in Ali's esteem when I told him I had lunched that charming woman in Copenhagen in November, 1939. I could do no wrong after that.

There are other settlers of this aristocratic breed who came out to Kenya to try and continue the life that they knew was doomed in England: that enviable life of the nobleman living on his broad acres. Lord Francis Scott came out to Kenya with this intention and a fair enough sum of money, which he lost; but he has made enough of it back now to retire contentedly on the stone veranda of the Edwardian mansion he erected facing the blue Kenya mountains beyond his flower beds: that irascible, aristocratic figure with the kindly blue eyes, who often tried to bend the whole Colony to his will. For a long and trying time (for those he disagreed with), Lord Francis Scott was the Leader of the white settlers.

He was seriously wounded in the First World War, and after years of acute suffering has only recently had his foot amputated. When the weather was bad, or Sir Francis's foot bothered him, he went down to Nairobi and took it out on the Legislative Council, so they complain.

All these people, these early Kenyans, are now giving the benefit of their experience, not always happy, to the new settlers who have recently come out to Kenya. The Hon. Nellie Grant has been practically the patron saint of the Egerton Agricultural College. She probably knows as much about what *not* to do in Kenya as any man in it.

CHAPTER VII

Land Schemes

THE post-war schemes for settling in Kenya this time have been small. When the Tenant Farmers' scheme for settling ex-Servicemen had run out of the Crown land alienated for it, only 256 persons (including men and their families) had been accepted for farms. When I was at the Egerton Agricultural School in January 1948, only thirty-five of these farmers had actually been settled on their land. In all, including some big farms which have changed hands by private purchase, only 669 European settlers had taken up land in Kenya from the end of the war up to August 1947. And of these 481 were Kenya nationals, 147 were ex-Servicemen from overseas, and 41 were non-ex-Servicemen. Until it is possible to persuade some of the big European landowners in Kenya to break up their estates (and one or two should certainly be broken up), there will be no more new land for settlers in the White Highlands–unless, and this would harm the Colony in the long run, some of the big forest reserves are thrown open. As the water table is already sinking alarmingly in East Africa, I do not think that this will be done. But they were good schemes, handled with imagination, care and foresight–both in Kenya and at the London end. Good people were in charge of them; they were well conceived; nothing like the sad Soldiers' Settlement Schemes which disgraced the aftermath of the 1914-18 War. And just because both of them might be reopened again, they are worth describing. There were two schemes: Tenant Farmers and Assisted Ownership. Both these schemes required that a prospective farmer started with a large amount of *his own* capital.

A Tenant Farmer was supposed to have from £1,700 to £3,000. An Assisted Owner from £3,000 to £5,000. So that rosy dream of being able to "go out to the Colonies" and make a living just by the strength of your own good character and right arm was killed before any unfortunates could ever get out to Kenya. A pity, but those days have gone: these two settlement schemes were kind just because they were based on that hard fact. Moreover, a man would have a very hard job to pass the Selection Board at the East Africa Office in London if he did not show that he had at least some practical or theoretical knowledge of farming, or convinced those on the Committee—seasoned settlers themselves—that he was the sort who would set-to and quickly learn such things. In this connection, the personality of the wife was of extreme importance, and, though she may never have been aware of it, she was being analysed in the minds of the Committee as to whether she would stick Kenya or not.

When I was at the Egerton Agricultural School, where some ninety-five Tenant Farmers were being given a nine-months' course in arable dairy-farming, the backbone of the scheme, two graduates who had already been settled on farms had both just given it up—their wives "couldn't stand Kenya"! A few months later, when I came back to the school and was at the Njoro Hostel for its prospective settlers, a cable came while we were having tea from one of those men (both were R.A.F., with exceptional war records): COMING BACK QUICKEST POSSIBLE PLEASE ARRANGE, etc.—the two wives had changed their minds. That sounds vacillating; but both these R.A.F. officers and their wives were popular at the school and with their brother pupils, and I dare say that it has now worked out all right. But the woman in most cases is the unknown quantity in each farmer-settler's life. Sometimes, though, it is the man: Africa isn't what he thought it to be—"Why, this is nothing but damned hard work!"

The greatest change in this soldier settlement scheme from those which followed the 1914-18 War is that the type of people wanted now are those who would normally engage in tenant farming in England, but who had insufficient capital to undertake farming in a highly-developed country like England. In short, real farmers were wanted for Kenya. No more of that nonsense about the "gentleman," the public school boy, making the best type of settler—"because, by nature, he knows better how to get on with the natives." That false premise has been thrown into the discards. The yeoman type of farmer has already shown that he is the best man for the new Kenya. I saw several, and one made me smile: "I may not know much about Africa," said he, who had been parachuted into Yugoslavia, "but I am a farmer by profession. I know how much work ought to be got out of a man. Maybe that will be useful when it comes to handling these black boys." It certainly will! But I wonder how long it will be before the black boys begin to break his heart?

The Njoro Hostel, an old ex-private mansion with a lovely view from a high ridge, was an annex of the school: it provided accommodation for married men and their families, as an overflow from such quarters at the school, as well as a reception center for settlers before they are found farms and to give them time to look around.

Part-time courses for wives in dairying, cheese-making, poultry, etc., were given free at the same time. It was a rule that a married couple could not live outside while taking the course. The school was under the Headmastership of J. E. P. Booth, B.Sc., Agric.(Lond.), who held the Wye Diploma of Agriculture—and who had been at the Imperial College of Tropical Agriculture, Trinidad. He was a dry, intelligent, precise man; and to handle ninety-five people, ex-Servicemen and their wives, some of whom had been brigadiers—or sergeants—only a few years back, was a job that I believe would have broken the heart of Job.

"My God!" swore one of these to me (a Penguin, by the way). "Being sent back to *school* again! Damnable! After all the war, too!"

A D.F.C., sick from fever, lay on his cot in the Njoro Hostel and yawned wearily: "Oh, we'll get over it. Only, I wish they'd let us have that land in the Forest Reserve!"

Mr. Stuart Gillett, Director of Agriculture in Kenya, said he hoped that the Egerton School could be continued (it is now closed), and that another Tenant Farming Scheme could be started. He said that there were still "far too many insufficiently developed alienated farms," i.e. big European landholdings which it would be better to break up if they are not farmed to their capacity. This is a very sore point with many of the wealthy Kenya landowners; they will try to oppose this breaking up by every means they can—chiefly by their influence in the Kenya Legislative Council. If they persist, I think that either Sir Philip Mitchell, or the next Governor of Kenya, will have to get tough with these people, some of whom are absentee landlords, and legally make them sell part of their vast estates.

I encountered a strong feeling on this subject in Kenya, especially about some women who own vast areas in Kenya and cannot possibly live on their immense and widely spread estates, but just draw down the money that is extracted from their lands by paid managers—*that* is not settling. Unfortunately, some of these immense tracts belong to some of the most charming people in the Colony, people who are almost naïve in their simplicity, and who would be unable to be mean to anybody. You cannot confiscate land from people like this without imposing a Socialist ruthlessness. You can merely convince them that the time for cutting down these vast landholdings is here; and that for the good of Kenya itself, the land should be shared among more people.

There are others, of course, who are just land misers and should be treated accordingly. Believe it or not, I have met men who want to take even more land from the natives—such as the Leroki Plateau. Such people are social morons. They are unaware of what is going on in this world, and what will happen to Kenya if they persist in their selfish way. But it would be incorrect to say that they are not still powerful enough to make trouble. As you hear them talk, say in some up-country club, you feel like saying with Peer Gynt: "*Beautiful Earth, forgive me for having trodden thee all to no purpose*."

The most interesting, almost sinister, thing about the present-day settlement in Kenya is that it is not the younger, but the older men who want to go overseas. I had heard this before I went out to Kenya from friends of mine in the Civil Service whose work it was to place ex-officers and soldiers in employment. They said: "It's surprising, but the spirit to go out overseas seems to have gone. Especially from the *young* men!" There seemed to be two reasons that they could think of: the first was that this war seems to have exhausted the *soul* of many men, made them world-weary, and they do not want struggle any more. Under the various social benefits of the Labour Government, they seem to have been insured against real destitution or ill-luck such as sickness, unemployment, etc., if they stayed in Britain. So why go overseas and take on another fight? Next, the idea of settling overseas seems to have lost its romance. There is nothing exciting about it. "It is just a bloody awful grind in a country that is too damned hot to be comfortable in." And that is true. The great rewards of settling overseas—when you could grab off a 20,000-acre farm for six pence or less per acre in Kenya—have gone for ever. Farming in the Colonies today is a full-time, hard job. It always was, really, though the Romantics did not know it.

Finally, with the rise in the price of passage, etc., as well as the long time one must wait before getting accommodation, the difficulty and restrictions of reaching a new land—always with the necessity of having a fairly large sum of capital—have made many a good man not even try to go out.

I think this gives some idea of the smallness of the post-war immigration into Kenya and at the same time the soundness of the schemes on which it has been based. This unique Colony, that has been so much maligned and misunderstood, will probably prove that it has shown the most intelligence and moderation in handling its immigration problem of any of the African territories. If the new Kenya settlers work hard—and they will have to—these farms should succeed.

I went out to several of these new farms, which I shall describe in a later chapter. It is an invigorating sight to see a man breaking in new land or bringing back land that has been allowed to go to waste. The Crown lands that were occupied under the scheme were virtually virgin bush, where the Tenant Farmers lived in tents or temporary mud-and-wattle huts pending the construction of permanent houses. In this way, fighting the bush for their farm, they are repeating the thrilling experience of some of the early settlers. And you can get a pretty good line on what sort of settlers these people will make by asking them what sort of house they intend to build. The man who starts talking about a £5,000 structure (as one of them did to me) can, in my opinion, be washed out right away.

There is so much talk about making a success of farming these days that one almost forgets that it is a way of life. The faces of the young people at the Njoro Hostel wore a general air of impatient expectancy, showing how eager were these new settlers to start to "live" as they had hoped. It comes as a shock to them that they will have to compete, in most cases, with the older settlers. Especially those who will go in for dairy and market products, selling to Kenya townships. This is one of the disturbing realities that they will have to get used to; but they are as impatient as dogs waiting to be taken out shooting. One family we met—father, mother, two sons and two daughters—had brought out two jeeps from England and had driven up to Njoro from the coast with most of their worldly goods. A modern Swiss Family Robinson. Their enthusiasm was enviable; so was their innocence. They didn't know what they were going to raise or grow, exactly; "but Mother preferred lavender." One of the daughters had become engaged to one of the young ex-officer tenant settlers at the Egerton School—and *that* farm was already being talked about with delirious expectations. One lady from (say, Cheltenham), who obviously hated, and was frightened of, a farmer's life, said rather pathetically: "I left my old people and my sixteen-year-old daughter at home and it was awful, but I shall get used to it. My husband *would* come!" Others had paired up; and one old chap of the sporting type kept saying over and over: "I wouldn't go back [to England] for anything. I wouldn't live under *that* Government [Labour]. I am going to be a free man!" He had bought a £5,000 house with 120 acres and a 1,400-acre adjacent farm for his son. *He* may be able to feel free, but his son will have to get up at seven o'clock every morning to take the roll-call of his black laborers—and Kenya will be his master from then on.

One of the most naïve figures I met in Kenya was a young man who amused us all at dinner on a big farm up on the Molo Downs, telling its owner and family and the two white managers at the table (he was a pupil-assistant): "I left England because I wasn't going to have *anyone* tell me what to do! I wasn't going to be booted about by their Socialist restrictions. I won't *have* restrictions!"

"You—ah—won't have restrictions?" the owner of the farm gently said to him. "How *very* interesting."

I don't think that young man will last long, unless he radically changes his mind. What *looks* free and easy in Kenya very often is the smiling face of a Spartan régime. To go out on the big 8,000-acre farm of Walter Trench up on the Molo Downs, for instance (once President of the Kenya Farmers' Association), is such a pleasant and restful experience—for its vast, rolling landscape looks exactly like Wiltshire—with no one apparently being either fussed or very hard-worked, that, as the R.A.F. would say, it looks like a piece of cake. But every morning at seven o'clock, Walter Trench is out there in his farmyard with his youngest daughter riding pick-a-back on his shoulders, hearing the roll-call of those of his 137 boys who are on shift for that day. He stands there with his two young English managers (each of whom gets £29 10*s*. a month), and together they plot out each piece of work on the farm for that day—and which natives are to do it. One of the young managers is in charge of all the mechanical equipment, tractors, ploughs, combines, machine-shop, etc.; the other handles the labor force. Everything is as well ordered and smooth-running on that farm as in a good battalion's day. On his 8,000 acres Trench has 1,200 cattle and 5,000 high-grade sheep, with a large and variable number of acres always under cultivation. He is one of the most successful wheat and pyrethrum farmers in Kenya, and, aside from being President of the Kenya Farmers' Association, he was also Chairman of the Pyrethrum Board. A few of the fixed and inescapable charges on this farm are: wages, native = £1,200 yearly; Europeans' salaries and bonuses = £1,000; food for native laborers = £700; fertiliser = £1,500. That means at least £4,400 must be found before one penny of profit can be taken. For the year of 1947-8, he told me, he expected his turnover to be £17,000, with an overhead of £10,000. That sounds rather prosperous, yet—

In 1924, Walter Trench and his wife were living on this same property in a mud-and-wattle hut. They had come there in 1920, after Trench had worked with his friend, another Irishman, Frank Joyce, at Ulu, until he got the hang of how at least to start farming in Kenya. He bought 500 acres on Mau Summit and put up only a grass hut. They lived eighteen months in that grass hut, then another eighteen in the mud-and-wattle hut. They had no kitchen, cooked on a fire made between three stones, and the bath was out in the open, on the veranda. The room they had intended for the bath was found to be too precious—it was needed as a dairy. The hut had a mud floor. Their two first children were born on it, without the aid of a doctor. When two neighbors came along, as amateurs, to assist with the second child, the baby arrived before them, and they spent the rest of that night drinking the bottle of whisky they had brought along for Walter Trench.

Today the Trenchs have a home built of brown natural stone, with a deep fireplace which they built themselves, and a restful roof of red drain-pipe tiles, put on by the Italian prisoners of war, who seem to have done all the artisan work for Kenya before they were repatriated. (Kenya is now bringing 4,000 of them back again.)

The atmosphere of easy and good-living at the Trenchs', where you all sprawl before the log fire after dinner—in your pyjamas and dressing gowns—with everything, seemingly, so restful and secure, covers a background where, more than once, this farm was not the Trenchs' at all: when he was owned by the banks. In 1921 he bought his first 500 acres; he bought another 4,000 in 1924, and in 1927 he bought another 4,000 (at about £1 an acre); but in 1930 came the world slump and Trench was so heavily in debt to, and pressed by, the banks that he said to them disgustedly: "Take the whole —— lot! Otherwise, shut up and loan me some more money." They did. But in 1932 the locusts came along and cleaned him out again. And when the locusts come in Kenya, they can stop railway trains; their pink, repulsive bodies make such a mash that the wheels of the locomotive cannot get a grip.

Not until this war was Walter Trench able to clear off all the farm's indebtedness and begin to lay by some much-earned capital. World food demands practically guarantee good prices for all he grows now. And he, like nearly all the rest of the old Kenya farmers, is storing money up against drought, locusts, and all the unknown factors which make large-scale farming in Kenya such a big gamble. That heavy overhead can break a man in two years. So no one need grudge the Kenya farmers their prosperity; they are no more avaricious or hard-hearted than are the farmers in Britain—and they don't get one-half the Government protection and assistance.

Few guests of the Trenchs realise that while they are sleeping the farm is being worked all night. Tractors are ploughing: each tractor has a recording instrument which shows when it is running, and for how long and when it has been stopped. I was surprised to see that the night-cards showed more continuous operation than the day-cards. "Oh," said Walter Trench, "the natives like working at night." "Do they!" laughed his impudent young labor manager. "What you mean is, they are afraid to stop the tractor and get off—for fear the hyenas would eat them!"

The life of these young Englishmen who have come out to Kenya as managers or pupil-assistants is poignantly interesting, because they all intend to win a farm for themselves some day. At Trenchs' place the three lived in the Guest House, with its big communal fireplace, under the high thatched roof below some towering blue gum trees that sighed most mournfully at night. It is cold at 8,000 feet after the sun goes down. Our rooms were separated only by high partitions of papyrus reeds, called "Kavirondo mats," so that you could see, by his light, if any of the others were awake.

When these white boys come in from their work they take their hot bath, then get into pyjamas and dressing gowns, as every old farming family does in Kenya, and eat their dinner with the man who owns the farm, and his family. Depending upon how well they get on with the family, they sit for long or short lengths of time around the main farm's big fireplace after dinner. Then they go back to their own digs. The redhead who ran this farm's technical equipment left us early one evening saying he was going to write some letters home. I wonder what he wrote? For theirs is essentially a hard and lonely life; yet the vision of that farm—their own bit of land—is always before them. Very often they have selected the site. I mention this because it is in these young men that you see examples of those who can come out to Kenya with practically no money—but who have had the initiative to gain some useful knowledge before leaving England—who can, even in these days, still win a farm by hard work. But they will have to be of resolute character, and dedicate themselves to that farm as irrevocably as a monk does to his vows.

Walter Trench had recently bought an American bulldozer, and had already made himself a beautiful dam with it, blocking a valley with a dirt revetment over fifty feet high. A lake was beginning to form, with egrets settling in its bushy banks; water-lilies were appearing—and Trench had already declared the coming lake to be a bird sanctuary. Every migrating duck would be safe on it. Neighbors came in while we were staying with him, begging him to let them use his bulldozer. He will, if they can pay him for it. It will build many a dam in that Molo district before it is worked out; but Walter Trench was so "dam-conscious" when I was with him that he could talk of nothing else. He had dams in his mind's eye, all over his property, which has at least one fairly good trout stream. Dams are the best insurance against disaster in Kenya. And a young man who, today, goes out to Kenya with a bulldozer could make a good living and get a farm that way quicker than in any other I could think of.

Personally, I like changes of seasons. I would not miss the smell of the April earth in North Devon, where I own a mite of land on that lonely section of the English coast, for all the land in Africa. But if I *was* going out to Kenya, I would buy me a bulldozer, learn how to run it and repair it, then—*with plenty of spare parts*, almost another bulldozer, in fact—I would take ship for Mombasa. And I would not work for anybody except myself from then on.

"Pussy" Trench, Walter's eldest daughter, had bought 1,500 acres adjacent to his land, and now runs her own farm. Sheep, mostly; with 160 acres under wheat and flax. She has a tiny house-boy named Cheriot, who used to herd turkeys. When I first saw him, he was sitting on the top of a big racehorse. Now, aged ten, in a little blue robe and cap, he is the majordomo, and is so important that Pussy Trench has to take him down occasionally: "Oh, you're much too swell!" she teases him. "You don't know anything." "I do. I know *everything!*" answers Cheriot. He runs to meet her car, takes all her things, puts them away, bosses the other boys that dare come near the house, etc.—and now, as the cook left when he was not given the higher wage he demanded, Cheriot, aged ten, is the cook. The Admirable Crichton is not to be compared with him—this tiny, laughing Limb of Satan.

The house Pussy Trench lives in is a delightful example of the way the right sort of person can live in Kenya. It cost exactly £50 for its original owner to build some twenty years ago. It is made of cedar logs, the barked "outsides" that are usually turned into kindling by the saw-mills; its roof is dried grass thatched over poles cut from the forest that have never been dressed or trimmed; its floor of cedar is seasoned and deeply polished today, with leopard and sheep-skin mats. And she has deep chairs (home-made) before a deep stone fireplace, flanked with rows and rows of books. The whole effect is utterly satisfying, esthetically and for comfort. I can't think how any settler would want any better. Even at present prices, such a home could be built for less than £100. What more can a man want?

Walter Trench is engaged in numerous public activities, and during the war Pussy Trench ran his 8,000-acre farm as well as her own—ran it just as efficiently as he did, so all the other Kenya settlers say. So did Pamela Scott run Lord Francis's estate. And that remarkable young woman, Anne Joyce, ran her father's 20,000-acre dairy farm down at Ulu in the "brown country." She is still really the mainspring of that fine farm and gets up to do her day's work at sunrise every morning. These three young women have all made a name for themselves as farmers. And they all love it. They give most male farmers an inferiority complex.

Pussy Trench's chief ambition, however, is to raise and run race-horses. Biscuit-colored ones, preferably. She had a horse in one of the big events during Race Week while we were visiting her parents, and went down to Nairobi to see it run. She told us not to put our shirts on it. Luckily, we did not. If they had black jockeys in Kenya, I am certain that little Cheriot would be one. "I know *everything!*" In the rainy season the elephants come out of the forest and roam about Pussy Trench's estate. . . .

She has just what she wants, and I have met few who are so completely aware of it. Her farm, despite changing times, is the Kenya farm of many a man's dreams. A life in which every day is interesting. As one old Kenya settler said to me, when I was describing my delight at finding everything so *sensible* at Pussy Trench's home:

"Any prospective settler who starts belly-aching about his house—a big house—had better get out of Kenya. He's no good to the country."

These farms are at 8,000 feet altitude. The country is grassy. rolling downs, so much like Wiltshire, as I have said, that a photograph taken of it would be identical. They even have stands of trees on some of the hills around Molo that look like Chanctonbury Ring. The top forests are deep, grey-lichened cedar forests. There are great stands of pine (*Pinus insignius*), which give some of the sweeping valleys the appearance of the Bernese Oberland. The country is full of rufus hawks, their white breasts shining in the clear sun; its swampy valleys have golden-crested crane wandering among the rushes.

This is a great horse-raising country, and there is a lot of riding and hunting. There was a Hunt Ball at Molo that Christmas. But I found it too high for my liking: at 8,000 feet, I could hardly keep awake after dinner, and writing my notes was an odious job. Some people that I visited on their farm at 9,000 feet gave me the impression, definitely, that they were affected by the altitude—they were jumpy, taut, touchy—they had what is known as "Kenya Nerves." This was directly on the Equator; a nearby station of the Kenya and Uganda Railway is named Equator, after one called Summit. I think it has yet to be proved whether the second generation of white people born at that height will be altogether unaffected by it. I think this is asking too much of Kenya.

CHAPTER VIII

The Boers; New Settlers at Kitale

MOST of the post-war settlers have been put down on farms around Kitale, one of the most beautiful bits of all Kenya. It lies at from 6,000 to 8,000 feet across the Nzoia River and around the slopes of towering Mt. Elgon. Here is Kenya, the real thing, such as many people must have pictured in their dreams. To get there from the grassy Molo Downs you pass through mountains deep with belts of creepered, indigenous cedar and podo forests; grey forests, where the towering trees and their dangling parasites seem locked in a static combat, and the black-and-white colobus monkeys swing from branch to branch, travelling in their own world high over your head. There are forests of feathery bamboo on the highest ridges from 9,000 feet and up. And then you drop down past the saw-mills, to come out on the vast, golden, seemingly empty plain of the Uasin Gishu Plateau. This is the Boer country, first settled by the South Africans who came to Kenya in 1904-7. It is strongly reminiscent of the old trek Boer, with his undying passion for space, even to this day. It seems that you can go on here for mile after mile without seeing either man or beast. Just the dark islands of the wattle plantations standing on this feathery sea. Then you come to the town of Eldoret. The nicest thing about Eldoret is the road leading in and out of it, flanked for a mile or so by flowering gums; the beautiful Nandi-flames, with their dark green leaves and vermilion blossoms; the long side avenues, when you get into the town, of the hyacinth-blue jacaranda trees.

It is said that when the Boers first came to this part of Kenya—with its bare, flat-topped hills, and the round shale mountains so like their beloved *kopjes* in the Transvaal—that they out-spanned at once, saying: "Here is a land where our women can breed in space!" I don't know whether that is true or not. But years ago I travelled with the trek Boers, and I know how they love space! It is by far the nicest thing about them: the type of Boer who would in-span and trek on if he even saw the smoke of another man's fire on the horizon. The country was getting too crowded! You get that feeling on the Uasin Gishu to this day. The first Boers who settled here brought their oxen and their great wagons with them around from the Cape. They landed in ships at Mombasa, trekked all the five hundred miles up here from the coast, passing over the hump of the Kenya highlands and through green paradises that would have delighted the heart of any Englishman; they even passed up the Great Rift. When you know that a people have done that, you know that they have something in their psychology that is foreign to yours. When you get to know Boers, you know that the above is only a weak statement of the truth. The mentality of the Uasin Gishu is entirely different from the rest of Kenya.

I went out on the grassy plain to see one of these original Boer settlers; a grand man, still sitting on the same spot where he built his first mud-and-wattle house back in 1906. On an empty plain, he was sitting in a flowered garden before a pleasant old farmhouse, dark with the shade of towering gum trees. "The first night I was here," he told me, "I saw eleven lions, right from where we are sitting now. You could shoot almost any kind of animal you wanted in those days. . . . It was a lovely place!" Well, there is no game there now. These Uasin Gishu Boers still raid down into southern Kenya, however, where the distracted Game Wardens have all they can do to keep these skilful, and ruthless, hunters from turning every poor buck they see into *biltong*. This dried meat used to be considered the cheapest way to feed a native—and still is. No Boer really believes that a game law was meant to stop him . . . nor, I think, does he hold much truck with the idea of being "soft" with the natives. The consequence is that you get a strange feeling up here on the Uasin Gishu, and one not altogether pleasant: you also get the unmistakable impression that these people would like nothing better than to be left alone, to go to their "Dingaan's" Social Hall—where dancing is anathema—read their Bible, and to be allowed to feel their old feelings . . . towards their land and the black men who must labor on them. But, as you can never generalise about anything in East Africa, it should be pointed out that a great many Kenya settlers who have South African blood in their veins are now taking a leading part in the country's politics. I am convinced that most of them feel in their heart that one day Kenya must link up with South Africa. Their compass points there, not towards Whitehall.

Mr. W. A. C. Bouwer, Member of the Kenya Legislative Council, Member of the East African Central Assembly, and for years the most outstanding spokesman of these Uasin Gishu Kenyans, made a speech at Nyeri in March 1949, at which, according to the report given in the extremely reliable *East Africa and Rhodesia* (March 24, 1949), he was asked did he approve of Dr. Malan's policy of segregation in South Africa. To which he replied that there were already Native and European reserves in Kenya, that he thought Dr. Malan was on the right lines, and that "segregation was essential to European survival."

In my opinion, a major reason behind the effort of so many people in East Africa to create a further linking up of Uganda and Tanganyika with Kenya is to form a political state, or a bloc, which will be strong enough to "stand up to Whitehall," as they call it. And that their ultimate aim is to throw off the British Colonial Office administration in these territories. I do not think there has ever been a time when the Colonial Office, the traditional guardian of native interests, should be more on its guard, and supported by the British Parliament and people.

This old Boer was out of politics. But his grey-haired wife was an active public figure in her way. She had trained as a nurse in the Orange Free State, came to the Uasin Gishu in 1909, and since then, apparently, had delivered all the babies within a range of sixty-five miles of her. She had often made these trips by mule or ox-cart. And she had delivered many an African baby in its beehive grass hut, kneeling half the night through to help a native woman who had been maimed by the fierce Nandi female circumcision. She was a grand person too, in the old-fashioned Boer style.

The old Boer reminisced. "One of the first settlers we had here—man named Van Bredal—he was murdered by the Nandis. Why?" He chuckled. "*Cherchez la femme!*" "How could you?"

said his wife. "Well, it's a fact. That's why they killed him. Everybody knew that." He sighed to tease her: "Yes, yes, yes. . . . This was a great country . . . when we first came to it."

We sat there drinking coffee: and I thought of days up in South-West Africa; Boers just like this. They've unquestionably got something in their soul that we haven't got, something which gives them peace. And a strange sort of expansiveness. They have none of the inhibitions about class distinctions which fret the life of British colonies. They will shoot any animal they see moving, even when it is across a river and they know that they cannot get it. These Dutchmen, as the Kenyans call them, have among them some of the most pitiless ivory poachers in East Africa. Yet when you are out on trek with them, sit with them around some campfire, watch them go to sleep—still wearing their old hats and with their beloved rifle always by their side, very often with the old pipe they have been smoking still in their mouth—you know that they have got something close, very close, to the bedrock of contentment.

Up at Kitale—"Where the colonels are clustered like grapes!"—you come into another Kenya. This is the Englishman's paradise. The Club, with its golf, dancing, the happy-go-lucky chatter over a sundowner in the bar, the happy foregathering of old friends at luncheon on market day; men (and now many women) who have worn the King's uniform in all parts of the world, in all services over, in and under the sea—and who are laughing all the time about the joke of life. The gay jauntiness of their lives! Kitale has one of the most delightful little clubs I have ever been in: I look back on it as a triumph that I stayed on the wagon there. Perhaps that is why I enjoyed it so much. We arrived on the early morning of New Year's Day, when those who were still up from the previous night's party, and blinking in the fierce sunlight, led us to a brick bungalow facing the long golf-course, and retired to their much-needed rest.

The soil is red here, and the drives around the club were blue with the snow from the jacaranda trees. Mt. Elgon, its blue range backed by fleecy clouds, its slow lower slopes covered with a patchwork of buff wheat-fields, gave no indication at all of its height—its huge extinct crater, 14,140 ft., was not climbed until

1911, when two Austrian climbers, Kmunke and Stigler, made the ascent—but its condensing clouds cool the air, give the freshness and green to the land around Kitale. And, enjoying a physical ease that we had not known for some weeks, we stretched out on our cots before we began the job of unpacking to use this hospitable club as a base. As I lay there I thought, with a smile, of some of the sparrow intellectuals I had known in London between the wars, who used to sneer at these "hearties," as they liked to call the men and women of the Service families who had seen odd bits of life in queer corners of the world, and who still wanted to live in "the wide open spaces," as the Café Royalists would jeer. How abysmally comic some of those conversations now seemed. As I lay there I thought of what the country had been like coming up from Hoey's Bridge. One scene in particular.

There is a tree you pass frequently here, little larger than an apple, leafless, which bears an upright flower shaped like a hyacinth, but a vivid post-box red. These trees seen against the distant blues of mountains on the far horizon are unbelievably beautiful. And then—you suddenly become aware that you are staring straight at four giraffes, who are lingering to examine you. Their checkered coats are blazing in the sun. The blue hills, the scarlet flowers, the giraffes shining in the sun: you will look back in your mind to see that picture again for the rest of your life. That is Africa.

I wanted to get a cross-section of the new settlers around Kitale. I had the records of some of them that I had obtained at the Egerton Agricultural School. Now I wanted to see how they fitted in, and what they were thinking about their new life.

In the next few days we went out with the Settlement Officer. There were two men, of what could be called the yeoman type, who had paired their adjacent farms and become partners. The wife of one, a staunch Catholic, had six children. Her husband had worked on his father's farm in Wiltshire all during this last war; but he had always longed for a farm of his own. When his younger brother, who had been a soldier, came back from the war and took over the parental farm, he and his wife wrote to South Africa, New Zealand, Kenya and Canada about immigration.

New Zealand couldn't take them for two years, unless they came entirely at their own expense: New Zealand was too busy establishing its own Servicemen. Canada answered. But a neighbor in Wiltshire, who had been in Canada, said: "Yes; go there—if you are prepared to work twice as hard as you do in England; but, in that case, stay and do it in England." South Africa did not answer at all. So they plumped for Kenya.

The husband went, as a pupil, to a Mr. Thorne at Rongai. He gave them a small manager's house, and actually built an extra room for them. Then the husband took the short course, of three months, for those who have already had farm experience at the Egerton Agricultural School. They were placed on a bit of land which had been partly farmed, and when we saw them they were settling down in sort of an "Irish chaos" of an old house, but with a fine little vegetable garden that they had already started—and wired against buck.

This was fine farming land, but a great deal of it had not yet been cleared. The husband had spurned the land which the Kenya Government first offered him, and picked this land himself; the Government had then, very obligingly, bought this land for him, under the Scheme. They were contented people, with no regrets; educated and gently bred. Just the right type.

The partner, the ex-parachutist who had been dropped into Yugoslavia, was a blond, blue-eyed giant, with a forearm that could have felled an ox. When I was taken out to be introduced to him, he was sweating with the engine of a new tractor combine; and as an example of what these new settlers have to face with their £800 to £1,000 that they are supposed to come on their land with—a caterpillar tractor today in Kenya costs £900. "And we had to pay cash. They won't even let us pay 50 per cent down and 5 per cent interest on the balance." These two capable men agreed that to start farming properly in Kenya these days a man must have a cash capital of £2 10*s*. *od*. per acre. The ex-parachutist put it at £8 an acre. I have checked that figure with several other settlers and they all agreed that £2 10*s*. *od*. would be the absolute minimum with weather and everything else going right for you.

These two men were using a disc-plough in dry weather, ploughing 14 inches deep to kill the roots. They were growing a "cover crop," which they would then disc in to prepare the land for wheat. They had only forty boys between the two farms; one of 1,800 acres, the other of 1,200 acres. This was very high-grade land, with two skilled and hard-working young farmers; yet they were both apprehensive as to how soon they could get their first cash crop, so that they would not have to go to the bank. The ex-parachutist, a Hertfordshire man, was running 600 milk cows with their followers on his 1,800 acres, with pasturage so rich that he could ranch one animal to 1½ acres. Even so, they said:

"We ought to have one tractor for every 100 acres. If a settler takes a thousand acres, he ought, in these days, to be content to work 250 acres arable—manage with one tractor and a couple of teams of fourteen oxen. And work his farm night and day. That's the only way to make a paying proposition of it." (Put that against the commonly accepted picture of the Kenya "polo-playing" settler!)

The native boys only work from 7 A.M. until 1 P.M., this being the custom in that area, as it is considered too hot to get any real work out of an African native in the afternoon. The white men work all the day. Women, too. The wastage of inefficient labor, said these two men, plus the price of agricultural machinery, were their two biggest problems. These two men told me that they did not think they would join the Kitale Club for several years: "Farms like these don't leave you much time for fun and games!"

I talked to one settler and his family who were breaking in some new land right on the outskirts of Kitale. They were living in an abandoned warehouse. They were pessimistic (no wonder, in such a doleful habitation), and said lugubriously that they would never make any money; all the old settlers seemed against them, etc. Yet the wife kept reiterating, as if to reassure herself: "It's a *great* chance! We will have a *good* life!" I sincerely hope they will. For if ever I saw a hard-working man it was this one. Also he has got some hard competition when he begins to sell market produce into Kitale.

On the other hand, I went to the farm of one of the new settlers who had started from scratch like a sprinter in a 100-yard dash. This was an ex-rubber planter from Malaya. He had been a prisoner of the Japs and had slaved on the Burma Road. He had already got a contract to feed the schools of Kitale; he had made and sold 70,000 building bricks—he employs one hundred and twenty boys; he has already started a milk round. Today he has a minimum of £80 a month from these side-lines coming into his farm regularly. His farm was a coffee plantation originally, which had been allowed to go to waste, of 500 acres. He took that and then bought, via the Schemes, 800 acres of Crown land. He had £6,000 capital to start with, and has already paid out £2,000 for machinery and implements. Speaking of himself, he said:

"You have to like the life—and you have to get on with labor. Perhaps that is where my past experience is now useful to me: from 1928 to 1942 I was a rubber planter, handling native labor. I worked like a blooming coolie all those years. I know what it is to be hungry. . . . For four years I was a prisoner of the Japs. That was a sobering experience. Don't think that I won't work to hang on to this farm!"

This man is now spoken of as "a dead-sure winner"—one of the most sure to be successful of all the new settlers. Yet at Egerton Agricultural School—which he hated—he "raised so much hell that he almost broke up the place!" Now he smiles, and says that, looking back at Headmaster Booth, "I realise what a trial we must have been to him." It is the same story with nearly all these people who have been through Egerton; once they get on their new farms they forget all the annoyance they felt at "being sent back to school again!" Most Kenyans hope that the Egerton School will be revived and become a permanent feature of the Colony.

Up on Mt. Elgon I had lunch with a Yorkshireman who has been there twenty years. He grows strawberries as big as plums, and plums as sweet as honey, asparagus an inch thick, which he exports throughout Kenya. Also, under a benevolent podo tree, whose spreading branches come down almost to the ground, he has some stew-ponds where he is hatching rainbow trout to stock the mountain's rivers. The only thing that jars him is the presence of some 600 Kikuyu renegades, hiding in the forest above him—who are growing potatoes, etc., and selling them—"By motor-lorry, be God!"—into the Kitale Market.

This is one case where the African has put one over on the European. This irate Yorkshireman declared that these illegal squatters had sold 8,000 bags of potatoes and 9,000 bags of maize to the Kavirondo natives in the Kitale region the previous year. "And the Government won't allow any of us Europeans to go up on that land. It's a Forest Reserve, supposed to be of no use to anybody but the herds of bloody elephant!"

I must say that when I listened to him telling me of these adventurous Kikuyus, my heart gave a jump of surprised admiration. For this wasn't thieving or black thuggery. These people weren't spivs. This was initiative and enterprise: they were *growing* things, and marketing in a big way—with a motor-lorry! And in being on that mountain, in the Forest Reserve, they were not doing much different from the white man. Only the day before, a farmer on Mt. Elgon had shown me, with great envy, some big fields of wheat that lay in the dip of a valley behind his own farm. He told me that this farm was in the Forest Reserve, but that a South African farmer had been allowed to cultivate wheat there during the war owing to the need for increased production. "And I'd like to know how I'm going to get him out of it, because I *want* that farm." "But isn't it in the Forest Reserve?" "What difference does that make?" he asked me with a steely smile. Remembering this made me feel just as elated about these renegade Kikuyus as if I had heard that some of our American Indians—say, the Navajos—had broken away from the people who were trying to protect them; for if some people had their way, we would "protect" our Indians right out of existence.

We had one lunch here, with some friends, up at 8,000 feet on Mt. Elgon, where two of the four trout served were over 2 lb. each, all caught on their farm the previous day.

Summing up on the question of post-war settlement—and the settlers themselves—shows that they present two very different things. The idea that more whites could be brought into Kenya to increase their weight in the population ratio is, of course, sheer nonsense. No way can be found of making 29,000 approach 5,000,000, which is the present proportion of white to black. From the viewpoint of the new settlers themselves: first, they must face the prospect of being small farmers who will have to compete with large-scale farmers, both in the local markets and for export. Thus we see that they will have to work hard to make their farms a success. But why not? The final verdict is actually the real one: If they came out to Kenya to find a good way of life, they can have it. They will have only themselves to thank or to blame. Kenya still remains one of the loveliest countries on the face of this earth.

CHAPTER IX

"A Place to Fish"

KENYA has some trout streams that make you thankful just to be alive on the day you are fishing them. No visitor to that majestic part of the world should fail to take his rods with him. If you do, you will miss one of the most exhilarating experiences that the Colony can offer you. Sporting Kenyans themselves now fish the high mountains, with fewer and fewer going down to the great game plains. Kenya has the best trout fishing in Africa—and some of the most fanatic fishermen outside the British Isles.

There are two schools of trout fishermen in Kenya. There is the brown trout, or purist, set, who assert that "any fool can catch a rainbow," although I know one who will dispute that statement; and then there are the rainbow devotees, who magnanimously admit that while perhaps it may be a wee bit harder to induce the brownie to take the fly, once he has taken it he is a moribund fish compared to the dashing, leaping, flashing rainbow. I belong to both schools.

In the Thika, which is a rainbow river from six to eight thousand feet up, above which the brown trout breed—the two stretches are separated permanently by high falls and a 90-foot bamboo forest—in that beautiful river I lost the best fish I touched, because I could not adjust myself quickly enough to the *speed* of the Kenya rainbow: they tried to lodge me in rock ledges and, as happened in this case, to break me by fouling the dropper on a sunken log. On the Thika the wise fisherman who is out after big ones uses only one fly. On the Southern Mathioya, which is one of the coveted three rivers of that distinguished coterie, the Kenya Flyfishers' Club, I crawled up on my knees to the tail-end of a pool where the river split to pass an island and, after about twenty casts, finally got my fly down deep enough to attract the attention of a big brown trout that I had seen move out into the pool from some bushes on the far bank. My difficulty was to get the fly down to him in that swift water. Finally, I felt that indescribable "touch," and knew that I had him. But I did not see him for some minutes when, as he turned to take me downstream again, I saw the full beauty of his spots in the brilliant sun. He was exactly 3 lb., never jumped once, and the whole contest lay in thwarting his heavy drives to get up into the run above us, or to rub the fly out against the bank. My worry was not so much to land him as to keep him away from the land. And in that river I lost a huge brown trout which I fought for fifteen minutes under a crescent moon and which made me gasp when I saw his heavy body come to the surface and turn on its side, tiredly, in the moonlight. The African gillie, stabbing at it with the net, could not see the fish. He caught my dropper with the net. . . .

Both of these schools of Kenya trout addicts have some exceptionally fine and interesting fishermen. When I came in from fishing my second night on the Thika, with seven that totalled 3½ lb. and one rainbow of 1¼ lb., Mr. Pullen Burry was sitting before the outdoor log fire of the Governor's camp with three fish, one of 2¾ lb., two of 1¼ lb. He had been fishing down below the camp, where the big ones lie, and where it is only too easy to fish day after day without getting a rise. In fact, you seldom do get a rise, even with the fish you catch, for they lie low. Fish upstream (with a wet fly), fish slow and fish *deep*, is the rule for the Thika; and Mr. Pullen Burry makes no bones about it, and weights his cast with several lead shot. The brown trout school would call this "dredging." Maybe so, but Mr. Pullen Burry has a roll cast which he lifts off the water, and can stand with his back against a bank thick with bushes and shoot a line twenty or thirty yards as straight as an arrow. It is a sort of double Spey that takes a considerable amount of learning. He knows trout and all their habits! Mr. Pullen Burry, sisal farmer, was the man who put the first rainbow in the Thika, of which more later on. He prefers to fish downstream, winding up handfuls of line in his left hand, working every inch of the river. And it was a pleasure to fish with one who loved fishing so passionately.

Later on, just before I left Kenya, I had both the pleasure and the instruction of fishing that fine river with the Governor, Sir Philip Mitchell. He is a purist, and disdains lead shot. Instead, using a nymph as a tail fly, he can take rainbow out of rapids or from stretches of gin-clear water, so smooth and mirror-like that you could shave in them. He is a man of infinite patience—and deadly. Standing on the high bank above him, I watched him fish for fifteen minutes or so, trying to get the attention of a 2-lb. rainbow that we both could see clearly. It was a lovely sight, with its pink stripe glinting in the sun. Then the Governor's rod bent like a whip. . . . He took another one, only slightly smaller, from the same spot, the Canal Stretch, as it is known, in the afternoon. And at sunset, in an elbow of slow water, he got into a four-pounder that was more out of the water than in it with its ballet-dancer's leaps, until alas! it leapt into the branches of a half-sunken tree. Secretly, I was glad; I could not have stood much more of such perfection. I had tried for that fish for an hour myself.

At Tuso, as the guest of the Kenya Flyfishers' Club, I had the fun of fishing a few days with its President, "Billy" (W. G.) Rodway, surely one of the most amiable, expert fishermen who ever waded a stream. He gave me all the good runs and pools, and caught four fish to my one. I knew he would the minute I saw him use the 8 ft. 6 in. new rod he was just breaking in. But the five fish we caught between us the first day (his largest was 4½ lb.), would not have been a bad day for any river in the world. And our last was the evil day when I lost the whopper under the crescent moon. It is always well to leave some regrets —a fish that will haunt you and make you ache to go back to that river again; and I shall long remember our pleasant talks around the log fire after dinner when every one of the company had something to reproach himself for as he came in: "If only I had . . ." If you caught every fish you hooked, why, there would not be any fun in fishing at all. But you need not worry about that on the swift Southern Mathioya.

Both of these rivers race down from Mt. Kinangop, the last of the Aberdares. It is north of Nairobi, a fin-like mountain which raises its grey back like some prehistoric monster from the indigenous forests and wattle plantations of the Kikuyu Reserve.

Mr. Pullen Burry stocked the Thika, which is forty-seven miles from Kenya's capital, beginning in 1942, with seven-inch trout that he caught himself in the Ndarugu River, seven miles away. He brought them across in cans in his motor-car—four fish to three gallons of water. Since then, with their remarkable adaptability, rainbow have thrived in the Thika. They doubled their size the first year (the Thika is full of crabs and crayfish, as otter droppings all along its banks show), and a 6½ lb. one has already been caught. Mr. Pullen Burry, who is an Honorary Fish Warden, secured a closed season on the Thika for the first three years. There are now two spawning reserves on the river. One of 330 yards contains some of the finest tree-hung pools of all the river. One of the reasons why the fish lie so deep on this river, Mr. Pullen Burry thinks, is because too much of the bank brush has been cut away; the trout have lost the instinct to rise to falling insects, and there is so much good food down below.

These Thika rainbow exploded a pet theory of mine: that their pinkness depends upon the amount of crabs and crayfish in their diet; for you can catch two fish out of the same stretch, both in equally fine condition, and one will be pink as a salmon and the other pale. The Kenya brown trout school contends that a rainbow feeds for about eighteen hours a day, and finally eats himself out of both house and home, diminishing both in size and numbers. This grim epoch is not yet in sight on the Thika. But as the Thika is a public river, where anyone may fish who has a licence (10*s.* for every three months), the water gets a lot of whipping. There were twenty rods on it the Sunday of the first time I fished there. Eleven people caught nothing, and I was one of them.

The brown trout of the Kenya Flyfishers' Club were brought out from England and Scotland as ova; some from Loch Leven, though most are Howietoun trout. They were spawned in stew-ponds, up in the forest, at 7,800 ft., and fed on the orthodox grated ox-liver until they reached fingerling size. The opening day was September 16, 1928. Since then one 10-lb. brown trout has been taken. (I wonder how big mine was—the one that got away.) And here are the scores for two years, which will give you some idea what Kenya fishing can really be. In 1947, out of 452 rod-days, 877 fish were retained, 709 were returned: total weight retained was 786 lb. 1 oz. The largest fish was 6 lb. 2 oz., and there were twenty fish over 3 lb. In 1946, out of 714 rod-days, 1,238 fish were caught and retained and 919 were put back into the river; total retained weight equals 1,238 lb. 3 oz. (Singular similarity, making the average exactly a 1-lb. fish.) That year thirty-three fish over 3 lb. were taken and the largest fish was 6 lb. 2 oz. It can be taken that most of these were caught on No. 8 flies, with Coachman leading, Watson's Fancy next favorite, and then anybody's choice. The Coachman is *the* fly for the fighting rainbow of the Thika. And on both rivers a black fly, hackled, like a Kenya Bug, is good after dark. It is only in the darkness that the big pools of the Southern Mathioya will give up their monsters.

Enough of size and number. To fish in forests of bamboo or wild fig and olive, under the darkness of giant podo trees, to see that startlingly beautiful sight of hundreds of little golden weaver birds shoot into their hanging nests over a pool you are fishing, or a white-breasted fishing eagle shining in the sun—yes, even to feel shortness of breath, as you wade, say, at 7,500 feet, up towards the bronze-blue rocks of a mountain towering above you—these are all part of the delight of handling a rod on any Kenya stream. There are no closed seasons on these rivers: Nature takes care of that. During April and May the heavy rains make the Devon-red dirt roads up into the mountains almost impassable, even dangerous, where the road skirts a cliff face. Then, from the beginning of July to the end of August few people come up, because of the heavy mist that hangs in these wooded valleys. There is a book in Nairobi which must be signed, as there are ten beats on the Southern Mathioya; and a member can stay for only ten days, having to give up his place if another member wants to come up. It is, quite possibly, the most exclusive club in Kenya, and has 110 members now, with fifty-six on the waiting list. To be made a guest is about the nicest compliment that Kenyans can pay you, for the test is how you can handle a rod.

The African gillies are an adventure in themselves. And if you can't talk Swahili, you are all set to find out some startling things about the black man's character, and your own. At first, so it is said, they thought that shoving a net under a fish was just a child's pastime. (A certain amount of hearty cursing, I imagine, cured them of that.) Now they are much more keen to net the fish than you are. Too keen by half. "*Pole! Pole!*" which means "slow" in that *lingua franca* of the East African coast, was a word that I forgot every time I saw my own gillie on the Thika, Kihongi, leap into the water. With the smaller rainbow that did not so much matter; that moonlight night on the Mathioya it meant disaster. I could not call the gillie away from the fish. These agile natives leap from rock to rock like a water-wagtail, and balance just as deftly.

The Thika was the first river in my life where I have had my gillie leap from rock to rock and unfoul a fish that had caught the other fly on a rock or snag, for I was, foolishly, using two. With one fish of only ¾ lb. Kihongi unfouled me from one rock ledge with a small fall pouring over it, and—zip—the fish had fouled me in a ledge down below. Kihongi, water-wagtailing, got down and got me free from that. Then—and that was the only time I saw him do it—he lost his balance; his soft brown eyes had no expression whatever as he arose, dripping, from the pool. He was the prince of gillies; mute, his face registering no emotions, until one sunset (we were both in shorts) we sat down to change a fly in a colony of black ants. . . . They bite you, with their red-hot pincers, in the most extraordinary places, and all I can say is—Kihongi and I had it!

These black "boys," upon whom so much of the white man's life in Africa is based, are somewhat of a departure from their British counterparts. They think, as gillies, that you are right whatever you do. And they are very solicitous. I sprained my ankle my first day on the Southern Mathioya, stepping into the hole of an ant-bear while I had my eyes on the river, casting. In England or in Scotland I would have been laid up. But not in Africa. Like a shipwrecked mariner being hauled from the waves, I was held up by two of these black boys every time I had to cross that swift stream. There was something charming in their silent friendliness. The boys are engaged by the Game Department at the Thika camp, which employs a headman and some very capable servants. You pay your gillie *1s.* a day. There are three thatched, log-slab huts there, aside from the Governor's private camp; a bed costs only *2s.* a night. You can buy milk, chickens, and some vegetables from the local Kikuyus. Which reminds me that we bought a chicken, but Government House's Third Cook, which we had been loaned, forgot to kill it. We became so attached to it, tuck-tucking contentedly around the camp for some days, that we could not eat it. We gave it back to the Kikuyus.

The Governor's camp, which Sir Philip had built, is my idea of a fisherman's heaven. It has a fire at both ends: a big stone platform for the evening fire at the open veranda end, its heat thrown back to you from a red-clay bank, and a 40-gallon petrol drum in which water is heated for your bath at the other. A big room with double-decker bunks lies in between. No fisherman needs to be reminded what a heavenly feeling it is when you come in, wet and dead beat from a day's fishing, and then lie down luxuriously in a soul-restoring hot bath. No other bath in life can touch it. Then, after a dinner eaten before the big log fire, to sit there in the open and watch a crescent moon slowly top the flowered mimosa trees. "This saves my reason," sighed the Governor when we fished that river with him some four months later. He had just left when I fished it the first time, getting fourteen trout which totalled 18½ lb. He also left me some Coachman flies and three of his precious gut casts, with a note:

> If you should go up into the forest, be careful of elephants. . . . You can always hear them feeding your way—their insides rumbling like aldermen after municipal banquets; get out quietly and stay down wind. If you are sure that you are down wind, get behind a stout tree and stay *still and silent*. If, by great ill luck, things should go wrong and elephants should begin to behave intemperately, get behind the largest tree you can find (unless, of course, you can get twenty degrees up one) and remain *stiller and quieter*. If none of these valuable counsels avail, be sure that you will leave a fragrant memory and that I shall write a most sympathetic letter to your widow. If, of course, you can manage to write her off, too, that would save me a letter of the kind which is very difficult to write. . . . [His italics.]

I hate walking near elephants. The elephant herds were some miles up the river, and I told my wife that she could go up there alone if she wanted to. But fishing the beautiful Thika had made a fanatic out of Eve. She began with the master of all of us, "John Bickerdyke," up in Norway, years ago. After a summer's patient tuition, he said to her: "Now you are just getting to the point where you just might begin to catch a fish." Using my rod while I was writing one morning, she got four fish, one of 1½ lb.

Then the rains came on, and she fell crossing the stream on one of the slippery log-slab bridges, but with great presence of mind she held my precious rod aloft, so that no harm was done except a loose tooth, a slightly strained back and a leg gashed open on a grass-hidden rock.

Thirty-five of the Kenya rivers are now stocked with trout, mostly rainbow. A most interesting and useful thing to know about these fish is contained in the 1945 report of Mr. Hugh Copley, the Fish Warden: "Our big trout in the lower and much hotter waters only properly feed at night, for the waters are then cooler. Temperature also affects the amount of dissolved oxygen in the waters of a river. The amount of dissolved oxygen falls with any rise in temperature. Hence, in heated water the trout lie under the waterfalls, large or small, all day, and come out after dark to feed, when the water is cooler." From 60° F. to 66°, he says, is the optimum growth temperature: if it is hotter than that, the trout begin to stop feeding.

Major Cavendish-Bentinck, the Minister for Agriculture and Natural Resources, had been out fishing the Thika over Easter, and came out to the aerodrome at Nairobi to see us off as we said farewell to Kenya (surely the most hospitable country in the world): he had a couple of flies still stuck in his old veld hat. "The water was low," he said in a hoarse whisper, "but I lost the fish of all fish on a —"

The glaciers are retreating on Mt. Kenya, and the rivers from the Aberdares are appreciably lower than they were even so short a time back as 1932. That makes it all the harder to take a fish. It also makes the Kenya fish fans all the more determined to stock and keep a high pressure of fish in their streams. When I was up on Mt. Elgon, on the other side of Kenya, I lunched with two gentlemen who wouldn't come in to lunch, unable to leave their fascinating pursuit of counting 987 small trout that they had been rearing in stew-ponds under the shade of a benevolent podo tree. These hopeful fingerlings were to stock a new river in that vicinity. And when I asked Mr. Pullen Burry why he gave up so much of his personal time (he was then in the Sisal Research Department) to take the Thika in hand in 1942, building bridges, dams, even some twenty miles of road to get into it (aside from the heartbreaking task of clearing the jungle from its banks), he thought about it for a moment, unable to find a convincing answer; and then gave me the real one. "Oh . . . I just wanted a place to fish."

So far so good. When I was fishing below the Governor's camp that first, fishless, Sunday, I was tying on a change of flies when I heard laughter and cries of "*Jambo!*" from the wooded hillside above me across the river. "*Jambo!*" is a greeting. I looked up and saw that a bevy of Kikuyu girls were calling to me. The forest background was so dark that I could not make out their faces, only their white teeth when they laughed. To my wave, there was another chorus of "*Jambos!*"—and then happy laughter. Their European dresses were so vivid that I made a note of their colors: vivid scarlet, next a sapphire, then gold, amber, emerald green, cream and so on. They were as colorful as tropic birds. They came from a Mission School over the hill. Then another bevy came down the red-earth trail; boys and girls, dancing, singing, with their arms around each other's shoulders—more "*Jambos!*" They went on down the river bank. And as I began to cast again I heard their laughter until it was finally drowned by the rumble of a lower waterfall. That night I wrote in my note-book that while the Kikuyu may be suffering from political and social unrest and were very troublesome to the authorities, "they are unquestionably a happy and lovable people."

We did not know it then—we did not learn until Tuesday, when we dropped in to say good-bye to the D.C., twenty miles below—that at the very moment when I had been writing these pleasant things about the Kikuyus, and my wife had been fishing that river alone, except for Kihongi, a band of twenty-nine Kikuyus had been fleeing right past us. They had just ambushed and murdered a European assistant police inspector and his two native constables at a little village between us and Kiambu. They had mutilated the bodies in a most gruesome fashion, slashing the inspector's face open across the eyes and mouth; this after he had fallen to a spear in his back. And one poor native, with his hand half cut off, they had paraded around the village, telling him that he was on his way to a ceremonial execution. He was saved by a reinforcement of police, which had been rushed to the scene. These were "The Men of God" (*Wata wa Mungu*), one of the fanatical religious cults that are now breaking out, as if something was poisoning the "body politic," all over East and Central Africa. You will hear more of them later on.

CHAPTER X

The Kikuyus

THE Kikuyu woman's skull is long and flat, with an indentation from a head-strap across it that begins to form at the age of six and deepens as life goes on until she is a bent, withered old hag at fifty. They are the most ill-used beasts of burden in all Africa, not excepting the transport animals. This is a good thing to keep in mind when talking to a Kikuyu male, the most politically-troublesome people in Kenya, when he begins to tell you what burdens the white man has laid upon him.

This terrible scene of the Kikuyu women trailing in to the markets along the red, dusty roads, bent almost double under heavy back-loads of bananas, faggots, manioc, etc., with often their latest baby perched on top, will shock you everywhere you go in the great Kikuyu Reserve, once some of the most fertile, finely watered land in all Kenya. All their lives these Kikuyu women labor under loads almost as heavy as themselves, even heavier: they will often carry a sack of maize which weighs 200 lb.; and in the forest reserves, from which a native is often allowed to take all the firewood that can be carried at one time on one's back, they will stagger out to the border with 300-lb. loads. You will never see a Kikuyu man carrying such a load, not even on a European's farm. When wattle trees are cut down in the Kikuyu Reserve for tanning bark and firewood, it is the Kikuyu women who swing the axes and split the wood. The men stack it. The Kikuyu women cultivate most of the reserve with hand hoes or merely digging-sticks.

These women sit in sullen clusters in the market-places, legs stretched on the ground, wares at their feet; and, it seems, an unappeasable cold rancor lies behind their work-distorted faces, with their flat dugs, and perforated dangling ear-flaps filled with the mocking finery of wire-strung pink beads. You feel, when their inimical stare meets your eyes, that you are really looking into the face of Darkest Africa. I think you are. It lies in the soul.

Meanwhile, about all the able-bodied men of the vicinity who can get there are lolling on the stone tiers of a bogus Roman amphitheatre which the Administration has constructed, while they leisurely listen to the Native Tribunal (the local court) judge the case of two Kikuyu youths who had engaged in a street fight some time back, and a third man, who got his arm broken when he tried to stop one of these men from biting the hand off the other man. Nine Elders of the village, judges appointed by the District Commissioner (and paid eighty shillings a month, out of the fines they impose), sit with great solemnity on the dais of the Roman amphitheatre, marking off the points made as the testimony proceeds by throwing down tally-sticks. They have the same self-conscious solemnity, the desire to impress you with their omniscience, that you will see on the nine faces of the U.S. Supreme Court or the Lord Chief Justice and all the King's Bench. In that respect, the mumbo-jumbo with which the Law is wrapped up is the same in all instances.

This seems a nasty way of describing it. Yet when I saw this same pseudo-Roman amphitheatre at Kiambu ten years before, I had the uneasy feeling that there was something spurious in its proceedings. Now I am sure of it. I have been accused of being an Anglo-maniac often enough in my life to feel free to be candid when I am certain on some point. I think that the Englishman's incurable weakness to live more for the *form* of life than for its substance, his insatiable love of pomp and pageantry, of wig and gown, and gold braid, his passion for processions and ceremony, his yearning for bombastic buildings in his territories overseas is the weakest feature of his remarkably just administration. Witness the vulgar ostentation of Sir Edward Lutyen's monstrosity for the Viceroy, "The most magnificent palace built since Versailles"—actually, it is bigger—in New Delhi, and the pompous aloofness it implied, to say nothing of what has happened largely because of that self-conscious superiority.

The overseas Englishman's obsession with the size of the buildings he puts up, rather than what goes on inside them, is familiar to anyone who has travelled the Empire. These needlessly imposing structures come as a constant reminder—that their day is over. The Englishman still believes that they impress the native: they do, but it is the wrong type of native. It could almost be said that they *create* a type: the native who yearns to sit in one of these ornate erections, with a white-collar job, to lord it over his own countrymen, rather than become an artisan, farm instructor, bridge-builder, skilled mechanic—the very type of African which every colony is desperate for. That is, if the African is to progress, to be *able* to get away from the land and find useful, paid employment elsewhere, and play a dignified part in making the colony a success. Too many fine buildings can ruin a colony.

That is why I write against the pseudo-Roman amphitheatres to hold a football crowd of black Africans, who will argue all day about nothing. "But that is an old native custom!" the supporters of such a system will tell you. So was cannibalism, or the cutting out of one testicle to improve one's charm, and female circumcision; as is the filing of teeth to a shark's-tooth point a native custom to this day. But there is no need to go on with them. One thousand pupils being taught in mud-and-wattle huts are of far more use to a colony than imposing stone edifices which, when they ever are completed, will hold only a handful of pupils.

I know that the institution of the local Native Tribunal lifts a lot of minor litigation off the District Commissioner and out of the British Magistrate's hands; these appointed native judges can fine a wrongdoer two thousand shillings; they can sentence him to six months in jail, if the D.C. signs his consent; and in judging and punishing cases which are peculiar to native life—such as "removing girl without consent of the parents thereof," i.e. running off with a girl without paying the bride-price—they can be of immense value. I am well aware that the Native Tribunal is a definite step of the British to hand over responsibility and begin local self-government, and that thus it is hoped to transfer the democratic idea to the African.

The fairness of the British intentions is beyond reproach. The result is more questionable. I (still thinking of the indented female skulls and head-straps) believe it is madness to encourage what is already the male African's almost orgiastic passion for wordy speeches and his love of prolonged litigation by giving him these imposing edifices to waste time in. I think it only further adds to his cynical suspicions of the white man. The African sees the "show" of the whole proceeding; *he* knows that behind these long-drawn-out arguments in the Roman amphitheatre the traditional bribery and intimidation are still at work; and he thinks, "Well, if the white man subscribes to this sort of business, let's encourage him; hide the face, and let's see what else we can get away with." I have had many an Englishman, disgusted with such time-wasting tribunals, assert that it would be far better to continue the once-held native belief that the white man "has something"; to have the old system, where the District Commissioner or the Magistrate, who *knew* his people, would say: "Yes; I hear what you say; you didn't do it. And you've got eight friends here to swear you weren't even on the spot that day. All right–six months!" With seldom an injustice done.

I am taking these two discordant spectacles, the bent women trailing along the red roads and the men lolling under the eucalyptus trees, not as a condemnation, but to show the pathos of the whole Kikuyu race. Their jarring note sent a deep shaft of sophistry into my wish to believe in the model farms and so forth that I was shown in the Kiambu District–most progressive in all the Kikuyu Reserve. They made me doubt the authenticity, the practicability, of any present reform: that is, whether it would ever "take" or not. They made me feel that the leading Kikuyus I met were so far out in front of their own people that they could not be taken as being even representative of the advancing Kikuyus as a whole. They pointed to a wrong turning; to a road that went off in the wrong direction–from which one ought to go back and find the right turning.

I want to give a few facts and figures that are indispensable to the proper understanding of the black man–both as to his life and his complaints. I take wages first. They are the African's average rate of pay when he goes to work outside his reserve. So that I may not be accused of any personal bias I am taking them from official sources: *Report of the Taxation Committee, Kenya, 1947*, commonly known as the Plewman Report.

There are several interesting things about these figures. Perhaps the first of them is that while there are something over five million Africans in Kenya, less than 200,000 of them are shown, by this report, to be working for Europeans.

	Number of Employees	*Average Wage per Month (shillings)*
Domestic servants	17,364	19.4
Unskilled labor in private industry	90,725	11.6
Agricultural workers . . .	29,635	11.6
Other workers in private industry	16,964	20.5
All employees in public service	28,160	20.7
	182,858	14.6

And the average wage paid the black man is less than six pence a day. (I believe that with a certain amount of even lower-paid "squatters," etc., it can be said that nearly 250,000 natives are working outside the reserves.) To the above wages must also be added eight shillings a month, which is what it costs an employer to feed his farm "boy" with *posho* (maize meal) and house him. This wage of less than six pence a day looks absurdly, even criminally, cheap. The most significant thing to realise about it is, of course, that it is not so cheap as it looks, because the African laborer is so woefully, often deliberately, inefficient. "You give us the job and we will finish the tools!" is only too often the African's happy motto. "You may be able to get African factory workmen for as low as five shillings a week," as one leading businessman in East Africa said recently, "but you will only get five shillings' worth of work out of them." And another fact to be remembered—perhaps the most dismaying truth of all—is that African employers have found from bitter experience that raising the African's rate of pay will hardly ever make him work any harder. In fact, their greatest problem today is to find any incentive—except drastic hunger—which *will* make an African work. It is a heart-breaking job to try and give an African the "money urge."

Furthermore, when analysing the above rates of pay, we must come back to the reserves. For the average African worker also has some land in the reserve. He can return to it. With a married man, this plot of land is always being worked by his wife or wives and thus adding a substantial bit to his income. The women seldom go out to work; it is only in the rarest instance that you will see a black woman working in a European's household, even as a child's nurse. My own driver, who was in Government employ and was being paid sixty shillings a month, had a fine little farm of some 31 acres in the Kikuyu Reserve, twenty-five goats and three cows; but only one wife to run it for him, however, as he was a Christian. He was an extremely well-educated and intelligent Kikuyu, and one of the best drivers I have ever sat behind. I had him for four months. It was only when I said good-bye to him that I learned the Government was paying him only sixty shillings a month. (He is now getting more.)

On all the European farms the boys get *posho* and lodging; and in the big, well-run Kericho tea estates, some of which employ over 5,000 boys, they not only have splendid barracks, free hospital service, well-organised amusements, but a diet which in calorie value far exceeds that enjoyed today by any citizen of Great Britain. These tea "gardens" also employ child-labor. I give this picture of wages so that you may see what the African expects to get when he goes out of the reserve: less than six pence a day is the average pay.

Here are some facts from inside the reserve. The Kiambu District of the Kikuyu Reserve is its most prosperous district, containing, as I have said, some of the best-watered and most fertile valleys in all Kenya. Yet today its land is so over-populated, overworked, over-grazed (and badly farmed) that it is admitted officially some 10,000 of its 28,500 families must be moved elsewhere. Forty per cent of its 196,181 population is already landless. And an official report runs: "On the assumption that 40 per cent of the population is already landless and that 10 per cent of that figure are engaged in non-agricultural work, on the present density in Kiambu some 90,000 persons might become without means of support within a short time: *something which cannot be faced with equanimity.*"

I italicise that last sentence because the Kenya Government is doing everything but regard the situation with equanimity. It knows that the population-pressure on the invisible walls of the Native Reserves has now reached crisis proportions. An intensive soil-research campaign is now being conducted from Nairobi, with teams in the field, as well as teams of agricultural experts in every reserve, fighting (it *is* a psychological battle) to make the natives adopt sane, if not even modern, methods of farming their land.

"Terracing" is the magic but extremely simple process by which the Kenya Government hopes to persuade the natives inside the reserves to save and reclaim some of their eroded hill-sides. Like the "hill-billy" farms in some of the more poverty-stricken southern States in the U.S.A., the average African (except such tribes as the cattle-raising Masai) cultivates on the slope of a hill. With his present wasteful methods, the Big Rains every year wash an increasing amount of his substance away. The rivers run red with the soil of the Kikuyu hills, and the Tana River makes a discoloration in the Indian Ocean that can be seen twenty-five miles out at sea. In some areas there is no top-soil left. The natives, one would think, should be only too glad to terrace. But terracing is very hard work; and where it has been enforced too rigorously by a European Agricultural Officer or an appointed native headman, the natives have some legitimate grievance in saying that they just have not got the strength to do it. But *politics* have stopped terracing more in Kenya than any physical exhaustion—or even native dumbness. Although the African's stupid suspiciousness is the chief reason why a native "agitator" can persuade his brethren (the women) to stop terracing. He says, and it is believed: "Terrace that land; and when you have done it the European will take it over." So—they stop; the rains come, more land is washed away, less food and grass is grown for man and cattle, people become weaker, more surly, from being hungry for the greater part of the year; riots break out when the District Commissioner tries to plead with them. . . . The life of a District Commissioner, those underpaid, earnest men who are the very backbone of British colonisation, requires to an appalling extent the daily use of those three cardinal virtues: patience, courage and determination.

Owing to the perseverance of the D.C. at Kiambu, and a very forceful Agricultural Officer, some model farms have been got going—run by the exceptional Africans. Chief Magugu, in this district, has 9,000 people under him; and his brother Wanyutu runs one of these farms. It is about 19 acres. He employs black labor, and this in itself tends to add to the number (40 per cent) who are landless in the reserve; it adds to the bad custom of the more successful farmer buying up his less far-sighted brethren. And Wanyutu, who employs both men and women (a European farm uses only males) pays them twenty-four shillings a month alike, as well as giving them their food. On a European farm they would get fourteen shillings or less. The situation sounds ideal, and it was a well-run farm to look at: rolling land of maize, beans, onions, English potatoes, some sweet potatoes grown for his own use. The cash crops were onions (for which he hoped to get £100 for his present crop in Nairobi), English potatoes and beans.

The farm was well terraced, so that the rains would not sweep his soil away. Wanyutu was planting grass, "igorka," something much like the coarse English couch grass, and told us he was making 20-30 tons of compost, giving it two months to rot down. I did not see how he could get that much. He was reclaiming some land from the ditches along the brick-red road and from paths—this, the Agricultural Officer said, usually amounts to 20 per cent of a potential holding—and he would soon have enough land to graze sufficient cattle to manure his farm. He had seventeen tiny cattle, of which the cows did not give 1½ pints a day each. At the moment he was buying Masai manure: 3–4-ton truck loads, which, including haulage from the Masai Reserve, worked out at anywhere from sixty-five to seventy shillings per load, of which he seemed able to purchase all he wanted.

The proximity of the Nairobi market should make such a farm almost a certain success, owing to the capital's demands for fresh vegetables; though how he could get £300 a year from only 19 acres, which I was assured this farm would produce, is still puzzling me. Anyhow, the whole thing was predicated upon the ideal working, weather and market conditions. And if African farm laborers could get twenty-four shillings working inside the reserve they would never go outside it to work at fourteen shillings on the farms of Europeans; so you would think. But, of course, this and two or three other farms I was shown in that district must all be regarded as laboratory experiments. I saw no evidence at all, either at Kiambu or in other parts of the Kikuyu Reserve, which led me to believe that these model farms are being followed on a large scale. They are good to show to Creech

Jones and visiting political tourists; they are not in the least representative of the state of the reserves. They can't be.

During my four months' stay in Kenya I learned that this particular farm was shown to every visiting personage. One visiting Socialist, high up in the colonial administration of the Labour Government, came out there, walked around it, did not ask questions of any of the attendant, awe-struck Africans, went back to Nairobi, and announced that what he had seen was splendid. He had been immensely impressed.

By what? These farms keep no books. If he had been a little more inquisitive and properly sceptical, he would have known that the prodigal use of imported manure on that farm (a thing which the average African cultivator can almost never afford), has yet to show that it has paid for itself. And if he had asked any of the doubting Africans in the district, they would have told him that if this demonstration farm showed a loss—and the real position of its finances would have to come out *some time*—then the whole effort to get model farming started in the district would go back.

This is the man who was in a reserve seething with discontent—from *real* miseries—who returned to England and said of Kenya:

"Race relations are excellent!"

For the sake of the record, and so that you might see the actual facts of the case—the situation, given without bias, that both European administrators, agricultural experts and the Africans themselves inside the reserves are up against—I am going to give this report of the Kiambu District. And keep in mind as you read it and see some of the difficulties, that this is the best district in the entire Kikuyu Reserve.

Kiambu Reserve

A. Land

I. *Total Area:* 423 square miles, or 270,720 acres.

II. Land Unsuitable for Agriculture: 27,072 acres, i.e. 10 per cent (Forest, rocks, steep slopes, roads, etc.).

III. *Balance Available for Agriculture:*

(*a*) Arable and temporary leys	135,360 acres = 50 per cent
(*b*) Permanent grazing . .	108,288 acres = 40 per cent
Total	243,648 acres.

B. Population

I.	(a) Married men	28,548
	(b) Polls	12,731 (approx.)
	(c) Women	55,893
	(d) Children	99,012 (at 43.5 per cent of total population)
	Total	196,184 (1946)

II. *Number of Families:* say, 28,500.

(See note on surplus women/children, concubinage, etc., below.)

C. Densities

I. *Present Position* (see note on *landless*)

(a) Arable and leys . . .	4.83 per family
(b) Permanent grazing . .	3.87 acres per family
(c) Total	8.70 acres per family

N.B.—(i) The above calculation makes no allowance for the large numbers of women who are, apparently, surplus. It is assumed that these women have migrated from other areas and are occupied in capacities connected with the proximity of Nairobi. The incidence of prostitution is high, and some may be living in concubinage. No doubt some of them brought children from elsewhere and may have had children during residence in the Kiambu Reserve.

(ii) The apportionment of arable to permanent grazing is, of course, based on the ideal division. The actual proportion may, in fact, be quite other. The total, however, remains the same.

(iii) No allowance is made in these figures for "landless" families and/or "Ahoi." Mr. Colin Maher places the landless in Kiambu as high as 40 per cent. (See Memorandum at end.)

"Ahoi" are people allowed to cultivate a plot of land temporarily. They can keep the whole proceeds, but they can be disposed at the landlord's will.

II. *Capacity in Relation to Density*

(a) Allowing 8 acres arable and temporary leys and 6 acres permanent grazing per family, maximum capacity of reserve will provide for . .	= 17,000 families
(b) Present number actually in reserve . .	= 28,500 families
Surplus to capacity	= 11,500 families

(*c*) Approximate number of stock units in reserve . . . . = 60,000 head

(*d*) Approximate capacity of reserve . . = 64,300 *

D. Memoranda

Several conclusions arise to modify the general conclusions, viz.:

1. Land Tenure, etc.

(*a*) The fertility of the soil and the proximity of Nairobi, with its ready market for vegetables, flowers, etc., would presuppose an opportunity for the successful working of "*Smallholdings*," but it is known, however, that the tendency in the reserve is towards the creation of a class-owning large acreage, with the inevitable result of an ever-increasing proportion of *landless families*. The figures given above and those given in Mr. Colin Maher's report ignore these facts in as much that the actual subdivision of the land is not exactly known.

(*b*) The landless families are no doubt occupied in other pursuits than farming *or* are employed *at low wages* (which means that Mr. Wanyutu's scale of pay cannot be taken as the normal one; nor is it) by the larger landowners. This is a breakdown of the old "Ahoi" system to a certain extent, although employees are still called "Ahoi." In the event of a general "slump"—not unlikely in the near future—and the consequent fall in prices for market produce, the condition of these people would cause considerable anxiety and produce a pauper problem of some magnitude. On the assumption that 40 per cent of the population is already landless and that 10 per cent of that figure are engaged in non-agricultural work, on the present density in Kiambu some 90,000 persons might become without means of support

* Figure taken from Mr. Colin Maher's Report. This figure assumes a proper distribution of land to arable, temporary leys and permanent grazing, *and the reduction of the population by some 10,000 families.* It is obvious that with the present density the number of grazing units is insufficient to maintain soil fertility or to provide an adequate diet. For the present population the figures are:

(*a*) Stock units per family 2.2
(*b*) Stock units per head 0.32

After reducing the population by 10,000 families and increasing the stock to the carrying capacity of the reserve, the figures would be:

Number of stock units per family, 3.8 approx., which is much nearer to normal requirement. A further increase of 0.20 units per family would be desirable.

within a short space of time: something which cannot be viewed with equanimity.

II. Surplus Women

The very large discrepancy between the numbers of married men and the numbers of women—the latter outnumber the men by two to one—is accounted for by immigration into the reserve from *less fortunate areas in the Kikuyu lands.* No doubt these women are living to a large extent with relatives or as members of families, but it is certain that the "easy money" of prostitution provides the livelihood of many of them. A "slump" would, of course, affect these surplus women, but it seems unlikely that they would return to their original homes unless and until the areas whence they came could provide a reasonable livelihood. There would even seem to be less chance of their returning home than of reducing future immigration.

III. Soil Fertility

(*a*) The number of grazing units in the Reserve is, as has been noticed, insufficient to maintain soil fertility, but of late many of the farmers there have been buying large quantities of manure (dung) from the Masai. This, of course, is no permanent alternative of Mixed Farming, but it has done a good deal towards keeping up the fertility. However:

(*b*) One of the results of the above is that large profits have been made from the increased production of market produce sold in Nairobi; with these profits, those farmers who have so treated their land have been able to "buy up" more and more land from their less well-informed, fortunate or provident neighbors, thus creating the problem discussed at *D.I.* (*a*) and (*b*).

(*c*) This manuring of parts of the Kiambu Reserve cannot be regarded as a solution to the problem created by over-population and over-grazing, etc. It is and *can* only be regarded as a *temporary* measure and in no way affects the "long-term" problem we have to face. [Italics by author of this report.]

(*d*) Further, any considerable increase in dung purchases over a period would in all probability exhaust the available supply, and this of itself would create other problems of great import, such as a decrease in the supply of market produce, further exhaustion of the land and widespread discontent. It also implies the using of manure in one area to the detriment of the areas where it might in the first instance have been used with advantage. [*Me:* I believe it is already forbidden in certain areas for Europeans to buy manure from the Masai.]

IV. Summary

It can be said, therefore, that the problem remains substantially the same as shown earlier in these notes, viz.:

(i) The proper apportioning of the land between the arable, temporary leys and permanent grazing.

(ii) The reduction of the farming community by some 10,000 families *and the provision of alternative means of livelihood for the displaced.*

(iii) The encouragement of "intensive" farming for the Nairobi market.

(iv) The discontinuance of female immigration into the Kiambu Reserve from elsewhere.

(v) The initiation of sound farming practice *throughout* the Reserve, implying *the whole-hearted co-operation of the people themselves.*

There you have a picture, in capsule form, of what it is like to be in charge of a reserve, what it *feels* like, for a native African, to be in one, and also a good chance to see for yourself just how complex, even insoluble, some of its problems are. Take this question of the roving women who can't go back to where they came from, as there is not enough land to support them there. What do they think about life? And the white man? "Race relations are excellent" sounds a pretty shameful observation when you have some of these facts in mind.

To those who might feel bored in having such a detailed picture given them, I can say that it will not happen again. To those who are interested in lives other than their own, I would say that I find such a report as this fascinating to read over and over again. And what may be even more to the point—I found the Kiambu District fascinating just because I had this record in my pocket. I did not have it the first time I was there, and therefore I felt more or less at sea when I looked over the few model farms. I did have it the second and third times I went out there, and it made the whole scene come into focus. For one thing: you can see yourself, from the above report, that I was making no unwarranted statement when I said that "the problem of the reserves cannot be solved inside the reserves."

I was in all the big reserves. And in the huge Kavirondo Reserve, over on the shore of Lake Victoria, which holds over 1,500,000 Africans, where the population rises to 800-900 to the square mile in some of the worst districts, I have seen four families, twenty-five people, living on and trying to make a living out of 2¼ acres. As I know this statement will be challenged, I give the exact location: it is on a hillside called Lotego, near Majengo, in the South Marigoli District: four families, four huts, twenty-five people, on 2¼ acres. All farmers! It was a Salvador Dali nightmare of granite boulders among which the natives were huddled like rabbits. And as I stood under the sun, looking at the pathetic terracing which was intended to help some cassava, maize and sorghum to grow, the Agricultural Officer who had taken me there said a few words which expressed both our feelings; then added:

"We can sit on the safety valve for so long . . . but that is all we are doing. Something *big* has to be done—something *outside* the reserves—and we've got to be damned quick about it!"

One of the reasons why I wanted to cite that report on the Kiambu District in full was to give you some idea of what these District Commissioners and the Agricultural Officers are up against, the detailed care with which they go into the problems, the *realism* with which they report their conclusions—the honesty of their observations is striking—and also so that you should have a sympathetic feeling for the black man. But also to show that this must be tempered with the knowledge that the black man is not co-operating in the very plans which are meant to better his condition today. And only a few miles from where I was shown these model farms, all run by superior Africans of the Headman type, sat an even more intelligent and widely-travelled African who, so the authorities say, had just stopped the terracing at Fort Hall.

CHAPTER XI

"Jomo and His Kingdom"

JOMO KENYATTA lay sprawled on the grass, as in the title of his book, facing Mt. Kenya. He told me that he was between forty-five and fifty years old; he did not know exactly. He had had seventeen years of Europe: London School of Economics, under the great anthropologist, Professor Malinowski (who wrote the preface to Jomo's book, *Facing Mt. Kenya*); Bloomsbury and Café Royal; Berlin and Paris, with the beer-hall and sidewalk café conversation of the Intelligentsia of those two capitals. And then an unspecified long spell of Moscow, where he lived in the Lux, the hotel maintained exclusively for the international members (and students) of the Comintern. Hardly a record of foreign travel that would endear him to the British now trying to solve or better the mixed racial relations of Kenya Colony. But an impressive sojourn in the white man's country, behind the lines, so to speak, with which to persuade the black man to accept his leadership. Surely a man with all that time in Europe must know something about the white man, his weak points, and how to handle him. There is no question that most of Jomo Kenyatta's power in Kenya is based on that belief, and he is the most powerful African in it. But it is also true that Jomo Kenyatta's long and sophisticated experience in Europe has taught him something about the African, *his* weak points and how to handle him. But for whose benefit? That is the riddle of Jomo Kenyatta.

A big, paunchy man, bearded, with slightly bloodshot eyes, a theatrically monstrous ebony elephant-headed walking stick, a gold-rimmed carnelian signet ring about the size of a napkin-ring, an outsize gold wrist-watch fastened to his hefty arm with a gold strap, dressed in European tweed jacket and flannel slacks—with as pleasant, ingratiating and wary a manner as you have ever met. He has a series of grunts—"*Unh-hunh!*"—whose rapidly switching inflections might mean anything. He struck me as being a born actor, an evident leader, and, perhaps just because of this, a man born for trouble.

I met him the first time when I was in the company of some of the European administrators. The D.C. and Mr. Gollop, the Agricultural Officer—"Manure" Gollop, as he is everywhere known because of his passionate crusade to make the Africans use that precious substance. And it was in answering Mr. Gollop's joking but highly pointed comments as Jomo led us around the little demonstration garden which he had started at the Kenya Teachers' College that I realised just how guardedly evasive, yet retaliatory, those little grunts of his, those "*Unh-hunh's,*" could be. For it was a taut situation—Jomo having to talk to an inquisitive stranger before the very officials who were certain that he had obstructed their agricultural program—and he served Mr. Gollop's derisive criticisms of the model garden back to him as skilfully as any Wimbledon finalist places passing shots down the sidelines. Had it not been for the uneasy feeling that this grinning black man was being given a "treatment" right before me, I would thoroughly have enjoyed it. For it was amusing to see the way he kept his end up. Now I was on the receiving end.

"Tell me, Mr. Kenyatta, why did you stop the terracing at Fort Hall?"

"I *never* tried to stop the terracing at Fort Hall!"

Jomo sat up. There had been something disarming in his injured surprise, almost a lamentation; and now, actor that he is, those eyes of his travelled from my wife's face to mine. And what eyes! They made me think of Leo Slezak, the great Hungarian tenor, when he was playing Othello; and I had watched him bending over Desdemona, through my peep-hole in the backdrop. Jomo's eyes came to rest on the astounded ground between us: "Why, I'd *never* do anything so silly as *that!*"

"Well, who did, then? Because somebody told them to stop."

"*Unh-hunh?* Well, it's just like I was telling you . . . these young men—they call themselves the 'Forty's'—they came out from Nairobi, and *they* told the people at Fort Hall that I had given the order to stop terracing. *I* never said anything."

"Very likely. But couldn't they have been your stooges? You would not have to give such an order *directly?*"

Now the "Forty" is an organisation, purporting to comprise men of the 1940 circumcision age group (Kikuyu); young men, many of whom have been in the Army. And while the influence of the returned *askari* upon native life has not been so subversive as was expected, there is no doubt that this "Forty" group contains a large number of young men who earn their living by a combination of politics, hooliganism and burglary—as the Nairobi police records show.

Jomo Kenyatta is President of the Kenya African Union, the black man's biggest political organisation, viewed by the Kenya Government with just about as much favor as Washington views the Communist organisation in the United States (although K.A.U., pronounced "Cow," is not Communist: it is a political attempt to organise the black man on the basis of what it conceives to be native rights); and the Forty group could be said to be K.A.U.'s activist left wing. Many Europeans believe, I think correctly, that the "Forty" group has Jomo on the spot, and that he is afraid of them. But nobody except Jomo Kenyatta can tell you how much he actually uses the "Forty," or how much it pushes him. There is not a man in the whole Kenya African Union that is one-half the man that Jomo is. Yet he must always be afraid that this left wing group will do something in the name of Jomo Kenyatta—their dark and half-educated minds will lead them to the use of force—that will put a stop to his present profitable and very pleasant way of life. For aside from being President of the K.A.U., he is also President of the Kenya Teachers' College, with a well-lardered home on its high hill overlooking one of the most inspiring views in all Kenya. And to be "put away," deported, to live up in the barren Northern Frontier District, would be like losing a Kingdom.

Jomo, so far as he himself is concerned, can always be counted upon to stay within constitutional limits. "Why should I want to stop those people up at Fort Hall from doing the very thing I had just *told* them to do? I went up to Fort Hall, and I said to Mr. Coutts [the District Commissioner], I said to him that if he would let the women off from doing the heavy work (*remember that head-strap*), and if he would let the old men off it, I would make a speech telling the others that *they* had to do it—the *young* men. And so I did. You ask Mr. Coutts. . . ."

And so he did. I had asked Mr. Coutts. But—there was not the faintest chance that the young men would ever do such work. When they come out from Nairobi to the reserve they do not come out to dig ditches.

It must be just as well to give a picture of this scene. The Kikuyu Reserve, which begins less than ten miles west of Nairobi, runs north along the slopes of the Aberdares and around the flanks of Mt. Kenya, all the way up to Isiolo, gateway to the barren Northern Frontier District. It covers 1,400 square miles and holds about 600,000 people, with some 250,000 Kikuyus living outside the reserve. It once held much of the best-watered, most fertile land in all Kenya. Today large parts of it are becoming a wasteland of raw, red erosion and shockingly bad native cultivation. I have given the report on Kiambu, which is notoriously over-populated. But for the rest of the reserve (such as the region around Fort Hall) the story can be said to be a race between over-population—according to the present methods of native cultivation—and a growing skill to make the land support a larger population. Terracing and lateral ploughing are, of course, the essential beginnings of such a skill. Anyone who tries to put a stop to this terracing works against the best interests of the reserve—and his own people.

The finest trout streams in all Kenya still run down from the Forest Reserve on the upper Aberdares. Indigenous forests of bamboo, cypress, wild fig and olive, and the giant podo trees; deep, dark forests, hung with heavy grey creepers. At around 7,000 feet the Kikuyus have been persuaded to plant wattles, both as a cash-crop (tan-bark and firewood) and as a soil-saving catchment area. But from there on down you see their toadstool clusters of thatched bee-hive huts, with their little pocket-handkerchief patches of cultivation—maize, sweet potatoes, finger millet, etc.—and the cattle and goats eating the very skin off the earth. Part of this is due to the congestion of the people on the land; more, at the present moment, is due to stupidity—the native refusal to go in for better farming; and now a large part of it —how large only the worried District Commissioners can know— is due to political obstructionism. Such as the stopping of the terracing at Fort Hall. And here on a high hill at Gethunguri outside Kiambu, in a region where African private, instead of clan, ownership has already started, such as on these few model farms; where there are waving fields of fine maize and watered valleys rich with the luxuriant green of broad banana fronds, in a vast landscape on which you can see Mt. Kenya to the north and the blue mountains of Tanganyika rising above the plains to the south, stand the mud-and-wattle huts of the Kenya Teachers' College—900 to 1,000 pupils—of which Jomo Kenyatta is President.

Here, inside its own bamboo stockade on the hundred acres of the school grounds, stands his pleasant thatched house, built in the European style, with two symbolic spears and a shield stuck, rather ostentatiously, on its lawn. And the books: a room packed with the books of H. G. Wells, Galsworthy, G. K. Chesterton, Nietzsche, Schopenhauer, etc.—so many books that you wonder, as you often do in a European's library, if he has ever tried to read the half of them. And in a big, empty, cement-floor living-room (in which he seldom lives, because it is so much more enjoyable to eat and talk out on the lawn) are the photographs of Roland Hayes, Claude McKay (as I remember them)—and of Paul Robeson.

This (with one of the best cooks I enjoyed in Kenya) is Jomo Kenyatta's home. "Jomo and his Kingdom." Jomo lived with Paul Robeson when that great Negro was doing the movie, *Sanders of the River*. They had a flat near Charing Cross. Jomo told me that he was the African expert on that film. He consorted at that time with most of the London liberals and left-wing intellectuals; and as I have many friends among that pink-and-dappled herd I was able to give him the latest news of some mutual acquaintances. He listened eagerly. (So eagerly that I began to find myself wondering just how long Jomo Kenyatta intends to remain in Kenya.) It was in 1934 that Kenyatta lived with Paul Robeson in London, teaching him to sing the African songs in *Sanders of the River*. But at the same time Jomo was also teaching Kikuyu in the London School of Oriental Languages. For further information on this most powerful African in East Africa, and what he has to say about the customs of his own people, the Kikuyus, I refer you to *Facing Mt. Kenya*—particularly Professor Malinowski's preface. Malinowski speaks admiringly of the primitive black man's society, whose people, he says sarcastically, "have not suffered from the benefits of our higher education." And the more I see of what some of the poorer or just plain stupid type of white man have done to the black man, and would like to continue to do to him—read some recent pronouncements, a spate of them, about "the African must work his passage"—the more I agree with Professor Malinowski. Because, after the almost unbearable conditions arising out of the over-population of the reserves, the next source of ill-will between the black man and the white is the determination of the latter that the African must come out of his reserve and work on the European's farms or in his factories: a determination which, on one or two occasions in Kenya's short history, has been just one step this side of a demand for forced labor, and, in my opinion, is now working up to that point again. With the "direction of labor" now being enforced in Great Britain, where every free-born Briton, man or woman, may be forced to take a job—no matter how uncongenial—it is perhaps only natural that the British in Africa should seize this as an excuse for imposing forced labor on the Africans. The Labour Government in England, as it happens, has not enforced this "direction of labor" on more than a few dozen very recalcitrant people; but many people in Kenya would like to use it as an excuse to force labor on the black population. They are already advocating it:

> When practically the whole world is short of food, and when the Native reserves of the Colony are liable to periodic famines, it seems difficult to justify the failure to take effective steps to combat the unwillingness to work which is so widespread among the Africans today. I favor the direction of labor being applied to all communities. Most Native authorities dislike to see their young men living in idleness.

This was the election address of Mr. Gerald Hopkins, who won the Aberdares in the recent elections (May 1948), to the European Non-Official Members of the Kenya Legislative Council. (And there is a lot of truth in his last sentence.) Here is the statement of the man who was defeated, getting third in the contest for the Aberdares, Mr. Arthur W. Sutcliffe:

> Strict control and supervision of Native reserves must be established. Obstruction, inertia and supineness of chiefs and headmen

> must be dealt with firmly, and areas under unsatisfactory control should have military units billeted in them until discipline is restored, all public services, agricultural, medical, educational, and so on being meantime withdrawn.
>
> The state of the world demands the maximum work output of everyone, either in private or official capacity. I would advocate a non-racial universal conscription by age-groups and direction of labor to civil or military work as appropriate and requisite. If this is not done now it may be too late. It is already later than we think. . . .
>
> The alternative to labor for public services or military undertakings or agricultural requirements should be considered, and the age-groups requisite would be called up irrespective of color, race, or creed, as in Britain today. Otherwise Italian, Chinese or Tamil labor must be available for importation on contract to increase production and perform essential work on public services, roads, etc.
>
> One thing is certain: the days of vacillation, equivocation, hesitation and procrastination are past. Everyone in Kenya of every race, color or creed in every walk in life must get on or get out.

You can read into these two declarations what you like. I think that people thinking of going out to make a life in Kenya should read them. The interesting thing is that both of these gentlemen have had long years of administrative work in Kenya: Mr. Hopkins had twenty-five years as District or Provincial Commissioner; Mr. Sutcliffe was for twenty years in the administration of Kenya. At one time he was District Commissioner of Nairobi. Both are farmers in the Aberdares constituency, flanking the Kikuyu territory. There is one thing that you will have to read in the statements of these two men: both are worried about a labor shortage in Kenya. And with reason.

In 1929 Jomo Kenyatta first came to London as a paid emissary of the Kikuyu people to present a petition to Parliament against what they claimed, at that time, was an attempt of the Europeans in Kenya to impose forced labor upon them. It might have looked, at that time, that the Government was going to be talked or bullied by the settlers into a direction of labor via an order to the District Commissioners in the reserves; the D.C., for example, being instructed to "see to it" that the required amount of labor came out of the reserve to work on the European coffee plantations. But that attempt was never made; the Kikuyus' fears were exaggerated. And in 1930 the slump began to set in and European farmers began turning Africans away instead of trying to recruit them. So it cannot be said that Jomo Kenyatta's mission to London resulted in any appreciable benefit to the Kikuyu people; but it did result in Jomo remaining in London and on the Continent, maintained, so it is said, very largely by contributions from his people at home. He did meet a lot of the Leftist and Labour intellectuals, who were very strong in the London of those days, in the House, Bloomsbury, Café Royal, etc.; and with his charm he made many friends, some of them quite influential. Lord Passfield (Sidney Webb) and Ramsay MacDonald, apparently, made a great fuss of him, as they would. This is the man, with *that* background, who, after seventeen years, returned to live in Kenya. . . .

The result could have been written in advance.

I have talked about the stupidity of the white man in dealing with the black man. The build-up for Jomo Kenyatta's allegedly subversive return to Kenya had been well prepared by that very thing. Jomo's predecessor at the Kenya Teachers' College had been the man who founded it, Peter Koinange, son of a senior Kikuyu chief, and he had started it because of a grudge. Peter Koinange ("lost to the fold" altogether, I am told) was an exceptional Kikuyu who went abroad, had one year of Cambridge, then went to Harvard and Columbia Universities, and returned to Kenya full, as may be expected, of great expectations—only to be offered a teacher's job at one-half the pay that its former occupant, a white man, had been getting. Pointing out the fact that the money he had had to pay for his own education had not been halved because he was a black man, he refused to accept the post. I have heard various interpretations of this episode, but not one which has convinced me that it was not the most stupid, bone-headed act that any governmental education department could have invented. It showed just no imagination. The upshot of it all was that Peter Koinange founded his own school—the Kenya Teachers' College—and I have described in *Behind God's Back* how I had driven in vain, ten years ago, 100 miles down from the Great Rift to see him, only to find that, for some mysterious reason, he was to be found nowhere at all that day.

I have often wondered why. The authorities knew I was coming. Anyhow, I saw that school, which then had 600 happy little African children; and I wrote with admiration of the fine sight it was to see an African school, run by an African, which seemed to have such an eager spirit—a thing so seldom seen in our schools at home.

And now, ten years later, there were 900 children and older boys—with even more eagerness. I will make one or two qualifications later; but the *spirit* of that school, the alertness and discipline with which they were paraded and went through a series of gymnastics with almost an Aldershot precision, was the most inspiring exhibition of youthful enthusiasm that I saw anywhere in Kenya. What they were being taught—and how well—is another matter. And here, I would say, the character of Jomo Kenyatta—whatever that is or will be—will play its most powerful part in African life.

I think there is something sad about the whole set-up. Peter Koinange and Jomo Kenyatta would not be the first colored men whose lives could be said to have been automatically cast into the rebellious opposition because they had returned to their own country after, as Malinowski might have said, having received the benefits of an English education. They find it very difficult to reconcile themselves to life in an English colony after that. Peter Koinange's younger brother is now teaching at the Kenya Teachers' College. I met him, and he impressed me as being one of the most capable and keen teachers that I met there. Though I did not see many teachers; nowhere near enough, it struck me, for a school of 900 pupils. I was told later that, as he could not pay them enough, most of the original teachers who had come there during Peter Koinange's time, some of them even from Makerere College in Uganda, had left; and that now the Teachers' College itself was having to rely upon unqualified teachers.

The chief teacher at Jomo's school for teachers did not even pass his exams at Alliance High School, so it is said, and was a rejected medical dresser. If so, I wonder what those 900 eager young Africans, whose ages range from seven to eighteen (a nine-year-old may be in the top grade; the fifteen-year one in the lowest, because a pupil's age seldom means very much in African schooling), are really being taught. For the first book I picked up on entering one of those mud-and-wattle classrooms was *Race Conflicts in Africa.* And I am sure that when, or if, his young pupils ever graduate—and they come from all parts of Kenya, from nearly all the tribes—that they will teach the young Africans more of what is in such a book than what the Iron Duke did to Napoleon at Waterloo.

I don't want it to be taken, just because I refer to certain facts that are in the black man's favor, that I am arguing the case for Jomo Kenyatta. Did he stop the terracing at Fort Hall? I don't know; and I have heard a lot from both sides. I have not one single bit of evidence which convinces me one way or the other. I am inclined to think that he might have, having learned something of his technique; and, in a way, it must have been a pathetic act in its very self. For it was really against the good of his own people. And, so everyone seems agreed (except Jomo), he did it to raise funds. This is the way one African put it to me:

"Jomo came back as a god [when he returned from Europe] . . . a defender . . . a sort of adviser to the Africans . . . and because he is an adviser he gets money. 'The women don't do any heavy work in England,' said Jomo. . . . 'Why not stop women doing any heavy work here?' He stops it—gets money—is popular. . . . You will never catch Jomo making any speeches showing how we aren't getting along—showing that *he* isn't having a success. No, no!—he's much too clever for that! *He'll* never commit himself. . . . He'll always do it through somebody else. . . ."

Consequently, if Jomo Kenyatta could call for political contributions, after getting the women off the terracing at Fort Hall (they had stopped, as a matter of fact, *before* he came up there—very likely from an order sent through "somebody else"), you would think there would be a large number of female pupils at Jomo's school. But there is not. There are only thirty girls there out of the 900 pupils. And I am still wondering why. Jomo Kenyatta's way of life today is maintained almost entirely by these voluntary contributions. So far as material things go, he has a very comfortable life.

I know, also, that Jomo Kenyatta has addressed large public meetings of his own people on many occasions, telling them that they will have to work, work hard—"and learn how to work intelligently"—if they ever want to be justified in getting any large advance in wages. He speaks more plain words to his own people than a white man can—for they listen.

The desire of the African for education is touching. What he gets is even more pathetic. It is estimated that out of an African population of over five million, there are well over two million people of school age in Kenya. Out of these not more than some 200,000 are in school at any one time, but they are not the same students throughout even their short school life. One-half of them leave school within the first two years, never to return. Only about 10,000 ever finish their primary school; only some 6,000 of these go on to the secondary, but of how many complete this course no record seems to be kept. None that I could find, anyway. Only about seventy Kenya students ever go on to enter Makerere College, which is over in Uganda and is the very peak of education in East Africa. A few brilliant Africans (and this is increasing) receive bursaries, and because of that and, very often, their own superhuman efforts go on to the London School of Economics, Cambridge, Oxford, and in exceptional cases even go on to study in the U.S.A. Mr. Eliud Mathu, one of the four African Members appointed to the Kenya Legislative Council, went to Balliol for a time, and, if I am right, finished his studies through a correspondence course. It can be seen that the teaching of teachers in Kenya is lamentably inadequate; and in fairness to the régime it must be said that if all the black children of school age in Kenya did go to school, there would not be one-tenth enough teachers. That is the position today.

Practically all of the Kenya elementary schooling is left to the missions: God-fearing and earnest people, and in some cases remarkably far advanced. There is a Roman Catholic Mission School near Thika, of which an exceptionally well-educated young African said to me: "I am very proud of that: a child can go there, get elementary, and go all the way on for a Senior Certificate for Cambridge. Very good teachers. Very good discipline." And after a thoughtful pause he added (for he had gone to two universities outside of Kenya): "A school like that gives you a very wide view of life . . . for when you return to your people." There are mission schools like that, but with a great many of them it must be admitted that the education they provide is sketchy; and as for a wide view, they make you think of Dorothy Parker's comment on the acting of Katharine Hepburn: that she ran the gamut from A to B. Each mission—C.M.S., Church of Scotland, Roman Catholic, Seventh-Day Adventist, or Church of National Holiness, Chicago, U.S.A.—has its own interpretation of life, both here and hereafter, and the proper education with which to meet it. Africans have to make the best of it. But I have seldom heard a literate African speak ill of his mission days; and I have had one or two speak with what could be truly called a deep and abiding love of the missionaries who gave them their early education.

The secondary part of the Kenya African's education, most of which is run by the Government, is odiously academic. It seems to have been designed almost entirely for a white-collar class, a class of clerks, whereas the one thing that Kenya needs most, in the way of education, is an artisan class: skilled African craftsmen, people who have been taught how to work with their hands, and, most important, are proud to work with their hands. As it is, this "top-hat" education has the same taint of snobbism that used to be attached to what is known as a "varsity education" in Britain, and is very often applied in Kenya by persons who have been given an inferiority complex back in Britain simply because they had not been to the right school, and the result with the African, as so pitifully few of them ever do graduate, is that he attaches a snob value to his own education that actually puts him further away from his own people than is even the European. He does not lead from *among* them; he is an Olympian, aloof figure, concerned only with the "higher things." As such, he is totally uninterested, even offended at the idea, of having anything to do with an African kindergarten class. That is beneath him. The African teachers themselves are thus in a state of transition. And this is one of the chief reasons why, as no real *African* interest is taken in their early teaching, one-half of all Kenya's African schoolchildren leave school within their first two years.

But other reasons which have been given to me by the Africans themselves why they leave school or do not go to school at all are (*a*) the expense: these are prohibitive for all but a few African parents to undertake. (*b*) The distances: schools are so far from many of the Africans' huts that a child receiving a day-school education will often walk four or five miles each way, and that takes considerable endurance, and persistence, on the part of the child. (*c*) Then there is the parents' chronic objection, "Who will look after the goats?" for it usually is the children who herd the goats, sheep and scrawny cattle. And it must never be forgotten that the African parents look on their children as a source of income: child labor of from six to nine years old is heavily employed in the coffee-picking season and on tea plantations. So it can be seen that an African who really does manage to get an education has some reason to feel proud of himself, and can therefore be excused for placing such a high, even snob, value upon his learning.

Then, too, in these days of increasing suspicion and doubt between the black man and the white man—and it is folly to try to deny this obvious fact—when these weird and fanatical religious cults are breaking out all over Africa, as a result of *something* that is poisoning the blood-stream, I think it would be well to take some of the following things into account. A great many Africans fear that the Europeans are "cheating" in the education of their children; that they are teaching them things which will take them away from their people. Others think, and quite rightly in this case, that a European education is making class distinctions among the Africans. There can be no doubt about these two feelings.

What is open to doubt—and it is with this reservation that I state it—is that it seems a pity that so much of the early education of the African has been left to the Missions. In this I am not criticising the Missions; I am criticising our own failure to live up to the Christian standard of life that, regardless of their particular creed, all Missions preach. I think that even while he is at the Mission school the average African begins to suspect that we do not live by the precepts that we talk to him so much about. Later he is sure of it. How could he help it? Eventually comes the alarming conviction that we do not believe in the God that we are still trying to make him believe in. And from that, that we are trying to teach him to believe in many things that we do not believe in ourselves. And that we are doing it for our own good, not his. In that way I think we have debased the African; at any rate, we have made him lose confidence in *us*. After talking to many Africans, I have come to the conviction that if we had placed less stress upon the teachings of Christ we would have let him in for less disillusionment and suspicion of our motives. I believe that a straightforward secularist education would have given him a more realistic and useful code for life as it really is, and for getting along with Europeans. It is not the Missions I am criticising: it is us. And I can understand why many an African, in the face of all our specious declarations, regards us with contempt.

Then there is the experience of two wars in which the Africans, as porters or *askaris*, have seen the Europeans destroying each other with the very mechanical perfections that we have taught them to respect us for. Finally, there is the European's doubt, in these worried days, of himself. The European, even in Africa, is in no way so sure of himself as he used to be. I think that this is contagious, and that the African has caught it. And when we start to transfer what we know as democracy to the African by the method of conferential discussion—"How, do you think, should we set about doing this?"—he, with all these other doubts in his mind, jumps to the conclusion that we are asking him because we don't know ourselves!

Such are some of the difficulties of coming to grips with the native mind. They are formidable. Ask any District Commissioner who has to deal daily with these dark doubts and suspicions, and he will tell you that a proper and widespread education could mean everything. The present assortment of inconsequential facts that it is now being tried to stuff into the African's woolly head can perhaps best be portrayed by a remark of Sir Philip Mitchell—possibly apocryphal, though it would be characteristic of his candor—when he was being conducted around a new African school:

"What," he said, turning to his A.D.C., "can the naval policy of the Phoenicians possibly mean to these poor people? Or, for that matter, to *you?*"

"The Europeans," said Jomo Kenyatta as we were eating a fine lunch of fried chicken under a shade-tree on his lawn, "lay a lot of stress that education must come from the *top*." He made a graphic gesture with his hand. "*I* say that it has to come from *below*. I tell my pupils that they have to teach from *among* their people. They have to be one of them. You ask me what kind of a line I am taking? . . . Well, I think the best way to put it would be to say that I am cutting the dead wood out of a lot of our old African beliefs, and I am reinforcing what I think are some of the best things of our African ways of life. I am sending them out with something that I hope is going to *work*. I want them to be proud of being *Africans!* I don't want to make a lot of Black Englishmen!"

"Female circumcision? Do you tell them to cut that out?"

He grinned. "No-indeedy! I'd might as well close up school! I've got to be *practical*. . . ." His eyes, wary and thoughtful, came to rest on the stone church, which is also in the school's grounds.

"Does that church preach against female circumcision? Against polygamy?" I asked him.

"It does not. Why should it?"

The Kikuyus' own efforts to give themselves the kind of education they want, and a religion which fits in conveniently with some of their most strongly held beliefs, were shown both in this school and the presence on its grounds of the church. Both are called Independence. Both were founded as a breakaway from the Mission and its schools when the Church of Scotland almost provoked a rebellion among the Kikuyu in its fierce crusade to abolish female circumcision. This was in 1929. The Kikuyus forcibly circumcised some Mission girls. And I have cited in *Behind God's Back* the case of one Kikuyu girl who sued her father for forcibly circumcising her—and won her case. The first and, so far as I know, only lawsuit of its kind in Africa. There was also the terrible episode of the Scottish missionary, who had always strongly opposed female circumcision. The Kikuyus broke into her home one night and forcibly circumcised her in the most brutal fashion. She died from her injuries.

Female circumcision is practised by nearly all the tribes of Equatorial Africa. It is unquestionably their most savagely held custom. Though the most curious, even sinister, thing about it is that few Africans can give you a satisfactory reason for it. I have never heard one. When it is done by the old and practised midwives of the tribe, it cannot generally be so harmful as Europeans try to make out. Otherwise how could the Masai women bear such splendidly-formed men? But when it is driven underground (as is abortion in European life), then malformation, death in childbirth and all sorts of human misery may result. It is a custom that some tribes, such as those in the North Kavirondo Province, are (or were, until it was re-started again by a religious cult) gradually giving up of themselves. But it is something so deep-rooted in the African consciousness that it cannot be put a stop to by any law. The Local Native Council at Kiambu, for example, passed a resolution forbidding female circumcision; and it is also an example of how fanatically this custom is adhered to to say that the Kikuyus there have kept right on doing it. Neither the Independence School nor the church teaches or preaches against female circumcision.

When those Kikuyus who broke away from the Mission schools in 1929 attempted to found their own schools, they met active opposition from the missions who, in Jomo Kenyatta's words, went to the Government and said: "We have the monopoly here. Don't let them open competing schools, the 'Independence Schools.' They will not teach religion!" And the Independence Schools, according to Kenyatta, were closed by the Government from 1929 to 1932. Since then the active opposition has stopped; licences began to be granted in 1932; and today there are 180 Independence Schools in the Kikuyu Reserve, all entirely maintained by the natives themselves, with an attendance of some 34,000 pupils. Even the Local Native Council, which will give a grant to mission schools from money raised from the natives themselves, does not give a grant to these Independence Schools. The L.N.C. of the Kiambu District, which has 196,000 people, gave a capital grant of £5,000 during the fiscal year 1946-7 for the building of schools, mostly mission, which shows how, contrary to uninformed opinion, the African is paying largely for his own education.

They raise their own funds, but here again comes the danger of generalising about anything in Africa, or even of accepting things at their face value: it is impossible to assess the quality of the teaching in these Independence Schools. Their teachers may be eager—in fact, they must be—but they may not possess the necessary qualifications. Those who disapprove of the Independence Schools assert that they have never graduated a pupil who has been able to matriculate at Makerere, the college to teach teachers, over in Uganda; and that, as the Government has no control over their syllabus, they may be able to produce people who can read and write, but they are turning out a great mass of half-educated Africans who will become a dangerous problem in the future.

The Independence Church was started in 1935. The Kikuyus wanted a religion, but it was to be a religion that fitted in with most of the things that the Kikuyus wanted to practise. The Independence Church was not to preach against polygamy, as a plurality of wives is the basis of African economy, peasant farming, and even of social life. Chief Wambogo, near Nyeri in the Kikuyu Reserve, has today 120 wives and, as one African put it to me—"some big village of children"! Chief Kibathi in the Kiambu District has twelve wives, and eighty children. And they are both said to be good chiefs, wise and capable leaders.

To get their own priests, the Kikuyus brought up a black Bishop from South Africa—from the Orthodox Church, which is almost like the Greek Church—and a Negro pastor from the U.S.A. named William Alexander, and said to them: "We employ you for a year or two, and during that time you ordain some of *our* people." William Alexander was in the Kikuyu country for eighteen months; during that time he ordained eight priests. Since then nine more priests have been ordained. And these seventeen padres of the Independence Church travel throughout the Kikuyu Reserve like judges on circuit. They baptise children, marry people, and say nothing whatever against polygamy or female circumcision. It seems a very obliging religion.

Jomo Kenyatta's school, the Kenya Teachers' College, was paid for by an age group of Kikuyus—all the people who were circumcised in that year. These age or circumcision groups are the strata on which Kikuyu life is built. They have an entity, a unit-consciousness of a university's class. They function throughout life. They raise subscriptions *as* a group, have an *esprit de corps* that is peculiar to its group, and, as I have indicated with the "Forty," they may even provide a terrorist group: this largely, it should be said, owing to the political and moral infection from the black African slums of Nairobi, which has about 22,000 more Africans than it can hold, with black spivs and unemployables sleeping on the floors of warehouses and in the bodies of trucks and abandoned motor cars. This infection pollutes the whole Kikuyu Reserve—and race. Each circumcision group has a name. When the first aeroplane came to East Africa, that year's group was named "Aeroplane." Another group was called "Japan," because it was in that year that the Kikuyus were struck by the cheapness of Japanese goods (about 1937, I think). Jomo Kenyatta's group was called "Big Knife"—due, he said, to that being the year when the Europeans began to give their African farm laborers the big knife such as natives use in the cane brakes, and with which the present-day African almost cleans his teeth. He would feel naked without it. A pair of shorts, a ragged shirt and that knife are very often the African farm laborers' only wearing apparel. Jomo, who obviously has a lingering love for some of the old customs of his tribe, said that "Big Knife" might also have come from the custom of the witch doctors, who put a knife in the fire and make a suspect lick it to prove his innocence. There was an ex-witch doctor (and I don't think he was so much "ex") walking around Jomo Kenyatta and us during most of our three talks. He was dressed in an immaculate pressed suit of Indian-made khaki drill. Circumcision is as great an event in Kikuyu life as a young English nobleman's coming-of-age. Said Jomo: "The young are very keen on it."

I said: "The theory is that circumcised women remain more faithful? They get less fun out of it?"

He protested: "But it *doesn't* destroy their pleasure!"

"How do you know?"

Jomo grinned. "They are no worse off."

"But are they any better?"

Jomo hesitated. "W-e-ll—you never know. . . . *Psychologically*—so some of them say—it *is* better. . . ."

I cannot speak any further from practical experience. These circumcision groups go by a seniority scale, with certain privileges—and obligations. Jomo, for his Kenya Teachers' College (and perhaps other ventures), had demanded 12,000 shillings from each Kikuyu age group. Some of them had already paid up. And as his school is inter-tribal he has got contributions from other parts of Kenya. The money, said Jomo, was going mostly into a big stone building that was going to house the new school.

So far, it was just an unimpressive oblong cut into the ground, with some stone tiers laid at its bottom, which Jomo pointed out to me with his elephant-headed stick. It made me think of old Chicago days, when we used to wonder how much of the State taxes ever went into the roads. And here again was that pathetic bar across the road of African development: an Indian was the *fundi*, the foreman on the job. "Oh, one day," said Jomo, sighing and pointing to some native carpenters working on a nearby building, carpenter's work being a thing for which Africans have a natural aptitude, "one day . . . we'll have it so that they can do it *all* themselves!"

This inter-tribal school takes pupils from the Kavirondo Reserve over on Lake Victoria, Kipsigis, Nandis, Lumbwas; and Wakambas and even some of the tribes down on the Coast send their children to it—tribes that ordinarily hate each other. In the school the brotherly feeling among these young Africans was exhilarating; they made you think that some day there really could be such a thing as a unity of Kenya Africans. But when, shortly after, I took my Kikuyu driver over into the Nandi and Lumbwa country, he complained that the house-boys there would give him nothing to eat; and in one place he was so concerned for his own safety that he slept in the locked car. Joseph and his Brethren, which could be called the story of my driver, was a daily surprise of contradictions. It made me wonder who the British ever could hand over democracy to in Kenya. And Joseph, as I have said, was as good a driver as I have ever sat behind.

I saw Jomo Kenyatta on three occasions, with widely spaced intervals during which I went over nearly all of Kenya; from the warrior Masai country on the great game plains on the border of Tanganyika up through the waterless thorn-scrub and lava deserts to the frontier of Abyssinia; from the swamps of Victoria Nyanza to the clove trees and Arab civilisation in the dhows at Zanzibar; and the more I saw the more I realised what a terrible long way it is that we have got to bring the African—that is, if we have any right to force our education upon him at all. Which I am beginning to doubt seriously. If it were possible, and I know that it is not, I would say leave the Masai and the Somali nomadic camel tribes alone to live their wandering pastoral life.

They have a life with more real wisdom than that package of superficial information we press upon people instead of knowledge. But as I know that such tolerance is impossible in the way this world of ours is going—to permit a numerically weak people to continue to enjoy its primitive way of life—I would at least say to the Fabians and their like at home that they are preaching outmoded things, that they are really out of date in striving to make the Africans struggle for independence and self-rule; and, just as the Soviet Russians have abolished all personal liberty in the name of liberty, their well-meant efforts will deliver the desperately backward or half-educated Africans into the worst political and industrial bondage they have ever known. This is not mere rhetoric. The kindest words I have read about the African since I went back to Kenya in November 1947 (and I am not a Catholic) were printed, on June 5th, 1948, in the *Tablet*, which said:

> We have to say to the peoples of Africa that it is the experience alike of antiquity and the twentieth century that mass politics, democratic forms operating among very uneducated and very poor people, lead straight to demagogic tyranny; that genuine freedom and a sense of personal security can come only as a middle-class and an educated electorate are brought into being. It is the truest charity to explain these facts of social life to people who have not had any experience such as we can draw on of what is necessary for economic advance, and what for political liberty; for it is a spiritual work of mercy to tell people things they do not know and need to know. And twentieth-century Europe would be a better and happier place if there had been less amiable fostering in the last century of dangerous illusions about the ease and simplicity of human progress which are having to be paid for in this.

I think that this, coming from the Catholic Church, which maintains some of the best missions in Africa—best, so it is generally admitted, because the Catholic missions place so much stress upon self-discipline—is one of the most profound truths I have ever heard about that Dark Continent. It is almost impossible to make people who have never been there realise just how backward the people of Equatorial Africa really are, particularly in East Africa. When the British began to build a railway up from Mombasa in 1890, the natives inland, in what is now known as Kenya, had never heard of the use of the wheel.

They had no calendar or notation of time, no means of writing, no numbering except on their fingers or making notches in sticks or knots in fibre strings. They did not know of any tools except small hand hoes, stone axes, and wooden digging sticks. Nor did they have any government beyond a few tribal chiefs and patriarchs. (They had poisons, though, which could kill a man or an elephant within half an hour.) All this is astounding when one considers what was found in the tomb of Tutankhamen up in the valley of the Nile. And when one thinks of the great emirates of the West Coast of Africa, and even of the civilisation which the Arabs had brought to the narrow coastal strip of East Africa and the island of Zanzibar. It is just unbelievable, one of the greatest riddles of all Africa. But it is a fact.

On the other hand, we no longer feel quite so confident in measuring them by that so-convenient yard-stick which we used to call "civilisation." For in many ways they had worked out a pretty elaborate system of rule and self-rule which fitted in very well with their circumstances of life. The Baganda have a dynasty of "Kabakas" (Kings) which has a direct descent pre-dating any Royal House in Europe.

The Wakamba, whose reserve is now next to the Kikuyu, may never have heard of the wheel, but they were making snake-chains out of copper three hundred years ago, as pliable as those steel ones you buy for your key-ring in Switzerland today. Dr. Leakey, the archaeologist, showed me these chains when I went along to the Coryndon Museum in Nairobi to get *his* explanation for this mysterious backwardness of the East Coast Africans. He said that after 5,000 B.C., when the Sahara began to dry up, the deserts dropped like a shutter north of the rain-forests in Equatorial Africa; the floating swamps of the Nile's *sudd* prevented the Egyptian civilisation from coming south; and the deserts of what is now the Northern Frontier District formed a shutter cutting off any civilisation coming down from Abyssinia. It was a coincidence almost too unbelievably apposite to be cited that, as I left the Museum to walk back to the Norfolk Hotel, I saw a Kikuyu woman in the swampy patch below it breaking up a bit of land for cultivation *with a digging stick*. But it is exactly such contrasts that you will find in all East African life. Sixty years ago they were all using digging sticks. Today's educated East African is just emerging from *that.*

Therefore, when you do meet an African who has gone all the way through, surmounting every obstacle to get his education—one who has *not* allowed his learning to turn his head—you will know that you are meeting an exceptional man. They are some of the most charming, refreshing and encouraging people you will meet in all Kenya. They are the real leaders of their race. *They* know that they have to interpret the white man's world to the African, they have to make him fit in, because the white man is taking over the African's world; and they just ache to make their people learn. They seem to suffer, some of the keenest among them, from an almost unbearable anxiety. I think that as time goes on more and more of them will begin to discard what they can of the white man's values in teaching their people.

Like Jomo Kenyatta, many of them will try to find out which were best and begin to re-fortify many of the old beliefs. The whole term "education" is up for revision in Africa. And I think that the white man should put something new into his educational policy, something that will better educate the African for a life—*in Africa.* The frantic desire of the African to be left alone to develop his own Africanism is the paramount impression I got from all these outstanding Africans. It was the same impression I got over in Uganda in 1939, where the natives are much more highly educated than the Kenya Africans. They firmly believe, and I know they are right, that the only defence of the native population against the encroaching demands of the white man is *education.*

But that is only met with in the literate Africans: the ones who, as they say in Kenya, have "come out of the tree." I saw several of what I would call modern—even model—attempts of the British to give the African a really serviceable education; notably the school for ex-*askaris* out at Kabete, where, in classes of about 250, some of the most promising soldiers from the last war are being given a short but very practical training in such crafts as shoe-making (very good), tailoring, tin-smithing, carpentering, elementary motor repairs and the running of shops; and where half of the pupils are being trained exclusively to become African welfare officers and go back to work in the District Commissioner's office. I went through the Railway Workshops in Nairobi, where African apprentices are being given as well-planned a training to become skilled mechanics as they could get anywhere in England. Two things they seemed to bring out: the first of them rather tragic. The African seems to think that there is some *magic* difference between the European and the African, and that education is the answer to it. Give him the same education and he will be the same man. He takes no account of evolution. The other is the inability of the African to think in abstract terms, but give him a routine, specific job to do, and he will keep on and on and on—just so long as you keep after him. I came on one or two brilliant exceptions to this, which I will show in their settings.

I went through the Government Secondary School over at Kakamega, which, so far as an academic education is desired, struck me as being better run than many a European school, though this was almost entirely due to the personality of the Principal, I believe. But the more I talked with the Africans themselves, the more I came to realise that this aching desire for an education—as I have even described it myself—is a thing you hear only from people who have stayed through the school course, who have graduated from the secondary schools, or from parents whose children had got that far. You hear nothing except silence from the great mass of Africans who have withdrawn their children after the first year, or who have never allowed their children to go to school at all. Inarticulate Africa!

Education is not compulsory for Africans in Kenya, it should be remembered. It is for European children throughout the Colony, as it is for the Indian children in all the townships. But the African can take it or leave it, as he chooses. And the reasons why there is practically no female education in Kenya, except a few mission girls, bring out, in my opinion, some of the most fundamental, and at the same time backward, features—both of the "darkness" of African life and the surprisingly little imagination that the European has used so far to overcome it. The roots of these reasons are deep; they go down through the thin layer of European civilisation to draw their nourishment from the wells of savagery that lie below all African life.

CHAPTER XII

Game Country and Native Poisons

I DID not take a rifle with me this time to Kenya, the desire to kill things having finally petered out, except for the odd duck or goose. The only large animal I shot was Roger Wilkinson, District Commissioner of the Masai, into whom I put two No. 7 shot, which I shall describe when and where it happened.

This is down near Tanganyika. The great game plains lie restfully in the setting sun. The short grass takes on a golden hue. The nearby acacia thorns are touched with emerald. The mountains on the far horizon turn a slaty blue, and look like the backs of prehistoric monsters crouching along the skyline. There are openings between these blue and green mountains that lead into other bits of game country, some of which are still unknown to the new type of white hunter that has appeared in Kenya. For most of the afternoon we had zigzagged all over the open plains, making false leads with our lorries' wheels, barging into deep brush occasionally and then back-tracking down drifts, to come out of stony stream beds again where our wheels would not be likely to leave any trace. And then we had resumed our main direction towards a particular gap in the mountains to the west. This was done so that the three big game *safaris* which were known to be shooting somewhere in that part of Kenya would not be able to track us to our camp on the upper Talek River, to a stretch where there were some water pools, beside which the Game Warden had his camp.

The whole day had been a panorama of wild animals. We became bored, even annoyed after a time, with the sweeping herds of little Tommy gazelles, who would insist on racing us, trying to cut across our cars. It meant frequent stops to let them settle down again. Kongoni and topi sometimes did not even look up. More Tommies . . . bouncing, stiff-legged, like rubber balls, sure sign that they were enjoying life. The plain was full of young things. The wildebeest seemed to be dropping their young everywhere, little dun-colored wildebeest, trying to keep pace with their mothers, flying at full gallop with their manes tossing in the wind. To have one of these bearded and wild-maned gnus race your car at night, particularly a rainy one, is like pacing something straight out of Hell. Giraffe waited inquisitively at openings where the old Lupa Goldfields Road went through the stands of candelabra euphorbia, then rocked off, their thudding hoofs stampeding many animals which had not been frightened until then. At one place two herds of zebra, and we estimated there were about 250 in each, raced across our bows in a running stream of stripes that looked as if all the convicts in Sing Sing had just made a jail-break. Fat as butter (I have never met anyone who has seen a thin zebra), with the brownish colts running beside their mothers. Zebra were by far the most plentiful large animal on the plain. It seems like sheer murder to kill them for lion-bait; yet with every full licence you get the right to shoot four zebra, to hang up in trees. Then, theoretically, you crawl up and shoot the lion which is eating them the next dawn.

Don't imagine that just because I did not take a rifle along I am going to rhapsodise about "shooting" big game with a camera, and tell you it is the same thing. It isn't. With a camera you make no enemies. But when you bring your rifle to bear on a big animal, you say to yourself: "It's now or never." If you hit him and he doesn't drop, then the odds begin to equal. If he's a lion, and wounded, if he doesn't charge you at once, he will go into the bush, and you have to go after him. That's the unwritten law. And no man (who wants to call himself a man after that) dare break it. It is even more nerve-racking (yet tensely exciting) to follow up a wounded buffalo in high grass. Consequently, you have a curious bond of hostility; an entirely different psychology from photographing or watching animals. And you also have a sympathy. Henri Bergson, in one of his books, tells of a wasp which sticks her proboscis into the nervous system of a spider, paralysing it up to a certain survival point—to when the eggs that she has laid in the spider hatch out and the larvae have fed on the spider until they can take wing; and the word that he uses for this curious relationship of the wasp and the spider is —*sympathy*. In the old Greek use of it. Therefore, when people wonder how it is possible for, say, a white hunter to feel fond of the animals he is leading you to kill, or when, as is really the case, the big game hunter feels a sympathy and an admiration for the lion he is aiming at—there is a bond between them. Finally, there is the ultimate thrill of making yourself experience danger, for no man tastes life unless he puts it in the balance.

There is something esthetic in it; it is the lust to acquire the beauty—to *get*. This is not a justification for big game shooting; that is another matter altogether. This is just a statement. And for these reasons men will go all over the world to shoot big game.

"And no man has the right to press the trigger," has said Captain Archie Ritchie, Chief Game Warden of Kenya for twenty-five years (half of that Colony's life!), "unless he is prepared to accept the possible subsequent obligations."

During the morning we had come down through some scrub-bush country that was the domain of the bigger birds. Readers of this have probably seen a pine grouse trying to lead you away from her nest, feigning a broken wing; or possibly you have seen a merganser coasting about, up and down, off a patch of reeds, trying to distract your attention, while her beady-eyed little black-and-yellow balls of fluff try to hide themselves in the natural protective coloring of the reeds or under the overhanging branches from the bank; but to see an ostrich—a *male* ostrich —try to lead you off is a sight indeed! When we were going through a patch of whistling thorn in fairly open scrub country on our way down to the game plains, we saw a big black-and-white cock ostrich running ahead of us, and then, to our astonishment, we saw him trip, slide, in a flurry of dust; then get up and trot joltingly off again, dragging his ragged wings. Just for an instant we were taken in. Then we saw the hen ostrich, with three little dun-colored chicks (about the size of barnyard turkeys), cutting off at top speed in a side direction. "And greater love hath no bird than this!" sighed the Game Warden, Temple-Boreham, who was driving beside me.

Then he showed me a thing about whistling thorn that I had

never known, although the lion that I had shot ten years before had been in a grove of whistling thorn. Each of the little black balls on these thin thorn trees, slightly larger, but about the same shape as horse-chestnut shells, was packed full of tiny black ants. Millions of them! How or why they should be there in such quantities is a riddle; but in the next few days I broke open these whistling-balls time and again, and always found them full of ants. The whistle comes, of course, from the hole they have made in the shell when the wind rasps past it. We had plenty of time to examine them, I may say, for the old *safari* truck in which Eric Sweatman, the Officer in Charge of the Masai, was travelling, had decided that its time was up. And the African boys from our three lorries—we had eighteen boys to begin with—spent their time crawling over and under that lorry, like black ants themselves. It gave us plenty of time to enjoy the landscape; also to see how one or two Africans among our crowd of mixed natives had something close to genius when it came to machinery, whereas others had not the faintest conception of what made a car go. We were all surprised when this one did go.

Eric Sweatman was the officer in charge of this trip. For at the end of it we were going up on the Loita Plateau, the "Country of the Magicians," where all the Masai medicine-men come from, where he was going to hold an open-air court, sitting in judgment on twenty-one bad hats of that most mysterious and troublesome clan. "And I can tell you one thing," said Sweatman ruefully as we set out on this *safari*. "When you have me along, you will never see a lion. I am a jinx. In twenty-six years of Africa I have never yet seen a lion." This was an astonishing statement from one who had been for years in top charge of the Masai country. Yet we did not see a lion. In eight days, in a district where ten years before Sydney Downey and I had seen four lionesses our first night and where we had lain all one afternoon behind a knoll watching a lioness play with her cub, we did not see one lion. In eight nights we heard only one roar, and that from a long way off.

The camp on the Upper Talek was in a lovely spot. The Temple-Borehams' big marquee had been set up in a grove of 50- or 60-foot acacia thorns which made a crescent facing what was left of a pool in the drying river. On the tops of these trees sat hundreds of marabou storks, bills on their chests, with their drooping, naked sacs, the most depressed-looking aggregation of birds I have seen anywhere in Africa. It rained that night, and as the drops hit the canvas and I could smell the wet earth, I thought of all those marabous sitting on the tops of the acacia thorns around us, like mourners . . . as if waiting for us to die. Nothing moved them. Not even the huge brushwood fire before which we ate our dinners on the succeeding nights, whose flames lit up the acacias until we seemed to be sitting in a golden amphitheatre. Going beyond the realm of glow, looking up into the night, the stars of the Milky Way seemed to be streaming across Africa, and close at hand, as if you were looking up into the misty spaces between them. The whole feeling of the camp filled you with disgust for what the white man hopes to do with what is left of Africa.

I have been reading the words of one great British industrialist. "To me," he said, "there was something exciting and dramatic about Que Que. Here is a steel-smelting plant of the very latest type that has been put up right away in the middle of the veld. . . . Here again is an illustration of the conveyor principle used. To see these latest methods being installed in the virgin veld under the hot African sunlight is, to an industrialist, most exciting and inspiring." He added: "Baboons that commit suicide on the high-tension cables are particularly troublesome." Who can blame them?

In the mornings, feeling fresh as if they were the first day of Creation, we drove out into the sunrise for a pre-breakfast survey of the surrounding plains, nearly wrecking the car in the bouldered beds of some dried-up rivers around us in our efforts to find a lion. There was almost an ominous silence from them. Indeed, we all began to feel that these plains and brush-filled river banks were haunted by the lions which had once roamed them. Big game *safaris* had shot 109 lions in the Narok district that year; later, almost a year's closed season was given them, a short rest from extinction. But it did not give the poor old king of beasts much time to breed again. I think the lions are on the way out, that we can see their end already in sight. And with the way game is being handled in Tanganyika, we are probably watching the end of a lot of other animals too.

The attitudes of Tanganyika and Kenya are almost directly opposed about game, though the blame cannot be placed on the shoulders of the Tanganyika Game Department. It should be placed on the doorstep of the Governor and the Secretariat in Dar-es-Salaam, and to lack of imagination in London. In Tanganyika the natives are allowed to have rifles, allegedly to shoot game for their own food; and some 30,000 rifles are registered with the police, with the police thinking that 50,000 would come nearer the number of rifles in native hands. And what the natives do with these rifles is worse than murder. These are muzzle-loaders, but with them the natives are supposed to be killing *about 180,000 head of game a year*. Just think of that figure for a moment. This rather takes the curse off Southern Rhodesia, which shocked world opinion some years ago when it frankly announced that some 320,000 head of game had been killed in its tsetse-fly campaign of 1922-45. The natives are by far the worst enemy of the wild game of Africa. They are not supposed to sell meat, but everybody knows they are doing it; hunting it with motor lorries. More game was killed by native hunters in two years in Tanganyika than the Southern Rhodesian anti-tsetse-fly campaign killed in twenty-four years.

Under the Tanganyika law (unless it has been changed while I am writing this book), an African can provide himself with a muzzle-loader, take out a one-shilling licence, and shoot almost every variety of game without any limit as to numbers. And it is not only what they kill: it is what these old-fashioned rifles and unfeeling hunters wound. Captain Keith Caldwell, making a survey for the society which hopes to protect the vanishing fauna of the British Empire (what is left of both), reported that he had found seven dead giraffe in the Tanganyika bush which had not even had their tails cut off: proof positive that the native hunters had never found them after they had wounded them, for giraffe tails are highly prized for the making of bracelets. In Kenya, natives are not given licences to carry arms except for one "native or Somali employee" licence, which a farm-owner may take out for one of his boys, for whose actions he is personally responsible. It may be argued that morally the native African has more right to kill his own animals than any New York millionaire or British sportsman, and the argument would be right from a moral viewpoint; but with the Indians organising it and the native hunters killing everything they could get within range of—for meat, skins, ivory—Africa would soon be the graveyard of the most beautiful creatures which now walk this earth.

The greatest danger which Kenya game is facing now is the "biltong hunter." Some Dutchmen used to invade the Masai Reserve annually with the determination to supply themselves with a year's dried meat to feed their farm boys. Temple-Boreham, the Game Warden we were with on this *safari*, has chased these South Africans all the way back to Eldoret and caught them on their farms. But usually it is impossible to tell from a lorry load of sun-dried meat how many antelope went into the making of it. Big game sportsmen do very little harm. One reason —they are sportsmen. And for those who might like to go out and shoot in Kenya I give the latest list (there may be some periodic changes) of the game they might both kill and see. It is a long list, but it gives some idea of the wonderful wealth of animal life which is still left, and being rigorously protected, by that most game-loving colony of them all.

Kenya Full Licence (for one year): for a Visitor, £75; Serving Officer of H.M. Forces, £20; Kenya Resident, £7 10*s.* 0*d.* (A fourteen-day Visitor's Licence is £15.)

I. Full Licence

1.	Lion	1
2.	Leopard	1
3.	Cheetah	1
4.	Hippopotamus, but only in Lake Victoria and within five miles thereof	1
5.	Buffalo	3
6.	Common zebra	4
7.	Grevy's zebra	1
8.	Eland	1
9.	Greater kudu, male only and only in Turkana and N.F.D.	1
10.	Lesser kudu	4
11.	Bongo	1
12.	Sable	1
13.	Roan	1
14.	Wildebeest	3
15.	Waterbuck, defassa	1

16. Waterbuck, ellipsiprymnus 1
17. Oryx, beisa 3
18. Oryx, callotis 1
19. Topi 3
20. Hartebeest, Coke's, excluding the nakuru and Neumann's hartebeest 3
21. Hartebeest, Jackson's, excluding the Kenya hartebeest . 1
22. Hunter's antelope 1
23. Sitatunga 1
24. Impala 3
25. Bushbuck 6
26. Reedbuck, bohor 4
27. Reedbuck, Chanler's 1
28. Grant's gazelle 4
29. Peter's gazelle 2
30. Thomson's gazelle 9
31. Gerenuk 3
32. Klipspringer 1
33. Steinbuck 3
34. Oribi, Haggard's 1
35. Oribi, Kenya 1
36. Oribi, other than Haggard's and Kenya, altogether . . 6
37. Duiker, all species altogether 6
38. Dikdik, all species altogether 6
39. Pigmy antelope 3
40. Blue monkey 1

II. Fourteen Days' Licence

From the above list delete Items 1 to 25 inclusive and substitute the following items:

1. Buffalo 1
2. Common zebra 1
3. Lesser kudu 1
4. Wildebeest 1
5. Oryx, beisa 1
6. Topi 1
7. Hartebeest, Coke's, excluding the nakuru and Neumann's hartebeest 1
8. Impala 1
9. Bushbuck 2
10. Reedbuck, bohor 1
11. Grant's gazelle 1
12. Thomson's gazelle 3

13. Gerenuk 1
14. Steinbuck 1
15. Oribi, other than Haggard's and Kenya, altogether . . 2
16. Duiker, all species altogether 2
17. Dikdik, all species together 2
18. Pigmy antelope 1

Kenya's sympathetic attitude towards game preservation is almost entirely due to the personality of its chief Game Warden, Captain Archie Ritchie, but he is on the point of retiring now, and what the new man will be like is causing a great deal of worry to those who will be responsible for his appointment and to all game lovers in East Africa; for Kenya has set a world model for good game control. A man with the most dazzling assortment of university degrees in zoology, ornithology, etc. (such as one brilliant naturalist who was recently tried out for the post) would be a tragic failure unless his character was big enough, as well as his knowledge of men, to be able to take on white hunters, settlers, all the visiting millionaires and V.I.P.'s who wish to kill Kenya animals, and be able to stand up to the Government as well, and that on many an occasion. For twenty-five years Captain Ritchie (the finest Game Warden that Africa has ever known) has fought a running fight against all these elements in his protection of Kenya's wild life (he was seconded for eighteen months to Malaya to establish game control there), and no man can really replace Archie Ritchie. That is admitted.

In Kenya the threat to elephants carrying large tusks owing to the sharp rise in the price of ivory (and the largest elephants in the world are found along the Tana River) was met by doubling the price of Elephant Licences. In *addition* to the £75 for the cost of a Full Licence, it now costs £50 for the first elephant, £100 for the second, and not more than two Elephant Licences (two animals) are allowed to the holder of one Full Licence in any one year. In this way the Kenya Game Department has put a stop to the practice whereby a hunter took out a Full Licence for himself and special Elephant Licences for his father, mother, wife, sisters and cousins to act as dummy licence holders while he cleaned up all the ivory in the vicinity. This has caused a great indignation among the money-making fraternity. In fact, one or two letters which Captain Archie Ritchie has received, and which he read me, reached heights of abuse which brought tears to my eyes as we laughed at them. No author could have invented the double-barrelled names which rage rose to coin for Kenya's Game Warden. I remember one phrase—from an Australian, I think, which I thought particularly cutting; its author informed the "syphilitic son of a baboon, etc." that if he thought he had any chance of bringing *him* to book he had "as much hope as trying to stick a pound of butter with a red-hot needle up a wildcat's arse!" (I've forgotten whether that one was written to Ritchie or whether the Aussie was just showing what he thought of some "down under" official.) One old ruffian of a white hunter, a notorious character, sent word in to Ritchie that he was going to come in there, to the Game Department, and shoot him. In his dark and gory past this man was supposed already to have knocked off one man, and he was slightly mental—he had only a short time back "accidentally" put a bullet through a rival white hunter's windscreen while that gentleman was seated at the wheel of his *safari*-car—so Captain Ritchie was ready for him. . . . I won't say whether or not there was a revolver in Ritchie's half-open drawer, but I do know that there was a bottle of gin in the plaited grass market-bag beside his desk. And only the little black dachshund which always sits behind Archie Ritchie's back in that swivel-chair knows the conversation which sent that fire-eating white hunter off, still muttering threats of bloody murder, but with Captain Ritchie, ex-French Foreign Legion, Grenadier Guards, still left unshot. Ritchie has pacified many an irate settler, too, with that famous bottle of gin. "Come on, let's have a drink on it. . . . And then we can discuss this little affair in peace. . . ."

The sharp and mysterious rise in the price of ivory during the war years was caused entirely by the fact that the Indians of the East Coast of Africa thought that Britain was going to lose the war. They thought that the British pound and the East African shilling would be worthless; they wanted to get their savings into something that would have permanent value. They were, and still are, the master-brains who organised all the poaching and killing by poisoned arrow along the Tana River and in badly controlled Tanganyika, and who, by the most ingenious methods, still smuggle this ivory on board ship and send it to India—together with rhino horn which, they firmly believe, when ground into a powder, make a most potent aphrodisiac. (I wonder if it does?) The prices of ivory have been as follows:

	Per lb.
1940	9 shillings
1941	8 "
1942	9 "
1943	13 "
1944	14 "
1945	13 "
1946	17 "
1947	14 "

with a drop at the latest sale I have any record of at Mombasa, in 1948, to twelve shillings. First, they thought that England would lose the war; later, when the war was won, they were undoubtedly scared of a capital levy or confiscation of loose cash.

Big game shooting was stopped, as such, during the war years; and in 1946, when the shooting started again, it was thought that the average weight of a tusk in the Tana area would be around 100 lb., or well over, if a hunter took his time. But this was not so, and by the end of 1947 shooters were well satisfied with an 80-lb. tusk or even 70-lb. There are still huge elephants left along the Tana, but they are in the "byways and don't frequent the highways," as the Game Department puts it. "If you want a really big elephant now, you must hunt for him—unless the Lord is very much on your side!"

The majority of elephants illegally killed in Kenya are shot with poisoned arrows by the local bush tribes, the Mboni, Msanye, Wakamba, etc.; and, in the Northern Frontier District, by the Boran and, of course, the poaching Abyssinians. But the elephants illegally killed (in Kenya) do not anywhere near compensate for the natural increase of the elephants, who appear to be the last animal, odd as it may seem, threatened with extinction in Africa. No Europeans are in the ivory-poaching racket; the Indians organise it and collect it in interior regions and up in the N.F.D. It is collected in the Coastal region, from the woolly poachers, by Arabs; and by far the majority of the illegal ivory that is got out of Kenya is picked up by Arab dhows, and goes to India either direct or via Arabia. India takes the majority of ivory, legal or illegal, that leaves Africa, and pays higher prices than London. Some ivory goes as far east as Hong Kong. The exports of illegal ivory that do not go by Arab dhow are smuggled out in bales of hides or crates or sacks of other stuff marked "merchandise" in European steamships. And some good ivory is undoubtedly substituted for inferior stuff, *after* the latter ivory has paid the lower tax. The stories of Jack Bonham, Game Warden of the Coast, and his battle of wits against the ivory poachers enlivened the hot nights as we lay on the coral strand under the casuarina trees of his camp near Malindi, as I will relate in the final chapters of this book, when I was "goggling" with him and Archie Ritchie in the emerald and sapphire pools of Barracuda Reef.

The poison used by the Kenya natives (and those on the Tana and Sabaki Rivers are supposed to be the best poisoners in Africa) is a blackish substance that is applied in a viscous condition for some 3 inches below the head of the arrow. It looks very much like burnt, sugar-coated almonds. Until the arrow is required for use, the poison is protected from the air by a very thin strip of animal skin wound around it. It deteriorates in potency very quickly, and stale poison will certainly not kill an elephant, although it might make him pretty sick. Jack Bonham, handing me "stale" poisoned arrows down on the Coast, handled them carelessly. (I didn't!)

The common and largest ingredient of the poison used by Kenya natives is made from a concoction of the branches of a tree called *Akocanthera friesiorun.* This tree looks very like a wild olive, and, oddly enough, the leaves of the tree hold practically none of the poisonous element that is obtained by boiling down the wood itself in water. The poison is a glucoside and is known as *ouabin.* The poison from *Akocanthera* is apparently liable to become brittle and dry, and there is accordingly a certain amount of euphorbia latex (talk about dumb natives!) mixed with it to keep it tacky. A certain amount of another substance, a concoction of a shrub called *Sapium madagascarensis,* tends to make the poison more quick-acting and virulent. (Jack Bonham told me that when he asked a native of the Tana how the poison worked, the man cut his own arm so that the blood ran out; then touched a freshly-poisoned arrow to the foot of the blood-trickle. "And it *frothed*—bubbled! Then the blighter wiped his arm, and said: 'Like that.' ") *Sapium madagascarensis* is known to act as an intense irritant, tending to draw blood to a wound, and apparently its effect is to get the *Akocanthera* more quickly into the bloodstream. People making arrow poison in places where the *Akocanthera* is not obtainable substitute for it the *Adenium*, the "desert rose," that fat-rooted plant with its pink-and-white flowers which grows where nothing else can, in the blazing deserts of lava-rubble.

It is difficult to give any exact figures as to the length of time the poison takes to act. Ritchie (from whom I got all the above facts) told me that he had seen the remains of a lion which had died not more than 15 yards from the point where it had been shot with an arrow. He had evidence of a buffalo having fallen dead, or at least died, within 30 yards of where a heavy falling arrow from an arrow-trap had struck it. Jack Bonham said to me that he had come on two native poachers just as they put a poisoned arrow into an elephant; he saw it run—and drop dead within half a mile. Apparently, with quick death, the poison makes the blood just boil in the heart. On the other hand, there are instances where elephants have gone for an hour, or even a day, before succumbing to poison. An enormous amount depends upon whether or not the poison is really fresh, and also as to whether the arrow penetrates at a point where the poison is quickly absorbed into the bloodstream.

Over in South-West Africa, when I was taking notes on the poisoned arrows of the Bushmen, a Bushman who was a Camel Police Scout at Fort Namutoni told me that a wildebeest would usually drop dead within a maximum of two hours after being hit, but that the beautiful little springbok always took much longer to die, sometimes a whole day. From that he shrewdly deduced: "There must be something in the poison that the springbok eats." No European yet knows the full ingredients of the Bushman's poison; and only one or two men in each tribe, its witch doctors, know the secret. They pass it on to the younger witch doctor after they initiate him—that weird "Doctor Dance" which I was lucky enough to witness (few Europeans have ever seen it, if I may say so without boasting), in which I saw, with my own eyes, a young Bushman *danced* completely into a state of hypnosis. It took them hours to bring him back. He was cold as ice when I felt him as he lay unconscious on the sands.

Ritchie writes me: "It may interest you, with regard to the poison used on arrows, if I tell you a little story. I asked one of the Bushmen (a Msanye) who had used the poison all his life what was the purpose of a certain charm that he wore around his neck, and what it consisted of. He told me that it was a piece of a certain wood, and that it was an antidote to the poison used on arrows. I asked him if it was an effective antidote, and he said it was absolutely and invariably effective. Having heard that there was no known antidote for the poison, I was both surprised and interested, and asked for further details. Did he know of anybody who had received a wound with the poison, and who had been saved by this charm? He said that in fact he did not, the reason being that the application of the charm itself was insufficient, and that the repetition of certain invocations or formulae were also necessary, and that no one within his knowledge had lived long enough for a sufficient repetition of the invocations to render the charm effective!"

One of Jack Bonham's boys was shot by a poisoned arrow meant for Jack Bonham, whom Jack saw die within a few minutes. I met a young native who had been in the party of ivory poachers who shot that arrow at Bonham. Bonham caught him and kept him prisoner for a time, then released him to go back to his tribe. A year later he turned up on Casuarina Point and asked Bonham to take him back again. This handsome, smiling youth is now Jack's house-boy.

The Game Department in Kenya is vastly different from that in any other British territory. Its personnel could not be duplicated!

In Tanganyika, the high price of ivory has caused an increase of 1,500 per cent in the number of Elephant Licences over prewar years. The Game Warden requested, with no success, that the price of licences should be raised, as had been done in Kenya. But when this plea was placed before the Finance Committee—"and a number of important folk who knew little about Game Preservation," as Captain Keith Caldwell, late Game Warden of Uganda and formerly Assistant Game Warden of

Kenya, says in his report—the reply was: "Revenue would suffer. . . . The price of Elephant Licences should be lowered, not raised."

That report which Keith Caldwell made in 1947 for the Society for the Preservation of Fauna in the Empire is well worth the reading. Of some most recent Tanganyikan developments, he said this:

> How much game control will be needed to assist the Groundnut Scheme is uncertain, but I am inclined to think that game will fall back before the intensive cultivation and clearing which is taking place. In any event, I hope that the Game Department will take over such control and it will be carried out systematically on expert lines and not left to the whims of the Groundnut folk.

Of whom he says:

> I met one of these in the train on my way to Shinyanga. He said he had been out on survey near Mwapwa and saw a lot of animals, "Wot looked like donkeys with straight 'orns" [oryx?]. But "we mowed 'em down from the jeep; 'ave to get rid of them." I doubt if he actually did much "mowing," but I hope that control will not be attempted by the unco-ordinated efforts of untrained individuals.

Of course, there is always the *other* side to all these questions. There is the side of the pastoral Masai who say that the tsetse-fly is pushing further north each year and is carried by the wild animals, chiefly wildebeest and zebra, who invade their grazing grounds—which is true. There is the same complaint from the European cattle-raiser. The elephants are increasing instead of decreasing in Kenya; a certain amount of control shooting will have to be carried out along such places as the Tana River, not only to protect the native cultivation there, but to cut down this surplus elephant increase. The 1,000 rhinos shot in one year in clearing the Makueni district of the Wakamba Reserve for native settlement revealed an astonishingly greater number of rhinos than even the Game Department experts imagined could be there; and a 400,000-acre bush-covered area in that vicinity still promises good sanctuary for that dangerous animal. The Game Department, even in Kenya, is always in the invidious position of having to make the decision whether or not it is right, from a moral as well as a settlers' point of view, to clear an area of game. It is a question of judgment which can only be right if it is based upon years of experience. But the Kenya attitude is on the side of the game, whereas Tanganyika's is most definitely not, although that is probably more official fat-headedness than hard-heartedness.

The tsetse-fly controversy is too complex and scientific for me to get into it. But some things stand out. Two-thirds of Kenya, Uganda, and Tanganyika are under the fly and are therefore unsuitable to cattle and domestic animals. It is spreading, for instance, northwards in Kenya at the present time into the Masai Reserve—yet this is accompanied by a *decrease* in the game animals in all those territories. It has yet to be proved that killing all the animals in an area will completely clear it of all fly; for some species will remain. They might even be carried by rodents. And while some authorities, such as Professor P. A. Buxton, F.R.S., assert that man and tsetse-flies are ecologically incompatible, and, if I don't mistake him, that the wild animals should all be killed in order to make room for human habitation, there is another school which contends that this is not the *only* way to make land habitable for man and cattle, and that more research might find a way of "proofing" cattle against the fly. (This *seems* to have been found by the new drug, antrycide. But a lot of people are reserving opinion upon how the millions of cattle in Africa can be periodically inoculated with it.) There are big farms within sixty miles of Nairobi today on which there are both game and cattle, and the owners of those farms deliberately protect their wild game. Furthermore, the Masai seem to have found a way to immunise their cattle (at least partially): it is an age-old custom of theirs, when they learn that a plague of rinderpest is in their vicinity, to drive their young cattle into that area—deliberately to infect them—for they have learned long ago that the younger animals usually survive the sickness and have immunisation from then on. With pleural pneumonia, the Masai will take the saliva from an infected animal and inoculate another beast by cutting it with a knife. They have always recognised two forms of rinderpest—mild and acute—and they take the blood and urine from animals reacting to the *mild* form of the disease and rub on the noses and in the mouths of healthy animals. They have learned, in their own fashion, that if the animal "reacted" it would be safe from, immune to, the acute disease. (It is also asserted that the Masai had a form of vaccination against smallpox. But this seems doubtful; I never met anyone who could confirm it; whereas the above measures against pleural pneumonia and rinderpest are well-known Masai customs.) Similarly, the Samburu of Kenya (cousins of the Masai) regularly drive their cattle, including the calves, into tsetse-fly infested areas, and such cattle are supposed to develop *and maintain* a resistance to *trypanosomiasis.* The Samburu "stand their ground," as it were, proofing their cattle and thus consolidating themselves on their grazing territory, instead of retreating before the fly. They can't retreat, it may be said, as there is no other land left to which they could go.

An interesting thing to note here is that many game animals, of species which abound in tsetse country, succumb to *trypanosomiasis* when they are reared in captivity and artificially infected. They have not been "hardened," as it were.

Kenya killed 1,000 rhinos to clear the bush at Makueni for the native settlement scheme, but that was because the natives were afraid to go into an area infested by such dangerous animals. Kenya Game Department has killed between eighty or ninety elephants a year along the Tana River, but that is to keep them back from the river, where they destroy native cultivation. The elephants learn, and do stay back until thirst drives them to the river; antelopes and gazelle, wildebeest and zebra, however, never learn, and invade the green Kenya plains with every season of the Long Rains. Kenya, so far as I know, has not yet gone in for any large slaughter of animals on a strictly anti-tsetse-fly campaign. What the new Game Warden will decide to do—or agree to do, which may be a better way of putting it—is impossible to foresee.

Every year on the edge of the Long Rains there is an immense migration of game into Kenya from the plains of the Serengeti down in Tanganyika. Hundreds and hundreds of thousands of them: so many head that they cannot be counted. Such an immense passage of wild animals that it has been necessary to establish cordons of game-rangers to "shoot them back" at times, otherwise they would overflow up into the Masai country and eat up all the grazing. The game leave the Serengeti partly because that plain is of volcanic ash and becomes a quagmire when the rains come on—motor cars caught there just remain until the next dry season—but the main reason why the game migrate up on the fresh green plains of southern Kenya is to have their young. The plains were just dotted with young things when we were there. The little Thomson's and Grant's gazelles, dropped on the open plains, which have as short grass as a golf-course, can get up and run as soon as they are dry. A wildebeest calf can run beside its mother the afternoon of the same dawn it is born. Lions and leopards, belonging to fiercer families, are not so mobile: they have nothing to fear. It was a wonderful sight to watch the different families on those plains, and then, in the longer grass, to see the buck lying down and basking in the sun. Some of them jumped up and raced us just for the fun of the thing. I clocked one kongoni that raced beside us, about 100 yards off, for over fifteen minutes. He seemed to be doing 20 feet between bounds. And at times the car was doing 30 m.p.h. Finally, he gave it up, stopped, shook his head, and then lay down in the sun again.

Foxes, silver jackals, little families of mongoose shooting across the green plain; the blue mountains lying before us in the sun-haze; the growing green of the grateful plains—the whole scene filled me with the delight of being back in the very springtime of life.

CHAPTER XIII

The Proud Masai

AS AN example to those who make it a practice, almost a profession, to criticise the Colonial administration of the British Empire, I would like to hold up the treatment of the Masai in Kenya and Tanganyika. The British got off to a bad start. It is all very well to say that you have made a treaty with a native tribe, but you know that you have exploited their ignorance and taken advantage of their faith in you: they have taken you at your word. The Americans have had plenty of experience in this sort of thing in our dealings with the Indians; so they will understand how it was that the British broke a solemn treaty with the Masai, the finest warrior tribe in all Africa. Kenya settlers get overblamed for such land-grabbing merely because it was so recent; it happened less than fifty years ago. We have been able to forget ours.

In 1904, under the pressure of the white settlers who wanted the great grazing plains, the Masai were evicted from their fine pasturage around Lakes Naivasha, Elmenteita and Nakuru, along the Uganda Railway, and forced to settle up on the Laikipia Plateau. I have described this former paradise of theirs in the Great Rift; and how the first settlers, knowing less than nothing about local conditions and possibilities, said to each other: "If you can get hold of land where the Masai have been grazing, you can't go wrong. The Masai know more about cattle than any people in Africa." Commissioner Sir Donald Stewart, who knew that the settlers would then demand the land up on the Laikipia Plateau—as soon as the Masai had grazed and improved those lands—made a treaty with the Masai which guaranteed their right to remain on Laikipia in perpetuity. "*The settlement now arrived at shall be enduring as long as the Masai as a race shall exist,*" ran its promise. . . . "European and other settlers shall not be allowed to take up land in this Settlement." It was a promise that was kept for exactly six years and two hundred and sixty-one days.

Sir Donald Stewart died. In 1911, again under the political pressure of the land-grabbing settlers, the Masai were evicted from the Laikipia Plateau. And the settlers rushed there. The Masai chiefs, or *laibons,* applied for an injunction in the High Court; it was granted, temporarily restraining the settlers from breaking the 1904 Treaty; the Masai took their case to London, and there (it seems hardly believable) a decision was given, in December 1913, that the Courts could take no cognisance of the case, because the Masai were "a foreign nation and not British subjects." And although the Masai were under the protection of the British Crown, the justification given was that it was outside the jurisdiction of the British Courts to enforce engagements (the 1904 Treaty in particular) between sovereign parties founded on treaties. I know nothing about the law, and must assume that the decision was legally correct; but that does not make it any the less unpleasant. The only bright spot was that when the greedy Europeans did get on the Laikipia Plateau, they found it was not good grazing land at all.

Nevertheless, since that day no large wrong has ever been done the Masai by the British. They had a rough time with the Germans, however. At one time a clan of Masai had closed the passage and was living hidden in the ten-mile-wide crater of Ngorongoro, an extinct volcano, until a dog led a German big game hunter to them, whereupon the usual Hun heavy-handedness was applied to them. But the Masai are past masters at the art of evasion, and when the 1914-18 War ended and German East Africa became Tanganyika, the Masai military organisation was still intact. Today, some 45,000 Masai live in Kenya on a reserve of 15,000 square miles—larger than the entire European White Highlands; and some 30,000 live in Tanganyika, on an adjacent reserve on which the British confirmed them after the First World War. To an amazing and admirable extent, the British in Kenya and in Tanganyika have been leaving the Masai alone, to live just as they please. That is all the Masai ask. They claim that they are both politically and economically self-sufficient; they pay their poll tax without any trouble, being the richest in cattle of any tribe in Africa. The average for a Masai and his two or three wives is 300 head; many Masai own over 1,000 head of cattle, and it would be a poor Masai indeed who owned less than fifty (the mathematics of it are colorful: 49,000 Masai living on 15,000 square miles own 700,000 head of cattle). In addition, they own several million sheep and goats.

But the Masai do not raise cattle either to sell or to eat. They are not meat-eaters. They live with their herds, drinking the milk and the warm blood, which they extract from the living animal by shooting a plugged arrow into its neck (leaving the animal none the worse for it); and to them their cattle are a sign of wealth, used as currency to pay fines, poll tax, the bride-price, etc., with an increase in the investment of so many new animals born every year that is more dependable and larger than any interest paid by the bank. Therefore a cow, in no matter what condition, is still a cow, be it ever so crumpled, as a worn one-pound note is still a pound. Also, they love cattle; say, a particularly beautifully colored animal, which has been hand-fed from birth.

In Tanganyika, the Masai are still allowed to keep their 7-foot steel spears and their painted, heraldic shields of buffalo hide; in Kenya they are allowed to keep the spear but not the shield. These razor-sharp spears are nearly all steel, having a haft of only about 8 inches of wood. The shields, painted red, white and blue with a Masai's own particular armorial bearings, his coat of arms, have as historic a blazonry as those sanctioned by the British College of Heralds. They have a pathological effect upon the Masai, the sight of them invoking memories of the days of the blood-dripping spear with which a Masai established his right to manhood. The shields will often throw Masai warriors at a ceremonial into paroxysms, where they will froth at the mouth as in an epileptic fit, at which times they are held down and kept away from their spears by their comrades. But on the whole, if not interfered with within their reserves, the Masai are a very tractable people; they are not litigious, like the Bantu Africans, having had very poor luck with the law, and all they ask is to be allowed to live in peace.

Their trouble is that they have become almost a museum

piece in the races of emerging Africa. What to do with them? One school of thought believes that if they are left alone, to live as they want, they will eventually "breed themselves out," and, suffering from widespread venereal disease as they are, that they will soon pass into history. The other school, which is the prevailing one at the moment, asserts that the Masai must be "educated" and made to fit in with modern times. The Masai don't want to be educated; they loathe civilisation, as we understand it; and, in the opinion of most thoughtful white men who have had to deal with them, we will ruin them if we try to force our ways upon them.

Most District Commissioners who have been placed over the Masai end up with a feeling of puzzled respect for them, and are, I believe, of the school which would leave the Masai to live out their own destiny, even to dying out. Some of the more esthetic among the Commissioners will even tell you that they are jealous of the Masai, that they envy the tang which those red warriors get out of life. One District Commissioner whom I knew (he is dead now) became such a passionate admirer of the Masai that he went to live with them: hunted lions with a spear, lost his job in the Colonial Service, and as a result became a distinguished lecturer on anthropology at Cambridge. Many a time he has sat on the floor of my drawing-room in Walton Street, London, declaring it would be murder to force our civilisation upon such a fine race of human animals as the Masai. He said this before he left the Colonial Service, said it too frequently and too angrily. R.I.P., Jack Driberg.

The Masai are beautiful men. Quite possibly, with the exception of their cousins, the gazelle-like Rendille of the Northern Frontier District, the most beautifully-built men anywhere in the world today. To see a Masai with just his red skin blanket tied over one shoulder, 7-foot steel spear in hand, running across his plains as effortlessly and as free as the wind which sweeps them is a sight that fills you with admiration. Most of them are 6-footers, or over. Nilo-Hamites, a mixture of Bantu and Semite, coming down into Africa from the head waters of the Nile, have features which could have served as models for the sculptors of ancient Egypt. The men are so delicately built that they look much more effeminate than the women. They are aristocrats, and quite conscious of it, from their delicate ankles to their finely cut nostrils. They often have eyes slightly oblique, like the Mongolian, but their noses are nearly always a pure Caucasian type. Some of them can only be described as "fiercely" handsome. They have a sense of "effortless superiority," even over the white man, which comes from their previous dominant position in East Africa, when they used to roam over, raid and terrorise an area larger than all Europe west of the Rhine.

They are copper-bronze in color, but they paint themselves red with ochre, plait their hair in red blobs with mutton fat, and during their warrior years they wear a pig-tail built around a leather strap. They have 3- or 4-inch holes in their ear-lobes, enlarged by a succession of wooden plugs, from which dangle heavy copper ornaments, bracelets of coral beads, with usually a stylish safety-pin clasped through one of the small holes in the ear's upper rim. They knock out their lower incisor teeth so, say some, that they can be fed if seized with lock-jaw; others, that they can spit better. An old-fashioned Masai would spit on you to show that he likes you, and would have been delighted if you spat on him. Even today some of the Masai Elders will invariably spit on their hand before, with a superb dignity, they put it out to you.

They are the greatest fighters that Africa has ever known; better than even Chaka's Zulus, some of the old settlers in Africa think. They kill the lion with their spears, crowding around him in a circle; one man, crouching down, always taking the charge on his shield—and the lion on his spear; yet they absolutely refused to go either as *askaris* or as porters to either the 1914-18 War or this last one. In the First World War an attempt to conscript them failed dismally. They have so far managed to refuse education. On the other hand, a Masai doctor at Fort Hall is said to be one of the best doctors in Kenya for native complaints. They are exceptionally intelligent—when they want to be. Their brain power is supposed to be superior to the Bantu African's. A Masai artist, teacher at the tiny school for Masai at Narok, can show you paintings which would collect an interested crowd of fellow artists at any London gallery. His sense of form is the "post-blue" period of Picasso. They are without a doubt the most puzzling, decorative, economically useless natives left in Africa. They just grin when a Governor comes down to make a patriotic speech, saying that they ought to do their bit in the development of Africa, if only for their own good; or that, as soldiers, they should fight to defend "civilisation" against "barbarism." They *despise* the white man. That is the most charming thing about them.

The Engidongi Clan, to whom Eric Sweatman, the Officer-in-Charge of the Masai, and the rest of us were going, had been quarantined up on the Loita Plateau for several years. The reason is that this tribe of witch doctors, which supplies all the *laibons* for all the Masai, is believed to have supernatural powers, and that they use their powers to cause trouble. I am not being facetious when I say that they do have some "power" which seems a little beyond the natural. At any rate, when you see one of these Engidongi, wearing the black cloth that they bind round their heads (when on business), stroll into a Masai cattle-sale, you will notice that all the other Masai begin to look uneasy, and will even cover their faces or turn their heads away from him. And, what is very peculiar, nearly all the Engidongi look alike; they are *ugly* men, with aquiline noses, that all look as if the bridge had been broken, with a most repulsive way of baring their teeth at you. None of the men from the Engidongi tribe are allowed to leave the Loita Hills without a signed chit from the District Commissioner at Narok. Few of them get it.

The entire Masai life is based on a military organisation, and on age groups which regulate every act, even sexual, and even all thought and conversation that a Masai has from the day that he is circumcised to the day that he dies and his body is carried out on the plains, and left there for the hyenas and the vultures to eat. No Centurion of Julius Caesar had a more rigid code of military conduct. All his life, a Masai lives by rules. The power of the *laibons* over them, which seems almost supernatural in itself, is as yet not fully understood by Europeans, the District Commissioners, etc., who have administered and studied them. I know that this time Eric Sweatman and Roger Wilkinson, the D.C. at Narok, and I spent days discussing this, with no final conclusion as to what a *laibon* really *is*. Neither of these Masai-experts could agree on every point. A *laibon* is not a chief; he is something *more*. . . .

A brief schedule of a Masai boy's life gives the best picture of their civilisation. When a Masai baby is born, a sheep is slaughtered for all the women of the village, the *manyatta,* except for the mother; a bullock is killed and fat from the bullock is fed to the baby. The mother eats the meat. This seems to be about the only regular eating of meat indulged in by the Masai. This slaughter continues at intervals, to feed the baby with fat; the baby is not weaned from the mother's breast for eighteen months. At six years, the boy starts to herd calves near home; he comes home for the midday meal. At seven or eight he goes out to herd bigger calves, sheep and goats; he does not come home for the midday meal. At this age his two central lower incisors are removed. When eight, nine or ten years old, he gets a knife and is given a small spear, and may be entrusted with full-grown cattle by himself. Realise that this is alone, out on the great empty plains. At eleven or twelve he may kill a lion while herding—and is supposed to be capable of doing it. This is an honor that, I think, scarcely a Masai boy has ever earned. Yet they are told that they *ought* to be able to kill a lion at that age, and they go out on the plains with that responsibility on their shoulders. As an example of inculcating self-reliance, I would call attention to this. At fourteen the Masai boy begins his sexual life with the young girls of his own age or thereabouts—and continues that free-for-all cohabitation until, about the age of 32, he cuts off his warrior's pig-tail, takes the first of the two or three wives that he will soon acquire and settles down to become a staid family man.

But from puberty on, despite his sexual freedom of action, a young Masai enters into a set of rules that are just as inflexible as those of any monastic order. This is where a Masai differs from any other native in Africa. The rest of his life, from the day he is circumcised, is devoted to the absolute obedience of Authority. They break it, of course, as young men will; but the authority of the Elders of the Masai clans is not rotting away the way it is with the rest of the African natives, and they still hold their *laibons* in great respect and awe. Respect for authority is the Masai's greatest virtue, after his courage. This has baffled the British, because they thought it would be possible to exercise "Indirect Rule" through the *laibons;* but it has invariably failed.

The Masai still believe in their *laibons'* supernatural powers and stand in great fear of them; but when the British tried to utilise that power of the *laibons* over the clans, it slipped through their fingers like quicksilver. And such hopes have now been abandoned.

Masai boys get circumcised around sixteen or seventeen, but some even wait until they are twenty. I don't know at what ages the girls are circumcised; but the two I saw down in Tanganyika, just after the operation, looked about fourteen or fifteen years old. From circumcision the Masai's status is settled as to his warrior group: he becomes either a left-hand *moran* or a right-hand. The left have a brown wood haft in their long 7-foot spears, the right a black one. The age groups are also established by circumcision; and it usually takes four years to circumcise one-half of a generation, four for the other half; and two generations are always linked together in forming the warrior groups, like a descending set of stairs: A–B; C–D. A are circumcised and for seven years are junior *morans;* about the fifth year of that period B gets circumcised–and A fights the senior *moran* of the generation born before it which, when it sees that it can no longer stand up to them, gives over and lets them become senior warriors. The whole set of steps, B, C, D, therefore moves up one step. A are warriors of the right hand; B of the left. This is complicated, I know; but the interesting part of it is the two classes of warriors–a left-hand *moran* can never be a *moran* for as long a time as a right-hand *moran;* and the senior *morans* will never give in to the oncoming junior warriors until the younger warriors show that they can beat them in a straight fight. Masai are even now sometimes killed in these fights. When the senior *morans* hand over, cut their pigtails off, and retire to become elders, they know that they have left enough warriors of *proved* fighting ability to protect the tribe. This "standing army" of the Masai exists to this day. And the elders become the political advisers of the warrior groups.

Formerly, a Masai was a junior warrior for five to seven years, then a senior warrior for ten years. That is, for a right-hand *moran.* Lefts were several years shorter. During all that time (seventeen years for a right-hand) it was the custom–and still is–for them to sleep with the young unmarried girls of the tribe in special barracks, the fighting men's *manyattas*. The only stipulation was that the girl was never got in the family way.

A *laibon* is *not* a chief. He is a "diviner," a consultant, a go-between with the supernatural. He can give charms to assure fertility or faithfulness; not that the Masai care much about the latter! If a Masai's wife bears him a child by another man, *that* man automatically becomes his best friend. (In Europe it is usually the best friend who does it, and whose status changes after that.) It is believed by the Masai that no *laibon* ever dies unless he has been killed by the witchcraft of another *laibon*. *Laibons* themselves confidently die in this belief. It is noticeable that most of the noted *laibons* have died young—nearly always of heart failure. There is definitely some mental connection with their sudden collapse and their belief that they have been bewitched by a stronger *laibon;* and that therefore there is no hope for them. Lenana, however, the greatest *laibon* of them all, died at a good age, only in 1911. He was one of the two leading *laibons* of East Africa long before the British began to colonise.

To get up on the plateau of the Loita Hills requires a hard day's driving—not in miles so much as in rough going. It is often easier to go across open country in Africa than where roads have been used. You sink so deep in the wheel ruts that your engine sump frequently grounds on the ridge between them. So, for the first part of that day, we drove cross-country over open plains that, with their sparse covering of low shrubs, looked like the mesquite deserts of New Mexico and Arizona. It was great bird country, full of francolin, greater and lesser bustard, thickets along which the sand-grouse concentrated and along which the guinea-fowl scurried like grey mechanical mice. On the skyline, thirty or even fifty miles away, a line of blue mountains undulated in the heat waves. It was a country which affected one's mind, giving immense scope to the imagination, like the boundless steppes of the Russian Ukraine in the spring, and, to pay them full tribute, the Masai appreciate it. We had to take to the road when we came near the dry river beds, as this was the only way we could get down the brush-choked banks. The Maggi Moto (Hot Water) River was still running, about the temperature of a comfortable warm bath. And here, as the D.C. tried to talk to some Masai who live near that fording place (they were about as responsive as the traditional Englishman in the train), several of our boys went behind some bushes, stripped, and lay down in the steaming and stinking sulphur water. It is supposed to possess curative powers—for V.D.

The Masai are getting worried about syphilis. So many of their young girls have been rendered barren by it that the Masai are now marrying Kikuyu girls. The V.D. infections are spread, of course, by this uninhibited custom of the warriors sleeping with all the young girls in their *manyattas*. There is no such thing as a virgin among the Masai, among the girls older than fourteen or fifteen. By such mass-marrying of Kikuyus, the Masai tribe is being bastardised. It is strange that Masai should marry Kikuyus, their historic victims and enemies, and *vice versa*, for throughout the centuries they have fought the forest-living Kikuyu with his bow and arrows and the plains-living Masai with his long spear. The Kikuyus have always managed to hold the forest-line, where the bow is so deadly. There had recently been a fight of just such a character on the Masai-Kikuyu border, which resulted in two deaths on each side, the Masai raiding warriors getting away, however, with quite a large number of Kikuyu cattle.

At the small but good hospital for the Masai at Narok, the Medical Officer there told me that out of the 8,000 Masai which he is supposed to be concerned with, some 800 had syphilis. "I give each case twelve shots of 606." Then he made a strange observation: "There is hardly any G.P.I. among the Masai. Syphilis does not seem to affect their brains. Whereas there are many 'mentals' among the Kikuyus, almost certainly due to syphilis." Another queer thing about the Masai: the only vitamin stuff that a Masai consumes is milk, yet they never get scurvy. But then, of course, they drink the blood of their living cattle. A rich mixture!

He had a Masai in his morgue who had just been killed in a bow-and-arrow fight. A Masai shepherd had come on this Masai, making off down a stream bed with twenty of his sheep. He called on the robber to bring back the sheep. The other man laughed at him. The owner of the sheep then put an arrow to his bow-string and winged the robber in the behind. The robber then drew his sword, a vicious-looking weapon which the Masai carry in a scarlet sheath, and made for the other. As he turned to come up the bank the bowman put an arrow right through him, sideways, entering through his ribs at the right side and protruding from the left.

"I never realised before," said the M.O. at Narok, "what a neat little hole an arrow makes!"

The Masai who had killed this man said: "He ran down the river bed. I followed him. He fell. I saw he was dead, so I took my arrows out. I went back later with another man to see if the hyenas had eaten him. They hadn't, so I have come to report myself."

The hospital had been keeping the body three days in its morgue until it could be shown as evidence. "But it got too whiffy," said the M.O. when we went over to the morgue to inspect it. "I'm sorry, but it seems they had to bury it this morning. I'd have liked to have shown you that hole. I don't know what they'll do to the man who killed him. Not much, I hope."

Masai will very often die, just wither away, if kept too long in jail. The severest sentence is to impose a heavy fine on a culprit, which, as he can't, his whole clan will be made to pay. It is usually imposed in cattle. This was what was taking place when our party first came to Narok. I had been told that, aside from the cattle being sold to pay the fine, it would be the biggest *voluntary* sale of cattle ever held within the Masai Reserve. The latter did not materialise. Not more than 100 cattle were brought in to be sold during the two days I was at Narok. They were auctioned off in a cattle-pen, all to Somali stock-traders. It was a picturesque little demonstration of compliance, for that is really all it was. The corral was a five-rail pen, on top of which sat Masai, several Englishmen, the men and women of our party, with two local Masai chiefs (not *laibons*) who had been appointed by the Administration, jovial old rascals, politicians, wearing their badge of office, which is the brass Colonial Office lion, worn on the front of a khaki solar topi. And the four Somali stock-buyers, in white turbans, they being Mohammedans, standing in an aloof knot. As each animal was knocked down and driven through what they call the "crush," i.e. the railed exit from the auction-pen, leading to a corral where the cattle were to be kept until the Somali buyers took them away, a native with a set of branding irons, all reddening in a wood fire, pushed that particular Somali buyer's brand into them with a hiss, a whiff of smoke, and the smell of burning hair and flesh. People who have ranched in Africa will never forget *that* smell! The cattle brought about £5 each, which was considered a very good price. But these Masai had been fined 9,000 shillings for their part in the raid against the Kikuyus (it took place on the night of August 31st-September 1st, 1947), and ninety of these £5-cattle had to be handed over to the Officer-in-Charge of the Masai, Eric Sweatman, or else a fine-tax. "We've left it to them," smiled the D.C., Roger Wilkinson. "They have worked it all out among themselves. Old 'Ole' here [the Purko chief] thinks they won't bring enough cattle in if we just commandeer them; so we are taking four shillings a beast off every animal sold. In that way, we don't stop the Masai from bringing their cattle in. They get the bulk out of every sale."

It was this way, in a forced sale of cattle, that Major Hugh Grant, Wilkinson's predecessor, had been killed in 1946. Accounts differ about this. Some say that he was an impetuous Scot, too inclined to be high-handed with the Masai; others that he had been vetting inferior cattle all day which the guileful Masai had tried to get past his inspection, and that when it did come to this question of "the white cow," that he had been rightly exasperated beyond endurance. Anyway, he refused *not* to commandeer a white cow that a young Masai warrior begged him not to take. This white cow, it turned out afterwards, was one that this particular warrior loved passionately; he had hand-fed it since it was a calf. He came back to Major Grant time and again, offering him an increasing number of cattle; *ten* of the best of his other cattle, finally, if he would *please* not take this particular white cow. Grant was obdurate; he had agreed to accept substitute cattle several times that day, but now he had lost patience. He is said to have told the Masai to leave him alone, and ordered the white cow to be sent into the auction-pen. The young warrior went off and sat down on the ground beside his long, slender steel spear . . . and Grant, turning his back, leaned over the rail of the entrance to the pen. (Some versions of this murder say it was over a black ox.)

Suddenly, before anyone could be aware of what they were watching, the young Masai *moran* walked up behind Grant, took his stance, and sent the 7-foot steel shaft completely through him. Grant died instantly. The spear was sticking in an opposite rail, trembling.

Two things went against that young Masai which prevented him making the excuse (not that he would have made it) that the murder was unpremeditated. The first was that he had *greased* his spear. Masai warriors grease their razor-sharp spears when they intend to use them on human beings. The second was that he belonged to this clan of the Engidongi–the witch doctors' clan. He was hanged in Nairobi.

As you near the Loita Plateau you begin to feel some of the mystery, the eerie aloofness of this fastness of the medicine-men. The Masai plains lie at about a 5,500-foot level; the Loita Plateau is 8,000 feet. It is a sort of tableland going up into the clouds, with, of course, higher mountain peaks that stay in the clouds permanently. H. G. Wells could have picked such a plateau for another story paralleling *The Country of the Blind*, or Conan Doyle for another *Lost World*. It had this feeling of inaccessible remoteness. And this was not diminished when we tried to get up it.

The road was a 1-in-4 gradient in many places, usually on the sharp turns, and was composed of a peculiar harsh sand made from crumbled red quartz-rock that slid away from the wheels, letting the heavy lorries sink down. Near the top you enter a deep cedar forest. And then–!

We came out into an alpine valley, whose immense rolling plains, shining in the setting sun, seemed as smooth as a golf-course, and were as vivid a green. This sophisticated landscape was at once shattered by the sight of some russet impala that came out from a grove to stare at us. The grove is also something which seems to belong to another world, for the bunched trees looked like English holly, with their dark green leaves, burnished now by the sun. This is one of the poison-trees I have spoken about. And then, on all the surrounding ridges of the nearest hills, we saw the great stands of deep cedar forests . . . and, like islands on these vividly green plains, the painted herds of the witch doctors' cattle. It was a strikingly beautiful scene. I am sure that if the white settlers had ever come on it years ago, when they were pre-empting Masai land at will, this would now be one of the most cherished parts of European Kenya.

The Engidongi clan is quarantined here. Lenana, as I have just said, was one of the two great *laibons* of Kenya when the British began to colonise. His Masai are known as the Sighirari Section, and do not live on this plateau. The other great *laibon* was Sendeu, and his descendants form the Engidongi clan. This clan now supplies all the *laibons*, the medicine-men, even to the Sighirari Section. There has always been some form of quarantine over the *bomas*, the actual homes of these Engidongi, but the formal quarantine of the persons of the Engidongi themselves dates from August 1946, when Hugh Grant was murdered. A Police Post was built on the Loita Plateau after that, and all the Engidongi are supposed to live within view of it. That is so that they may be kept under constant observation; all the Engidongi have to report weekly at the Police Post. This is so that they do not try to leave the plateau. Also, under the Witchcraft Ordinance, two *laibons* who had made trouble had been ordered back to the plateau, to be quarantined there. Sweatman, as Officer-in-Charge of the Masai, had made this *safari* to hold a *baraza* on the morrow, at which twenty-one of the worst "bad hats" of the Engidongi were to appear before him. Need I say that the three worst did not appear . . . and also need I say that the O.-in-C., Masai and the D.C. were not in the least angry or fussed about it: "Oh, they'll be picked up in time."

We had our three tents set up in an opening of the towering cedars, some distance back from the open plain. I thought it peculiar at first, but not when I went out on the plain! It was alive with flies that had been feeding on the Masai cattle. What looked like a paradise instantly became hell. There were thousands of guinea-fowl on the plain, trotting off at human approach in a long, irregular line like objects being washed ashore by a long line of coastal surf. We tried for some guinea-fowl, and I, in full view of all our party, fired into the "brown" of some thirty birds which rose with a whirr between me and some other guinea-fowl I was stalking—and missed the whole lot. That spoiled my first evening, a lovely, cold, star-lit night around our log fire.

Next morning, taking Roger Wilkinson's advice that no sporting nonsense was ever allowed when shooting the elusive guineafowl—"Pot him on the ground, because you're shooting for the pot!"—I put two No. 7 pellets into Wilkinson. He was the least concerned of any in our party about it. "This has upset you much more than it has me," he grinned as I stepped from the bushes and saw the blood trickling down his arm. An episode, I may say, that still makes me go cold all over.

In here it should be well to stress that the tribe's attitude toward a *laibon* is one thing; the *laibon's* attitude toward the tribe is quite another. Whether or not a *laibon* actually does believe he has supernatural powers—and the evidence is that he both does and *has*—he loses no opportunity to use the tribe's belief in his connection with the other world to increase his worldly possessions in this one. This is particularly true concerning the matter of wives: the *laibons* expect to be *supplied* with them. One *laibon*, Parrit, collected five young girls on a *safari* he made with the British when they were demarcating the boundary of Southern Masailand. A girl married to a *laibon* is supposed to be lost for ever to her tribe and family, all the ordinary relations cease to exist. Parrit was "murdered" by another *laibon*—he is supposed to have collapsed from a spell—in 1928. And, of course, as one of a *laibon's* chief duties is to advise who to raid, when and how—they are very expert at organising such cattle seizures—they become rich from the percentage of cattle which they are given, as their fee, after every successful raid.

There were two young Masai, handcuffed together, locked up in the Loita Police Post from just such a raid. They had raided in Tanganyika, losing three men of their own party, who had been killed by the Tanganyika Masai but, as they had killed five of those Masai, they were regarded rather admiringly by the other Engidongi as they were led out to face Eric Sweatman. He, Roger Wilkinson's wife and mine, sat on chairs which had been placed for them; Wilkinson and I sat on the ground. And in a semicircle, facing Eric Sweatman and the police *askaris*, lay, prone on the ground, as ugly a lot of Masai as I have ever looked at. These were the medicine-men.

Sweatman, a sophisticated, London club-man type, did not go in for what usually spoils such occasions, any "high hat" official posturing. He sat there smoking a pipe, letting the Masai voice their complaints, or alibis; turning to have a chat with Wilkinson after each case had been heard. Then he gave a decision on the spot or directed further investigation. There was an immense dignity preserved on both sides. A Masai who would stand up, his face all twisted with his emotions—anger or whatever they were—would soon become calm, begin to state his points clearly, and eventually sit down, having accepted the verdict. Not that this in any way means he was satisfied. But the whole clan heard him freely state his case, and also heard the Administrator's answer to it. This, of course, was a lesson to everyone present. Two Engidongi who pleaded earnestly for permission to leave the plateau were flatly refused it, and before all the others. The reasons why they were not given permission were not stated full out in this case.

One of these was a *laibon* who had imposed himself on the Masai who live along the railway south of Nairobi, on the way to Mombasa. They had been terrorised by him. They had come to the Government and asked them to remove him. "This man is *Shaitani* [Satan himself]," they said. "He is a very bad man. Don't let him stay here. You must understand that, in his presence, we cannot say these things, otherwise he will *do* things to us. So please take him away!"

There he stood, with his blanket wrapped around him, wearing a Balaclava helmet (which is very popular up on the cold plateau); and the reason why he was there could not be explained, for the simple reason that the O.-in-C. and the D.C. could not betray the other Masai who had come to them secretly. "Just tell him he is going to *stay* here," said Eric Sweatman, taking his pipe from his mouth. "The others all know what a bad hat he is." Another was a *laibon* who had been put in jail in another district of Masailand because he had been intimidating the Masai there; and they had come to the D.C., and said, "This is not good enough. He can still do us a lot of harm from that jail. Please take him to some jail that is miles and miles away from us!" So he had been locked up in Nairobi, then quarantined here among the Loita Hills. He, also, was merely told that he had to stay where he was. Most of them who were pleading to be allowed to leave the plateau, I was told, had the intention of immediately making a break for Tanganyika Territory. This worst one, Koyaki, who could *do things* to people even through a jail's walls, now has to live within 100 yards of the Police Post at Loita. His father, also a witch doctor, had "bequeathed" Koyaki to the Kapoteirei clan of Masai, who live along the Nairobi-Mombasa stretch of railway line. When he went there, they declared, he put a curse on their present *laibon* by breaking a gourd and shouting incantations during the lightning flash of a thunder-storm, and their own *laibon* immediately became unwell. Koyaki was supposed to be about forty-five years old, and was a most unpleasant-looking customer.

The trouble when dealing with these witchcraft cases is that, though you may not believe in the force yourself, you are dealing with people who most undeniably do live in fear of it, and your way of settling such affairs must be such that, to their primitive minds, you have found a way to defeat the witch doctor. This requires considerable histrionic ability and power of suggestion on your own part. The greatest difficulty, of course, is when you begin to feel a bit uncertain yourself. What if this man before you has got some power that is beyond that of ordinary men?

You can't put such things away from you. The Masai, watching the night through by his herds, stares up at his Moon God. We don't know what he is thinking or what powers he gets from it. We see him with his skin blanket wrapped around him, his spear stuck in the ground by his side, as free as the wind that sweeps his lion-colored plains. It is true that if he could be persuaded to de-stock his plains, sell half his cattle, that both he and the remaining animals would be far better off. It is true that the Kenya Government cannot be morally called upon to bore more water-holes for them when the young Masai men refuse to work themselves. But it will require a lot more reasoning than I have ever heard to convince me that it would be best for the Masai to force our ways upon them.

The Masai, more than any race in British Africa, present the problem of whether it is morally, or even economically, right to force European civilisation upon indigenous natives. A United Nations Trusteeship Commission visiting Tanganyika could, of course, recommend the ideal solution: leave the Masai strictly alone. But the facts of modern life in themselves won't let a race like the Masai remain isolated from the rest of Africa. Their life today on their reserves, immense as they are, is really nothing like their old life. It can't be, for in the old life the Masai were the ruling race, the dominating race, which roamed at will. The beauty of their life was the way they would roam to seek pasturage, moving with their immense herds to seek the fresh green after the rains. Now they are enclosed, they cannot roam any more, and both in Tanganyika and in Kenya the Masai lands are being eaten bare by at least twice the number of cattle that they have any hope of supporting. That is one of the facts of modern Africa which precludes real isolation: the rest of Africa will not, and cannot, let them have enough grass for their animals.

I would like to have what I say now taken with more seriousness than any statements I make in this book. The British are almost at their wit's end as to what to do about the Masai. This in itself shows a genuine concern for them. By every means that they can think of, the British are trying to make the Masai fall in line and accept some of the vital compromises which they must make in order to exist in modern times. They have used every power that they have, short of requisitioning large numbers of the Masai cattle (which they have had to do at times), first, so that the herds are reduced to something like the number which the range can bear, but chiefly so that the Masai will get into the habit of selling their excess animals, and thus begin an economic existence which will actually permit them to carry on as a separate race.

In trying to achieve this, the British have been particularly careful to place just the right men over the Masai. The Masai, quicker than any race in East Africa, will spot a second-rater. And have no use for him. With such an administrator, the necessity of giving drastic orders, even those leading to the use of force, is always a danger. With the right man, the Masai can be coaxed along the road. In this *baraza*, the open-air trial, which

Eric Sweatman and Roger Wilkinson held on the twenty-one trouble-making Masai up on the Loita Plateau, the entire proceedings were characterised by the fact that this was a discussion between—well, if I have to use that word—gentlemen. Although the power of force lay in the two administrators' hands, at no time was it allowed to enter the discussions as a threat. I could not imagine a German, Italian or even a Frenchman being so patient in such a discussion. The British administrators were patient because they knew that the whole of the Masai respect for them lay in the fact that their judgments—to a fighting race—must come as from honest and intelligent men.

This *personal* touch is the very thing which no U.N. Trusteeship Commission could even attempt to acquire. It is established by years of association, during which, as I have said, the British administrators have acquired an immense, if puzzled, respect for these red warriors, these museum pieces. And the Masai have come to have confidence in and respect for them. The British will not confiscate any more land from the Masai. It has been suggested that some of the excess population of the bursting Kikuyu Reserve might be settled in Masailand, across the Mara River. But in those discussions Cavendish-Bentinck said: "We will not break another treaty with the Masai. If we can manage to get the Masai to accept some compensation, then we could go ahead; otherwise, no."

I have seen the British administrating the Masai both in Kenya and Tanganyika. I can say honestly (and I would like to put it on record) I have never seen a more tolerant, well-meaning, even a more intelligent effort to get a fine race of natives to accept modern times. I think it would be plain murder to let any U.N. Commission have anything to do with them, even to recommending what should be done. I think it is a tragedy for Tanganyika that it was placed under a Trusteeship, anything that would mar that personal contact between the British Colonial Office administrator and the natives under him. The theoretical and the practical are usually at the opposite ends of the pole in Africa. And native problems should never be made the playthings of international politics and propaganda.

When I went out to live with the District Commissioner on the Masai Reserve in Tanganyika some ten years ago, a top official in the Secretariat at Dar-es-Salaam, even though he had arranged the visit for me, said: "How dare you go out and write about my Masai?"

"*Your* Masai?" I laughed. "What do you mean, your Masai? Do you have some proprietorial interest in them?"

"Yes!" he said, flushing unconsciously. "I was with those people for years. I think they're splendid people. Marvellous people! I'm only afraid that you won't do them justice."

There may be many settlers in Kenya and Tanganyika who are tormented by the sight, or the thought, of the stubborn Masai having the right to wander over such vast areas of potentially good grazing land. But they will not count in the long run. The Masai are going to come under some new rules regarding their disastrously large herds of uneconomic cattle; that is a certainty. But, unless I have been wrong in everything I have just said, the Masai will continue to be allowed to live out much of their old way of life . . . "as long as the Masai as a race shall exist."

CHAPTER XIV

Nairobi's Separate Compartments

TOO much attention has been paid to the effect of the white man upon the black man; practically none to the effect of the black man upon the white. This is a most interesting field. The deleterious effect is shocking. It accounts for the unbearable rudeness with which you will see the average white man (and the women are far worse) treating the average African today. I said average. I don't want to be unpleasant. We all know (read the stories of Somerset Maugham) the white man who has gone to the colonies and who, with a dozen servants leaping to obey his command, has risen to a position he could not have dreamed of attaining had he remained at home. He is one of the most odious little snobs you will meet in all your travels. He has his business and his club; and that is usually about all. He makes no effort whatever to learn the local language; nor is he interested in the customs or the history of the people among whom he spends his life. The natives are aware of it. This man has done more to lose Empire than is generally realised; and the best type of Viceroy, Governor, Indian Civil or Colonial Service official cannot make up for him. Compton Mackenzie has quoted General Gracey as saying: "We lost India because we never learned to say 'Please' and 'Thank you' at the right moment." The children of such parents, if born in the colonies, believe that you cannot be too rude to a native. I quote from the speech made by the Headmaster of the School for European children at Arusha, the best white preparatory school in East Africa:

> Do we wish [he said to both the pupils and their parents] to be accused when we come into contact with outsiders of being ignorant boors, dull and stupid with heads full of nothing but conceit? Do we wish to see educated Indians and Africans taking

> our place in every office and business? We are fond of talking about the shortcomings of the Native, but do we appreciate our own?
>
> The small child has an *ayah* (African nurse), and the *ayah* does things for the child that the child ought to do for itself. She cleans up his messes and puts away his toys. It shocks me to hear some children talking to native servants. They disobey their *ayahs;* they shout their orders at the house-boys; they lose their tempers when they do not get what they want.
>
> Then these children come to school. They make their messes as usual, but resent having to clear it up themselves; they disobey their teachers repeatedly, because disobedience with the *ayah* has become a habit; they are accused of being rude, and cannot always see where they have offended, because nobody thinks it is possible to be rude to a native.

That child, when he grows up, may think he knows all about the native; it seldom occurs to him that the native also knows *him.* Watch the face of the house-boy as he serves at table on a certain plateau in Kenya, and you will see a resolutely controlled mask of hate. Drive on fifty miles further, or back, and the boy is smiling as if it was the greatest pleasure in life that he can bring you in your morning tea.

"Good morning, *Bwana!* Nice day?"

"Good morning, Bugwa. Bugwa, where did you learn your English?"

"I teach myself, Master. I teach myself! How do you feel this morning, *Bwana?* Very well, I hope?"

That has cleared away many a headache. And that is probably all the English that poor Bugwa knows.

But Kenya has no class of "poor whites." And until they get that there will be nothing like the bad feelings between the two that you see every day in South Africa or in the southern United States. Most of the old Kenyans have a genuine affection for their house- or farm-boys; a queer mixture, alternating between something close to real love and furious exasperation. For you can start with the supposition, and be 100 per cent right, that having to handle Africans is almost enough to break a man's heart. Even the man who comes out to Africa as an idealist will almost certainly tell you in the long run, "There is no such thing as an honest African!"—and believe it. And they do such

> of diners-out burgled by organised squads in lorries; trains boarded by mobs; the roads of the reserves on Sunday infested by brutal drunken youths. [A serious tribal offence sixteen years ago; now tribal intervention risks a minor massacre of tribal authority.] And the King's Ministers stoned on the King's railway. These are some of the fruits—and the first fruits—of the new complacency. . . .

So now we know.

CHAPTER XV

The Joyce Farm

THERE is another side to Kenya life; and a glorious one it is. So far it may seem that I have been interested in only the dark problems of African life; and many Kenyans will doubtless say that I have deliberately called the spade a bloody shovel. But that is far better than a coat of whitewash, which the Colony does not need. I can say honestly that I met more people in Kenya this time who seem to have found just the life they were made for and who were living happier and more interesting lives than at that time (1947-8) I would have believed possible on this troubled planet. Things are much better in England now. But the other day I received some photos from Kenya—of a wedding. They were of a young farm manager, just born to farm in Kenya, and the girl who had run both her father's and her own big farm up on the Molo Downs. They were riding off, on horseback, after the wedding, dressed in the loose khaki clothes that settlers wear on their farms in that country (nobody wears a necktie)—and the sun was on their faces. As I looked at the photos, I felt a wave of nostalgia sweep over me; a longing to get back to those wide vistas again—this, although I have said that I would not miss the smell of the April earth in North Devon for all the land in Africa. I want to give the story of another farm; and of the three men—and one girl—who made it.

The farm is down in the "brown country" at Ulu, between Nairobi and the Coast—20,000 acres—where the vista, as you look out from the stone veranda, is fifty miles straight out over an open plain to where the blue mountains undulate along the far horizon; a bare, treeless country, looking at first sight almost as naked as the Somali deserts. Then you notice that it is covered with feathery, ankle-high grass, the color of a sand-grouse (you will never find a shot grouse or francolin if you don't mark closely where the bird fell on it), and after the Big Rains—which the Joyces proudly (and thankfully) call the Green Season—you will notice that a light bloom has covered these plains as if they had been merely dusted with an emerald pollen. Sit on the top of Joyce's hill under that bright blue Kenya sky and, 100 miles to the south of you, you will see the snows of Kilimanjaro shining in the sun. Look north and, 100 miles away, you will see the glint from the glaciers on Mt. Kenya. It is needless to say that the Joyces love that farm—love it with an emotion that almost brings tears to their eyes. This *is* Kenya.

Frank Joyce is one of those Kenyans I have described earlier in this book, when I spoke of the oak timbers of Kenya in the Rift Valley, who would never have fulfilled themselves had they remained at home. Like many of the original Kenya settlers, he left a life of comfort and secure social position, knowing full well that he had renounced nothing when he came out to try his luck in Africa, simply because such security had never owned him. Like all the old settlers who gave this colony its delightful way of life, he had never renounced his free will, always preferring real freedom—even the freedom to fall in love with adversity—to mere personal well-being; though God alone can tell you, for they can't, what some of those early Kenyans must have paid to keep it.

For years he had been one of the most active members of the Kenya Legislative Council, together with that other grand Irishman, Victor Shirley Cooke, in upholding the best interests of the Africans. The charge has been frequently made against him that he is "too pro-native"; and he had just resigned from political life altogether when I came down to stay with him. "I am putting to work here," he said with a smile, "a few of the things I have been trying to get through legislature." Of his 20,000 acres he has set aside some 5,000 for the Wakamba natives who live on his property; "squatters," as they call them. But he is trying to give a new meaning to that word by working out a way of life for the 1,400 Africans who live on his land which will make both them and himself contented. There is a lot to be said for that. If one man makes it his business to look after, make happy and raise the standard of life of some 1,400 other people, then you can say that he is making a generous contribution to African life, he is pulling his weight. And if some of the other big farmers in Kenya could do the same thing, and *if* the Africans could be persuaded to live properly on such farms, which is indeed far from being the general case, then Kenya's dangerous Native Problem would have at least one working partial solution proposed to it. I stress the *if;* because this is an arrangement—it should be called an agreement—which must cut both ways. Joyce's is entirely an arable dairy farm; and on the 15,000 acres which he has reserved for himself he is ranching 1,500 head of high-grade English cattle, which works out at one beast to every 7 acres, taking into account the land which is set aside for fodder crops. But 1 ton of seed-cake is used every day on that farm. When I sat down on his shaded veranda and expressed my regret that he should have retired entirely from public life, Joyce, in jodhpurs and open shirt, smiled. "I am getting acquainted with my farm again . . . and now I am going to direct the rest of my life to my *own* Africans." He is a sensitive man, and nobody looking at him could realise some of the things he has done. Speaking of the early days on his farm, before the 1914-18 War, when he had to fight for every yard of it, he said, in description of the rather humiliating performance of a young, untutored Irishman, green to Africa, trying to break in some irreconcilably stubborn oxen to the plough:

"I beat them, beat them, beat them . . . until, why, sometimes both the ox and I fell from exhaustion. . . . I could have murdered them!"

Frank Joyce, who had been for three years an officer in the regular British Army, came out to Kenya in 1912 and started ostrich farming on this same land he has now with a British regular Navy captain, F. O. B. Wilson (just knighted in the 1949 Honours List). Wilson had previously obtained a Government grant of 5,000 acres. They took in another partner, a man named Lambert, who had been Captain of Cricket at Eton, who had secured another 5,000-acre grant. Lambert died of enteric. The 1914-18 War came along and both Joyce and Wilson went off, serving the whole of it—both with distinction; Wilson sensationally so, though on land, in the East African fighting. Joyce saw four years of France and was badly wounded. When Major

Joyce, M.C., came back, he got a Soldier's Settlement of 3,600 acres. Ostrich feathers had gone out, Joyce and Wilson switched to cattle. They made their own roads, built their own house (the one that Joyce lives in now) and Joyce, who was paying so much a month into the partnership to become a half-owner, including half of the dead Lambert's share, even ran a sisal farm for a time, the manager of which was dying of the D.T.'s. (He can tell you some weird stories about that!) They bought more land, and when this splendidly successful partnership broke up only a few years ago—for they had raised dairy farming to its highest perfection in East Africa—they each owned 20,000 acres, where they now live side by side.

But the going was never easy. "In 1921 both the grass and the loans dried up," as Joyce now smilingly puts it. The banks had been too free with their money, though they were loaning at 8 per cent interest, "and so an overdraft doubled itself within seven years." Which is the reason why even such a remarkably successful farmer as Frank Joyce only came into the full possession of his farm (like most of the old Kenya settlers) during the boom period of this last war, which brought a heaven-sent chance to pay off these crushing overdrafts. This was the period when his daughter, Anne, ran this 20,000-acre ranch single-handed, for the Joyces never had a farm manager.

The composition of Joyce's squatters and the way they work and live on the farm is highly interesting. Some idea of the ratios of sex and age in such an African group can be gained by the fact that out of the 1,350 Wakamba natives who were living on Joyce's land when I was there, there were twenty-two men too old to work—but some of whom were acting as the Elder Statesmen of the tribe—159 married workers (Joyce employs men only), 45 unmarried, 376 women and 758 children. That makes the children total over 50 per cent, which is not much above the average in an African group. A man may have several wives who work his land; and each family on Joyce's farm has its own hut or huts—according to the number of wives—and its own cultivation plot, where it grows maize, beans, millet, etc. There are 690 head of the squatters' cattle being grazed on Joyce's squatter property. Each family may have three cattle, or two cattle and three sheep (but no goats), three sheep being counted as one head of cattle. Each head of a native family is allowed his own 8 acres of grazing land. With a few natives who do not live on his property, Joyce has 240 native laborers to draw from, of whom two-thirds are at work at any one time, making 160 "boys" working on his 1,500 acres, and each male squatter living on his property works 240 days a year for Joyce. The remainder of the time is his own.

Now, the chief good point of such a squatter form of farm labor is that the native is not forced to live away from his family. He is not drawn out of the "sump" of a reserve, having to leave his wife and his children behind him, to become a detribalised, devitalised, often a desperate man or, worse, a smart-aleck, drifting foot-loose into the towns to become a black spiv. Here on this farm was every good reason for a growing and happy community of native life: Africa lives in tune with modern times.

The average Kenya farm laborer, as I have shown earlier in this book, is paid 14*s.* a month. The average is 20*s.* on Joyce's farm, with 12*s.* being the lowest. "But that is for the very worst type of farm worker, a 'boy' that is hardly worth employing." There are twenty-one herds on the farm who get 25*s.* a month; six bosses of the milking *bomas* who get 36*s.*, and twenty-two "fags"—elder children who help the herds, for each herd has his fag—who get 7*s.* These herd hands all get *posho,* maize meal, beans, salt, etc., and meat once a week. They also have their own plots of cultivation as well. By African standards, these squatters are very well off. Then there is a superior class of skilled Africans who work in the actual dairy itself—and very good they are too—who get from 35*s.* to 60*s.* a month. These are full-time, all-the-year-round jobs, and it is a pleasure to watch the Africans in Joyce's model dairy pasteurising the milk, running the big engine, loading the clean cans into bullock-carts for the railway, for Joyce ships *700 gallons a day* of the richest milk in Kenya to Nairobi and Mombasa. Non-squatters get on the average 17*s.* a month and their *posho,* and, as it happens, the highest paid native on the farm is a non-squatter, who gets 160*s.* a month.

There they live. Frank Joyce deals with his squatters, so far as their own private lives are concerned, through two old squatter elders, the equivalent of appointed chiefs, amusing yet very dignified old coves with horrible, sharply-filed teeth, whose grins make you think, with a shudder, of the old cannibal days. And under these chiefs, to give the tribe a share in running itself, there is a sort of tribal council of fifteen of the old men—unfit for manual labor—who do political work and get an honorary stipend of 5*s.* a month. They thus govern themselves with an applied working democracy. There is no white foreman on Joyce's farm.

But even Frank Joyce, who actually is receiving a gratifying amount of willing and active co-operation, showed me red gullies in his hillsides that had been made by natives always driving their cattle down the same track to get to water, and large areas of land inside the 5,000 acres of his squatters' land, where, despite his orders that such and such a section must be left at rest and no animals grazed on it, the natives had put their cattle in and killed the coming grass. Despite the fact that many of them had been on that same property with Joyce for thirty years, they *still* looked for some selfish self-interest behind the instructions which the white man gave them for their own protection. But then, that is the native; and Joyce, knowing it, is a firm man. His way, when a native has been caught violating one of these instructions about grazing, etc., is to fine him so many days' work, in which, without pay, he must do so many yards' terracing, planting grass, etc.—remaking, in a form that he can understand, an equivalent to the land that he has harmed.

Joyce showed me one area in his squatters' reserve which had been put aside for rest, in a valley of which he had caught a native who had been secretly grazing four head of cattle in there for some time. "Very well, I fined that boy thirty days' work 'dabbling-in' seed in the bare places. He could do it himself or he could get thirty of his friends to help him and do it in one day. I didn't care which, but the 'dabbling' was done." This, mark you, was not on Joyce's, but on the land he had turned over to the squatters. "*That* sort of fine teaches them to look after their own property. They hurt the land; very well, I make them repair the land, and no argument about it. The moment a native refuses to do that I send him back to the reserve."

It is interesting to point out that although most of these Wakamba families have lived for years and years on Joyce's land, they still hold the right to cultivate or graze certain land in the Wakamba Reserve. Joyce does not encourage them to give up that right; on the contrary. The fact that he can, without any injustice, send them back into the reserve is the strongest argument he can bring to bear on them; and bit by bit, family by family, more and more of Joyce's Wakambas are giving him the active co-operation which will make their unwritten agreement a successful partnership.

The natives have eleven dams of their own for watering their cattle and fifteen grazing areas. They do communal labor among and for themselves, and it is here where the authority of the chiefs comes in—under Joyce's power of veto. It is, in fact, about as close as can be got to an independent native community living on Joyce's land. It even has its own elementary school, present enrolment sixty pupils, whose parents pay 2*s.* 6*d.* yearly for tuition fees and whose teacher Joyce pays 40*s.* and food per month, as well as giving him a house. The school has its own farming *shamba* where elementary agriculture is taught, and one of Joyce's most interesting projects in hand now is the enlargement of this school. How far can he go in teaching the young Africans how to protect and use the land, for that is the one education which the modern African needs most?

Such a life has dignity (if the natives want it) and self-respect. Joyce pays about £170 a month into that squatter community by way of wages. It runs its own store, with forty shareholders. One of the two chiefs has put 700*s.* into the store, and Joyce holds some £250 of his savings for him, on which he pays this business-like old African—with the filed teeth—4 per cent interest. "But I make *much* more money out what I have in the store!" the grinning old Wakamba had Joyce translate to me. It is the son of this old chief who is now the Chief Foreman of Joyce's farm—the man to whom Anne Joyce gives the orders for work at the conference which she holds in her office every day at twelve noon.

That farm will always remain in my imagination as Anne Joyce's farm. I got up shortly after daybreak and went out on her rounds with her one morning. Usually she rides a horse (and few girls have ever looked nicer in jodhpurs); but this day she took me around in a new American motor-car she had just bought. Some of the bore-holes are ten miles apart. Those ineffable little blue starlings were darting about in the yellow-flowered mimosa trees as we drove down Joyce's hill to get out on the great, brown Athi Plain. The white clouds still filled, like a river, the valleys of the Kilungo and Mukaa Hills behind us, in the Wakamba Reserve. These are some of the things that Anne Joyce did before we drove back for breakfast:

First: we saw some natives trying to chop through an enormous tree; it had honey in it. Slender Anne Joyce, in her beautifully fitting jodhpurs and checked shirt, got out of the car, surveyed their futile efforts, then suggested that they try splitting *tactique*. The "boys" grinned as they reversed positions and started to split, instead of trying to chop through, the great trunk. Two: we stopped at a long shed where the day's ton of seed-cake was being cut and proportioned, being sent off in bullock carts to the outlying cattle *bomas*. There is a daily passage of animals of the trek oxen. All working animals on the farm are zebus—the grade cattle cannot stand up to working in the heat, and these staid, humped cattle, originally from India, evoke thoughts about ancient civilisations and of the friezes of the temples in the valley of the Nile. The little Boran cattle, with their dewlaps and oval intelligent eyes, would seem to have no connection with these lumbering, biscuit-colored beasts, yet a couple of thousand years ago, on the plains of the Ganges, they might have had a common mother.

Three: we stopped at a milking *boma*, where Anne checked the book. There were seven cows tied to posts, each munching with contented sighs the cotton-seed cake, bran and molasses placed in the wooden trough before it, while a black boy—washing his hands in warm water first—squatted down on his hunkers to extract that cow's daily quota of rich milk for the Nairobi and Mombasa markets. There were seventy or eighty cattle at each milking *boma*, which moves, of course, with its own herd's shift of grazing. These milch cattle are beautiful, straight-backed Ayrshires and Aberdeen Angus. Each milking *boma* has its own black boss, who has seven boys to help him—seven cows are milked at one time—and a little fag who chases about, and usually seems to be collecting firewood, for a big steaming kettle of water is always kept going for the boys to wash their hands in.

When one cow had been milked, the boy loosened it and simply spoke to another cow—exactly as if he was talking to it—which then obediently walked up to the milking post. This relationship of the natives with their cattle is a thing to see. On the Sese Islands in Lake Victoria I have seen the Nilotic herdsmen there whom the Baganda employ to take care of their cattle speak to a line of advancing huge animals—these are the cattle with 5- or 6-foot spread of long horn—and the entire line came to a halt, with a row of grey noses pointed at us as if asking the herdsman why he had stopped them. When he spoke to them again—just a low word—they moved on. The cattle-owning tribes are everywhere the aristocrats of Africa.

Then we drove out across the vast plain to where some black islands of the beef cattle were grazing. These live off the land, getting no seed-cake. They are half Boran and half Aberdeen Angus, black as pitch. Here Anne Joyce superintended the dipping of 101 cattle, always checking the book which each herd boy keeps. It is said that the *totos,* the little fags, first learn to read and write this way, watching their elders, learning numbers, etc., from the brand marks; although a native—one who cannot count—can take one look at a herd of cattle and tell you instantly whether or not some are missing. They know them personally, so to speak. The boy at the dip whistled to the black cattle. They came in through the railed enclosure, paused in the shed at the edge of the cement dip—then jumped. Woosh! They had to go completely under in that jump, then walk in the liquid some distance before they could scramble out at the other end. When they emerged they glistened like satin under the hot sun. In a country where tick-fevers can decimate herds and ruin a rancher almost overnight, this dipping has to be carried out with an inexorable regularity. The movement, as you feel the tempo of life on a big farm like this, is like that of some great machine, turning slowly over and over . . . always with the same rhythm.

A black native clerk rode out to meet us here on a bicycle, and wrote down *on his arm* the number of cattle that were being dipped. He carried no book or paper with him. Then, lifting his solar *topi* to Miss Anne (the Wakamba call Anne Joyce *Kalakye,* which, I think, means "pigeon"), this educated young black man then mounted his bike and rode off. But it was queer to think how close behind him lay his entirely savage background. When one of the old chiefs on Joyce's farm became a little too much of a tyrant over the natives, or so they thought, they began to poison his wives. The Wakamba are one of the finest fighting tribes in all Kenya and make splendid *askaris*. They distinguished themselves in the last two wars.

"I love the dry country . . . the brown country . . ." said Anne as we drove off across the plain to one of the bore holes, "but there is nothing so refreshing as the sight of that water."

There are eighteen bore holes on Joyce's ranch, all drilled at enormous cost; and ten of them have already dried up. This, itself a terrible warning of the desiccation of East Africa, must be always present in the Joyces' mind. There are trees around these bore holes; shade and water are of priceless importance. There was a pump at this bore hole, pumping water two miles. Anne Joyce went into the shed where the engine was running and checked the fuel in its tank.

Then she drove up on a grassy hillside where, under the shade of mimosa thorns, some young calves were being bucket-fed. A young European assistant (getting £30 a month) who had just come to the Joyces' farm, was inoculating these calves to cure them of "scour." They were inside wire enclosures, separated from one another, and their mothers lay contentedly on the grass outside the wire. They would not be allowed back to their mothers until it was seen how the inoculation was working. Steam was rising from the basin in which the young Englishman was sterilising his hypodermic syringe. A little black fag held a calf's head over a bucket, dipped in his cupped hand for the milk and held it to the calf's lips. . . .

Each one of these *bomas* has its own bullock cart, and sometimes a fête day is celebrated on the farm in which each *boma* races its cart against the other. They get a great kick out of it. But if *two* men are seen riding on a bullock cart so as to save walking, then the boy who should not be on that cart is instantly fined. That is an unbreakable rule on the Joyce farm, so as to prevent undue tiring of its trek animals. Also, each boy at a milking *boma* is given one half-pint a day of its milk for himself. "Otherwise," smiled Anne, "he'd take it anyway . . . and perhaps more."

I said that the Africans were artful dodgers. "Aren't we all?" smiled Anne.

It was hot now, though only about nine o'clock; so hot that, it seemed, even the birds did not want to sing. The blue starlings were sitting in the mimosas like chips of iridescent metal as we went in to breakfast.

CHAPTER XVI

Wakamba Reserve

JOYCE and I went out to shoot sand-grouse and francolin after tea on the edge of his big dam. That great plaque of riffled water, with the rafts of duck riding in its center and the marabou storks and stilts wading around its edge, was one of the most luscious sights I had seen in all Africa. I wanted to drink the whole of it. Nothing makes a Kenya farmer so happy as just to stand and look at a well-filled dam. They get quite sentimental about them, for water is *life*. And Frank Joyce, if I remember correctly, had shared his pleasure and gratitude for so much water by making it a sanctuary for the bird life on and around it, just as had Walter Trench on his big dam up at Molo. There is something endearing in such a sentiment; man, harassed himself by the desire for water, finds himself able to store it in large quantities; and, in his thanks, instinctively shares his good fortune with all the other lives that he can. That, at any rate, is my interpretation of the subconscious impulse which moves many a Kenya farmer to make a sanctuary of his dam.

The sand-grouse and the long-necked francolin were all over the brown plain, but were mostly concentrated along a green *lugga*, or dry stream bed, that led into the dam. There was plenty of cover in the brush which filled this wandering gully, and in one or two places where some moisture must have been very close to the surface there were dense thickets of vivid green thorn, topped by the flat mimosa trees with their yellow blossoms. We were walking the birds up. We had an old faithful pointer with us; but he was a little too exuberant, in memory of his happier hunting days, and ranged far afield, putting up coveys of birds long before we could get to them, then yelping pitifully when Joyce smacked him. (It wasn't much of a chastisement.) He was suffering badly from tsetse-fly sickness, was moth-eaten in appearance, and had no sense of scent left whatever. Out of one covey which rose less than 40 yards ahead of us, Joyce and I each dropped one bird—stone dead, so it seemed; but so amazing was their protective coloring that it was only after ten to fifteen minutes' search that I saw the bird. Joyce's bird was never found, although we could easily have seen a runner in that short grass, and we knew that it was lying there dead somewhere. The pointer still pointed, one foreleg raised and tail quivering when we came on some birds; but he might just as well not have been there at all when it came to finding a dead or wounded bird. After about an hour's stroll, we came back with four sand-grouse and two francolin, and considered that we had had a good day. It is at this hour, as the sun sinks over Africa, that you most appreciate your first drink and then the life-restoring bath before dinner.

Most of the old Kenya settlers just get into pyjamas and dressing-gown and mosquito boots after that hot bath, and eat dinner in that comfortable costume, having only a short chat afterwards before turning in. Ten o'clock is really late in such families—people who are accustomed to get up with the dawn. This habit has been bred into them by the long, hot days during which they have had to fight for their farms, when they were doing physical labor such as would have appalled any gentleman-farmer of their type in England; and if you look at their hands you will see that even the most sophisticated and cultured Kenya settler of the old school has work-gnarled fingers that look like grappling hooks: the horny-handed sons of toil, in all truth. When you don't see an old settler with hands like that you know that he is not up to much; he has always been able to employ a manager or white assistants to do his job. But you will see few of such type even among the much-maligned and misunderstood Happy Valley lot—those who were accustomed to begin their drinking at sunset and end it with the dawn.

It is in these few short hours after dinner and at early dawn when you see the sun rise over Kenya, that the deep sensual pleasures of owning, running and being responsible for a big farm are most enjoyed. The life of such settlers is as far as could be imagined from the harum-scarum, happy-go-lucky existence of the polo-playing, hard-drinking Kenyan which seems to be the commonly-held opinion about them. This is the certain reward of a hard day, when the plains simmered like a stove in the sun—when most Europeans in Kenya lie down for a short siesta after luncheon, to escape from the pitiless heat. You feel then, when you think of everybody taking a nap, that life sort of slides by; that the white people there are somehow not getting the best out of things. Even that they sleep too much of their lives away, for want of something better to do. But early settlers like Joyce can look back to the days when there were no siestas after luncheon, when there was precious little for lunch as well; days when it was touch and go whether they would ever manage to make their farm pay, and they "worked like a nigger" to save it; so that they can lie down for a nap after lunch now without feeling they are becoming degenerate. It is always amusing to meet one of this breed in a London club, a man with the face of an aristocrat and the hands of a dock navvy, for Africa—and this is no bromide—has stamped its mark upon them.

The long, spiky sisal hedge on the high hill behind Frank Joyce's home marks the beginning of the troubled and badly over-populated Wakamba Reserve. From his house you can see—immediately on the other side of that hedge—the raw, red earth which marks where their "ruinous" way of living begins. I put that in quotation marks because there is a lot to be said on both sides in this case, for until the native is willing to co-operate, there *must* always be two sides. The Wakamba do ruin their land and they do run a suicidally large number of wizened, uneconomic cattle in their reserve; but the facts of the case are that they are rich neither in land nor in cattle; and for nine of the last eleven years a large number of the 250,000 Wakamba in the Machakos District directly adjoining the farm of Major Frank Joyce have been carried by the Kenya Government on something like famine semi-relief, being allowed to buy grain, etc., at one-half the market price. The other Wakamba have even paid this half-price for them in some cases. It is said that 37 per cent of the land in the Machakos district is today completely worn out, eroded down to its subsoil and beyond. Unless some 150,000 people are removed from that half of the reserve it will never be possible to bring the land back.

In 1946 the Kenya Government set aside £80,000 to feed the Machakos district, of which the Acting Financial Secretary said in the Legislative Council: ". . . However favorable, the rains cannot produce more than a fraction of the food required to maintain the inhabitants until that district has been rehabilitated. . . . The fact is *we must regard it as on the dole for the time being and provision for famine relief will be necessary from year to year.*" [My italics.]

The conditions in the Machakos District of the Wakamba Reserve, alarmingly paralleled by some sections of the Nyanza Province and, as I have already shown, parts of the Kikuyu Reserve—*with no workable answers yet found to solve them*—show incontestably that the days of the wide-open spaces in Africa have gone forever. Most thinking Kenyans know it. Furthermore, the obsession widely held in the high places of Great Britain (born of Great Expectations out of Fear), that there are thousands of square miles in Africa only waiting to be cleared of the tsetse-fly to be made great areas of successful cultivation, is also not held in Kenya; the man on the spot knows that the tsetse-fly may in all truth be a very beneficial thing, for it keeps large areas uninhabited and under bush and grass, which hold moisture and cover on the land, which prevent wind or sheet erosion on large areas that might very likely be turned into dust-bowls if thrown open for modern mechanised cultivation. Land under the plough, it is said, goes towards exhaustion fifty times faster than it does under the native hand-hoe. But more than anything else Machakos shows that the time is now definitely at hand where either persuasion or *force* must be used to make the natives de-stock their ruinously over-cattled grazing districts; and that force will one day have to be used—the demand for it is urgent—to make the natives accept group farming, rigidly enforced under European supervision until the Africans see for themselves the absolute necessity of abandoning their present "mining" of the soil.

The key to the whole thing, of course, is the native mind: how to get at that; and it must be admitted that in this the white man is making no progress—is even going backward. The most dangerous element in all this situation is that the mind of the white man itself also needs a drastic overhaul; it must refuse to accept explanations of these native problems which always place the blame on the native and, as a direct consequence, lead to projects to solve them which of themselves take none of the real and dangerous facts into consideration. It is a crisis; and should be seen as such.

For instance, in Kenya, when you hear Europeans talking about the Wakamba, you get the idea of a wilful lot of incorrigible natives who are stupidly grazing vast numbers of useless cattle on their lands; who, if they could only be brought to see reason, would sell half their stock—and everything would be fine in the Wakamba Reserve. The facts are directly the opposite. The Carter Report (that remarkably realistic and non-partisan Kenya Land Commission) showed in its findings that the average farm for a family of five of these partly pastoral and partly agricultural people in the Machakos District, was approximately 3 acres, while 1½ acres lie fallow. The average number of stock owned by a family of five was approximately five head of cattle and six and a half head of sheep, and—"the people might well have more stock without the number owned by the average family being unduly high." But owing to the appallingly eroded condition of the land, in some parts of that reserve as much as 20 or even 30 acres would be required to give one head of cattle its proper grazing; and over in the Kitui District the cattle there sometimes have to go twenty to thirty miles for a drink of water.

Statistics, as we know, can be twisted to prove anything, but those concerning Machakos do not need any doctoring. In 1938 it was estimated that the Wakamba Reserve was having to support some 250,000 head of cattle, 269,000 goats, and 50,000 sheep, whereas "the maximum number of cattle which the reserve could properly support without further damage was well under 60,000." Another estimate gave it that the Wakamba Reserve was carrying "three times its proper number of cattle and many tens of thousands of sheep and goats" and "the

Wakamba have been known to die of starvation rather than kill any of their stock for food."

Put those two things together, the Carter Report, that the Wakamba could have more cattle "without the number owned by the average family being unduly high," and the other saying that Wakamba Reserve is "stocked with more than three times its proper number of cattle," and what do you get? That the Wakamba need more land. They certainly do. The soundest report of an agricultural expert on that district states that over 40 per cent of the Machakos population is superfluous, and that to give the land its proper rest, as I have just stated, some 150,000 Wakamba ought to be removed from that area and settled elsewhere; which, it at the same time admits, "will be a herculean task." Now a large-scale project was launched at the beginning of 1945 to try to answer just this very dangerous problem of the Machakos semi-starvation area, and it would be illuminating to the doctrinaire liberals in London and elsewhere to show just how the natives themselves have blocked this project. They have reduced it, in my opinion, to nothing more than a mere token demonstration.

Put briefly, there are roughly 350,000 people living in the Machakos District on an area of roughly 1,000,000 acres, with an adjacent area of some 250,000 acres that up until 1937 was lying under tsetse-fly. In 1937 a fly-belt three miles long by a mile wide was made to stop the tsetse-fly from invading the inhabited district of Machakos.

At the beginning of 1945 it was decided to carry on from this fly-belt and clear the whole 250,000 acres of the Makueni District—for that is its name—of the fly, and settle as many Wakamba as could be induced to go there on this new land—under the conditions of restricted grazing and modern cultivation.

At first this fine scheme—for that is what it was at the beginning—envisaged groups of natives farming large co-operative farms something like the Russian collectives. But the Wakamba refused to go on the Makueni land, which they said was already theirs, under any "set of rules," as they put it. They also refused, and still do, any idea whatsoever of any communal or co-operative effort. This, mark you, in the face of the fact that native life is largely communal of itself. The result is that the idea of co-operative or collective farms had to be abandoned in the face of this adamant unwillingness of the natives to combine for work, and a scheme of model 18-acre farms was adopted instead.

This, it was hoped, would be such a vast improvement in the scale of living that they were accustomed to in the Machakos area—where the average farm was 3 acres—that the Wakamba would jump at it. Instead, it was not until October 1947, that Wakamba opposition to going on the Makueni land was broken, and only then when a highly literate native Chief, Mutinda, who had 500 acres of his own in the reserve, agreed to accept and cultivate a model 45-acre farm, and brought twenty other native families along with him. They were given 40-acre plots to encourage them. At a cost of some £67,000 (which does not include the cost of the fly-belt), some 13,000 acres have been entirely or partially cleared, wells have been bored, and the land for eighty-four families was ready for occupation when I went to Makueni in February 1948. Any white brain in Kenya which accepts *that* as a project which will answer the Machakos situation is not only misleading itself but the people higher up in England who will have the say in making grants from the Colonial Development Fund. It is just no answer at all.

On the other hand, it is as intelligent and hard-working an effort to make the natives farm properly as could probably be found in all East Africa. In fact, when you survey these model farms and meet the men who are in charge of them, you see that the Makueni development is an admirable scheme. *If* only the natives could be made to work it. It is no answer to Machakos, but it is, most definitely, a deeply sincere effort of the Kenya Government to persuade the Wakamba to adopt a more sensible way of life. Persuasion—and then, I am certain, force—will have to be used at Makueni. The natives must be *made* to co-operate, for their own salvation.

A sad item that may be given to show the type of land that is being cleared for the Makueni scheme is to say that 999 rhino had to be shot by white hunters before it was considered safe to open up clearings beyond the tsetse-fly belt. The rhino is an ugly beast, this hangover from prehistoric days, and because his short sight and chronic nervousness make him charge at anything that moves, is probably the unsafest animal in all Africa. Yet it seemed a shame, if the Makueni scheme is not going to be accepted by the Wakambas, to have slaughtered so many of even these unsociable animals. Thinking of that as I sat in the valley of the Keite River, I felt very much as did a white man who had been clearing the tsetse-fly out of a section of Tanganyika in 1939, who told me then: "Goddam it! When I think of some of the men [white] who are going to come in here, I'd rather have the fly!" Our jeep had to stop and be de-flyed several times in the two days that we were going in and out of the fly sections at Makueni: a black boy squirting D.D.T. or some other insecticide on our wheels and chassis. Some 4,200 acres have been completely cleared, and 9,000 acres had been "discriminately" cleared—that is, de-flyed, but with a certain amount of shade trees left standing. It is a rolling, and now open, country, at about 4,000 feet elevation, lying between wooded, undulating hills. About as pleasant a spot to live in, it struck me, as any man could wish.

Here you have a large-scale scheme which is intended solely for the African's benefit. No white man will, or could, make one penny out of it. In fact—which is a thing to give the Kenya Government full credit for—the fulfilment of that scheme will mean a large drain on the Colony's exchequer. It is the Africans themselves who are responsible for the slowness with which the project is getting under way, and who, unless they change their unco-operative attitude, will be almost entirely responsible for its failure. The two top men in charge of it on the ground at Makueni could not have been better cast. One, the District Commissioner, is a quiet-spoken man of the university don type, the calm, deliberative Colonial Office official who will sit there patiently and let the native have his say, and thus do much to win the confidence of the black man in the integrity of the scheme: he will be *reasoned* into complying with the necessary restrictions of the scheme rather than ordered into them. This is the psychological advance; a gain greater even than clearing the bush. It is the one thing that will make the native work his land properly. This District Commissioner is also extremely happy in such a post, because he is a fanatic ornithologist, expert enough to contribute regularly to the *Ibis* and other British bird periodicals of the more scientific nature. He lives in a big marquee tent, as does his colleague, and his delight that first night was to show me the set of Audubon prints that will eventually glorify the wall of the small house that is being built for him. The other man there—and these two form a remarkably complementary couple—was King's Own Scottish Borderers in this last war, also an officer in the King's African Rifles, holds the unique distinction of having fired both the first and the last shot in the Abyssinian campaign, with a break as Lieutenant Colonel in Burma in between. He is an agricultural expert and a fanatical research worker into all the problems arising from the environment itself on these model farms for Africans. He is the "driver," the type of fanatic who "gets things done." Both in its conception in the Agricultural Department in Nairobi and in the application on the spot, this scheme lacks nothing in either heart or intelligence or white man's effort. The only thing wanting is the co-operation of the natives.

Eighteen acres on paper look one thing; 18 acres of field, as you stand on them, look entirely different. I can't see how one family of, say, five natives will ever be able to work 18 acres. And I don't think that Major Frank Joyce, who probably knows as much about farming as any white man in Kenya, could either. That is, to judge from his remarks. Yet here is a strange thing, to show how insatiable is the native's lust for land. As we were leaving Makueni, my driver, Joseph, a Kikuyu, asked me what I thought of the Makueni scheme, and I, thinking that one family could never handle so much land, said: "Well, the Wakamba certainly can't complain that they are not being given enough land in this place!" "Oh!" said he. "Eighteen acres is nowhere near enough land, sir!" So there you are. The white man's conception of such a scheme as Makueni is to set going a type of modern farming which will enable more people to live on any given area of land; the black man's idea, when presented with such a scheme, is to ignore that and merely demand more land. The idea of intensive, *permanent* cultivation is the hardest thing to get him to accept.

The very core of the Makueni scheme is to get the native

to give up his old habit of shifting cultivation; to show him that he can live on the same section of land, and, by the proper rotation of crops and resting his land, how he can get a greater and assured return from it. It goes further in showing him how, by centering his farming around his own personal cattle *boma* (5 acres of each of these 18-acre farms), he can manure his own land. Fundamentally, it is to teach him that you can't always be taking something out of the land (the kitty) unless you put something into it. By induction, even with these separately worked 18-acre farms, it will also show him how to market his cash crops *as a group*. That, if the Kenya Administration can bring it about, would be real co-operative farming on, say, something like the Danish model.

I saw the main experimental farm for the Makueni scheme, where valuable knowledge is being gained of what strains of grass, fodder crops, maize, millets, groundnut, etc., will promise best in the conditions likely to be encountered when the bush has been cleared. But I could not help feeling that the very precision of this rotation and so on was too intricate and delicately balanced, much like a laboratory experiment, and, with the native psychology being what it is, will never be carried out in practice. In that respect, Makueni was too good to be true. At Makueni 1 acre is supposed to be enough for one head of cattle. On adjacent European farms one beast gets 7 acres.

The question of land tenure in native Africa is always troublesome, and far too complicated for me to go into here. Yet it can be said that at Makueni an 18-acre farm is a man's own property, but he is registered together with all the people of his family living on it and the number of his stock. He cannot break it up or sell it, but he can nominate his successor. So, if the successor is considered an efficient man to work the property, it could be said that these 18-acre African farms are entailed. All water is communal at Makueni; but—here is the native obstructionism at work again—difficulty has already been found in how to work communal water and/or manure carts. A communal cart could spread manure over these 18-acre farms, each family using it in turn, far faster and with less labor than any individual family could do it by hand. But a native hates to have any other native even step foot on his property.

Makueni is an area where *experience* may be gained by both black and white in the best ways to clear bush of tsetse-fly, the simplest but most effective methods of providing water in a dry land, what order in which to rotate crops, and especially what crops are best suited to the soil. Experimentation is now going on at Makueni in all these things. Even though the acceptance of the project has been disappointingly small up to date, the day may come when it will take on momentum—here comes that psychological problem again—and real and willing *active* co-operation of the black man with the white man will have been started in Kenya.

It is still difficult to persuade the Wakamba to take up these 18-acre farms at Makueni.

What is the reason for the African's increasing suspicion of the white man and of his good intentions? Nobody knows. It is an interesting point that the Commission of Inquiry which the British Labour Government hastily sent down to inquire into the reasons for the riots and killings that broke out at Accra on the Gold Coast in February 1948, in which twenty-one Africans were killed and 228 injured, and in which the Gold Coast Governor, who withdrew the right of *habeas corpus*, and claimed (without yet being able to produce any evidence) was a Communist-incited disturbance, had to report:

> By far the most serious problem which the Administration has to face in the Gold Coast is the suspicion which surrounds Government activity of any sort. Its origin, apart from political propaganda, is disperse and often obscure. It does not attach to persons or individuals in Government service. It is an attitude of mind based on no specific grievance. That it exists we have evidence on all sides. That it must be overcome is the hard core of the problem of healthy relations between Government and governed.

That, word for word, can be taken as typically true of the native state of mind in Kenya today, much as some visiting political tourists of the Labour Government would like to deny it. If they continue to deny it and keep on trying not to face the facts of African life, then every scheme in East Africa will be built on a false basis. The native must be persuaded to believe in the white man's good intentions. What is more, the white man must *have* them.

CHAPTER XVII

"An African Churchill"

CHIEF WARUHIU of the Kikuyus was about the only man I met in Africa in whom I felt that the teaching of Christianity had completely fulfilled its mission. This was merely an impression, of course, and it will probably seem unfair to several other godly people I met, including some very unselfish and hard-working missionaries and one arch-deacon. But with the very-Christian white man, I have usually found that he is a bit egotistical about it; he makes a pose of his humility. Whereas with the black man, possibly because he is less sophisticated, he not infrequently takes the teachings of Christ literally. And his composure, coming from the fact that he feels in his heart that he is living a Christian life, is the most rock-like thing about him. Such a man in the reserves is the best hope we can have for an understanding between white man and black. And without such an understanding there can be no hope for Africa.

This morning, when I began this chapter, I came on a passage by Matthew Arnold, written in 1853, which struck me as being so strangely apposite to life in a Native Reserve that I want to quote it. Declaring that a situation cannot be simultaneously painful and poetic, he said:

> What, then, are the situations, from the representation of which, though accurate, no poetical enjoyment can be derived? They are those in which suffering finds no vent in action; in which a continuous state of mental distress is prolonged, unrelieved by incident, hope or resistance; in which there is everything to be endured, nothing to be done. In such situations there is inevitably something morbid, in the description of them something monotonous. When they occur in actual life, they are painful, not tragic; the representation of them in poetry is painful also.

That describes the frustrated, hopeless life in some of the over-populated districts of the native reserves, where "suffering finds no vent in action; in which a continuous state of mental distress is prolonged, unrelieved by incident, hope or resistance; in which everything is to be endured . . ." better than anything I have ever read. For idleness, as we all know, is not a happy state, and the disfranchised warrior, lolling about with nothing to do, nothing that he can find to do which he can really take an interest in, is in my opinion the most morbid man in all Africa. Your answer is: Well, let him work, then. True. But first we will have to find the psychological key to his make-up that will persuade him to work. And then we ought to see that it is interesting work. With a simple man the best key to this last question is to find some way, or manner, by which we can give him a proprietorial interest. In South-West Africa I found that the African would very often rather work for the old trek-Boer, the man who invariably paid him the least and beat him the most, simply because that old type of farmer would say to his boys: "Look here. Tomorrow we're going to start building a dam over there. . . ." It was the "we" part of it that did it. The English settler, scrupulously fair, never got that personal, co-operative contact with his boys. I cite this, for what it is worth, as one means of the psychological approach to the African when trying to enlist his interest in the various schemes and programs that are now in hand for his betterment in East Africa. And men like Chief Waruhiu could be pilot-Africans in such endeavors.

An education in *understanding* is the only thing that should be gone in for in Africa today. And with haste! It should be the pilot-scheme to all the big master plans. It should be a complete, ruthless revision of the whole box of tricks that goes today by the name of a European education. The dates of the Kings and Queens of England should be utterly discarded. An education about Kenya, white settlement there, would be a far more useful thing, embarrassing as some of its incidents might be. It could be shown that the British colonisation there was the least unjust of any in Africa, and that the present plans of the Kenya Government for the native's benefit are probably the most promising of any others on the continent. In my opinion, the Information Departments of the three territories that make up East Africa should spend their time in explaining the European to the African, and bother less about trying to attract British and American tourists to their countries. Then they would get somewhere. That sounds very dogmatic. It is so obviously true that I almost hate to state it. But the African does not have to do all the learning. The Englishman has to learn how to say "we" to the African, to know the urgent reasons why he should soon begin saying it—in political life as well as on the farms.

Chief Waruhiu has 26,000 Africans under him and six chiefs. He is, very possibly, about the closest thing you can get to an hereditary chief among the Bantu Kenyans. That is, his father owned large stretches of land where he is living now, as did his grandfather, and they were the natural headmen, the elders, of the Kikuyus around them. When the British confirmed the appointment of Waruhiu as chief some twenty-odd years ago, they were only confirming an established fact. The authorities try in every case, in their appointments to the positions of headmen or chiefs, to give the official recognition, and power, to someone who has already achieved a position of authority among his own people. But in many, if not most, cases they are persons who have no hereditary right to be given such power, and as a result they are usually looked upon as being mere agents of the Government. There is a distinction here which is very important. A tough African who, say, distinguished himself as a sergeant-major in the 1914-18 War may, if he is intelligent enough and his nerve does not crack, be able to boss a great number of would-be unruly and suspicious Africans. But that is not the Indirect Rule which Lord Lugard envisaged; far from it. And in the "show of hands" by which Local Native Councils become appointed, intimidation functions more often than not—the threats of the young men—and the wrong men get selected. These are some of the truths that you become conscious of only after you have talked with a few African "chiefs." To find one who rules because of an inherent power of character and personality is rare indeed.

Chief Waruhiu seems an outstanding example of what a mission education can produce when it has the right material to begin with. It is said that because of his character alone his is absolutely invulnerable to any African "agitator" (although Jomo Kenyatta lives in the same district, the terracing was not stopped among Chief Waruhiu's 26,000 Africans); and while the influence of the old men, the leaders of the tribe, is rapidly waning in African life, Chief Waruhiu's stands undiminished. He is spoken of as an "African Churchill."

He has a home, built in European style, with a decorative monkey-tree in its well-swept drive, a hyacinth-blue border of jacaranda trees, which were in full blossom when I was there, climbing yellow roses on its walls, and a beech-like *manunga* tree on its lawn under whose cool shade we had tea, looking out over that same spacious vista to where the misty blue outline of mountains rose out of Tanganyika to the south. Nearby, under the peace of some sighing gum trees, lay the graves of the two American missionaries who had educated him and his seven children. The Kikuyus are now building a school facing that spot in honor to their memory.

They were a Mr. and Mrs. Knapp, of the Gospel Mission Society, and the moment I led the talk in their direction Chief Waruhiu's face took on a radiance, the light of loving remembrance. Mr. Knapp had died first, and was laid to rest in the grove of towering gum trees that flanked the mission school. Mrs. Knapp carried on. Then she died.

"The Gospel Mission wanted them taken back to the United States," said Chief Waruhiu, "but we didn't want that. . . ." So the Council of Elders at Kiambu sent a strong petition to America, asking if Mr. and Mrs. Knapp could not be buried where they had taught. "That was granted to us. So we carried them—we wouldn't let any Europeans do it—to where they lie now. It is just over there. . . ."

Then he was silent. He is a man of great dignity, and we went on with our tea and left him alone with his memories. I asked him if the Knapps had ever told him about the life of Booker T. Washington, the great American Negro educator. He smiled gratefully. That was the most encouraging book they had ever given him, he said; it was in his house now. The story of Booker T. Washington, and of Tuskegee College, had been translated into Kikuyu. What had so impressed him, said Chief

Waruhiu, was to know that Booker T. Washington, the Negro who had dined in the White House with President Theodore Roosevelt, had been born a slave. Then I told him what I knew of that other great slave-born American Negro, George Washington Carver, the agricultural chemist, who had just died, whose research into the industrial use of peanuts has raised the standard of thousands of lives, both white and black, in the southern United States; how his name was to be placed in the American Hall of Fame, a bust was to stand in the Smithsonian Institution; and how he was to be the second Negro in U.S. history (Booker T. Washington was the first) whose face was to appear on a postage stamp. His curiosity about Carver, and my account of the impressive number of brilliant Negroes who are now appearing in all walks of American life, led inexorably towards the color bar. But he never mentioned it. Instead, by one gentle question after another, he led to the major question: Did the American Negro have a free and equal chance to use his talents? And that was the very question that I did not want to discuss. For I have found, in practically every instance where I have met an African Negro who has returned from the United States, that he has given his own people an entirely false impression of the American Negro's status. Perhaps not intentionally; he has just hoped that that was the way things would work out when he has cited celebrated Negroes like Jackie Robinson, Paul Robeson and Roland Hayes as being typical of Negro advancement. One finds it only cruel to point out that they would have been exceptional and distinguished people, no matter what their color. It seems to be taking away hope.

But I did take the opportunity to indicate how the increasing number of Negroes who are appearing as successful doctors, lawyers, teachers and businessmen in American life, aside from their outstanding actors and artists, was of itself working for equality of opportunity. I implied that one day there would be so many of these prominent Negroes that they would burst the bonds of the color bar. He smiled wisely and said: "Yes, I suppose it is numbers . . . not just a few brilliant exceptions," leaving me with the feeling that, although he had listened to me politely, I had not shifted his feelings one inch, whatever they may be, about what the white man thinks about the man who has a darker skin. He was a statesman. And I had to smile secretly when his son, David Waruhiu, afterwards told me the advice that his father had given him when, in his official capacity, he had to deal with other people: "My father said, 'Never let them know *all* of you!' " I left with the impression that Chief Waruhiu feels that the color bar is a despicable thing, but that it was useless to discuss it.

This was in strange contrast to a conversation I had with Jomo Kenyatta only a few days later. For even that highly intelligent African seemed to think that it was only the white man's greed and fear that was causing him to hang on to the color bar, and that other, more advanced white men, if they wanted to, could abolish it by a law. "Until that is *abolished*," he insisted, "we will *never* have any comfort between the races! Take me. Here, on this hill, I am free! I *hate* to go into Nairobi. I want to run away from towns. I am always afraid that some day some ignorant white man will come up to me and say: 'Here, you. Get out!' That might happen to me *any* day. . . . I never know when. . . ." As I had seen him sitting in the audience of the Kenya Legislative Council, with his elephant-headed stick, while a debate about some of the very troubles he was supposed to have instigated was in progress, I asked him if he had ever met any such treatment from a white man. "No," he said truthfully. "It's just the fact that it *might* happen. . . ." I don't think it will. That is, unless Kenya by any ill-chance starts to get a class of "poor whites." As it is now, the racial relations in Nairobi are less uncomfortable than they are in Washington, D.C. The African Africans have more things to be thankful for than they know.

Here is how David, the first son of Chief Waruhiu, got his education. In 1926, at the age of nine, he went to school at the Gospel Mission Society, the same school which had given his father his education. He stayed there until 1932, studying geography, history, agriculture, Swahili and mathematics. Then in 1932 he went to the Church of Scotland Mission at Kikuyu, staying there until 1935, when he got his Primary Certificate. Then he went to the Alliance High School at Kikuyu (maintained by the Government) for three years. Then, after fifteen years of such schooling, he went to King's College, in Uganda, where he studied two years. The original idea of King's College was to train the sons of African chiefs so that they could go back and administer over their own people. He then went to Adam's College in Natal. The fee at Adam's College is only £20 a year, including board and lodging, but with books, clothes, etc., this amounted to about £40 a year, which was an expense that his father, Chief Waruhiu, could not keep up. So David Waruhiu started a tuck-shop at Adam's, buying goods in Durban and selling them on the campus; he started a Students' Co-operative Society, which made him its Chairman; and the Principal of Adam's, doubtless impressed by the energy and resourcefulness of this student, then decided to pay one-half of his school fees. Nevertheless, that was still more than his father could manage, and David Waruhiu had to leave Adam's.

Now, here comes the most interesting part of his education, for he went as a day-scholar to Natal University in Durban. It was due to the Indians in this institution, the way they found a place for him to live and gave him a job whereby he could maintain himself, that this eager young African got the remainder of his education. Durban is the most "English" city in South Africa. Yet it was to the Indians that this African finally had to turn for help.

"I lived in their society," he told me. Out of the 200 students in Natal University at that time, among Indians, Chinese, and "coloreds," there were twenty Africans, and David Waruhiu was the only one from East Africa. When he was there as a day-scholar the Indians got him a flat in Durban to live in. When the wife of the Prime Minister of Uganda, a Mrs. Kawlya, came to Durban to live for two years, she came to David Waruhiu to help her find a flat, "which I did, among the Indians." For Europeans in East Africa, who constantly complain that the Indians and the Africans take a common front against them, I would say that here is one example of Indian interest in the Africans that might help to explain it. The race riots in Durban this year (1949) have been among the lowest members of the Indian and African communities.

David Waruhiu worked as a commercial traveller for A. I. Kajee, a Mohammedan, who is the Leader of the Natal Indian Congress, the same man that I interviewed in 1939 (see *Behind*

God's Back), when he was the Secretary of that powerful Indian group. The population of Durban then was:

100,000 Europeans
90,000 Indians
6,000 "coloreds" (mixed breeds)
34,000 black men

And 70,000 more Indians live within a seventy-mile semicircle drawn around Durban, working on the everlasting sugar plantations, living in fantastically wretched hovels, running, it seems, every shabby shop in the country districts. David Waruhiu, this young and ambitious African, went out among these, as well as up into the green rolling hills of Zululand, to sell goods to the Africans, even as far as Johannesburg. A. I. Kajee gave him a car and driver, £25 a month and—this is particularly important—arranged in advance everywhere that he should have hotel accommodation or a private home, always among the Indians, where his color would not be allowed to embarrass him. (During his first summer vacation, when at Adam's, Waruhiu had worked for three months as a sweep in a Durban hotel, as a checking clerk in its cloakroom, and finally behind its bar. "I made a lot of tips there!" he told me.) During 1944, when he was working for A. I. Kajee, he was able to attend only the night classes at Natal University. But in 1945 he entered as a full student, and spent one glorious year, for him, studying political economy, history and English, during which he read a great deal of Dickens, Shakespeare, and made his first acquaintance with Milton and even the poetry of Rupert Brooke. In 1946, "My father called me back, as he no longer had enough money. My brother is studying to become a doctor." (Chief Waruhiu is paid 279*s.* a month by the Kenya Government.)

In September of that year David Waruhiu was made the Executive Officer of the Kiambu Local Native Council, which is the office he is holding now. He was sent to England in 1948 on a short-term bursary from the British Council to study agricultural administration, and stayed a few days with me in my home in North Devon. This is a great dairy country, and he was found "uncommonly interesting" by one of our own expert farmers here. His brother went to the Roman Catholic Mission

School at Mangu which I have described, and is now finishing a two-year course at Makerere, from which he hopes to get a bursary which will allow him to go to Edinburgh to study medicine. From 1926 to 1946 is the twenty-year period through which young David Waruhiu struggled to get his education, and his greatest wish now, he told me, is to succeed his father as chief—"To lead by example," to use his own words to me—over the 26,000 Africans that his father is now leading in the Kiambu District.

He smiled as he said to me that this would be an example of an "educated" African leading his own people; and that the young men of Kiambu would not be able to say of him (as the young Africans say of so many appointed chiefs or headmen): "Ho! That man was put in there by the Government! He only says what the Government tells him to say. He can't come that over us!" Young Africans of David Waruhiu's caliber will be the first to tell you that if the demand for self-government which so many African agitators are clamoring for today was granted before there was a widespread education, it would be abused: the Africans would not know what to do with such freedom.

There are usually over 900 black students from Africa in England, of whom over three-fourths are in London. They see little of British life, as it seems the Communists are the only people who take a real interest in them. Here is where hatreds and frustrations are born. It seems a pity that the Royal African Society does not take more real interest in these African students in England.

The duties of an African chief are almost undefinable, depending as they do almost entirely upon the strength of his own personality. The foremost of his specific duties is to collect the poll tax. Not a popularity-making obligation! But his real function should be to interpret the wishes and proposals and regulations of the Administration in every phase of its rule over the Africans to his own people, and, with an ideal chief, he should be strong enough with the Government, and wise enough, to be able to translate the wishes and the objections of the Africans back to the white administrators. It stands to reason that not many black men can be found who can fill that dual role completely. Essentially, he is really a glorified link between the

Government and his own people, and, as such, his best work is done off-stage, with neither side knowing how it was done. In the open, his attitude and character can be seen by the position he takes in the meetings of the Local Native Council.

The Local Native Council gives a wide measure of self-rule to the natives in a reserve if they take it in the right spirit and it has the right type of District Commissioner to function under —an official who should never let a question get to the point where he would have to use his power of veto. This requires intelligence, patience and a considerable desire to reach a mutual understanding from both sides. I would put patience as the one virtue which a District Commissioner simply cannot do without, and then say that the closer he gets to that ability to say "we" the better an administrator he will be. Though, he will never acquire "we" by merely becoming familiar with the natives. They are remarkably quick in spotting a weak man.

The poll tax in the Kiambu District is 20*s.* yearly for every male over eighteen years old; 14*s.* goes to the central Government, and 6*s.* goes to the Local Native Council, 2*s.* of which is set aside for education. The Kiambu L.N.C. was started in 1925 (Chief Waruhiu has been on it since the days of its inception) and consists of twenty members, serving a term of three years. Of these, thirteen are "elected" by a show of hands. The other seven members are the paramount chief—Waruhiu—and the three Divisional Chiefs and the three Headmen, who serve under him. At the risk of being tiresome, I will go into the methods of "electing" a Local Native Council. For, as the District Commissioner is always automatically made its Chairman, and he or the Provincial Commissioner has the final right to veto any of its resolutions, it is often said, by critics of the L.N.C. form of self-government, that the African has been given no substance of autonomy at all—which is not true of the way it works out in practice.

To begin with, the Africans put forward the names of their own people whom they wish to see appointed to the L.N.C. This is done at *barazas* (meetings) of some 500 or so people, at which the District Commissioner or the District Officer is always present. The people call out the names of those whom they wish to have represent them; they can shout out as many names as they like. The D.C. or the D.O. takes a list of these names. Then, picking them at random down the list, he calls for a show of hands. The D.O. takes these names in order of strength. He does not call out the names of the successful candidates, but when all the thirteen locations in the Kiambu District have "voted" this way, he gives this list of names to the District Commissioner, who then calls a meeting of the Divisional Chiefs, and they (and Waruhiu) go over the names and state which they, the chiefs, consider good men and eligible. The D.C. then sends the names proposed—say, thirty in all—to the Provincial Commissioner, who selects the final thirteen. It can be seen that this requires an intimate knowledge of the natives proposed, both on the part of the D.C. and the P.C. When the P.C. has made his final selection, the list is given to the Government Printing Office, and the names of the thirteen Africans thus elected appear in the *Official Gazette*.

A Local Native Council stays in being for three years, and meets four times a year. It has a multitude of duties, but the most important of them are that it has the right to make Resolutions about (*a*) collection of the poll tax, (*b*) all road-making and upkeep, (*c*) education. The Council has the right to detail a certain number of natives to work on the roads of the reserve: communal work, which is not paid. And on education it has the power to grant or refuse any application for the establishment of a new school. In the fiscal years 1945-6 and 1946-7, the L.N.C. at Kiambu gave a capital grant each year of £5,000 to the Missions to build schools. This is money raised by the Africans themselves. It has been forbidden by law to give any grant to the Independence Schools; and that, in 1947, struck the L.N.C. of Kiambu as being unfair. So it is interesting to point out the L.N.C. at Kiambu passed a Resolution to stop this grant to Mission schools until *all* schools have been made the subject of an Educational Survey. When I asked them why they had suspended that grant, they said that, aside from the fact that it seemed unfair to the Independence Schools, "We feel that most of the children are not getting the proper type of education. We have not sufficient control over the syllabus of all of the schools [here the Independence School was being hit at]; and only when that survey has been made will we feel certain that the money is being spent correctly." Now there is an example of the native mind working with a simple logic, which, if that Educational Survey is made, will probably not only advance the type of education as a whole in the Kiambu District but might as a result end by getting more qualified and better paid teachers in the Independence Schools.

The Africans themselves do not like this "show of hands" method of election to the Local Native Councils. They say that Africans, in the presence of other Africans, are very often afraid to vote for the man they want most, because they feel that they will have openly declared themselves for the wrong man if he does not get elected. And intimidation comes into play here, say members of the "Forty" group watching this hand-showing. They want the secret ballot, as it used to be in the peasant districts of India. There is no need to be able to read or write, they say; give each candidate the symbol of an animal—the natives know an elephant, or a giraffe, or a lion—and they can show their choice by making their mark against the animal. Furthermore, say some of the Africans, they would like to see people like Jomo Kenyatta elected to the L.N.C., but for reasons rather different from what one would think.

"What I say is," said one old African, talking to me, "all those noisy people . . . like Jomo Kenyatta . . . just put them on the Council! Let's hear what they have to say. Let's see what kind of speeches they are going to make when they know they are going to be printed in the papers! Let's see that they will stand up and say to the Government then—and to their *own* people—instead of doing all this talk from behind!"

At the present moment (end of 1948) the Kiambu Local Native Council has a reserve fund of £150,000, all raised from Africans in the Kiambu District (196,000 pop.), all to be spent on Africans by Africans. They would like to be able to elect their own Chairman for the next L.N.C., have the District Commissioner step down. Not because they do not have faith in him: "But we want the opportunity to run ourselves completely. If *we* make mistakes, if we find that under *our* Chairman the work does not get done, then we will be glad to have the D.C., as Chairman, back again."

The scene in any reserve is a maze of contradictions. Clusters of conical thatched mud huts, like toad-stools, all over the slopes of the red, eroded hills, with their little pocket-handkerchief patches of maize and other cultivation; and then, directly neighbor to the Kenya Teachers' College, the modern stone house, with its red tiled roof, of a rich African, able neither to read nor write, who had four wives, three motor lorries, a wattle forest from which he sold charcoal into Nairobi, and 300 acres on which he grazed many cattle. This is in a district so congested that 10,000 of its 28,500 families must be moved out, where 40 per cent of the people are landless, where, so I was told, he had bought the land from other families which had been reduced or which had died out. Jomo Kenyatta himself had a farm of 300 acres only four miles from the school. In a reserve itself there seems to be as great an inequality among its African inhabitants as there is in the ordinary life of Europeans. It is an old adage in Africa, and I think a true one, that the worst oppressor of the African in Africa is the African; and there is plenty of evidence to show that Africans make pretty hard landlords. It is impossible to assess the money that is made inside a reserve. Many people claim that, despite their constant lamentations and demand for more land, the Kikuyus are the wealthiest people in Kenya, taking native incomes as a whole. This is often given as the excuse for not giving them more land. The poverty of the average Kikuyu is, however, self-evident.

Then, too, in a race which it seems extremely hard to train as skilled artisans, or workmen who can be depended upon to finish a complicated job, if left on their own, you will suddenly come on a genius, an African Edison. There is a row of ramshackle little bamboo stores at the market place near Jomo's school, with one pathetic little establishment with a sign up—HOTEL. It had only a few chairs and a table at which some African males were having a cup of tea and some hot mashed potatoes. A native *duka*, or general shop, with a wretchedly small assortment of a few bolts of cloth and, chiefly, some blue-mottled bars of anti-insect soap. A butcher who wrapped up his purchaser's meat in banana leaves. The whole being rather a tragic imitation of a European line of stores. And then, working at full blast right behind them, was an African blacksmith who had invented his own forge, run with the spinning wheel of a motor car as a flywheel and a fan-belt to a blower, with a jet to concentrate the flame, in which he was melting down pieces of other abandoned motor-car chassis and scrap to turn out as neatly made bolts and hinges as you could buy in any European hardware store. The blower was his own invention. He buys the motor-scrap from Nairobi. He was booked up with orders, he told us, for as far ahead as he could see—and he had only one arm. His whole busy workshop was redolent of an inventive turn of mind. He had a grand sense of humor, and it was a delight to meet a man who was getting so much happiness out of the use of his brain. Every now and then you will come on an outstanding African like that. And it makes you think twice before making any generalisations about that enigmatic, often exasperating, but usually lovable race. They make you wish for some miraculous change in the white man's heart that would smash the color bar—wish for the impossible!

Before I left Chief Waruhiu, I summoned enough courage to ask that calm and restful African the one question that had become important with each minute that I spent with him. "I know it is an awkward thing to ask you point-blank," I said. "But tell me: has the Christian faith been of so much use in your life?"

He was a trifle embarrassed before the others. Then he said: "It has been everything."

CHAPTER XVIII

"The Men of God"

I DROVE across Kenya from Machakos to the shores of Lake Victoria where, in the great Nyanza Province, I hoped to study the Government team-work of the Administrative officers, the Provincial and District Commissioners with the Agricultural, Veterinary, Welfare, Maize and Produce Control Officers in that general advance along a broad front which the Kenya Government is now conducting with considerable skill and determination to help the backward African advance into modern times. There, around the shores of the great Lake, still so redolent of the great days of Lord Lugard and Henry Morton Stanley, where the missions are the most highly developed and concentrated in all Africa, I came on some of the things, deep and obscure, that are holding this progress back. Things which, if ignored, will make it difficult for the white man to come to grips with the African mind.

I have stressed all along in this book, and made it sufficiently plain, I hope, that the white man's greatest problem in Africa today is to get the African to *believe* in him and in his good intentions. That is a psychological problem. Instead of being solved, it is getting worse. Every big plan that is conceived in Europe for the "development" of Africa only adds to its gravity. I have said once, and I stress it: it requires no effort to prove that these plans are first and foremost for the European's benefit and tend to help the African, if at all, only in their stride. As I have said before, this knowledge is seeping through Africa. It comes on the top of older fears and disillusions.

I believe it was something more than a coincidence that when I arrived at Kakamega the first thing I should come on was the inquest on eleven Africans who had been shot as they were threatening to murder the Fathers of a Catholic mission.

These men belonged to a fanatic religious cult, the *Dini ya Msambwa* (the Cult of *Msambwa*), which had been started by a mission-trained lunatic who had been sent to the Mathari Mental Hospital in 1945, but later released against the advice of the Administration. They were shot when they attacked Assistant Superintendent J. Walker and his Kenya Police (who had come out to protect the missions) at Malakisi in the North Kavirondo Province on February 11th, 1948. That courageous officer held his men until the last moment and did not give the order to fire until he went down, for the second time, under the crash of a rifle butt which nearly brained him. I have seen that cut.

"Blimey!" he said (he is a fifty-five-year-old Australian) as we sat outside the D.C.'s office at Kakamega waiting for him to go in and give his testimony at the inquest. "They gave me a crack on the napper that nearly conked me!"

He took off his blue policeman's vizored cap and there, on a grey-haired and tonsured skull, was a criss-cross mark exactly like that on a hot cross bun. Inside, the little grey Catholic priest, an Austrian, was testifying before the Resident Magistrate of Kisumu how one holy Father had fired a shotgun into the air six times as the mob of howling Africans, with drums beating and spears waving, advanced across the lawn of the Mission; and then how he had fired one shot into the ground: a fatal thing to do, for nobody was hurt, and this only confirmed what the mob's leaders had told it—that the *Dini ya Msambwa* were immune to bullets. Jehovah would turn these into water.

I have related how on the morning of December 21st, when my wife was fishing up the Thika River—alone but for her African gillie—twenty-two "skin-men" with their leader, "The Man in Red," were fleeing up the valley in which she stood, trying to reach the obscurity of the high bamboo forest. They had just ambushed and murdered Assistant-Inspector Dominic Mortimer of the Kenya Police and two of his native constables. These were "The Men of God" (*Watu wa Mungu*), or the *Dini ya Jesu Kristo*, the Cult of Jesus Christ, as they sometimes call themselves.

For some reason—I cannot understand why, unless they do not attach sufficient importance to these cults—top officials in Nairobi like to give out that there is no political significance in these incidents; they are "merely the result of religious frenzy." But people who have had to deal with them, such as some of the more thoughtful Commissioners in the Kavirondo and Kikuyu Reserves, assert that something very much more than politics is involved. They say—and from what I have learned myself I am sure they are right—that these fanatic religious cults which are now breaking out like boils all over the body politic of Africa come from something deep down, some common cause which is poisoning the blood-stream of the black continent, something so deep and desperate in the African's mind, his sub-consciousness, that to look at it for merely its possible political significance, its anti-European aspect, would be taking a superficial attitude. But whatever it is may be as hard to identify as what causes cancer.

Disillusion seems to be the common denominator of all these sects. They are characterised by a sort of blind yearning to get back to the old customs, back to the primitive; yet at the same time they are also characterised by a marked desire to find a new way to God, and that not via the white man. Some of them even preach that Christ was a European (a white man), a man of flesh and blood, with, of course, a European's attitude towards the African; and they refuse to accept Christ as the medium between them and God, but prefer the more mystical medium of the Holy Ghost. They are all based on the Old Testament, with its violence, lust and cruelty as part of the Christian religion—a *perversion*, for political motives, of an old indigenous form of primitive religion which has been helped by a natural tendency towards violence and disorder of an immoral nature. They've got a basis of indigenous ancestor-worship, allied to a deep-rooted religion of the pagan *Were* (god); and, superimposed on that, the basic Christian teaching, which, however, has been debased by using the Old Testament texts to appeal to the people—and the whole has been taken as a political weapon. I have used the word *Were* for a pagan god here, but that is merely the god of the Bukhusus, who live in Uganda, and I use it here because the Kitosh (who are also Bukhusus) of Kenya have adopted that god (in a sect I shall describe later on) as part of their political effort to get their part of the Kavirondo Reserve turned back to Uganda again. That is political. Local gods may be taken as different manifestations of the same god. There are twenty tribes in the North Kavirondo District today, only fourteen of which are Bantu; and non-Bantu tribes, which ordinarily would have completely different pagan gods—such as the Nilotic Luos, who comprise one-sixth of its population—are gradually, it seems, beginning to find a meeting ground in these fanatical religious cults. The Kitosh are pure Bantu.

Some of these cults, as far apart as the Nyanza Province and the Kikuyu Reserve, exchange visits and seem to be affiliated. Some have rival prophets, and one tribe in a district may accept a cult while its neighbor tribe despises them for it. But the whole affair is incontestably strengthened by the issue of Old Testament stories in the vernacular to local mission boys, which has given them the impression that Christian belief is nothing new to them, but merely coincides with their own previous practices, and is especially used to bolster up the evil of these. It is interesting to note that several of the ancient African beliefs had a conception of the Holy Trinity.

I have said before that I think it can be shown that too much of the early teaching of the African has been left in the hands of the missions. For one thing, it places too much importance on the part that religion actually plays in the white man's life. It has given him the wrong idea of us. The susceptible African soon sees that we do not follow the teachings of the God that we are trying to get him to believe in. Sensibly enough, he does not doubt that God; he doubts us, and he doubts especially that we have shown him the right way to God. We have deceived him even there.

As a result, the African, whom we have cut adrift, now seems to have lost his faith in everything. I might put it this way: the African has lost his faith in the white man's interpretation of God; he has lost his faith in the white man; he has even lost his faith in life; but he still wants to find his way to God.

I think that is very important. It is because we don't believe in God ourselves—not really (I am speaking here, of course, not of the missionaries, but of the European administration officers and especially of European businessmen)—that we do not attach enough importance to the African's yearning to have faith. It is the greatest harm we have done him. Nothing less than a widespread and proper education would, it seems, be able to restore the black man's faith in the white man and his good intentions. I even believe that, until we do find some real faith for ourselves (and I am not professedly a religious man), the African will never have faith in us. When we believe, then he will believe; and not before.

I surprise myself when I find that I am writing like this. Yet the evidence is so strong that I am on the right track that I want to give some of it to convince you. I want to give the analyses of some of these fanatic sects that have been made by the District Commissioners who have to deal with them, and try to understand what causes them—thoughtful men who have devoted a great deal of time and earnest thought to the study of this subject.

Before going on, I want to state what an African layman, Mr. Christian K. Dovlo, told the World Council of Christian Churches at Amsterdam, August 27th, 1948. He said that three tasks faced the African Church: to break down the danger of denominationalism within the Church, to find ways of beating the modern methods of the medicine-man and new forms of Heathen worship, to ensure that educated Africans abroad do not return to their own country feeling Christianity as practised in Europe and America is a "great hypocrisy" and that in Communism they can find "that universal brotherhood which Christianity preaches but rarely practises."

Mr. Dovlo said the African medicine-man was trying to meet the impact of Christianity by telling his followers that his "fetish" was exactly the same as Christianity, but that, in addition, he could offer "special medicine" to avert the "evil eye" or assure them children in marriage. This "racket" made them rich, and the juju-men often gave large sums for Christian purposes.

Be it noted that at that same conference the youth members, 100, from forty-eight countries, were provocative and downright in asserting their views that the Church has become a "middle-class" institution and no longer has any contact with the working people. So it is not only the African who distrusts the self-appointed interpreters—the priests and parsons—and would like to go to God without those clerics. Keeping these facts in mind will perhaps give more interest and integrity to the studies made by the District Commissioners of similar African feelings that I now give below. I quote mostly verbatim. First, about the Men of God, who murdered Police Inspector Mortimer:

Watu wa Mungu—the Men of God
(Report from Administration Department, Kiambu, 1942)

1. As the number of adherents of both branches of this sect appears to be increasing rapidly, and certain activities of theirs, though hardly criminal, might be embarrassing to Government at the present juncture, some report of their activities seems desirable.

2. There is not at present much difference between the two branches except that the Saturday branch (who call themselves "The Seventh Day") treat Saturday instead of Sunday as their Sabbath.

3. Both branches consider themselves to be prophets (*Arathi*) and claim that all their actions (conscious or unconscious) are in obedience to the Holy Spirit.

4. All male members of the Sunday branch wear white macintoshes and white turbans, and those of the Saturday branch wear *kanzu*-like garments (like nightgowns) with a sash around the waist and white turbans. The Saturday branch have a large Cross embroidered in red on their *kanzus* (on the breast) on one side of which is "S" and the other "D" in red.

5. So far there seems to be no rivalry or enmity between the two branches, but there is little, if any, collaboration. The tendency seems to be towards complete disassociation.

6. The Seventh Day appear to maintain some sort of liaison with a similar sect in the Nyanza Province, and they are visited from time to time by representatives of the latter (particularly, it is said, by the Marigoli and Kisii), who wear similar vestments.

7. The *Arathi* (prophets) of the present resuscitation of the sect differ in some respects from their predecessors in that they do not go so far in repudiating foreign institutions and foreign customs and manners. They wear clothes of foreign manufacture and they do not (for instance) object to travelling by 'bus or bicycle or to using aluminium cooking pots.

8. But they still retain some of their original antipathies. They rarely wear boots and shoes, and their buildings (including churches and schools) must be built of indigenous materials, and one of their precepts (preached, but not necessarily practised) is that money is the root of all evil.

9. In various other respects they take a middle course. They repudiate ordinary education, such as that obtainable at Mission

schools, but run schools of their own (at which red flags are flown) in which all the education given is religious and based largely on the Old Testament. Their use of drums in revival meetings, their assumption of the Divine Guidance in everyday affairs and their total immersion in Baptism suggest sheer imitation of the Salvation Army, Oxford Group and Primitive Methodism respectively. The wearing of beards by their leaders suggests imitation of Roman Catholicism, and the wearing of turbans—as well as beards—of Islam. "Roaring like young lions" is based on the Fifth Chapter of Isaiah and the like, to which the original *Arathi* are so addicted, is not so fashionable with the newcomers. The Seventh Day doubtless get their ideas about the Day of Rest from the Seventh Day Adventists at Kisii and elsewhere. Agapemone of free love is probably the only spontaneous rite not based on imitation.

10. Imitation, indeed, is the basis of their ritual, and the "back-to-Kikuyu" principles of their forerunners (who themselves found it impossible to formulate any attractive ritual from native custom alone) is less in evidence. They even repudiate certain indigenous customs. Female initiation (circumcision?) apparently matters little one way or the other, and the use of alcohol and the "eating" of blood—Masai fashion—both well established in Kikuyu custom, are forbidden. So apparently is the payment of bride-price.

11. Authority is not officially flouted. The modern *Arathi* do not (as did their predecessors) carry bows and arrows for the symbolic destruction of evil spirits. The reason is that the Authority forbids the carrying of arms. They do not, in so many words, refuse to do Communal work, because Authority requires its performance. They render to Caesar the things that are Caesar's, and to God the things that are God's, but there is some difference of opinion between them and Authority as to which is which. When, for instance, there is Communal work to be done in one place, the *Arathi* are led by the Holy Ghost to visit another. The dictates of Authority, in fact, must be obeyed until they differ from the directions of the Holy Ghost, in which case the latter must prevail. Up to now the Holy Ghost would rarely appear to see eye to eye with Authority (the Kenya Government).

12. It is in this fact that the *Arathi* are likely to prove themselves an embarrassment to Government. Certain Europeans in the Limuru area (including Father Doody) believe that they actually discourage the flow of labor. They certainly show no sign of encouraging themselves in any beneficial occupation, whether inside or outside the native lands.

13. The *Arathi* offer a passive resistance to foreign medical aid and methods of disease prevention. They avoid inoculation against plague and take no part in killing rats.

14. They have leaders who are apparently considered High Priests. Some of these live in seclusion and never leave their huts except, perhaps, during darkness. Their meals are taken in to them by their followers.

15. Nothing the *Arathi* say may be permitted to prevent a *Murathi's* obedience to the directions he has received from the Holy Spirit, and if any person (a chief, for instance) puts any obstacle in the way, he is liable to be hurt. If anyone is killed in such a case, the *Murathi* marks the sign of a cross in blood on the deceased's forehead and all is well (with the *Murathi*). It is said that such talk induces the unsophisticated to part with their money on demand and to take no action against the recovery of girls who go unendowered to the leaders of the cult.

16. It is not immediately easy to understand why the *Arathi* attract so many followers. Perhaps the psychological background is simply a release reaction to the increasing complexity of life and the increasing competition for success in the new Kikuyu conditions. This may explain the *Arathis'* partial return to the simple life, their repudiation of education, and their desire to avoid outside influences while at the same time bringing themselves to public notice and satisfying their egoism without great effort. A religious compulsion provides an adequate sanction for non-conformity with custom, ancient and modern. We should not find it surprising that some such attempt at release should manifest itself from time to time when we consider how very rapidly a new and much more complex economic system requiring a more exacting struggle for existence and an individual effort no longer capable of a merger in a communal responsibility has overwhelmed a primitive African tribe.

17. However that may be, there is no doubt that the people concerned could hardly have chosen a more effective method of self-protection from the normal consequences of non-co-operation with the Government and their tribe than that of the justification of faith.

Paragraphs 16 and 17 hold the clue to the subsequent developments of these peculiar religious sects. I cite this report in full because it not only gives one the kernels of many an incident that happened afterwards, but because it also shows a brittle wit on the part of the District Commissioner and a thoughtful and compassionate mind. The report is as revealing of himself and his type as it is of the people he is trying to understand and report upon. A good D.C. is really the father and mother of the people under him; he can afford to be altruistic where, more often than not, a hard-pressed settler feels he can't. And, being part of the same social life as the settlers themselves, it very often requires great courage for a D.C. to take the part of the African against the feelings of the settlers in the district. Yet, almost without exception, they invariably do it. Thus, in a Crown Colony, the Colonial Office and its officers in Africa and elsewhere is always the final arbiter between the white man and the colored. When you consider that the District Commissioner at Kakamega has more Africans under him than the population of many a British colony which has a Governor, you can also get some idea of the responsibility and scope of their activities. The African population of the North Kavirondo District was given in 1946 as 475,852; this is greater than that of Bermuda, Barbados, the Bahamas, British Honduras and the Leeward Islands combined. Or compare it with the 300,000 Negroes in New York's Harlem. I think that, if the pay and pension could be made sufficient, many a Colonial officer would prefer to remain as a D.C. rather than go on to the higher, more exclusive rank of Provincial Commissioner; the D.C.'s become very fond of the natives they are dealing with and like to stay close to them.

This thoughtful report also shows how the *Watu wa Mungu* were only mildly evasive people in 1942; they were even not carrying the symbolic bows and arrows, because the Authority had forbidden the carrying of arms, and they were wearing European clothes. But by 1947 the *Watu wa Mungu* had gone back to wearing skins—hence the name "skin-men"—and they were carrying swords, the Kikuyu *semis*, with the intention of using them.

Thomas Dominic Mortimer, twenty-seven years old, was a newcomer to police work and had only just been made an assistant inspector—not a particularly high post, as natives also hold such rank in the police. He seems to have had a very poor understanding of native character. When he heard that there was trouble at Gatundu village, some twenty miles north of Kiambu, he went out there directly, taking only six native constables with him. For some strange reason, he split that force, taking three with him into the village and leaving three on its outskirts. This, I was told, was so that in case he met real trouble some of them could get back and report it. Then this brave man entered the Kikuyu village. Here is a report of what then took place, given at the trial of seventeen Kikuyu who were suspected as having taken part in his murder and in that of two African constables:

Assistant-Inspector Peter Mwami (an African) of the Gatundu Police Post, testifying before the Nairobi Magistrate, told how he and four other African police, armed with three rifles and twenty-five rounds of ammunition—all the arms and ammunition available at the post—and two *semis*, encountered a party of the "skin-men" on the Gatundu road. This was after a report had been made that a native had been wounded.

"I asked the leader of the party, the Man in Red, what his name was," the inspector continued. "He replied: 'Ask God my name.' He then told me I had better go away, adding that 'you Government people wearing uniform are the people who are preventing us from growing up in our religion.' He said that the police badge I was wearing was useless and that the 'crown' he wore in his red hat was empowered by God.

"I told him to tell his people to put down their *semis*, otherwise I would fire. The Man in Red retorted: 'It would be a wonderful thing if God were defeated by you Satans!' The 'skin-men' then began singing and praying and later advanced towards us. I told my constables to stand still, but when I realised I had no authority to open fire I asked them to retreat."

The Magistrate: "Why do you say that you had no right to fire?" "I thought I might be mistaken, because they had not attacked us."

"You now know you had as much right to fire as anybody else?" "Yes."

The Magistrate then said that he would not like people in the court to get the wrong impression of the powers of an African police officer: "I think it might have a detrimental effect on some of the audience [obviously the Africans] if they thought he had no right to fire."

The African police inspector then continued to tell how he and his police retired as the "skin-men" advanced, singing and stopping from time to time to pray (it can be imagined what a strain this must have been on the worried inspector's nerves, and how plucky he was). He then related how the "skin-men" took a side road towards a banana plantation, and whistled, whereupon other people dressed in skins rushed out to join them, after which the whole company—about thirty people—returned to the main road.

"I stood still with my *askaris,* and after five minutes the people retired to the village. I did not follow them, as I was expecting help from Kiambu.

"About fifteen minutes later Chief Muhoho arrived and asked me to go to the village, but I refused. The Chief then sent one of his tribal police to the village, and on his return he reported that the 'skin-men' had disappeared." This was where the ambush was prepared.

"I suggested that it would be a good idea to find out in which direction they had gone, and with Chief Muhoho and my party I went up the hill to the village. In one of the three huts were women dressed in skins. The Chief asked them where the men had gone, but the women remained silent.

"Two red flags—one bearing the words *Oben Heben*—were flying from the roofs of the other huts. Inside the hut were drums, skins and other objects."

The inspector said he had just started to break into the third hut when Assistant-Inspector Mortimer arrived. It was then that the "skin-men" burst from their hiding place: the ambush had worked.

"Mr. Mortimer turned to face the people," the witness went on. "One of the first people to reach him had his *semi* upraised. Mr. Mortimer fired his pistol at him. The first shot missed, but the second shot hit the native and I saw him stagger and fall. Three others then rushed at Mr. Mortimer; one got behind him and raised his *semi* to strike, but I hit him with my *rungu* before the blow was delivered. . . .

"I heard the swish of a *semi* behind me and a *semi* struck my tarbush and my greatcoat, which I was carrying folded across my shoulder. The crowd pushed me down and rushed towards Mr. Mortimer. I did not see him any more. I was about to get up, but as there were bullets flying about I decided to keep down. I saw and heard the Man in Red singing through a megaphone. He was going to and fro between the huts. I could only make out the name 'Samuel' in what he was singing.

"I later made enquiries concerning the whereabouts of Mr. Mortimer. I thought he had probably been killed."

This is a vivid enough vignette of the Men of God in action, and of that sinister little scene with the red flags flying on the thatched huts. When the body of Assistant-Inspector Mortimer was found, one *semi* slash had split his face across the mouth; another, across his eyes, had laid his brains open; there was a spear wound in his back. The body of a native was also found, hideously mutilated. The wounded native who was the cause of all this was a native tailor who had refused to make a red flag for the "skin-men" a few days before, saying that he had not the time. The Man in Red and his followers had dragged him out of a native hotel—a mud-and-wattle hut—and slashed his hand almost off with a *semi*. He was not killed, as I had been told at Thika, but he was told that it was "Jehovah's sword" which had cut him, and that he was being marched along the road to execution so that the "skin-men" could "wash in his blood." The arrival of Inspector Mortimer had saved him from that. "God's orders have cut you," the Man in Red told him.

For this crime four of the accused Men of God were sentenced to death at Nairobi on June 25th, two, under the age of eighteen, were ordered to be detained at the Governor's pleasure, and the remaining eleven were acquitted. But if the pursuing party of Europeans, led by an ex-Palestine policeman and including the D.C. from Fort Hall, had ever come up with the twenty-two *Watu wa Mungu* as they were fleeing up the Thika River—"if they had put up any resistance to arrest at all we would have brought back twenty-two corpses," I was told by one man who was in that expedition. This police search-party put their own lives in jeopardy during the extensive comb-out of thick forests. The Man in Red was caught on the Nyeri road, but six of the "skin-men" were only captured several days later on the slopes of Mt. Kenya, half starved and dead beat. The first thing they did was to beg their captors for food and water, which was given to them. It should also be said that most of the Kikuyus in the reserve joined in the hunt for the "skin-men" who had been terrorising them.

Perhaps the most sinister thing in connection with an outbreak of these fanatical religious cults is the quickness with which it subsides, its perpetrators feeling hardly any guilt. I was not there, but I can imagine the mute and obedient way in which they accompanied their captors back to jail. They at once become fatalists—it is "the Will of God" that they have been caught; and from then on they adopt a humble attitude. In the Kakamega Hospital I saw five natives there who were recovering from bullet wounds received in the riot in which the eleven other natives had been killed when they attacked Superintendent Walker and his party. They looked supremely unconscious of having done anything wrong. They were not locked up in a separate room, but were either lying on their coats—those still too weak to walk—or they were strolling about the ward. It would have been impossible to pick them out from any of the other patients had not they been pointed out to me. One had been shot through the back of the neck, by Superintendent Walker, I believe, and at close range; so there was little chance for *him* to claim that he had been only a bystander, as some of them did. When the surgeon was explaining how close the bullet came to his spinal column, he just sat there in stupefied submission. Easily excited, the African is just as quick to calm down, and it is impossible to tell which way he is going to go. Even he doesn't know. The six Kikuyus caught up on the slopes of Mt. Kenya in a deep and difficult forest, who immediately asked their captors for food and water, quite confident that they were going to get it, had only five days before been singing this song, when they thought that everything was going well with them:

"*What are you waiting for? Let us wash in the blood of men. What are you waiting for? The time is over.*"

It is folly to try to assert that these cults have no political significance. Their aim to escape white supervision, to get back to the past, is in itself political; it means that they are an influence in the reserve which would block the supply of labor from that reserve. And that is about as serious a political platform as any African could adopt in East Africa. When, as the D.C. says in the above report, they can link this with a faith, then "they could hardly have chosen a more effective method of self-protection from the normal consequences of non-co-operation with the

Government." And each one of these sects is liable to the most murderous flare-ups if the right sort of Prophet comes along. This is exactly what happened when Elijah Masendi was liberated from the Mathari Mental Hospital in 1945 to go back into the Kavirondo Reserve: he had a cult of his own going within six months.

Mohammed was an epileptic. I think that a study of the subject would show that most of the world's great prophets have been slightly mad. Dostoevsky claimed that for a few minutes on the eve of his seizures he always had a transcendent vision of the world and its beauty such as he never attained in his normal state, a "vision" which almost prostrated him. In the North Kavirondo Reserve there had long been established a cult known as *Dini ya Roho,* the Cult of the Holy Ghost. It was founded in 1916 by a native named Alfayo, who "dreamed" and was visited by *Roho,* the Holy Ghost. The leading group of the adherents of *Roho* lived at Masenda in South Wanga. They were Luos (a Nilotic race), and the Wanga of that district (a pure Bantu tribe) despised *Roho* and all it stood for. The Luos are not a particularly warlike people and their little cult was a comparatively harmless affair. Alfayo made known his dreams, but the movement died down and was not revived again until 1935, when a native named Lowe also began to dream and have visitations, after which the movement became firmly established. And a branch of the *Watu wa Roho* sprang up in the Marigoli district which promised to be a much more troublesome affair; they wore crimson *kanzus* (that garment like a nightgown) and beards, and gave every indication that this religious spark which had lighted in their district might one day flame up into a serious conflagration.

In the report which the D.C. of North Kavirondo wrote on the *Watu wa Roho* in 1942, he says that the two Elders or High Priests at Masenda were men of "quite respectful demeanor," that "the community always pay their taxes at first call and are law-abiding in every way," and that when he asked them were their teachings in any way anti-European, the two Elders replied "in the negative, adding that if they were they would not use European clothes, hats, boots, or advise their people to pay their taxes early and obey all Government orders." The two men I talked to were adherents of the C.M.S. (Church Missionary Society) previously, and I asked them in what way their present faith differs from the C.M.S. Their reply was to this effect:

"In the C.M.S. we were taught to worship Christ, but the 'influence' was not strong enough to prevent people sinning. We prayed for guidance, and the visitations advised us to worship the spirit which would be the stronger influence. We believe in God and His Son Christ, but we worship the Spirit." But in the same report I see that he says that the *Watu wa Roho* told him that they do not believe that Christ was the Son of God, but was a European (a white man) and a man of flesh and blood and not different from any other human. The son of one of these High Priests was a soldier in the Pioneers, yet the brother of the other High Priest—Paulo Rangenja—had gone into seclusion some years back (from 1942) and had now become the strongest "medium" for the *Watu wa Roho* between them and God. An interesting thing about this medium is that his "dreams" have been written down and have rapidly taken the place of all other religious literature among the *Roho;* yet this "Record," says the D.C., is "written in some language which is not known to any other person I have shown it to, including literate Africans." The *Roho* apparently can read this unknown tongue. Somewhat like Christian Science, this medium asserted that *Watu wa Roho* did not need any medicine, "for the Spirit can cure all."

The High Priest and Elders of the Masenda *Roho* wear a white *kanzu* and on their left breast have the letter "S" with a cross between it, and the image of a spear-head in red; the "S" stands for the Luo word *singiruk*, which means a binding oath, and its use in connection with religion probably denotes that its wearer has taken his vows; the spear-head is said to symbolise the spear which killed their leader, Alfayo, in the riots which broke out at Masenda in 1935.

Characteristic of their ceremonies is the drum-beating and frenzy and all the noise they can make at prayer. They prohibit smoking and intoxicating drink. They pay the bride-price, but do not recognise more than a second wife, although a new adherent with many wives may be accepted and not required to reduce their number, provided he is a faithful follower of *Roho*. They do not shake hands with one another, as they say that during the process the sins of one man may be transmitted from his hand to another. They use Saturday as the day of worship, though they say it was a divine direction and not imitation of the Seventh Day Adventists which caused them to adopt it. And now we come to the place where even this law-abiding sect begins to show its political aspect.

"It was not admitted to me by the two elders," says the D.C. in his report, "but other information indicates that there is a belief among them that many of our actions and words are not genuine and in the native interest, though we say so. An example given was in connection with the present immunisation of cattle from rinderpest. We tell them that it is a benevolent act for their benefit, but they say that it is merely a ruse so as to obtain accurate account of the cattle for commandeering purposes." For any layman who does not understand African conditions, let me state that the natives always violently oppose any count of their cattle, because they think (and on many occasions they have been right) that it is the prelude to the Government forcing them to make a willing sale of their surplus—the amount of cattle beyond that which the Government thinks the reserve can safely carry. When I was in Kavirondo this last time, the natives at Kericho and surrounding districts were even then trying to avoid such a tally.

When Elijah Masendi was liberated from the insane asylum, he began to form his new sect, and in June 1947, he went underground. He had originally been a native court interpreter, but had gone wrong and been prosecuted on one or two occasions: for being part of a small group, not a sect, which had tried to get rid of a local chief, and also for taking part in the burning down of three Salvation Army buildings, for which he had been certified in 1945. He was liberated after only six months at the Mathari Mental Hospital, owing to the intercession of the "Prison Visitors," despite the almost violent protest of the Provincial Commissioner, who did not trust Masendi's relatives and other natives who had gone his bond. A month or so after he got back into the North Kavirondo area the D.C. there heard that this madman had announced that he was a Prophet, and that he had started a new religious sect called *Dini ya Msambwa,* the Cult of the Good Spirits. A district that had been remarkably quiet during Masendi's incarceration began to give trouble: there was a large outbreak of female circumcision, for one thing—one old woman of fifty was circumcised—which had been on the way to dying out as a custom after the Local Native Council had passed a resolution prohibiting it.

Masendi managed to avoid direct trouble for nearly two years, but when he put on his white, blue-trimmed robe with the "I.H.S." on the back, it was said that he became quite mad. He said that he had a promise from God that He would send a Black Christ if Elijah could succeed in liquidating all the Europeans from his area. He went about with a dozen or so men whom he called his Apostles, and held meetings, not only in the Kavirondo Reserve, but up in Trans Nzoia on the farms of the European settlers at Kitale, Hoey's Bridge, and even over in Uganda. At one time he had a hide-out in a cave on one of the steepest slopes of Mt. Elgon, from which he could look down on the very police parties and farmers who were most anxious to catch him, of which more later on. He may have been mad, but he was most certainly not stupid. One of the first things he did to show his power was to inform the illiterate and credulous natives that he could lead them to places where the British had planted "medicine" to keep the Africans weak. He led a crowd of 2,000 natives to a surveyor's beacon. Not even many white people know that it is sometimes the custom of surveys to put their findings in bottles and plant them under the beacon bearings. Elijah went there with his excited crowd, told them to dig, and lo!—there was the bottle and inside it the paper with its cryptic markings. For another example of his astuteness, Masendi, like the witch doctors Dr. Dovlo warned the Amsterdam Conference of the Churches about, took the Christian religion, took a pagan god, and added some of his own "medicine" on top of *that* combination. Coming into a region which had already become used to cults, such as *Roho*, he went then one better. He wore "I.H.S." on his back, like a Catholic priest, carried a Bible with him; but said that he was Elijah, the Prophet of the Bukhusu god *Were*, in contradiction to the Christ of the Christian faith. (And here, as I shall show, he was on a sound political wicket.) But first something about his new religion, the Cult of *Msambwa*.

The origin of the cult is in the belief that after a man dies his spirit continues to live. (Spirit = *Amusambwa:* plural, *Msambwa.*) This spirit is more powerful than the living man and is said to be the cause of all the luck, good or bad, that befalls the family of the deceased man. (In this way he is not changing much from an ordinary witch doctor.) The family periodically propitiate the *Amusambwa* by offering sacrifices or consulting the witch doctor. They very often sacrifice a goat or some other not-too-expensive animal. This *Msambwa* spirit does not seem to have been evil, as is usually the case with a conventional spirit, but to have supreme power over mortals. The witch doctors of the *Msambwa* Cult differ from their less advanced brothers of the traditional type by becoming something like the Delphic oracle—or Elijah Masendi himself. This ancestor or spirit worship was then identified by Masendi with some famous and possibly legendary warriors.

I will not give the names of all of them, but Nalukali is supposed to be the ancestor of the Bukhusu tribe over in Uganda. And Masendi presumably picked that god to be the prophet of, as he knew that possibly he could get his strongest converts from among the Kitosh-Bukhusu, a tribe that had been split in two when the Kenya-Uganda frontier had been laid down, and who in recent years have been agitating to have their section of the Kavirondo Reserve handed back to Uganda, which is a predominantly native country. It was the Kitosh, I may say here, who attacked and tried to kill Superintendent Walker and his police *askaris.*

This god of the Bukhusu is all-powerful and works through three "messengers," *Were* Mrumbi, *Were* Makkoba, *Were* Khakaba. Each of these gods performs a different role within the character of the Bukhusu *Were*, or the main god, and are thus a kind of Trinity. The long eight- or nine-foot rod that the Cult of *Msambwa* carry, split into three prongs at the tip, is the symbol of this Trinity. They were carrying these rods when they invaded the Catholic Mission at Kababii, screaming and singing words to the effect that "Europeans have long since troubled us. Now we have got our own God."

These three that make up the Trinity are good gods; but the *Msambwa* also have two bad gods, an evil god of land and a jinx for river or water. And all this, as I have said, is built upon the lusty foundation of the Old Testament, with all its violence, lust and vengeance. This cult's faith goes a long way back; in fact, some books, i.e. *Hebrewism in Africa*, identify the Bukhusu's *Were* with Yahweh. And this belief is fortified by a tradition of the Bukhusu that they were long ago led out of a country to the north in flight. They came to a sea they could not cross, but they were swallowed by a frog and spewed out on the other side. Another version of the Red Sea story, and equally believable.

It can be seen that Elijah, the Prophet of the Bukhusu god, had come a long way since he was a Mission boy at the Friends African Mission, those gentle Quakers. With this pantheon of deities, he seems to have appointed himself to represent just about everything. And in June 1947, this so-called lunatic and his sect (it must be remembered that he was *discharged* from the Mathari Mental Hospital) held a meeting at Lugulu of some 5,000 people. Now, Lugulu is the place where the fighting Kitosh made a last stand against the British. The remains of the old Kitosh fort are still there. The meeting of the *Dini ya Msambwa* at that particular spot coupled a glorification of the historical last stand of the Kitosh warriors against the invading British force under Captain Hobley with an instant anti-British feeling. To have picked the site of this old fort, so reminiscent of departed glories, was good politics, to say the least.

The District Commissioner of North Kavirondo, when he heard of this mass meeting, immediately asked the chief of that district to bring Elijah down to meet him at Kimilili camp. "When I got there I found a note from Elijah saying he was unable to come. I went to his house and found it empty. I have never seen him alone until he was recently arrested." This was the testimony the D.C. gave at the Kakamega inquest when I was there. The D.C. gave orders to the police to bring Elijah in. From June 1947, until March 1948, Elijah the Prophet was "on the run." At one time his trackers thought that they had come up with him, trapped in a cave in the Mt. Elgon region overlooking some European farms. They were sure he was inside: but when they entered he was nowhere to be found. Then, so one of that party told me, "we noticed what appeared to be a blunted pyramid that for some strange reason rose up from the floor of the cave. And when we scaled it we saw that Elijah could reach a hole in the cave's roof, which we had not noticed before, and through that haul himself up and escape into the bush, into the back country—which is exactly what he had done!" Elijah was clever. He was not present at the threatening advance upon the fathers of the Catholic Mission at Kababii nor when eleven of his followers were shot and killed in the attack upon Superintendent Walker and his police at Malakisi.

The Catholic fathers at that Mission must have been extraordinary people. One of them had actually taken a photograph of the 1,000 or so natives as they advanced across the lawn, spears waving, drums beating, horns blowing; a frenzied mob whose leaders were bearing aloft those sinister 9-foot, three-pronged papyrus rods in symbol of the Trinity. It was about as macabre a photo as I have ever looked at. "They were singing and dancing, unbalanced and disorderly," in the words of the Kisumu Magistrate who took the testimony at Kakamega. The holy fathers had been warned the day before that there was a likelihood of their coming. Now they stood inside the Mission and watched the crowd hold an excited meeting: though it finally decided to do nothing—not just then. But the district was "up."

The D.C. was playing tennis at Kakamega when this news reached him at 5.30 P.M. He at once assembled one of his District Officers and an Assistant-Inspector of the Kakamega police and drove the forty-six miles out to the Mission with a small force of *askaris* and tribal police. At midnight he telephoned Kisumu for police reinforcements and Superintendent Walker went out to Kababii the next morning. One section of the small force—I think it numbered only thirty all told—was sent to Malakisi to protect a Salvation Army Officer living there with his wife and family, who had had trouble before with the natives. The D.C. held a meeting of the local chiefs and told them that meetings of the *Dini ya Msambwa* were forbidden in the future without written permission from him. At that meeting of the chiefs, one of them came to him and said that he had just heard that a meeting was being held even then, of some 500 *Msambwas*, at a nearby place called Sangolo. And the D.C. went there!

Here he found men and women stripped naked, rolling on the

ground in a frenzy and frothing at the lips. I heard him give his testimony and it was exemplary of him and his kind that he stood there and talked to these frenzied people for about an hour, until he partially pacified them. He is a Cambridge Double Blue himself and a quiet man; and, as I understood it, he just stood there and talked to them about religion. They started to disperse, but before they had gone 100 yards their leaders managed to get them into a frenzy again: "And so, as I did not want to hurt anybody if I could help it, we formed the police into a line and 'walked them away.'" It is in little statements like that, given in a casual manner, with the Magistrate taking down every word of the testimony in long-hand (as is still the custom in East Africa), that you sometimes get your sharpest picture of what it means to be an administrative officer over such a dark and unstable population. That mob of 500 frenzied natives had its drums going and its leaders inciting it to stand firm, even attack, but . . . "we walked them away."

That took cold courage. These disturbances had been going on since February 7th. On the morning of February 11th, at Malakisi, Superintendent Walker arrived on the scene just as a huge mob of the *Dini ya Msambwa* was marching on the Police Post there with the evident intention of rescuing three natives detained there in connection with the Kababii Mission disturbance. The Indian store-keepers at Malakisi rushed up to Superintendent Walker, telling him that they were frightened of the crowd; then immediately cried: "Oh, here they come!" There were only four Kenya police and three tribal in the Government Camp. The crowd already assembled with sticks and drums was surging into it. Walker spoke to the crowd in Swahili and a corporal of his police translated into Kitosh. This was met by cries of "Let's go forward" and "We cannot be stopped by these people; they are nothing," and shouts of "The Europeans are troubling us. It is better to kill them."

Superintendent Walker is fifty-five years old, and he had never fired on a native crowd before. He stood there with his handful of native police lined up behind him. The crowd rushed him and he went down under a blow as one man tried to wrench his revolver away from him. He got to his feet and shot that man. A rifle had been taken from one of his *askaris*, and with this Superintendent Walker was again hit over the head. As he fell to the ground, he gave the order to fire. . . .

He said to me, as he sat there smoking a cigar, waiting his turn to testify at Kakamega: "I don't even know now whether I even shouted '*Pega!*' which is the order to fire. Bless me, I was so groggy I hardly knew I was on the ground. My revolver was all dusty afterwards, so I know I must have been." Some thirty-two shots were fired by his police *askaris;* seven natives were killed outright and four more died in the Kakamega hospital. Walker, although seriously wounded, got to his feet and directed the fire until he saw the crowd begin to break and disperse. Then he stopped it. The Magistrate's summing-up said:

"This officer has been in the police for twenty-five years, and he has never before fired on a crowd. He showed great restraint and courage. All witnesses are unanimous that he withheld fire until the last possible moment, and that the small detachment of police would have been murdered if they had not fired."

"A fourteen-year-old girl (ninth witness) has given evidence how she was initiated into the sect" is also included in his summing up. "On February 9th she and others were told in a meeting that the next day they should go to the Government Camp at Malakisi and find out why the *askaris* had come. The preacher said that they would have to fight Europeans if there were any with the African *askaris.* Also it was preached that bullets fired at them would be only water. The girl probably believed it until a bullet grazed her shoulder the next day."

Superintendent Walker was taken to the hospital at Kakamega.

Elijah Masendi was caught on February 16th, with several of his followers, outside the cave which had been dug for him at a place called Chesamis. He gave himself up without any trouble, although he had a following of 200 to 300 men. By order of the Governor-in-Council, Elijah and three others have been deported to live in the old Arab settlement of Lamu, an island off the coast of East Africa above Mombasa. The Cult of *Msambwa* has been proscribed. But a new cult, the *Dini ya Mboja*, has sprung up among the Kipsigis of the Kericho (European tea-growing) district. This has also just been proscribed, and its followers will be prosecuted.

It may be argued that I have attached too much importance to these sects. I don't think so, and I think that most of the D.C.'s, etc., in Kenya will agree with me; at any rate, most of them did when I was there. The political aspect of these cults has already been made plain from the three that I have just described. And, shielded by that mantle of being a religious cult, these sects can go a long way—right up to the riot point—before the political reason for any outbreak is disclosed. Meanwhile, as the D.C. of Kiambu said in his report, the African native could hardly have conceived a more effective method of self-protection for not co-operating with the Government.

In some parts of the South Marigoli District in the Kavirondo Reserve, the population is over 900 to the square mile. I have stood on one plot of land in that territory where four families were trying to make a living, and making it, on 2¼ acres. I know this statement will be challenged by the incredulous, and I do not blame them. Let me give the exact location: it is among a maze of grey boulders in which the Kavirondo are huddled like rabbits, on a 47-degree slope, at a place called Lotego, near Majengo, in South Marigoli—four families in four huts; twenty-five people, on 2¼ acres, planted in cassava, sorghum and early maize. I don't say this is typical of the Kavirondo Reserve; far from it. But I do say that the inability to redress such a shocking example of destitution at once does show the conditions which must exist in the remainder of that alarmingly overcrowded and worked-out reserve. As one Agricultural Officer who heard I had been at this place exclaimed bitterly:

"We can sit on the safety-valve for so long. But that is all we are doing. Something *big* has got to be done, *and not in the reserves.* The only answer is the alienation of big blocks of land for big schemes, using machinery. It is useless to tell Europe that the native way of agriculture is insufficient unless you give him the land where he can cultivate in European fashion. At the present moment, if all the land in this reserve was cultivated by the natives in the very best type of smallholdings, it could just barely give a living to the present population, but it takes no account whatever of the future."

The British, in the vast Nyanza Province, are working at high pressure in what could be called at least the most advanced *effort* possible to raise the standard of life and safety of some 1,500,000 native Africans. So far as the native is concerned, the Nyanza Province is the greatest grain-growing territory in all Kenya; its war effort was sensational. Yet—and I quote from the foreword to Mr. Norman Humphrey's report on the sociological and agricultural problems of North Kavirondo, and he is the *Senior Agricultural Officer of Kenya*—the people "as a whole, are on the border line of mass destitution. In another generation, if the present trend continues, distress is certain to prevail. *And there can be now little doubt that this same trend is operative in most of the native lands of Kenya. . . .*" [My italics.] The foreword asserts:

> Above all, we must get the common people on our side, and this will mean a social revolution—a revolution which will take our authoritarian set-up back to where it started, at least to somewhere fairly near it. For only thus shall we induce the tribesmen once again to take that living, active, co-operative interest in their own concerns without which all the efforts of the expert will be in vain.

This brings us back again to what I said about the greatest problem in Kenya being the psychological one: to find some way in which to come to grips with the native's mind, in order to be able to persuade him to believe once again (if he ever did) in the white man and his good intentions. "Our Chiefs and agricultural instructors can perhaps command compliance (till their backs are turned)," this foreword concludes, "but they cannot command co-operation." These are not my words nor, in the last sentence, are they my parentheses, but I think that that statement, coming from the Chief Agricultural Officer of Kenya, is sufficient to prove how only too often visitors to Kenya are shown an example of compliance as an example of native co-operation. Kenyans even accept this false face themselves. And that is what puts off the big, all-embracing plans that are demanded by the circumstances. The truths are not faced.

CHAPTER XIX

Kakamega

KAKAMEGA is a beautiful place. Its high rainfall makes it one of the greenest districts in Kenya. The golf-course there is famous throughout East Africa. Its greens are real grass, close-knit, clipped smooth as the baize on a billiard table. All the big championship matches are played there. It is not at all an uncommon sight to see H.E.'s (the Governor's) black car streaking at 70 m.p.h. across the Great Rift Valley from Nairobi; so that he can captain a team of East Kenya against the West at Kakamega. The golf "greens" in Nairobi are just circular discs of pressed bare earth. Kakamega stands on a ridge. The site of the D.C.'s home and those of his three European District Officers, with the Doctor's house, set in their wide green lawns, were all once the center of a big forest experimental station. Immense towering blue gum trees, with their mottled, scaly trunks, shade the flowered gardens; romping children play with their *ayahs* under the beautiful Cape chestnut trees. An avenue of towering gums flanks the road where it runs down the hill to the corrugated iron roofs of the Indian *dukas* in the bazaar, with their Singer sewing-machines always humming at full speed on the sidewalk (I counted thirty-three at work one morning), and the secretive Somali village of stock-traders where the almond-eyed girls flirt with you, half-veiled, with pouting lips, and the soccer team of Kakamega Township's Africans is playing the Africans from the Rosterman Gold Mines. The soil is Devon red. And a ring of misty blue hills surrounds Kakamega in the distance. It is, without a doubt, one of the most salubrious posts that a D.C. can get on the entire African continent.

The D.C., Cambridge Double Blue, a quiet and unruffled man, proceeds along the line of that truest of sayings, "If your Reserves are healthy, your Colony is healthy," and is a man who firmly believes and lives up to the precept that a District Commissioner must be the very father and mother of the people entrusted to his care. It is a sight to see the everlasting crowd—it never seems to get smaller—of the half-hundred or so people who are always waiting to see him. To a newcomer on the scene it always looks as if something unusual is happening. But it isn't. This same scene is enacted outside a D.C.'s office everywhere in Kenya, every day. Also, there seems something ominous in those mute, poker-faced creatures who are waiting their turn to go in. But there isn't. The odds are that it will be the most trivial complaint. Or it may be for some advice: a son who ran away, and the D.C.'s advice and help are being asked for (with touching confidence) so that he may be found; a cow has been stolen or a wife has run off; an old man who wants to go "straight to the top" to explain why he should not be asked to pay the 19*s*. poll tax. Or it might be just the opposite: the piteous wife of a Goanese clerk who has taken cyanide because he found that his accounts were going to be investigated; or the D.C. is writing a letter to England to the relations of a schoolmaster (European), who also took cyanide for reasons of his own. (Both these things happened a considerable time before I got there: cyanide is easily obtained in a region where there are so many gold mines.) Or it may be just a chief who has known the D.C. for years and has come in for the pleasure and privilege of having a good gab with him. A nun has come in from a nearby Mission, dressed in spotless white and wearing a white solar topi; she leaves a pale-faced young novitiate in the Ford station-wagon while she goes in to see the D.C. An Englishwoman, settler's wife, comes to the *boma* to get her mail, and loses her fox-terrier in the D.C.'s office: he won't come out. All these must be seen and satisfied. The crowd stands in mute, expectant silence. The happiest figures, one morning when I went over to see "Ngomby" Williams, were a ring of twenty-two convicts from the big red prison at Kakamega who were sitting on the square of greensward before the D.C.'s office, having a happy little chat. Later, I would see gangs of them building roads around Kakamega. They always struck me as being weak: they don't work very hard, not even cutting lawns. That morning a European settler came in, presumably to consult the D.C. as to the best way of discharging a new English pupil-assistant he had just hired.

"Fancy!" he said to me. "The fool asked: 'But where do I get my *dancing?*'

"I told him Nairobi.

"He came back and said: 'But you've got to be *introduced* to the girls in Nairobi!'

" 'What the hell did you expect?' I told him. Then I said: 'Listen, mister. Africa is no place for you. You've come to the wrong address.' *Dancing*—be God! The fool had to have his *dancing!*"

The D.C. and his three new European District Officers, slightly helped by two of the new African Assistant District Officers, the Welfare Officer, Revenue, Agricultural, Marketing and Health Officers, handle this bag of mixed complaints and petitioners for advice every day. The Secretary of the Local Native Council (flippant young man) is at the tail-end of most African complaints, and a highly efficient Goanese clerk, wearing an expensive gold wrist-watch, bedevils some half-dozen ambitious Africans into keeping some sort of order in the office work of the *boma*. The "machine" goes on: the greenness, the shade, the quiet; the sighing gum trees, hedges of flowering poinsettia and scented frangipani; boys cutting the grass with their long-handled sickles or clipping the box-like hedges of the *macrolapa* bush; the heat. The D.C., sweating as the sun climbs over the blue hills, puts on his topi and drives home in his Ford *safari* car to have a good breakfast. Eating is one of the pleasures of Africa, although the food is seldom exciting. Heat seems to have burnt the taste out of everything before it could get to a stove. You are living in one. . . .

The Union Jack hangs listlessly over it all.

The D.C.'s three new District Officers, bottom rung of the Colonial officers' ladder, were a young man who had been a brigadier at thirty-two and who had commanded a battalion of Nigerians with Wingate's Chindits, a one-eyed test pilot, with a black patch over the other, who had fought in the Battle of Britain and who had been shot down in Burma as a squadron leader, a young, curly-haired captain from the Ulster Rifles—all keen as mustard on their jobs.

Their duties demanded quickness of perception and the ability to improvise without looking about for a precedent. The ex-test pilot, who had also flown Hurricanes at Malta, was helping the P.W.D. and the Maize Control officers at Kisumu to select sites for building new market-places in the Kakamega district; the Ulster Rifles captain, who had been out searching for Elijah Masendi (who thought he had trapped that prophet in a cave), was now engaged in taking the Census figures in Kakamega and was, as a side line, investigating the *Watu wa Roho* and in getting some sort of line on the Somali stock-trading community in the village. There are members of two opposed tribes of Somalis at Kakamega, and they are always burning each other's houses down. The exterior of these houses, invariably made of bashed-flat paraffin tins, is rusty and unpleasing. But inside they are walled with silk, with silk coverlets on the beds: all the finery, some of it very costly, of a well-to-do Mohammedan's harem. The Somalis usually have at least two wives.

The Ulster captain was extraordinarily handsome in his fresh, laughing way, and the Somali girls flirted with him outrageously when I went in with him to their secretive settlement, but he went off to get married even while I was there. The ex-brigadier, grinning, went off in a 3-ton truck, laden with police *askaris* and camping outfit, to sit down in the Malakisi district, where the rioters had been shot, as that region had now been declared a "special" area. Have you ever seen a hunting dog when his master takes out his shotgun and goes for a walk . . . ?

The village of Kakamega is just some dirty streets lined with Indian shops—you never see an African one—whose corrugated iron roofs project out over the sidewalk and form a shady meeting-place where idle Africans gossip all day. The Indians work from dawn to dusk.

The office of African Assistant District Officer had been started by Provincial Commissioner Kenneth Hunter over in the Nyanza Province, where he has spent all of his career. It is an experiment. It is almost impossible to convince other natives that they are not "agents of the Government," for that is exactly what they must be. Up to date, I would say, their function has not progressed a step beyond that of being a glorified interpreter, given official rank as well as being empowered to carry out whatever duties are delegated to them in the administration of the reserve. They have to find their feet and are, quite naturally, nervous and a little apprehensive as to what is being thought of them by their white colleagues. But I met all six of the African A.D.O.'s that are in the Province, and they all struck me as being earnest, impeccably honest and coming young men. Perhaps they themselves will never arrive—reach the self-confident state when they can take a white D.O.'s place. But their *sons* might. . . . That was why Hunter established the office of the African A.D.O.

Of the two at Kakamega, both of whom were Makerere graduates, one was a husky African in his thirties, with two lower and two upper incisor teeth taken out (this had been done by his parents when he was young, and most of such mutilated Africans among the Makerere undergraduates are now petitioning the Kenya or Uganda Governments to pay for the cost of having false teeth put in), who had been a schoolteacher for some years before he was taken into the straight Government service. The other, a younger and very handsome man, was an Intellectual of sorts, and always sat in his office, which was that adjoining the D.O.'s, with a copy of Aldous Huxley's *The Perennial Philosophy* prominently displayed on his window-sill. This was not just for show: the eagerness of these advanced young Africans to dip deep into the white man's philosophy is, I am ashamed to say, far more widespread and consistent than is ours into theirs, except for—I would like to stress this point as much as I can—every one of the *good* officers in the Colonial Service.

I held a *baraza* with these two young A.A.D.O.'s, together with three chiefs and the Secretary of the Local Native Council, who was the son of one of the chiefs. I did not expect any revelations, nor did I get them, except for one thing that came at the very end, when one of them (I won't say which) got me in a corner by myself. To my first leading question (which I always asked in Kenya) as to what did the Africans want most, what *immediate* things did they think could be done, one of the old chiefs, when this was translated to him, answered pat:

"Equal pay for equal work. Why, when an African does the

same work, should he be paid less for it than a white man gets?" Would I please explain that?

I leave it to you how I tried to wriggle out of that one. It was not quite so easy, as you may imagine, to assert that the African never did do as thorough a job as the average white man could. But I tried it. I even cited certain trades and works—such as mining—where the African did not have the technical training. This gave me the gambit to shift to Education. Did not the assembled company think that, instead of so much book-learning, the African should be given more instruction as to how to build bridges (wooden, of course), houses, culverts—"all the work that I see the Sikhs doing all over Kenya"?

"But where are the *schools*, sir?" asked one of the A.A.D.O.'s. "Where are the *teachers?*"

And so on. I was getting more than I had asked for.

Finally—and I could see it—the three old chiefs began to get suspicious. Who was I, anyway? was the unasked question in their eyes. And what was the good of talking to me? I would only go off, very likely, and repeat something they had said, something that would get them into trouble with the District Commissioner. It was better to get out of this conversation as politely as possible, so they seemed to be thinking. I closed the interview. The Secretary of the Local Native Council, who had expected to play the lion, said angrily: "It is all the question of color, sir. We can't hope for equal treatment until the color bar is abolished." "Which isn't a question of any *law*," I said to him, a trifle testily. "That is a question of *time*. And it depends upon you, just as much as it does upon us, how soon that invisible barrier between us is going to be rubbed out. We'll never do it if the African keeps on suspecting that everything that the white man does is solely for the white man's benefit. I ask you: Would you say that that was the way that the D.C. and the D.O.'s act here?"

"No, sir!" came emphatically from the two African A.D.O.'s. And, when it was translated to them, the three old chiefs nodded in solemn assent. It was only the frustrated Secretary of the L.N.C. who left that little confab with any unpleasantness in his heart. So I think. One came to me afterwards:

"Sir," he said quietly, "I'd like to ask you some questions, if . . . you don't mind? (I nodded.) Tell me, sir, how would you answer this: We are accustomed, sir, to dealing with three types of European: the Administrative Officer, the Missionary, and the Settler. The Government officials are always supposed to be neutral between us and the Settlers. Now, tell me, sir. How is it going to be when a Government Officer becomes a settler himself, when he *knows* he's going to be a settler . . . even right now? . . ."

This direct bull's-eye was due to the fact that the Governor of Kenya is known to have bought a farm up at Subakia to retire on. Nowadays, as so many of the Colonial Officers are now retiring in the lands in which they have served—"England is too expensive, I find it impossible to live there on my pension and give a good education to my children"—the Africans are becoming widely apprehensive they will take "the Settlers' point of view," even while they are in office.

"Surely," I said, "you don't think that Sir Philip Mitchell, or Mr. Williams here—you don't think that *they* would do things now, take a settler's way of looking at it, just because they know that they are going to live in Kenya in the long run? Or do you *really* think that?"

He rubbed his head. Finally he gasped out: "I just don't see how it's *possible*, sir! It's . . . it's just too Christ-like to be true. I don't see how *any* man wouldn't be influenced by what he knows—or thinks—are going to be his own best interests . . . even if he's got to wait some years to get them. *It just isn't human!* What about the sub-conscious, sir?"

I was worried. He had put to me one of the hardest cases to argue I have ever come up against. Colonial officers can be said to make almost a profession of altruism. They spend the whole of their careers in looking after other people, and, doing so, they invariably become very fond of them. But some of them do get over that. One or two of the worst reactionaries in Kenya, to judge from their words, are settlers who previously had long and distinguished careers in the Colonial Service. On the other hand, the most consistent champion in Kenya official life of native African rights is a senior member of the Legislative Council, who for over twenty-five years was a Colonial officer in Tanganyika and Kenya. And one man like him is worth a round dozen of the others. My only answer could be to this genuinely worried African:

"Well, let's suppose that we look at it this way. Africa is changing; that you will admit. So are the settlers. So are the Administrative Officers. Now, a good Administrative Officer in Kenya today knows that to call a man pro-African is only a tribute to his intelligence, for if a white man isn't pro-African in the Africa of today his days are numbered. Only the stupid could deny that. Then, take this: it is also a tribute to a man's intelligence to say that he is pro-settler. For Kenya is essentially an agricultural country, and if the settlers fail, then this country fails and everything goes back to chaos, with everyone in it. You'll admit that?"

"Oh, yes, sir! Readily."

"Well then, it just might be of an *advantage* to have so many Colonial Officers going out from the Service and into normal Kenya farming life. They have spent the best years of their lives in contact with you Africans. They know, because you have told them and they have seen for themselves, what it is that you want, and—I think you will admit this—they know the compromises that both sides have to make . . . in order to get on together. Don't you think that it might be an advantage to have so many of your former colleagues on the—shall I put it?—'the other side,' so to speak?"

He thought it over. Then he said, dubiously: "It might. It *would* be wonderful if—ah—things should work out like that. What do you think yourself, sir? Tell me honestly, if you don't mind my asking you so point-blank."

"That you seem to me incurably suspicious—suspicious of everybody. Even in *your* post!"

The Kakamega gold-fields were rediscovered in 1930, but the reef has already petered out. The gold-mines are dying quietly. I went down 1,000 feet in one of them that was still working, and never had I felt such a sense of depression as in that soft, damp heat, lighted by a few lamps, where some black men were clearing a space where a bored white man would drill a hole for one more charge of dynamite into the vanishing reef. Nor at luncheon afterwards, when, in a vast stone mansion, built with Edwardian magnificence in the gaudy days of the boom, in a dining-room walled with most of the world's classics and all blinds down so as to shut out any sight of Africa which might destroy the illusion, we ate cold spiced ham, washed down with champagne, together with a beet salad and a "trifle" that might have been served to you at the same time in any big English county house during a cricketing week. It was all so unreal. The debonair English manager, a famous mining engineer who had been all over the world, in the Andes and Siberia, had shaken us some iced cocktails, at the same time joking about the ill wind, the failure of the reef, that was going to blow him back to civilisation again. There is a social club at that mine with a big dancing floor and no one who feels like dancing. . . . At the other big mine in the district all mining for gold had been stopped and it was now making fire-proof tiles, etc., from its refuse dump. When gold was first found in the Kavirondo country and the big rush began, there was a lot of talk in the world's newspapers (and I wrote some of it) about how the British had broken their promise to the Kavirondos and invaded their reserve. But I think just the opposite now. They pre-empted microscopically small bits of land; went under like rodents. And these big organisations with money, like the big tea estates over at Kericho, give their workers an excellent life. Not only do they feed their black workers better than they had ever hoped to live; they have given many an African a technical skill, a sense of ambition and self-respect, that has incontestably lifted him to a higher level. An American in the district will be long remembered by many an Englishman in Kenya. During the very lowest depths of the depression, he worked his mine almost entirely with white men, giving work and pay to 120 Europeans at one time.

He paid them £5, £10, up to £15 a month: "All right, you're a married man with two children: £15 a month for *you.*" He was a fierce old man, slightly deaf; and he always poked his trumpet at you. If he didn't like a man, or wasn't interested in what he was saying, he put his trumpet down.

During the height of the gold boom, Kakamega saw new hotels being put up, champagne flowing in rivers—one hotel was called "The Corkscrew Inn"—and wild days and nights reminiscent of Bret Harte's tales of the Rockies. Then it all faded away. . . . But I met one man there who was a good "story" even to this day: a hawk-nosed, high-cheeked man, a six-footer with grey hair and a wild blue eye; he and his brother had actually diverted the course of a river in whose head waters they were doing some placer work, "washing" gold.

"But what an act of impudence!" I said.

"Oh, I don't know. We were all crazy then. We just dug a ditch and turned it down another valley. . . ."

"But the natives? That must have been a surprise to them!"

A laugh. "W-ell . . . come to think of it . . . I expect it was."

But now he is doing just the opposite; he is remaking the land. He is one of that hard-working agricultural team which is trying, by every method known to man, to make the natives co-operate and take care of their exhausted soil, not to make gullies out of cattle trails, etc. The natives are so jealous of their own bit of land that they will not co-operate; they will not allow any other native's foot to tread their bit of earth; and soil is so precious to these hard-pressed Kavirondo that they will scrape back on to their own plots even the few handfuls that have been loosened in making a walk between their little handkerchief-sized holdings. They are insatiably land-hungry and almost incurably suspicious. It is a heart-breaking job to make them accept good agricultural methods. "I do it mostly by parables," said the blue-eyed ex-gold-washer with a wry smile. "There's always a lot of Mission-trained folk among them, and I talk to them in the language of the Bible. But sometimes it's damned hard work."

" 'Lord, let Thy servant depart in peace!' " I said.

He chuckled: "Oh, I'm very small beer."

"But you've got a good head on you," quickly said my wife.

That captivated him. "Hear that?" he called to his assistant. Then he said to us, "Come on. I want to show you more of this country—if it interests you so." And I found, in his modest way of showing us about, the living, encouraging example of the Government team-work I had come to find. He was "small beer" because he was not one of the career Agricultural Officers who get a pension. But he was the real stuff.

Incidentally, in one of the Kakamega streams where the

"color" was found which started the gold rush, a field-worker of the Coryndon Museum in Nairobi discovered a "water-porcupine" with a rattle on the end of its tail. The natives had told him about this queer creature. "What is it?" he asked. But they couldn't tell him. "Where is it?" he asked. The natives showed him a tree leaning over the stream where he could see that some animal had made a hideout in its roots, a sort of *Wind in the Willows* little home. "It lives there," they informed him. He said: "I don't know what it is, but I *want* it." And so the mortal remains of six of these engaging little animals—they do have rattles on their tails; I have tried them—now lie in the bird room of the Nairobi Coryndon Museum. The man who found them is an even rarer specimen, and I advise you to meet him. Both he and the water-porcupines have outlived the gold rush.

The Kavirondo country is a fantastic bit of the world. As you reach the edge of the parapet, the edge of the high land, and look down towards the shores of Lake Victoria, you come into an astounding chaos of round, grey granite boulders, like the balancing rocks of the Grand Canyon of Colorado. Some of them are 40 or 50 feet in diameter; some balance one on top of another, to startling pinnacles. Some are towers of smaller stones ending in a huge mushroom grey-head. Your eye and mind both refuse to believe what you are looking at. And in here, like rabbits, you see the Kavirondo living among the rocks, with their patches of maize growing like green hair. I tried with everyone I met to see if I could get some good explanation of this geologic madness, for the water of Lake Victoria could never have been up that high. So *what* could have rubbed these boulders round? And it was characteristic of Kenya that not one man or woman could tell me. The nearest I came was this: "Oh, well, there was an old priest here who had gone into the subject rather thoroughly; he had an explanation . . . but he's dead."

The Kavirondo Reserve is full of priests and parsons of every known denomination. And some that I had never even heard of before. The C.M.S. missions are usually quiet, unostentatious buildings, all built with native workers, of course; and one C.M.S. church that I saw there, which had only a thatched roof, was one of the most restful, deeply contented and contemplative atmospheres I encountered in all Kenya. An air of peace hung over its ground that made me hate to leave. Irrespective of denomination, it is the personality of the people in charge which gives a Mission its effectiveness; and the more I saw of these men and women the more I came to admire them and their work. Two visits to Africa, ten years apart, have left me with a strong belief in the value of Mission work.

At the Church of God, which cult arose in Indiana, we came on a massive brick cathedral with square towers like a medieval fortress, and two young, hairy-armed men of a size to go with it, of German-American descent, who, when I asked them where was their greatest number of followers, replied: "Why—uh—*everybody* belongs to the Church of God . . . so long as he—uh—*believes!*" Two young women in white, with solar topis and faces drained of all color by the tropics, when my wife asked them were they members of the Mission, yelled with laughter: "Yes! Don't we *look* it?"—and showed us their work-worn hands. They took my wife to the little hospital they were running, and I had all I could do to drag her away from the half-dozen little velvet black babies (actually, they were pale pink), which had just been delivered. African women have taken strongly to the "lying-in" hospital, with its chance to loaf a while and have the delight of being looked after, instead of having to get right up and out in the fields again. The Church of God had one building entirely given over to a printing press, a publishing establishment which was sending out its pamphlets throughout the reserve. I met German Catholic priests inside the reserve who left off cutting their supply of firewood to don their cassocks and discuss the Faith with me; and, over at Kisii, two rather pathetic young Seventh Day Adventists, man and wife, from Natal, who, with no motor car but great determination, were running a little Mission school for less than fifty pupils. The only discordant note I struck at these Missions was at the Church of God, where I saw a small boy playing with the bodies of two strangely beautiful birds of an iridescent dark purple, with scarlet spectrums in their wings and a yellow bill which carried on to form a shield before their tufted heads. They were called purple plantain-eaters, according to the boy. "And now . . . what are you going to do with them?" I asked as he tossed them disdainfully in the dust.

"Shucks! *They* ain't no good! We went out after *mon*-keys, but this was all we could git!"

The little horror. Having done the same thing when a boy, I knew I had no more to say to him. Both the Church of God and the Seventh Day Adventists in that region laid great stress on carpentry and "building things," that wise prescription which the White Fathers follow wherever they go in Africa. "For if you get a man [native] to work side by side with you, eventually you come to talk and he believes what you say. It is all in the sense of working together." But it was in the Nyanza Province, near Kericho, that the Church of National Holiness, Chicago, gave *The Last of the Mohicans* to its Mission pupils to read, with the result that politically-minded adults in the district said that that was what the British intended to do to the Africans.

There is also a very attractive little Mohammedan mosque at Mbale. It is for the modern Moslems, mostly in Aga Khan's *khojas;* but it made you think of the slave days, when the tough Arab slave-traders found this one of the richest parts of Africa to raid. It was so thickly populated, even in those days.

It is hard to define the personality of a Province. Kenya would not be Kenya without Nyanza, yet this great area by the lake, which contains over a million and a half of the colony's five million Africans, is as different from the rest of Kenya as if it were in a totally different part of Africa, both in its position and even in Time itself. There is an old-fashioned, even Victorian atmosphere about Nyanza Province. Its low-lying land near the lake, once so malarial, and the rocky hills have made it seem unsuitable for European cultivation. And in the steaming sugar-cane country you will even see Indians farming, a thing that you will never see in the European White Highlands. The land around Lake Victoria lies at an average of 3,750 feet, and is distinctly, often unbearably, tropical. Then it rises to 14,197 on the slopes of Mt. Elgon, on the eastern side of which lie some of the best farms of European Kenya. Kisumu itself, lying in the Gulf of Kavirondo on the shores of the great Lake, had, according to the 1947 yearbook, a white population of 350 and an Indian one of 2,500: forty-seven of its fifty commercial enterprises were being run by Indians when I was there in 1948, so the white people are just minute specks in this great province, even though they are running it.

I had come over to the Kavirondo Reserve, as I have said, to write about the Government's team-work: the Administrative Officers with the Agricultural, Maize Control, etc. But when I had been in it a time—this was the third time I had been there, on much the same quest—I became vastly more interested in the men who were running these enterprises. For, after all, it is they who will either make a success or failure of them. As Singleton, the old sailor, said in Conrad's *Nigger of the Narcissus:* "Ships! . . . Ships are all right. It is the men in them."

Very often you will find that it is not the career man, the man who will get a pension, but the "man left behind," the survivor of another epoch of African life, the unofficial man, who is really the most useful and practical man in the district. The man who might be short on book-learning but who has a long and intimate understanding of the natives. Sometimes this has soured him. And then you will come on a rare and thoughtful specimen—such as the ex-gold-washer—who can think almost like the land-hungry and desperate natives, largely because he has for a long time faced the problem himself of how to survive in Africa. The youngish career Agricultural Officer whose work I had come over to study had, with true official perverseness, just when he was making a good job of it, been shifted to Zanzibar, where he would have to begin all over again to study the disease called "sudden death" which is devastating the clove trees on that spice island. And so, *faut de mieux,* I was taken about by the old gold-prospector who had become almost as much a part of Nyanza Province as its grey rocks. I benefited accordingly, for he talked in terms of personal relationships and of problems which could only be solved, not by the percentage of humus in the soil or by rotating crops, but by a change of heart in the white man: some big scheme of land settlement for the Africans that would be a stirring example of the white man's wish to better their lot, and which might as a consequence help to solve our own problem as to how to restore their unquestionably dwindling faith in us. Such a mind goes beyond the statistics of agricultural technique to the much needed example of what the white man really intends to do.

When I said that the immense Nyanza Province had an old-fashioned atmosphere, I was using that term in its best sense. Actually, Nyanza is a very progressive province. The first Local Native Council in Kenya was started at Kakamega in 1925; its splendid hospital for Africans, built in 1919, has been the prototype for most of the native hospitals built in Kenya; Mr. Kenneth Hunter, the Provincial Commissioner for Nyanza, is the man who inaugurated the office of African Assistant District Officer; and the various Missions, as I have said, have probably reached their highest mass development in Nyanza Province. Even more important, as it is so thinly peopled by Europeans, the African development in this province has been permitted to continue along the lines and even fulfil some of the early ambitions of the British administering that territory when the ideal was being striven for. The Secondary School at Kakamega, for Africans, is undoubtedly one of these.

This school, with its quiet lawns and restful quadrangle of buff buildings with their weathered red roofs, its walks flanked by beautiful jacaranda trees with their hyacinth-blue flowers, with an immense Nandi Flame—like a horse-chestnut bearing scarlet candelabra—taking the place of the American college elm or the British oak, comes as near to a British public school as anything I saw in Kenya. This is what the early educators must have had in mind when they set out to educate the young African, for their original idea was to give him far more than book-learning: it was to give him a way of life, a code of conduct. Judged by statistics, the buildings are too imposing, too grand for the small number of pupils they house. Judged by the standard of a "way of life," however, they are just right. I cannot conceive how any African youth who serves his five years and graduates from that school—even if only 1.5 out of every sixty has shown the mental competence to go on to Makerere College—can ever let himself drop back into the squalor of African village life. Nor, after the training in character which he has had, would he allow himself to become one of the black spivs that one sees in Nairobi's streets. I kept thinking, as I walked around its grounds and sat with its calm and cynically-thoughtful Headmaster in his library under the photo of the bust of Cicero, "This is *Tom Brown's School Days* in Africa!" which is the briefest and best way I can describe it.

Kakamega has a hospital for Africans that looked as if it could hold its own with many a hospital in a white man's country: an excellent institution. As I have spent several of the best years of my life in hospital beds, between spells on the operating table, I think I know a good one when I see it. Three things about it interested me particularly: the five wounded Africans from the shooting at Malakisi; the V.D. parade of the Kavirondo women, who were lining up laughingly to get their injections for syphilis or clap—there were a lot of them; and a tragic little handful of under-nourished *totos* who were being sunned on the lawn. The most impoverished of them, little pot-bellied creatures, looked as if they had been *bleached*. Their black skins had lost their pigment and turned yellow; their kinky hair had become lank, almost blond. Incidentally hair has an important place in the physical criteria of race. Under the microscope, the hair of a European is oval in cross-section, and has no pith; the "woolly" hair of the black races (with the exception of the Australians and aborigines of India) is elliptical or kidney-shaped in cross-section, and has no pith; but the straight, lank and coarse black hair of the Chinese, Mongols and Indians of the Americas is round or nearly so in section, and has an easily distinguishable pith. Generally, hair curls in proportion to its flatness. The "frizzy" hair of the Papuans, which is a fourth type, seems to have almost its counterpart in some of the Somalis that I saw. Black, naked except for a loin-clout, they struck me as being astonishingly like South Sea Islanders as I saw them at the wells, drawing water for their camels.

Kakamega also has a tragic leper colony, of which a recent visiting specialist said that it contained the most malignant cases he had ever seen. This was nodular leprosy: dismaying people to look at with their distorted faces. But many lepers in the colony were walking about with merely missing fingers and toes and, apparently, suffering neither pain nor mental anguish. I noticed, though, that when we went through the colony all the wardens, who also are lepers, never came closer than 10 feet to us. They are supposed to observe that distance. They had a leper prison attached to the Colony, with leper wardens and leper criminals from all over Kenya. They had their own farm where they grew maize and other food, and, believe it or not, the lepers were allowed to go into town. No one knows yet how leprosy is transmitted from one person to another; for such as they are worth, records kept of married couples who cohabit show less than 3 per cent infection. So that did not make it seem so grim when I was told that in this colony many of the children there did not have leprosy, but were allowed to remain with their mothers. "It would be too cruel to take them away," said the doctor in a depressed voice. "God knows, if we can make anything easier for these unfortunate people we will try to do it."

Always that grim undertone of Nature striking at you, as if you had no right to live in Africa. Driving down to the low, flat valleys around the Lake with Kenneth Hunter, the Provincial Commissioner, we passed over a green, pouring river that looked particularly refreshing.

"You think so?" said Hunter with a grim smile. "Well, most of the people who live along this river used to go blind." And he told me the story of the "buffalo gnat," the simulium fly, which breeds only on the rocks under waterfalls. It belongs to the same family of fly which gives rise to elephantiasis, another common African affliction. The worms get encysted in nodules on the shoulders, arms, backs, legs and so on, and from these nodules pours forth a constant stream of minute worms. These young worms often make for the eye, which they destroy. Whole riverine villages will go blind. The disease is called onchocerciasis, and is absolutely incurable. D.D.T. has been used in this river to kill the pupa on the rocks, with good results—aside from killing most of its fish. But, said Hunter—"You can truly call some parts of this area 'The Country of the Blind.' "

After a time you get enough of writing about Africa. You want to *live* it. This desire had become overwhelmingly strong in me now. I didn't want to write another damned word of statistics. I didn't care how important they were. I wanted the Africa that I, personally, had come down there to get. I was, I must confess, bored with the everlasting story of how the European officials—always the same story—were trying to raise the standard of life of the Africans, and how the suspicious African was refusing to co-operate in every plan which is for his own betterment. My admiration for the Administrative Officers increased daily, but so had my aching desire to get away from all men—black or white. We spent a few days—and very pleasant they were too—with the Hunters in their wire-screened house overlooking the Great Lake at Kisumu. I raced a small yacht against another yacht, which would have beaten us had it had another half mile to go. It was weird to race a 16-foot "Rainbow" expecting a hippo to rise up before you at any moment. And then we missed our mooring when we tried to pick it up, to the delight of all the members sitting on the veranda of that congenial little yacht club. We went to Kisii, and had an exhilarating free-for-all argument with the team of administrative, agricultural and educational officers there who claimed, half in earnest, that education was only meant to make people discontented with their lot, anyway; through Sotik, where the sloppy European farming, such as that seen from the road, well confirms the saying: "All the slumps begin in Sotik."

We spent some days at Kericho, center of the big European tea estates. And here, as I have said, these big London companies, which have the money, have given their native laborers probably the finest living conditions in East Africa. It is one boy to each acre of tea: 5,000 acres, 5,000 Africans: as on the estate we were on. Its German doctor was a Jew who had survived Dachau concentration camp and who told me: "Kenya is Paradise." The house of the manager whose guest we were might have been any big "county" house in England: mahogany and Georgian silver, hunting prints on the walls, and a black-and-gold Chinese screen which had been looted from Pekin; it dominated the house. It was an immense piece of eight board panels, black, with the scenes in gold; one side showed the story of the big Chinese nobleman it was meant to immortalise at the wars—charging soldiers and flying arrows—and, the only other bit of color, scarlet pennants; the other pictured his domestic life, his "return from the wars," and the delectable life he lived from then on with his wives and concubines. A Chinese scholar who had visited Kenya came out to see this screen and said that it would now have been in a museum—even in China—if it had not been stolen by a British adventurer during the Boxer Rebellion. Staying in that house and adding greatly to its charm was "Boy" Long, who had been Lord Delamere's manager, the man who had hunted lions with Paul Rainey and his dogs on one of which expeditions a European Royal Prince had been killed, and who himself is one of the last and most attractive members left of that hard-living and free-loving Happy Valley lot.

At Kericho we met another person who seems to be filling the niche in life which she was made for, having, I may say, made this niche for herself: Miss Rachel Chilson, from Iowa, a Quaker who has started a spinning and weaving school there which now takes native girls from all over East Africa. They spin and weave silk, wool, cotton, linen, and even milk-weed, which they collect themselves in the vicinity. They make many of their own dyes, and their patterns are delightful. We took this chance to get some materials which were not cramped by British austerity; and a full set of sofa and chaircovers is now being made at Kericho for our home in North Devon.

Here at Kericho we saw some of the hard-faced men who are flocking out from London to buy land for more tea plantations. And more of the fine forests will be destroyed. They told me that one of these tight-lipped gentlemen was getting a salary of £30,000 a year. He can have it.

We drove through one of the deep, still, green forests of untouched Kenya, with the black-and-white Colobus monkeys romping in the branches, the birds calling, in innocence of the eventual doom that was hanging over them, and came out through a beautiful vista of blue hills dotted with scarlet cork trees into the country of the Nandi warriors around Kapsabit. About twenty of them, stock-thieves, were sitting in a contented circle outside the D.C.'s office, waiting their turn to be sent to jail for stealing cattle. "That is our greatest export around here," he told me smilingly; "stock-thieves. But they're splendid-looking people, aren't they?"

And so they were. And here was the last touch—almost an omen.

As we were driving out to Kaptumo to see the historic site of the old fort the King's African Rifles had built there in their hard campaigns to subdue the fighting Nandi, we came upon a naked woman on the road. She had a beautiful figure. She stood there with head bowed and one leg resting against the bank as our car drove past. "She is mad, poor thing," said the D.C. The view across the valley at Kaptumo, as you sit under the tall gum trees that the English officers planted in the Nandi campaign, is one of the most inspiring in all Africa: twenty-five miles across blue space to where you see the tea estates at Kericho. Near here, in a beautiful forest of flaked acacia thorn, a wild Irishman, with three Military Crosses, runs a pub—at least, he did run it, until he was euchred out of it. And when I spoke to him about some wealthy Londoners who were coming in here to cut down 8,000 acres of forest to grow tea, he said:

"Ah! They'll b— the whole world about, people like that . . . before they get through. Wonder where a chap can go these days?"

Well, the next day, when we were leaving Kapsabit for perhaps the most interesting *safari* on this trip, that up into the "uninhabitable" Northern Frontier District, we passed that naked woman again. This time there seemed something symbolic about her—a wood-nymph. She gave me this idea because, in her crazy mind, she had tried to clothe herself. She had wound a vine around her slim waist. And as we came near her she gave us a frightened look, and then stepped into the dark and protective forest, where she was safe. . . .

She was not mad.

CHAPTER XX

Gerald Reece and the Northern Frontier District

THERE is one-half of Kenya about which the other half knows nothing, and seems to care even less. This is the N.F.D., Kenya's Northern Frontier District. It is about 100,000 square miles, mostly volcanic desert, supposed to contain about 100,000 people, for they cannot be counted, even for poll tax, pagan cattle-owning Boran, and nomadic Somalis always on trek with their camels, lying between Lake Rudolph and the frontier of Italian Somaliland, and, north to south, from the green foothills of Abyssinia to the banks of the elephant-infested Tana River.

It is perhaps well to repeat here that Kenya is over two and one-half times the size of Great Britain and Northern Ireland; that the White Highlands, where practically all the Europeans live, comprise only about 13 per cent of all Kenya, and that over two-thirds of the territory is supposed to be uncultivatable. Then I can say that the N.F.D. is regarded by most Kenyans as the most *uninhabitable* part of their colony. Neither the British, when they began to establish their domain in Kenya some fifty years ago, nor the Ethiopian Emperor Menelik, when he joined the European Powers in their scramble for Africa, wanted this desert waste with its turbulent peoples. The first man to pass through it (and what a man he must have been) was the American naturalist, Donaldson-Smith, who, with astounding prescience, saw the strategic importance of this territory and warned the British that they should seize it:

> A line run from Ime, on the Webbe Shebyli (the River of Leopards), to a point immediately below Bonga in Kaffa, marks

> the southern limit of any country to which the Emperor Menelik can at present lay claim—either by virtue of peaceful occupation, by treaties with the native chiefs, or by conquest.
>
> It is absolutely imperative that the British prevent the Abyssinians from advancing to any great distance below the line above mentioned.
>
> It behooves England to act at once. If she does not immediately check the Abyssinians' advances it will only be a necessity deferred, and then when finally she is obliged to possess herself of the country east of Lake Rudolph, perhaps far to the south of the northern end of the lake, she will have lost all that magnificent, fertile and mountainous country, of great commercial value, extending a hundred miles north of Lake Rudolph, embracing Lake Abaya and the sources of the River Juba and the greater half of the Boran country.

Donaldson-Smith wrote that in 1895. His prophetic vision was not matched by the British. They lost the magnificent green mountain country that is now the southern foothills of Abyssinia, and, to create a buffer state, they had to take over, some forty years ago, the waterless, worthless waste (as most Kenyans still think) of the Territory which is now known as the N.F.D., at the cost (pre-1939) of £100,000 a year, to keep the peace along the Anglo-Abyssinian frontier. An Anglo-Abyssinian border-line, drawn by a certain Cap't Maud in 1902-3, cuts through all the best grazing and watering lands of the Galla Boran and Somali tribes, so that not one tribe of either Boran or Somali is complete in either territory, and as all the headmen remain in either Ethiopia or over in Italian Somaliland, life in the N.F.D. has been distinguished by Abyssinian bandit raids down into the N.F.D., continual fights between Kenya natives and Abyssinian tribes (and soldiers) over watering rights, inter-tribal battles between the Kenya tribes themselves over watering and grazing rights and, at times, outbreaks of nothing less than a religious war between the Mohammedan Somalis and the pagan Boran.

Sweeping south to the Tana River and also westwards is this inexorable push of the Somalis, which has been going on for fifty years, to get across the Tana River into southern Kenya, as well as to push westwards and swallow up the Kenya Boran tribes and their grazing country. This is to escape from the desiccated country they live in. The British Provincial Commissioner, with eight District Commissioners and a couple of District Officers (some thirty Europeans all told), have up to date been trying to keep peace and order in this country, which is larger than Great Britain, where 99 per cent of the people can neither read nor write, and live, most of them, as they did in the days of Moses.

In these tribal battles in the N.F.D., particularly those between the pagan Boran and the Mohammedan Somalis, it is the custom to cut off the private parts of anyone you have killed in battle, even male babies, and bring them home to show the girls of your tribe what a man you are yourself. This is still the ultimate test of full manhood up in the primitive N.F.D., and two little boys tending goats just outside Marsabit were murdered and thus mutilated about a week before I got there.

At the time I arrived it was still being thought that a tribe of local Boran who were camped just below the mountain had done this to wet their spears—they are a particularly sullen lot—but it turned out later that it was a band of raiders from Abyssinia. When I was at Marsabit, the P.C. and the D.C. were discussing the advisability of closing the local wells there until someone among the Boran came forward and, in secret, gave the names of the real murderers. With the wells closed, they would have to move, with their cattle, goats and equipment, sixty or seventy miles out into the desert before they again found water, but with the certainty that it would have no rich pasturage around it such as they were enjoying at Marsabit. It would have been a very effective way to make them talk.

There is no white settlement in the N.F.D.; the whole territory is Crown Land; and the only Europeans up there, apart from an occasional big game *safari* that penetrates into the barren country, are the administrative and police officers. It is said, half jokingly, that a white official can last only eighteen months in the N.F.D., after which he will either take one of those astonishingly seductive Somali girls for a temporary wife (they make the most sought-after prostitutes in Nairobi) or go dotty. Probably both.

This is hearsay. But eighteen months is about as long as any white administrator has lasted, particularly the married ones; they all begin to get jumpy after that and are moved away. The Kenya administrative officers have a uniquely clean record so far as mixing with the native women is concerned—quite the reverse of the Italian administrators in their Somaliland—and they do this in a territory which has no clubs, nor any of the amenities which make other remote stations tolerable. Furthermore, they all love it. In retrospect, they all speak of their time in the N.F.D. as being among the best days of their lives. The two men who really made the N.F.D. what it is, Sir Vincent Glenday, now the British Resident at Zanzibar, and Gerald Reece, now the Governor of British Somaliland, have, on the other hand, spent most of their careers in the Northern Frontier District. They dedicated their lives to it. The administration of nomadic pastoral people who are passing through a difficult stage calls for special qualities and abilities; the disadvantage arising from the physical and mental unhealthiness of desert stations are not negligible; and because frontier desert conditions require a good deal of physical and mental stamina, an *esprit de corps* has been built up among the men who have served their early years in the N.F.D. They have a tradition. It is born by having served in conditions every bit as arduous and uncomfortable as those met by the old French Foreign Legion.

I had the good fortune to go on *safari* with Gerald Reece just before he was taken away from the N.F.D. to be made Governor of British Somaliland. It is a trip that I shall never forget: the lava rubble deserts, the tensions along the Abyssinian frontier border, the 50,000 thirsty camels converging on Wajir, our nights sleeping under the stars—for we used no tent—and, especially, I shall never forget the company of Gerald Reece and the way he talked of the territory he had given his heart to for over twenty years.

It is a land where you can know the joy of working for something that is bigger than yourself. And I think that if they could only believe there is such a life, many an ex-officer in England today would just jump at the chance to serve in those deserts and wastes of lava rubble and choking scrub, where the Somali nomads live with their herds of camels and you see them passing you at night like grey ghosts under the stars. There is a tremendous amount of beauty up in the old N.F.D. It is awe-inspiring. Having seen and experienced it, I find it hard to understand why the British Colonial Office has not already established a special corps, something like the French Foreign Legion, to serve in that

was calling as he went about the house—his senior houseboy, packing books, clothes, reports, food, rifle and revolver, for our *safari*—"Mmmm-b-oy!"—the cook packing chop-boxes, and Reece inspecting everything. A three-ton lorry was being loaded out in the yard—tents, chairs, tables—and eight men in white robes, with blood-red turbans, were loading this lorry, always with the rifle that each one carried hung from its strap across his back. I asked Reece why they did not stack their rifles. "Because," he said, and now I saw that the end of his nose did sharply switch from side to side when he was interested in anything, "to be beaten in a fight in this country is no disgrace; it might happen to anybody. But to be taken by *surprise!*—that's inexcusable!" And so, these Dubas never take their rifles off. The Dubas are a *corps d'élite* which Reece raised, a sort of desert commando. There are two hundred of them, and, like everything about him, they were perfect. The white robe is just a long strip which they deftly bind around them and over one shoulder, and which is kept in place by a cartridge-belt. While Reece was neglecting his breakfast (he never seems to pay attention to any meal), I went through his library and found one of the most inspiring collection of books I have come on anywhere in the world. He seemed to have read everything—ancient and modern. On the breakfast table was *Horizon*, the issue with Cyril Connolly's gorgeous account of his visit to the United States: "Why do Americans fight in bed?" "Mnnn . . . keen chap, that," said Reece, taking another snap at his egg.

I finished my egg and went out to stare at the glaciers on Mt. Kenya—which dominates the scene all the way from Fort Hall to Isiolo—thinking I might cool myself off if only by staring at so much ice and snow.

Reece was in his bedroom sprucing up, putting on his tunic with the beige band of the Colonial Service P.C., to go out and inspect a contingent of desert Dubas that were being sent down from the N.F.D. as its contribution to "The Country Comes to Town" show that Nairobi was putting on. Reece's District Commissioner came in and said that he had received a letter from Nairobi saying that the Dubas must wear more clothing; a man dressed in nothing but a *tobe*—a double-width 15-foot strip of white cloth thrown over one shoulder, with a turn about the waist—might strike some people in Nairobi as being indecent, even if the sheet does fall to near his ankles. "They will go this way," said Reece, "or not at all."

The slim Sergeant-Major, a Rendille, one of the most graceful of the Galla tribes in Kenya, gave some high *yipe-yipes* of command, stamped his feet; and about forty Dubas, Rendilles, Somalis, Borans, Samburu—pagans and Mohammedans—stiffened into brown statues. Reece and the D.C. walked through them, Reece missing nothing. Then he stood off, took the salute; more *yipe-yipes!* and thirty of the Dubas marched off down the dusty road. "Mnnnn . . ." said Reece, staring after them lovingly. "Put more clothes on . . . indeed!"

A strange white man turned up, obviously not one of the administrative officers, in a Ford station wagon with an armed native policeman sitting in its front seat. From the car they took out two boxes which, though small, seemed heavy, and were linked together by a bright chain. Such a chain as you pull an ox-cart with. He looked inquiringly at Reece. "Ummm. . . . Put it in there," said Reece, pointing to the tail-end of the Ford V-8 closed car in which we ourselves were going to make this *safari*. I did not discover until we had reached Moyale, on the Abyssinian frontier, that this was £2,000 in notes and shillings that Reece was bringing up as the first part of the £67,000 compensation he had, after nearly five years, been able to persuade the British Government to withhold from the Abyssinians; being part of a British payment to Abyssinians, which, in his opinion, had to be diverted into an Abyssinian payment to relatives of N.F.D. natives who had been murdered by Abyssinian bandits; a *shifta* raid inside the Kenya territory in 1943. At that time Reece told his people that he would make the Abyssinians "pay for this!" and he said to me:

"A promise made must be kept." His nose switched to one side, then "pointed" like the tail of a good gun dog. "And so must a threat."

"Especially the threat."

"Oh, yes. They'll know you're no good if you don't keep that."

Except for the first night, when Reece had the Dubas put up a tent for me on the lip of a cold, high volcanic crater, and the next one, which we spent with his wife and children on the slopes of Marsabit, we slept under the stars. And the worn Webley .45, which his personal Duba loaded and placed on the green canvas camp-chair by his bed every night (together with a loaded Rigby Magnum big-game rifle placed along the steel cross-bars of his cot) was the same one he was carrying (and nearly lost) on the morning of March 20th, 1918, when he was shot through the chest during the rout of General Gough's 5th Army—"When we didn't know where we were."

In a disturbed area, full of *shifta* bandit raiders—such as is the normal state of the N.F.D. along the Abyssinian border—it is just as well to have a revolver by your bed at nights. But its most likely use would be against hyenas, who have a penchant for raiding a camp—and taking a bite at a white face.

A Rugby boy, Reece had begun to study Law after the 1914-18 War; then, finding office life insupportable, had come out to Africa, drawn, almost as if by compass, to the wastes and deserts of the northern frontier, where, off and on, except when he had been the British Consul in Abyssinia, he had been the last twenty years. Of leaving England, he smiled: "We came out here to find that everything we were doing was right and good. As we left Tilbury, we bought a Union Jack, prepared to carry on the White Man's Burden. Now—we know better."

After you leave Isiolo, the great Matthews Range lies on your left: grey granite cliffs shining in the sun, with green forests on top of what seem inaccessible tablelands. They are full of game and inhabited by little wandorobo, a tribe of hunters. Reece had been up all of them. "That was when I was young." Then we came to a dead river . . . the mournful sight of a red, sandy bed, wandering like a snake through the drooping Dom palms. These towering palms, which always look as if they are weeping, with their dead, drooping under leaves, have nuts nearly as hard as ivory which are cut up and made into buttons. Below them the high banks of the desolate river were choked with light green thorn. "Doesn't the water ever run here?"

"Sometimes," he said. "But this country is drying up."

This was the first of many dead rivers that we had to cross. To get the 3-ton lorry through the soft sand was no easy task;

the Ford passenger car was even more difficult. Besides the eight Dubas, with their rifles, we had a cook, two houseboys and the two African drivers: which, with Reece and myself, made fifteen men, or fourteen men to push. We needed all of them! The so-called road, which is often not travelled for two months at a time, was also a succession of obstacles. There had been nobody along it for four months, I believe, when we went up it. Some idea of it may be gained from the fact that I kept a log of our journey for the next thirteen days: we averaged, with all time taken out for meals, etc., just under 11 m.p.h. on the road up to Abyssinia.

While Reece and I were standing on the near bank of the dead river, watching the boys and the Dubas trying to push the lorry up the far side, an elephant slid down the bank about 100 yards below us and strolled casually down the sand. He was red (not pink, thank God) and he was not aware of us. As he put down each broad foot, he sort of flipped it up, then put it down with a satisfied pat on the soft sand. Reece called my attention to it:

"Look at him! Notice the way he puts that foot down? That ankle joint, so close to the ground. Seems pleased with himself, doesn't he!"

The boys, the instant they saw the elephant, began to shout to each other and talk excitedly. But what little current of air there was was drifting from him to us, and we watched old short-sighted Tembo stroll nonchalantly down the red river sands as if he was the lord of all Africa. Somewhere along it he would find a depression, where he would dig for water with his tusks. It is very scarce in these parts; this hot, dry land, where the territory leading to everything that had once been a water-course is littered with balls of dried elephant dung, a sight which also adds to the sadness of the scene. Then we entered the scrub brush. . . .

The brush in this relatively low-lying country about the Equator, at 1,500 to 2,000 feet, where the rainfull is in the main less than 10 inches a year, has a dry, hot terrible *intensity* that is the cruellest thing to be met with in the whole N.F.D. I emphasise that word, for the pressure of this brush on your mind is almost a physical thing. It has three forms. The least awful, which means stuff that you can walk through, is a desert grass-bush, with *Commiphora* (looking like leafless apple trees) and acacias spaced from 4 to 10 yards apart, seldom rising above 10 or 15 feet in height, with tufts of perennial grasses growing on the bare grey or Devon red earth in between. This, for the bushland, is comparatively open country; and there is a big stretch of it from where we crossed the first dead watercourse to where we came to the Uaso Nyiro River. In here we saw some ostriches, jogging along with their obscene, naked legs; the cock bird black-and-white, the hen and her chicks dun-colored. It was in here that Reece, as a *beau geste*, stopped the car and walked off in the hot scrub to pick me a Desert Rose. An adenium, almost prehistoric bit of flora which, with its pink-and-white petals and juicy thick stalk, is, I discovered later, the only thing that could live in the terrible lava rubble. In taking the flower from his hand, I began to learn something about Gerald Reece. The adenium also helps to make a poison for arrows which can bring an elephant down half a mile from where he has been hit.

In the depressions here, where some form of moisture must linger in the sub-soil and the grass becomes more dense, some of the pastoral pagan tribes graze their goats. And a young girl we came on suddenly, frightened, tried to hide herself behind a thorn tree not much thicker than my wrist. She was a Galla of some sort, judging from her straight nose and amber breasts; and the hair of her woolly head had been done up with fat and red ochre into a mop of little dangling red blobs. But, like the Somali girls, who are incurable flirts, and though supposed to be concealing herself, Reece asked me to note that she nevertheless kept one eye open, peeking around the tree—"with that come-hither look!" This was the only human being we saw in the 150 miles up to Marsabit.

The next type of bush, which is known as Desert Scrub and forms the red desert of Kasut, south of Marsabit, are vast patches where the stunted trees form a thin cover, never more than 10 feet in height, spaced only about 8 to 10 yards apart, with everything leafless in a drought-dormant listlessness. Only ephemeral grasses ever appear in these wastelands, following rain. Some are just devoid of vegetation; only the red soil meets your eye.

But along some of the lava ridges I saw an occasional tree in the far distance; and Reece told me, back in there, far from the road, lived other, always hiding, pagan people, pasturing their feeble cattle and goats on the dry and brittle grass. "Life here is a constant search to find moisture and grass."

Then there is the horrible brush, with 3-inch thorn spikes, which you enter just before you reach the Abyssinian foothills, and which, from Abyssinia down to almost the Tana River, seems determined to stifle you. In here the gnarled, spiky trees are so interlocking, so enmeshed, that you cannot see the earth between them. It is impossible to step one yard into it without a bush-knife; in fact, we often drove for miles before we could find a place to pull off the road for lunch or to pitch our camp. This is again these *Commiphora* trees, wrestling like Laocoön with climbing creepers and suffocating acacia thorn. Then, of course, there are the vast, open semi-grasslands on the edge of the lava plains, and that straight patch of "The Plain of Darkness," nothing but lava boulders, which is sixty miles wide. All this region, I may say, which is labelled as desert on the map and in descriptions of the barren N.F.D., never once produces the sandy desert that one is always hoping to see.

Reece, who also had Turkana under him, which is the "desert" to the west of Lake Rudolph, where live the savages who carry circular knives on their arms, and wear hooked rings to gouge out your eyes, had, in all, an area of 150,000 square miles, with 184,000 people under him, which he ran with only these eight District Commissioners, 1,000 tribal police, and the 200 admirable Dubas—men who are supposed to go across any country and carry out any hazardous mission, unprovisioned, living by their wits in any territory they enter. There are also 200 Kenya Police, with rifles, stationed at Moyale on the Abyssinian frontier. The livestock in Reece's domain, which also cannot be counted, "appear to be," says the official estimate, about 757,000 cattle (and the Boran raise the finest native cattle in Africa), 2,500,000 sheep and goats and some 328,000 camels. As Kenya's only foreign affairs must be those concerning relationships with the intractable Abyssinians and the restless Somalis, always moving southwards—and now stirred up by their Somali Youth League (which has not the slightest thing to do with youth)—his position is analogous to that of the British Commissioner of the North-West Frontier in India. And, indeed, he was, at the time I was with him, the Kenya Government's adviser on foreign affairs. But it is as a man that he was of far more importance. Especially in days like these.

We came to the Uaso Nyiro River, where a whole colony of *dom* palms seemed to be weeping in unison. As well they might. Some reddish water, carrying good soil from the Highlands, was still flowing through the shelving faces of rock, across which a concrete bridge had been built. The Dubas ran for the water, and, after some hesitation—"They are embarrassed at displaying themselves before the Distinguished Visitor," said Reece, just the faint touch of the rapier in his remark for my having started with a hangover at the beginning of such a *safari* —they then hastily unstrapped their cartridge belts, threw off the white sheet which bound their slender bodies and, one after the other, jumped like frogs into the water. Glistening then, they sat on the warm rock to let the sun dry them. I thought, as I stared at their lithe bodies, that it was no wonder they should look with disgust at some of the white men they encountered, especially the Sandow type of human perfection. Even the maimed or diseased in Africa seem more beautifully built than the great mass of the poorer inhabitants of European cities, the miserable human beings produced by our civilisation.

And there were some pretty miserable white men further up the Uaso Nyiro River. The Uaso Nyiro starts in the region of the Aberdares. Its tributaries come from the areas occupied by European farmers in the Nanyuki, Naro Moru and Rumuruti districts. After leaving the settled areas, it flows for a distance of 275 miles through the N.F.D. and ends in the Lorian Swamp. Though most of the country in the Uaso Nyiro watershed is dairy or ranching country, the Europeans have started to grow crops, such as maize, which they irrigate with water from the tributaries of the Uaso Nyiro. Many furrows have been made without permission of the Water Board (actually, they have been made in open defiance of it). These are not lined with cement (nor is the quantity of water measured), and in many cases the water is allowed to run to waste in the bush instead of being returned to the river, as it should be, so that what remains of it can benefit the natives living down in the N.F.D.

"Why the hell should the natives have it?" is a remark you will hear from many of these settlers. I was told of one South African farmer there, in a place where water was supposed to be measured, who was taking *seventeen times* the amount of water that was allowed to him: this to grow maize on black cotton soil, just so that he could squeeze the last penny out of his farm and cheat posterity, and that nothing was being done to him. I mentioned this to Reece, who was fighting to bring down all the water that he could for the natives of the N.F.D. He smiled, albeit bitterly, and said that such men should be shot. My opinion is that those who deserve shooting are the people who permit it.

The plain facts of the case are that for years successive Kenya Governments have ducked the issue of coming to grips with the farmers in that politically powerful region. The farmers themselves have not only refused to obey the half-hearted attempts that were made to restrain them, but openly announced that they would refuse "to accept any decision and intend to disregard all orders made in connection therewith by the Government." This was made in person by, of all people, the representative of the Aberdare District Water Board to the Government's Central Water Board. In other words, the Government could go to hell; and the Dutchmen and others on the Ngare Ngare tributary could still continue to grow maize on the porous black cotton soil, which, every agricultural expert knows, is rank farming treason. The natives along the Uaso Nyiro could also go to hell. This is white man's civilization on a high level, and was the state of affairs along the Uaso Nyiro when I crossed it in January 1948.

No wonder the *dom* palms are weeping. Because of this shameful treatment, even the great Lorian Swamp itself is drying up: one of the greatest sanctuaries for bird life left in Africa. All of East Africa is drying up, anyway; but deliberately to waste water growing maize in porous black cotton soil is openly robbing posterity. Kenyans will not like what I am writing—some of them—but those who know the facts will be grateful that some publicity is being given to this misuse of the precious water from the Uaso Nyiro River. The settlers originally got that land for grazing, and, as such, were allowed to get it at a lower price than if they had intended to grow crops on it. Now they are going to grow the crops. This is not so much innate selfishness, however, as it appears at first sight. Some Kenya settlers, because of their isolation and individualism, seem to get numbed in time to the realities of life; they seem unable to understand what is taking place all around them, to say nothing of the world outside Kenya, and so they persist in practices which are only destined to harm their own holdings in the long run. The big soil-conservation effort now being made in Kenya will probably save what is left of the Uaso Nyiro before it is too late. Meanwhile, thousands of native cattle will die during every drought.

There was a big herd of elephants on the far side of this river. In the high and leafy green vegetation, they first made their presence known by the high swirls of dust that suddenly shot up above the dense undergrowth. Then we saw their waving trunks, their huge, flapping ears and the sharp-ridged backs. They had got our wind. In a panic, the largest animals left on earth fled away from us. They had learned what to fear, although it was a comfortable thought to know that the elephant is increasing in numbers in Kenya and will probably be one of the last of its marvellous fauna to disappear. Just after passing the Uaso Nyiro, I saw my first gerenuk, the deer with the neck of a swan or a giraffe; certainly the queerest buck in all Africa. It was standing upon its hind legs, nibbling the leaves of a thorn tree some 10 feet above the ground, a perfect example of how animals change shape to fit in with their environment. We saw several after that, all standing in the phantom shade of slender thorn trees. For even they were trying to get some shelter from the burning sun. I am sure you could have fried an egg on any rock. In flight, these grotesque, strangely beautiful animals seem to float in the air during their long bounds.

It is up here in the desolate N.F.D. that you will see some of the rarest game left in Africa. I saw a herd of long-horned oryx sparkling in the sun on the far edge of a *lugga*, and a string of nine greater kudu walking along the green shoulder of Marsabit Mountain, that I shall never forget. We came into country where I saw several Grevy's or Abyssinian zebra, which look grey because they have such narrow black striping, the deep, liver-colored reticulated giraffe, with its dazzling checkerboard of white stripes. Poor giraffes, they are turned into buckets by the Somalis to get water from their wells, as only a giraffe's ½-inch hide can stand up to being passed up, hand to hand, from water that is 50 or 60 feet below the ground. The Somali and his giraffe-hide bucket are inseparable—just like an old-fashioned trek-Boer with his .303 Mauser.

We camped that night in a wooded mountain paradise on the lip of a dead volcano.

We got there in pitch darkness, the headlights shining first on the unexpected sight of high grass, then a lichened forest, with the rose-red eyes of animals. Reece had been doing this sort of thing for years and years. Never have I seen a camp pitched so automatically. The Dubas and the boys were like a troupe of trained acrobats. The instant the lorry stopped, after Reece had picked the site (he was always very particular about that), the Dubas jumped from the loaded truck, immediately set up two canvas camp chairs for us to sit on, and placed a table between us. Cook had a fire going and a big pot of tea on the table almost before I had finished my first cigarette. It was like rubbing the lamp. Dubas, rifles on their backs, were slashing grass with their long knives to clear a space for my tent, then raking it clear with an ordinary garden rake; a tarpaulin was being stretched out from the lorry under which Reece's bed was set up. My bed and wash-stand were put up, and a tarpaulin for me to stand on. And, although I never fired it once up in the N.F.D.—I didn't want to—my shotgun was placed by my cot. Soon the smell of bacon and sausages, spiced with wood-smoke, enlivened the cold mountain air. With a huge brush fire burning, lighting the faces of the Dubas and African boys, it was a fine sight that night under the stars, as a half-moon rose over Africa. . . .

The boys seemed to be enjoying it as much as we.

"Mmmmm . . ." said Reece, beginning the one cigar that he allowed himself each day, his contemplative after-dinner smoke. "Why shouldn't they? It is their old way of life. Or something very like it. If we could only restore these people's confidence and *belief* in some of their own old ways of life—

In the morning when I woke up, after a night of grisly dreams and half-awake quarter-hours of reproachful introspection—for I have reached the age where I loathe myself for taking too much drink, even though I do it—I looked out the tent mouth into an Elysian glade. There, in a state of perfect happiness, I saw another red elephant. He was not much more than 100 yards from my tent, ambling along, stopping at what looked like olive trees growing here and there in the golden grass, reaching up with his long trunk to eat some fruit or berries growing on their branches. These trees were *Bauhinia tomentosa*, very plentiful on Marsabit, whose seeds are much loved by the elephant. He was a fairly young elephant, flicking his short tail like a puppy. So different from the peanut-fed poor beast of the zoo or circus! Perhaps I ought to explain my predilection for seeing red elephants. They get this color from wallowing, and as the red earth, which holds iron, is cooler than the grey earth, they seem to prefer that. On this *safari* we saw the difference between these two earths when we camped at night. The red earth country cooled off instantly, and we had to sleep under heavy blankets; this in a country which almost seared your eyes by day. In the grey earth, land of the choking scrub, there was always a latent heat. The dawn wind was blowing strong from the volcanic crater, but for some reason its currents missed the elephant.

Reece came along. "There's two old men out there." I got up, and saw two more red elephants. They were strolling along, shoulder to shoulder, about 100 yards on our right. I thought then of the faithfulness, the solicitude which these great animals show each other, for if you shoot an elephant in a herd, and he does not fall, other elephants will sometimes get on either side of him to bolster him up and help him from the field. And many an elephant has been shot who lingered behind to try to help another elephant to his feet by trying to lift him with his tusks. These two "old men" were old elephants, possibly 100 years or so, who had probably been wandering around places like Marsabit long before the white man came to Africa. But they got our scent now. Their ears went up, they began to swing to and fro nervously; then increasing their pace, they made for the security of the deep forest. Nobody shoots an elephant now on Marsabit; at least, they are not supposed to. This is part of Reece's good work.

The red ball of sun rose like an angry eye over the deep volcanic crater. It is almost a perfect circle, with a floor, some 600 feet below you, that is a mile and a half in diameter. Reece and I stood on the edge with glasses, trying to see if there were any elephant herds in its damp bottom. Two natives came along, a man and woman; wild, yet with a timid look on their black faces. They were hybrids, said Reece, bastardised Gabbra, a tribe not very good to begin with, who, in the past, had destroyed thousands of acres on Marsabit by making forest fires so that they could graze their cattle. Their faces were not Negroid. The woman, with her straight nose and almond eyes, might even have been beautiful were it not that hundreds of flies were settled on her hair and around her eyes, attracted, I suppose, by the fat with which she had done her woolly mop. The man was carrying that strange bucket made from giraffe hide which, I was to learn, was the one thing that man and cattle and camel live by in the waterless N.F.D. The man had a spear, but looked a cringing creature. They belonged to a party grazing cattle, they told us, down in the pan of the volcano far below us.

We entered the lichen-covered forest to get into Crater Lake, with baboons and monkeys scampering among the branches; and if ever I saw motor vehicles take a beating, it was in jolting and swaying along that now unused road. The trees here are so interlaced that, with the one tree that has grown in and around another tree, it is impossible to say which is the host-tree and which the parasite. Wild olives were plentiful out on the grassy slopes. Here, with the exception of the cedar and the *muhugu* tree, of which there are none, and of ferns and palms, which are strangely absent, you will find almost every tree in East Equatorial Africa; orchids; and, in places, a red carpet formed from the scarlet poison lilies. Through this dim, green, almost secret forest darkness came the mournful note of the anvil bird. When we got to Crater Lake, which is now dry, one more sinister warning of drying East Africa, the pan of its bottom was full of black-and-white European storks. Thousands of them! They were after frogs.

In 1925, when the Johnsons were living there, this lake held so much water that they believed it was bottomless. Their Paradise! Well, they can see the bottom now. Baboons hastily retreated across it when they saw us appear on the lip. I sat on the stones of what had once been Johnson's house, while Reece, with the rifle—"In case I meet the odd buffalo"—went off into the forest to find if a pool was still there where he and his wife and their two children often bathed. They came in here frequently to bathe and picnic over a week-end, because of the wonderful bird life in this forest. Apparently it is a popular resting spot for European migrants in March and April. At that time it has myriads of swallows haunting the fringes of the forest, sand martins, grey and yellow wagtails, willow- garden- and sedge-warblers, chiffchaffs, white-throats, nightingales and red-backed shrikes. Some winter there. But the forest birds, which should be indigenous, are sadly lacking; forest guinea-fowl, the big hornbill and green pigeons, although every condition is suitable, are mysteriously absent. But ravens, eagles, vultures, hawks and owls are in all the cliffs and craters of the stony parts of Marsabit. The thing that impressed me most about the deep forest was its absolute silence. . . .

Abyssinian poachers, using cheap traps that the Italians first supplied them with, and alien Galla from over the border have almost exterminated the leopard in the N.F.D. Marsabit and Mt. Kulal, these two unique paradises, have been the scenes of regular and systematic slaughter. On the north side of Mt. Kulal, over near Lake Rudolph, there are whole cemeteries of elephants. Their bleached skulls lie thick on the ground. And never will their bones be seen again by any of their kind, as the herds have been wholly slaughtered and those remnants which escaped have now found sanctuary on Marsabit. The old myth that the elephants of Africa have a common cemetery where they go to die is now exploded; they drop when and where their time comes. But they have been practically exterminated along the Abyssinian border.

At Marsabit, where they are not shot at, the elephants have become, on occasions, entirely too tame. They will walk into the station and stand within a few feet of the houses. It amuses them to pull down a latrine or knock over a garage. They get above themselves and have killed cattle and, in times of drought, have done considerable damage to plantations and maize *shambas*. There was one old one-tusker who became the station's pet. When he strolled into its clearing, it was noticed that his wife always waited on the edge of the jungle for him. He once walked up to the D.C.'s house, with the D.C. and his American wife inside it, and ate all the creepers from its wall. "He must have known that we were sitting there within six feet of him!"

One moonlit night, when the D.C. was giving a dinner party, this old elephant came in and stood between the two halves of the house; and the servant, going out to the cook-house section to get the next course, walked slap into the elephant's behind. "With the boy yelling bloody murder and the elephant trumpeting, it sounded as if all hell had been let loose!" But this old one-tusker had, very reluctantly, to be shot. During a prolonged drought he began to lead a band of elephants into the station which used to break up everything: he was so unafraid that he had become dangerous. The D.C., whose father had once been the British Ambassador in Washington, had been seconded from the Coldstream Guards to the Somali Camel Corps, and loved Somalis. And his home and that of Reece looked down from their height on to the vast, sea-like expanse of the Dida Galgalla—the Plain of Darkness—the beginning of sixty straight miles of lava rubble on the road up to Abyssinia: one of the most breath-taking scenes I have ever looked out upon. On the lawns of these two homes are beautiful, wild brown olive trees, covered with little white flowers like lilies, which cover the ground with their white snow. Standing there my first morning at Marsabit, looking up to the ridge on which the dripping, lichen-covered forest began, at 9 A.M., with the moon still up in the sky, I watched nine greater kudu walk out along the ridge.

Here at Marsabit the moisture, condensed by this forest, makes magnificent grazing plains. And here you see the first of those mysterious wells that have been cut, it is not known by whom, from 60 to 70 feet straight down through limestone or gypsum rock. The Somalis and the Boran believe that they were cut by a race of giants who, they declare, were 10 feet high. They are cut with a precision that makes them look as if bored with a machine. And every drop of water that the cattle or camels drink is raised from the bottom of these wells by a line of men and women standing on the sides of the wall, passing up and down in a continuous line of giraffe-hide buckets. They are known as a twelve-man well or an eighteen-man well, depending upon the number of people required to make the line. It is one of the most stupendous sights in Africa to watch one of these wells in action.

The cattle wait until they are called. The two wells at Marsabit are down in a ravine and are therefore comparatively shallow: five-man wells. On a wall that was almost perpendicular stood five Boran. A man, naked from the waist up, stood on a wall of the ravine, put his hand to the side of his mouth, and uttered a loud cry. In a few seconds a couple of hundred light brown cattle, as frisky as playful dogs, came out of the grasslands and began bouncing down through the red boulders that lined the gulch. The five natives in each of the wells began a series of rhythmic shouts, "*A-ja-la! Hoy-ya-da!*"—a chant that had something mesmeric about it. It seemed to put them in a trance. Actually, the timing of this strange chanting linked them in unison so that the giraffe-hide buckets, about 8 inches deep by 6 inches diameter, were circulating as if on a mechanical revolving belt. The speed and dexterity with which the buckets were seized and passed up, emptied into a trough, then, empty, were being simultaneously passed down has to be witnessed to be realised. The Boran and the Somalis can keep this up for hours on end with the steadiness of a hydraulic pump. And, watching it, you get some sense of the intimacy between these men and their cattle and camels.

They can speak to their animals: and the alertness of those Boran cattle will make me hesitate before I ever use the expression "stupid as a cow" any more. As each batch of these nimble, intelligent little cattle came jumping down into the red ravine, they lined up automatically; and then, at a signal, a group of six or seven would advance to the trough and take their deep drink that was to last them for the day. (The camels, as I watched them at Wajir, take two long drinks—20 gallons in all—that have to last them for fourteen days.) There is a herd, with a stick, who whacks cattle back which have become too impatient. And this day, as I watched them, six fat little donkeys stood in an aristocratic group by themselves, taking a bite at any animal that came too near them until they, in their turn, were summoned to the trough. Elders of the Boran, with turbans and half-closed, threatening eyes, stood there with spears in their hands and knives in their belts in an attitude of dignity and defiance that had been handed down through hundreds of years of such tribal custom. When one herd had had its water, it walked slowly up through the red boulders to resume its grazing on the broad grasslands and —"*Haiiiiii!*"—the wild-looking Boran on the rock shouted for another group to come to drink. They seemed to answer his call without anyone on the tableland ordering them to come down. And all through that afternoon that incessant chanting was kept up—"*A-ja-la! Hoy-ya-da!*"—the Song of the Well.

As no other hide is tough enough to stand up to this, and rubber is no substitute, the number of giraffe that the natives of the N.F.D. slaughter every year to provide these buckets seriously threatens the existence of that noble animal, so easy to kill because of his insatiable curiosity, which makes him linger until you can get within 20 or 30 yards of him. For a rifle, they provide a pitifully easy shot.

Waiting on the veranda of the D.C.'s office, I saw the Chief of the Boran and several elders of the tribe which was supposed to have murdered and mutilated the two little goat boys a few days back. They knew they were under suspicion, and a menacing group they looked, staring at us insolently under their lowered eyelids. They were dressed in spotless white robes, red-sashed, with voluminous white turbans. Their faces were black, but high-cheeked, hawk-nosed, with nothing of the Negro about them. Their chief, a heavy creature—bone, mostly, for none of these Boran ever manage to eat enough to get stout—eyed Reece with a look of what appeared to be studied hatred. His black, bearded head and keen rugged features gave this look the edge of a challenging malevolence. Reece, returning the D.C.'s sharp salute, walked past them curtly.

"These are tough people," he said as he sat down in the D.C.'s chair, "and you've got to be tough with them." He looked over the station's report and saw the details of a recent cattle raid. "That is the beginning of the coming problem. If you don't watch out, these people will just ruin the country. If we can't find it out any other way, the people who actually did this job [the murder], I think it would be a good idea to close the wells to them . . . and be quite firm about it. They will probably be threatening. . . ." The end of his sharp nose quivered. "But as soon as they know we mean business, I dare say that some of them will come along to you—privately—and tell you who the murderers were. Pick 'em up. They can't live without water.

"And if they say, 'We will go back to Abyssinia' (where over half the Boran graze their cattle), then say, 'We will help you to go back to Abyssinia. Do go! We will even give you camels.'" A nose-twitch, this signifying satire. "The whole policy of this country is to push people northwards, anyway."

These turbaned chiefs out on the veranda had had Reece to do with for years. I could understand, as I listened to him briefing the cool young D.C., why they stared at his face with such sullen apprehension. They had a man to deal with. Reece, who had studied these people as keenly as could the most scientific anthropologist, passed to another problem: the southward migration of the unruly Somalis.

"The greatest danger is that you will let yourself get to like them too much. That's where they get you." He knew that the D.C. had been in the Somali Camel Corps and, as is inevitable, had fallen for the charm of these brave but most treacherous people. "As a rule, a man who is very pro-Somali or very anti-Somali is a man who does not understand the Somali. The usual rule is to start by being very pro, and then, when you see that when he is at his most friendly manner he is really plotting to do you down, you become very anti. Sensible people won't allow themselves to be violently one or the other." He gave a little cough. "Personally, I like the Somali.

"I like them," he went on, "because I like their good manners. I like the Somali's manliness, his love of children and his ability to fight with courage and to endure hardship and to suffer pain. I like his sense of humor and the immense zest and energy which he can put into what he is doing that appeals to him. Treat him with confidence and respect when—ahem—whenever possible. . . ."

The handsome young D.C. permitted himself a smile. Everyone knows that "Uncle" loves the Somalis. It might be written on his sleeve. It was just as bad to be too harsh as to be too lenient, was the summing up of his peroration; though, I deduced, it was not difficult to be hard with the Boran, a most unpleasant people. The chief difficulty with the proud and high-strung Somalis, of whom there are some 60,000 in the N.F.D., is that for years they have been regarded, and regard themselves, as the aristocrats of East Africa; and their dignity will not allow them to do any manual work. They have the high sense of self-respect, leading to an unbearable conceit, that seems to be characteristic of all desert-living followers of Mohammed.

The Borans are Pagans, and they worship snakes; but they have prayers to their own invisible deity that are strangely like the teachings of Christ. Is this savagery?

> With the corn which thou letst grow for us, men were satisfied. The corn in the house has been burnt up. Who has burnt the corn in the house? Thou knowest.
>
> The murderous enemy took the curly-headed child out of his mother's hand and killed him. Thou hast permitted all this to be done so. Why hast thou done so? Thou knowest.
>
> When the corn blooms thou sendst butterflies and locusts into it, locusts and doves. All this comes from thy hand, thou hast caused it to be done so. Why hast thou done so? Thou knowest.
>
> The corn which thou letst grow does thou show to our eyes; the happy man looks at it and is comforted.
>
> Oh God, thou hast let me pass the night in peace; let me pass the day in peace. Wherever I may go, upon my way which thou madst peaceable for me, oh God, lead my steps.

These are taken from *A Grammar of the Galla (Boran) Language*, by Charles Tutschek, published in Munich, 1845. This German accompanied one of the early explorative expeditions to East Africa. And when you see the deep love which these Boran have for their animals—a woman will hold a calf dying from starvation or thirst in her lap and weep—you begin to revise your definition of the word "savage." It is what you bring *to* a people that gives you the greatest ability to understand them: an artist looking at a painting has more understanding of that painting than a layman could; similarly, the definition of savagery depends largely upon the character of the man who comes among them. If he was a brute (and he often was), he thought they were too.

That evening the D.C. and I drove out across the grassy plains below Marsabit to pay a surprise visit on the tribe of Boran which was suspected of shielding whoever of its members had murdered and mutilated the two little boys. The pastoral scene was almost melancholily peaceful, considering the fact that we were calling on suspected murderers. Some camels, hobbled by bending up the foreleg and binding it to the next joint, gave a hint of the cruelty which seemed to be lurking in the landscape; and the stare of black hate with which we were met by the white-robed and turbaned men who came outside the brush *boma* to receive us said, without words, what a delight it would be to these black pagans to sink a spear into us. A group of six men, never saying a word or moving a muscle, stood behind their chief, glaring at us with this steady malevolence through half-shut eyes; and the chief, upright, rugged, and openly fearless, made no attempt to conceal that he was angered by our appearance. But the sophisticated D.C., who had been born when his father was the British Ambassador in Rome, and who had seen a great deal of diplomatic life in his time, smiled as if the red carpet had been laid down for us, and, with his easy good manners, asked the chief courteously if he might show me around the tribe's *boma.* At the same time he held out his hand. . . .

The chief, who also had good manners, suitable to the occasion, looked at the young D.C. steadily, and held out a black arm, fingers straight and pressed together—the Boran do not clasp your hand—and stepped back. This was the sign that, as the D.C. was the administrative officer in the district, and as the Boran could not help themselves, he could do what he liked.

The *boma* stood on a vast sweep of treeless plain whose knee-high grasses were being brushed with gold by the setting sun. It was some 40 or 50 yards in diameter, ringed with a light *zareba* of brushwood, and contained some dozen or so low huts made of grass mats. A few biscuit-colored young cattle, with the dewlaps of the Boran animals, stood in a little inside enclosure of their own. Smoke came from the evening fires inside the grass huts, not one of which was higher than my shoulder. Such a camp can be struck in a night, the grass huts and all household goods—and the smallest babies—packed on horses or camels, and the whole outfit be twenty-five miles away from you before sunrise, lost in the bush or in the mirage of the desert, a mobility which makes the agile Boran and the Somali extremely difficult people to handle. And they strike, in their raids, with the same secret, swift celerity. At the administrative post of Marsabit it was thought at that time that, if they were really guilty, these Boran might make such a flight any night and head for Abyssinia. All of this was present in my mind as we walked through this peaceful-looking little *boma* in the serene sunset. We were received with silence.

Inside each grass hut, immediately to the left of its entrance, was the traditional manger for just-born calves: attractive little animals, standing there so confidently in the heart of the family. Three or four in each hut being hand-fed with milk. They were about the size of foxhounds. Inside each hut, with its tail against the three stones which made the fireplace, dozed a little dun-colored puppy, completely at peace against the warm stones. Women in each hut were cleaning gourds decorated with cowrie shells with wood ashes for the evening's milk. Other eyes met us, from shy or hiding young girls in the back darkness of the hut. They have no lights, of course. Babies began to cry when they saw our strange white faces. That was the only emotion displayed at our unwelcome presence. And in one hut a tiny black child was sitting stark naked on the ground, hugging in its arms a tiny white goat that had just been dropped. Black-and-white storks were stalking about unconcernedly, feeding in the maize and millet just outside the *boma*. It was impossible, so it seemed, to conceive of a more contented and tranquil scene. Yet when we drove away I could feel that stare of hate boring into the small of my back. . . .

I remember it because in this case the Boran happened to be innocent. And in the bitter restraint with which they received us, making it so plain that they were only polite to us because they had to be, I could read the story of a very cruelly treated race. Over half the Boran live up in Abyssinia, where they graze their fine cattle in the green foothills of a territory known as Borana. This was seized by the great Menelik less than fifty years ago, who was copying the European Powers in their scramble for Africa. Since that evil day, Borana has been a colony of Ethiopia, administered by the usual corrupt and cruel Amhara governors who have made Abyssinian rule notorious. These Governors, who get their position by intrigue and who know that they will lose it by the same, have, with the rarest of exceptions, all worked on the principle that they must make enough money to put by in anticipation of the day when successful intriguers at Addis Ababa are going to deprive them of their appointment. The result with the Boran has been that, as nothing was done to better their conditions or to protect them from brigandage, they passed under a form of serfdom; and a fine cattle-owning people, who at one time occupied territory as far east as Mandera and also the whole northern half of what is now the N.F.D., are now probably dying out owing to the persecution of their neighbors and—I think this should always be taken into account—just the will to live. It is quite likely that before very long they will be entirely absorbed by the Somali tribes, who are pushing them westwards. The Kenya Government cannot interfere with Abyssinian rule in Borana; nor can it effectively prevent, or secure recompense for, raids from across the border of Abyssinia into the N.F.D. Boran territory. It can be gathered, therefore, that they have largely been made an unpleasant people. And it is in the protection of the Borans that Kenya has one of its most difficult foreign affairs' problems in relation to the present extremely unco-operative rule in Ethiopia. These were the people in whom Gerald Reece wanted to reinstate dignity and a reinforced confidence in their former—pre-Menelik—way of life.

"If we can restore these people's self-respect and persuade them to accept some of the compromises that they will have to make—to exist in modern times—then our rule here will be justified. That is the real education that we should give these people."

CHAPTER XXI

Plain of Darkness

IN THIS battered world, which we seem to be using up as fast as we can, it is a joy to come on a region which can defy the hand of man. If the pagan Boran and the wandering Somali can live in the volcanic desert between Marsabit and the Abyssinian frontier, then they are lucky. They have found a place where the white man can do nothing either for or to them. The Dida Galgalla, the Plain of Darkness, as these nomads call it, is an unbroken plain of lava rubble, some sixty miles wide from south to north, which begins on the edge of the grazing plains at the foot of Marsabit and ends with an isolated little mountain called Turbi, twenty miles south of Abyssinia. There is a fringe of blue mountains on its western skyline, high and jagged, which shuts off the Chalbi Desert and Lake Rudolph, and which dissolves in the heat-haze of midday. On the east there is nothing except a few isolated mountain masses, just blue bumps, meaningless, as a child would draw mountains, which begin to float in mid-air as the mirage begins, then enlarge or retract, and also disappear. Beyond them is nothing but choking thorn-scrub extending all the way to the narrow fringe of coconut palms on the edge of the Indian Ocean.

How any man or beast can live on this plain of two-foot lava boulders, shimmering like the air over a stove, is an unsolved mystery. You can *see* the heat. It is alleged that the beautiful oryx, which are rather numerous in some sections, can go for weeks without water. Yet in that baking wilderness I saw Grevy's zebra galloping away among the reddish boulders, Thomson's and Grant's gazelle, and occasional troupes of ostriches, which, with their wings spread out to cool them, looked like trees. There are no trees in that plain, except for a few green acacia thorns along the bed of a dry *lugga*. And the plain is so flat that, with the heat waves distorting everything, a little Grant's gazelle balanced on a boulder at 600 yards stands up like a monument. Yet in here, on the bank of one of these dry, sandy, dead watercourses, we came on the crumbling droppings of many cattle and the grave of an old Boran chief who had once had his *boma* in these parts.

It was a cairn covered with lava boulders, in which, according to custom, it is believed that he is buried in a squatting position, with his arms around his knees, facing the setting sun. I dare say that his pagan spirit fully appreciates the wild and hard beauty of the loneliness in which he had been placed to rest. He had died near Marsabit, said Reece, and his followers, "with rather a romantic touch," had brought him back to the *boma* in which he had known his greatest days. We had lunch there under the gossamer shade of an acacia thorn and a pale blue sky with little islands of white clouds that stood high over us. The only sign of life was a lizard, which darted into the perforated lava-rubble of the cairn. Many of these Galla cairns date from prehistoric days.

It was appalling to try to imagine the explosion which must have spewed the boulders over this immense flat plain. Sixty miles of lava. A road had been made across it simply by pulling the lava-rubble to one side. We averaged twelve miles an hour, which was not at all bad. When the sun was at its zenith, the red-black lava seemed incandescent with its original volcanic heat. But, unless you looked close, it had lost its color. All colors seemed to have been burnt out by the immense heat. The Somali call this lava desert the Land of Heat. The long-horned oryx looked white in the vibrating heat waves. Grant's and Thomson's gazelles lost their black stripes. In illusory images created by the mirage, the ostriches, as I have said, looked like trees; and some ostriches, when we came up to them, turned out to be merely the greater bustard. It was a landscape that a white man could easily lose his reason in. And this was believed to have happened to the occupants of an aeroplane which had crashed somewhere in this lava desert on a flight from Marsabit to Moyale during the last war, whose wreckage has not been located even to this day. The small passenger planes which are used now in East Africa are instructed to keep along the line of this road, so that if they do happen to come down there will be some chance of picking up the survivors, if there are any. And where some of the Boran live in here, for it is known that they are there, no one can be sure. The greater part of the Dida Galgalla, the Plain of Darkness, is still unsurveyed, even from the air.

It gets its name from the way the lava boulders turn blood red at sunset. It is then that the colors come back. The jagged mountains on our far left turn a deep indigo. Just before we came to Mt. Turbi, its woods and granite faces shining in the setting sun, we came on to an open plain of stiff, silvered grass. Hundreds of gazelle shot like arrows away from us. We entered a dark belt of low green scrub, swung around the flanks of Turbi, where the Italian Colonial troops had nearly ambushed a detachment of the King's African Rifles, and drove on through another monstrous forest of these tangled, leafless thorns that look like dead apple trees. And then, in the deepening blues of sunset, we saw what looked to be flaky white islands on the hills of the dusty green scrub country beyond, but which, another illusion, turned out to be herds of thousands of white goats. A scene to startle anyone, both by its beauty and the fact that we had come among human beings again.

The soil here was a dusty Devon red, and a little further on we came to a ravine made in the thick brush by the passage of animals. As we came abreast of its opening a couple of hundred white goats spewed out of it and began their satanic bleating. They were under the protection of an old native, with white hair and beard, a thing seldom seen with the black man, and a little girl dressed in skins. When we stopped the Ford and the big 3-ton lorry behind us came to a halt, the old man pulled his strip of Abyssinian grey homespun cloth around him and, spear in hand, strode across the sands towards us.

There was something noble in his bearing. "He walks like a Man!" I said to Reece. "Mnnnn . . . yes. And he's a Gabbra at that." I don't remember, now, whether or not they shook hands. But when Reece began to talk to him in his own tongue, the old man, as was apparently the custom with his people, sat down on the sands. "He says the hyenas are very bad around here," said Reece.

Reece, who was very supple, squatted on his hunkers, making a map with his fingers in the sand. From time to time the old Gabbra jerked his head towards Abyssinia. Reece made a mark; his nose twitched as he asked another question. "The *shifta* have been at it again," he said. Bandits from Abyssinia. The bearded old patriarch spoke with great dignity and had unworried eyes. "He's not changed much," Reece said in an aside to me, "since the days of Moses."

Then the old man suddenly stood up, pulled his spear from the hot sand, and touched Reece's hand. "He has just said to me," said Reece, " 'You must excuse me now. The hyenas are very bad around here. They take my goats. I don't want to be out after dark.' " As we drove on, they crossed the sandy stretch and began to walk the goats over the foothills to where other islands of goats were moving in the red sunset towards some big native *boma*, where the old man would stretch out his tired limbs and sleep by the warm fire. "Now, what good could our civilisation be to him?" said Reece. "What have *we* got to offer from our worried way of life! The wisdom of old men like that goes far deeper than ours: they live by the fundamentals. That is the life I am trying to get them to have faith in, not our complicated civilisation, or this damned nonsense that the 'Sewing Circle' is preaching!'

The "Sewing Circle" was the nickname that the administrative officers in the N.F.D. had for the Somali Youth League so that they could talk about it before a native they were questioning without his ever knowing it. There are something like 2,000,000 Somalis in the three Somalilands, Abyssinia, and in Kenya's N.F.D., without one tribe being complete in any of these five territories, with the result that the whole Horn of Africa was being shaken by political agitation, instigated—there is now no doubt about this—by the twenty "technicians" (who knew nothing whatever about medicine, but a lot about how to organise Fifth Columns) which the Russians sent to their hospital in Addis Ababa. From now on, from Moyale down to the camel center at Wajir, down to the elephant country along the Tana River, Reece and I would be in a country seething with Somali agitators.

We slept that night on the borders of Abyssinia. Somebody had started a forest fire in the mountains. It was in full flame along the ridges, glowing, in parts, as vividly as an open blast furnace. It created its own gale, sucking the wind and the sands through the barren stretch in which we had made our camp. In procedure, if not setting, the camp was always the same. Reece "hated to be overlooked," as he called it; so that the big 3-ton lorry, top-heavy with camp kit—and ten Africans riding on top of that!—was pulled in and parked parallel to whatsoever road we had been travelling. The cook made his campfire on the near side of that, and around this blaze the armed Dubas slept at nights, except for the one on watch. Further into the bush our chairs and camp table were set up. Further still, in a space that frequently had to be cleared with knives, the Ford V-8 was parked parallel to the lorry, and our camp beds were set up against it on the brushward side of that. A tarpaulin was laid on the ground between them, and our wash-table was set up at the foot of our beds. From then on it was just Africa. . . . Reece, unlike even the most hardened old-timers, does not put a lamp up at nights to keep the wild animals away. "Mnnnn . . ." he said. "If you do, and it's near your bed, a nervous rhino might charge it. It's only an invitation. If it's out in the bush, it is of no use at all in keeping the hyenas away. Some people put up two lights, one hung high up in a tree . . . if they can find one. Personally, I dispense with it." The mere fact of having to walk far out from the camp to attend to the calls of Nature, hidden from sight in the bush, is often too much for some people. Reece, who was very particular in his conduct before the natives, would walk 100 yards rather than be "overlooked." With only an electric torch burning, it is often a tickly job. And never have I thought it more so than when—Wa-yooo!-woo! wooo!—a huge hyena, not the little laughing variety, howled within 10 feet of my bare behind that night. He scared the life out of me.

Meals on that *safari* were always interesting. The big lorry was full of chop-boxes. And Reece, squatting on his heels, would take out the tins of whatever combination he thought would make a good meal. Mulligatawny soup, made with a hot Indian curry-powder; *Mackerel in Tamatiesous,* as the illiterate label of its Indian canning company read; and, as there was a dearth of white English potatoes in Kenya at that moment, we considered a big dish of these fried the treat of any meal. For a sweet we had, usually, canned Kenya green figs, as toothsome a morsel as ever went into any tin. And, of course, pot after pot of coffee. . . .

The lower half of a waning moon was rising over Africa. A whole mountain in Abyssinia was now outlined in fire. "I suppose some damned fool wanted a *shamba* (a farm). The Abyssinians don't care," said Reece as we stared at forests which began to glow like coals that were being blown upon. With the clouds of smoke filling with white flame and soaring upward, it looked as if the volcanic age had begun again. The fire was too distant for us to hear it. And as we sat there under the stars of Africa, staring at one that was particularly bright and low down, looking almost like a lighthouse, that night-bird which sings in a descending scale called, "Who? Who-who-who-who . . . ?" with a plaintiveness that touched the heart.

It was cold. Reece never slept in anything other than his sleeveless undershirt and a thing with a red border wrapped around him that looked like an ordinary kitchen roller towel. I believe it was one. He wrapped a wash-towel around his face to keep the moon off, said as he lay back, "Don't let the hyenas bite your nose off" —and directly beside us came that yowling "Wa-yooo! Woo! Wooooo!" of the big hyena again.

"Well, there's one," I said. "Right by your head."

But he was already asleep.

In the morning, the big yellow-billed hornbills were planing about us. The tall black Dubas were getting up from where they had been sleeping on the warm sand, wrapping their white strips around them. Then around their shaven heads they wound their blood-red turbans. The moustached cook and the little 70-lb. houseboy were getting breakfast. The world looked fresh and clean. And suddenly I was filled with a glorious sense of living. . . .

Reece was asleep, face bound up like a Tuareg. He was a man with a spirit that was always scaling pinnacles. But I think it exhausted him. His revolver lay beside him. Two hornbills sat, glinting in the sun, on the thorn bush by his cot. I sat up and lighted my first, delicious cigarette. The little houseboy brought us our tea. Reece's own personal Duba, a beautifully built Rendille (I think they must be the most attractive men in the world), came and took the revolver, breaking it to take out the cartridges.

The heavy old .45 was shiny from constant handling. But the big game rifle he kept loaded, putting it in its socket along the V-8's dashboard, with its little leather cup over the muzzle to keep the dust out. Reece sat up, rubbed his head, poured himself a cup of tea—and then forgot it.

"Mnnnn . . . birds," he said, staring at the hornbills. "You know, in Somali, the name for all small birds is just the same, *shimberi:* no name for any particular species. Aren't interested in 'em. Same way, in Swahili they have no words for the different colors. Not interested in the beauty of colors—the sun on that granite mountain, for example. But *sex*. My God, they've got a word for *everything—all* the variations!"

We shaved and washed. The smell of camp smoke and frying bacon made me, at least, waste not too much time over that. I hustled into my shorts and *safari* shirt. Reece was being much more particular. He was carefully putting on the full field uniform of an officer in the British Colonial Service. His little houseboy, who had been orphaned in a raid and who, I am certain, thought he had adopted Reece as a father, brought him a pair of freshly ironed slacks and a neat tunic, with the old 1914-18 and other decorations on it. Reece put on a pair of beautifully polished shoes, selected an uncrumpled khaki tie, looked at his solar topi to see that its insignia, the brass lion, had been polished properly. He dressed as carefully as if he had been going to take over the Guard at Buckingham Palace. Actually, he was going to take the salute of one sergeant and twelve men, all native, in a last, lonely little Kenya Police outpost a few miles above us. The moral of the correct example was ever-present in Reece's mind.

It was like being reborn to wake up on those mornings. Primarily, I think it was the delight at getting away from the general hoggishness of the white man. It was the world before Adam. Life seemed to have taken on an effervescent quality of curious, small, intimate, exciting interests. You felt yourself alone with the most pleasant thoughts. By the time Reece got to breakfast, his bacon and eggs and potatoes were stone cold, and he was lucky that I had left him any.

For some reason, probably because it had been stopped by a cliff, the mountain forest which had been on fire in Abyssinia during the night had gone out. There was not even smoke in the now tile-blue sky. The frontier was only a few miles away from us. We had hardly got out to the red, sandy road again before the Rendille sitting in our car saw a cobra. Our expedition stopped. I have never thought that I would be sorry for any snake; I'm scared to death of them; but when I saw this wretched, evil strip of greenish-pink which had got its head halfway down a hole under a bush and was hanging on there, horribly hanging on, refusing to come out, while the black men flailed away at it, I began to feel pangs of compassion. Finally, one of them, more reckless than the others, made a quick grab at its tail, flung it out on the red road, where it coiled, squirmed, turned over and over on itself in its agony. With a yell, nearly braining each other, the black boys rained blows on it until it was inert. A fine-looking Duba, majestic in his red turban, had taken part in none of this, and now, with a worried expression, he turned away.

"A Boran," said Reece. "A snake-worshipper. It might be his grandfather. . . ."

(Odd as it may seem, that was the only live snake I have ever seen in Africa, although I have driven a car from the Indian Ocean to the Atlantic along the Equator.)

After a few miles, we left the grim, gnarled *Commiphora* trees, the choking wait-a-bit thorn, the cactus-like candelabra euphorbia, and came to trees which began to look like trees. It was a delight to come to a tree with green leaves and wide branches, which might have been growing in any English meadow. I do not know its name. But I shall always remember the pleasure it gave me to see a rufus hawk sitting high up on its foliage, his brave white breast blazing in the morning sun, and to watch him stare down at us curiously, then turn his head away, completely unafraid.

Below the tree some ugly marabous got up and began to flap in circles over us. Hundreds of grey doves and smaller birds showed themselves, darting above among the thick green vegetation. This was around a "pan" that Reece wanted to show me. He had been getting the natives to dig these depressions all over the N.F.D. to preserve water; one of his chief efforts, he told me, to help raise their standard of life. Originally, I imagine, the sites must all have been picked from old elephant wallows—those solidified waves of mud that you will often come on in the jungle or scrub where elephants have been grubbing with their tusks for under-surface water. The earth is so damp that millet can frequently be grown around these pans. Anyhow, by scooping out the depression and piling it up to form a dirt wall, a very good catchment receptacle is made for any rains that may fall, and there is also the sub-surface water to prevent it draining away. In some parts of the N.F.D., any passing nomadic tribe has a right to water its cattle or camels, provided they never let the animals enter the pan and the water is carried to them in buckets. In others, in payment for one big bucket of water, the native is required to dig eight times that amount of earth out of the pan. This was their ancient way, not Reece's; and this was one of the ancient customs that he was trying to persuade them to revive all over the province. Animals may graze around these pans for months at a time, and thus reduce the strain on the grazing around the wells; and these pans, as I saw between Moyale and Wajir, where for one stretch of seventy miles there are no wells, yearly save the lives of hundreds of people and animals. Remember, the Somalis do not ride their animals (except in fighting), but use them as transport animals: usually three camels to each of a man's wives, to carry their portable hut and possessions—and seventy miles is a long trek on foot.

But the unsettled conditions along the Abyssinian frontier of the N.F.D. make it very difficult to persuade the local natives to make these pans. They can never be sure how long they will enjoy the use of them; and unless there can be a clear understanding concerning the ownership of wells, pans, and grazing areas, the natives will not take any interest in them and they are allowed to deteriorate. The frontier cuts straight through the grazing land of all the tribes; no tribe is complete in any one place. If conditions were the same on both sides of the frontier—I am speaking of political and peaceful conditions—they could wander freely back and forth. But conditions are by no means equal.

"Where I pass not one blade of grass shall remain!" is supposed to have been the boast of Attila, "the scourge of God"; similarly, of the people and lands "eaten up" by the Amhara soldiers and officials, that small minority which rules or misrules Ethiopia, there is the saying: "*Where the Amhara tread, the grass grows no more.*"

It has been claimed in some London newspapers that "of all the African races the Abyssinian is best able to govern himself." This may be true, but the real question to be answered is whether the Abyssinian is able to govern the subject peoples who live in his colonies.

On the Abyssinian side of the frontier armed tribal levies are used to deal with frontier disturbances, and untrained and undisciplined natives are allowed to bear arms which, when there are no disturbances, they use to loot and murder and thus create blood feuds. For the past eighteen years no British tribesmen have been allowed to carry arms on the Kenya side of the frontier. (This places them at a horrible disadvantage, as I will show later on.) No extradition treaty exists between Ethiopia and Great Britain, and all attempts of the British to get such a working arrangement with the Abyssinians have so far failed. While the British have handed over many criminals to the Abyssinians, Ethiopian officials have seldom, if ever, reciprocated.

So here in this tiny frontier post, with the impeccable Reece taking the salute of not even a corporal's guard, with black soldiers in a gun-pit covering us with their rifles as we came in to the closed gate in its barbed wire, and other black police, in a square of sand-bags, keeping constant watch across an open space to the bushes and trees which marked the frontier of Ethiopia, one could see in microcosm one of the tangled knots in the skein of conflicting foreign and colonial policies which the British have the unenviable task of unraveling at the moment. Britain's Mediterranean policy (now linked with that of Western Union) would urge her to reinstate the Italians in their Somaliland and in Eritrea, but that (I am quoting from deeply-felt letters to the London *Times*), "in the interests of Western Union, would be placating Italy at the expense of Africa." It would, in the opinion of many high British Colonial officers, also start a third world war. Leaving entirely aside the morals of Italian colonial administration, the fact remains that the Abyssinians would almost certainly attack the Italians if they were replaced in Eritrea. The Somalis of all the Somalilands, British, French, Italian, to say nothing of the 60,000 restless Somalis in

Kenya's N.F.D., would think that they had been betrayed by England's promises (they want a united Somaliland). And the Somali Youth League would have been provided with just the material it needs to incite a revolt among the 2,000,000 Somalis in the Horn of Africa.

But that the Italians will be given the trusteeship of their former Somaliland under the United Nations is almost a certainty. [This has been done.]

Reece had a map with him, establishing a new frontier line between Kenya and Ethiopia, adjustments which had been agreed upon between Addis Ababa and London (strongly advised by Reece) which would go a long way towards reducing the chronic inter-tribal disputes over water and grazing rights. For something like forty years the British have tried to maintain good order and friendly relations with the Ethiopian Government, mostly by the exercise of extreme, and at times even a shameful, patience; and this policy of appeasement has failed. Reece's hope was that "His Majesty's Government will now allow us to adopt a firmer attitude."

That, the promise of immediate physical reprisals, if the Abyssinians make a raid—plus the bribe of the "blood money"—will probably be the way that things will work out in the northern section of the N.F.D. One thing that has shown the end of British tolerance (though it might be revoked) is that the British have refused to abandon their police posts in this frontier territory or move them back in order to acquiesce with the perpetual demands of the local Abyssinian officials. Until an extradition treaty is agreed to between London and Addis Ababa, this little police post at Abo, and others, will remain—"to keep the peace."

The tiny post was in a great state of excitement when we got there. But not because of the Abyssinians. The previous morning, so the still-startled sergeant told Reece, there had been a noise such as none of them had ever heard in all their lives: "The earth under our feet trembled!"—and the granite top of Abo had fallen off! Reece translated this to me; and, looking up, I could see the fresh grey scar, like a freshly broken iron plate, where a great face of the mountain had sheered off. The police sergeant, a pagan, but a man nevertheless who had been decorated in the last war for saving a detachment of the King's African Rifles from being ambushed (at Turbi), said that they had talked it over among themselves, and they had all come to the conclusion that a big Boran chief must have died some place; the top of Abo falling off had been the announcement of it. Reece nodded seriously. Then he began to try to explain to the sergeant that what they had passed through had been an earthquake. But no! said the sergeant; not only had the top of the mountain fallen off but *springs of water had appeared.* And he pointed to the foot of the granite mass, where, he said, his police had come on flowing water that morning. These thirteen natives had never thought of putting the two things together. The top falling off the mountain; that certainly was because something of immense importance had happened somewhere. Of course, it might not be the death of a big Boran. But the newly-gushing springs. . . . Oh, well, that could have happened at any time. Reece's earthquake explanation just did not register.

"At any rate," said Reece as he turned to me with his smile repressed, "there's some new water in this district. That means that more Boran will be allowed to come in here and graze their animals. Some of God's good work. But it also means," he said after a moment's thinking, "another source of dispute with the Abyssinians. The border runs right here."

While Reece and the sergeant and I were talking there was a loud whirr overhead, and I looked up and saw the amazing sight of about forty or fifty brilliant little blue starlings shoot into the acacia tree above our heads. In the bright sun, their iridescent backs glinted like a handful of emeralds. They have brown vests and little white collars. They paid not the least attention to us as they went on with their nest-building.

So far as I know, for I did not see any machine guns (I saw Bren guns at Marsabit), this little police outpost was armed with only rifles. But the Kenya Police who are used up in the N.F.D. are highly skilled men, trained even better than the K.A.R. for their extremely individual work in the Bush and desert. The Dubas are trained to execute one-man missions, and are supposed to be able to get to any place they are ordered in these wastes, and to be able to live entirely off the country itself.

Outside the small police post at Abo was a *boma* of some

Gabbra, camped as close to it as they could get in order to be under its protection. Usually the kraal for the cattle is in the center of such *bomas*, with the huts on the perimeter, so that any attacker would have to fight and overcome the owners before getting at the animals, the most-prized possession of all nomadic Africans. But Reece asked me to note that this group's cattle kraal was openly exposed on the edge of their huts, so that if any large party of raiders came they would get the cattle without difficulty; and thus, presumably satisfied, would not slaughter the inhabitants. " 'To live again and'—flee another day," said Reece. "Some of them haven't got very much spunk left." Another rufus hawk sat, totally unconcerned about our presence, on an acacia tree which shaded one of the straw huts of the *boma*. The men slunk away from us at first, tried to vanish among the huts. In the morning sun some small girls, ten or twelve years old, tried to see us through eyes that were gummed with secretions of some infection; and one, who could not have been more than six, and who was carrying a tiny *toto* on her back, looked almost blind. The little *toto* had some disease which had swollen his limbs and face, so that his fly-rimmed eyes were also almost invisible, and they had covered his poor little swollen and sore-eaten legs with a concoction that looked like tar. "Syphilis, very likely," said Reece. "I'd give my eyes to have travelling dispensaries . . . making regular circuits of the N.F.D. . . ." Southern Abyssinia is full of syphilis. And the Boran are decreasing in number because of venereal disease just as much as they are from the persecution of neighboring tribes. When you study some of these decreasing tribes in Africa, you come to the conclusion that they have just lost the will to live.

Aluminium piping plays a great part in the *bijouterie* of the N.F.D. It can be polished to look like silver. The arms of these small girls were shining, not with clinking bracelets, but a spiral of bright aluminium tubing that ran from wrist to elbow. Their woolly heads rose from concentric rings of shining metal. Aluminium bangles dangled from their ears. The diseased little baby had a ring of red beads around its neck. In Africa the small babies are always being carried by somebody. They are never left on the ground, where a hyena or a straying African might get them. I've seen them lashed to their mother's back where the "duck-mouthed" women with the wooden discs in their lips work in the suffocating fibre-filled air of the sisal-pulling factories in Tanganyika, where it is difficult for even a full-grown man to breathe. You will see them perched on head loads, on backs, on hips, but hardly ever on the ground, except inside a grass hut. But this intimacy of the smaller children with the smallest children, this way that African boys, hardly able to walk, will stagger about with a fresh-born goat in their arms, the way you will see Somali boys of six grazing great herds of snarling camels—all this is part of the interlinking, the weaving of man with the earth. The fear and the finery, the bodily self-mutilation, are all part of the same amalgam. It is a base of life into which the "great white chief idea" of the white man (the European) never gets very far below the surface. The Africans don't believe in us; never have, except for a few rare examples. The fact that a Zulu girl will appear in the streets of Durban dressed in literally nothing but a head-to-foot coiling of copper telephone wire, sixty-five years after the Boers and the British had broken the power and the pride of the great Zulu race, shows how, in the hinterland of the soul, the black man is still unimpressed by the so-called benefits of our civilisation.

The Boran in the N.F.D. have an *eight-year* initiation period, called *Gedamoche*, during which the man wears a phallic symbol strapped to his forehead, somewhat like a silvered chessman, a castle with a pointed top, during which they speak words of a language which is now dead among the Boran, are credited with possessing occult powers for good and evil, are not allowed to do any physical labor—not such a deprivation—have the pig-tail on their heads, which indicates that its owner has killed a man or a big animal, woven with the hair of ancestors into a halo effect, and on the seventh year are circumcised—very often having had children meanwhile. Then they retire to stipulated holy places, bullocks are sacrificed, and with dancing and song the night is passed, the wife shaves off the halo-cum-pig-tail, buries it, the entrails of the sacrificed bullocks are examined to see what the future holds in store—and, lo! you have the sullen-faced Boran with the lowered eyelids staring at you, such as I saw at Marsabit. For it was here, from the wife of

Gerald Reece, who has written a great deal about the Galla and Somali tribes of the N.F.D. (and very interestingly) that I got these details of what must be the longest and weirdest initiation ceremony in all Africa. I never saw a *kalacha*, as the silvered chessman symbol of the *Gedamoche* is called. Reece said, as we stared into the impenetrable brush below the foothills of Abyssinia: "It is only in there . . . far, far from the roads, that they can live without repressions."

Further along on the red, sandy road that crawls like a cobra itself through this choking brush we saw three Kenya camel police jolting towards us. The black men were in khaki shorts and *safari* shirts, with blue pill-box hats, puttees and neck-guards. The camels were grey, but so thin, with their bellies pulled up almost to their spines, where their lean, muscled hind legs began, that they looked like greyhounds with their backs arched. The proud little outfit saluted Reece smartly. He told me, when they had jolted on, that they were looking for a raiding party that was somewhere in the bush. I, trying to see even 3 yards into the choking underbrush, said that I'd rather look for the proverbial needle. "Oh, no. These men are trackers," he said, proudly. "They'll pick up the spoor in there, and once they're on a man's track he'd better hit it back as fast as he can for Abyssinia." He was silent for some time.

"Of course, if some of these wandering Abyssinian black spivs come in here to poach, armed only with spears, er—ahem—you can't shoot 'em. Just have to pick them up and bring them in. But if they have *rifles*, and begin to get nasty . . . well—"

I formed the impression there would be no need for a police court.

The road going up the Abyssinian Escarpment is so steep, with so many V-turns, and African drivers have such an incurable love of changing down gears in the very worst places—more than one top-heavy motor-lorry such as ours has turned over on this road—that Reece made all the Dubas get out and walk behind our two cars. This was late in the afternoon, after we had lunched in a thicket of mimosa thorn under a sky that was practically colorless, it was so hot. And now came one of the most abrupt changes I have ever seen in my life, so far as the sky was concerned. For when we got to the top of this escarpment the sky above us had suddenly become a bright Reckett's blue (I have never seen such a vivid, almost pulsating, color in any sky), and only about 1,000 feet above our heads floated thousands of clouds, white and brightly luminous, like a ceiling of steam jets, fixed, motionless, over the green hills. Hundreds of scarlet termite hills stood all about us. It was unbearably hot.

Gandhi had just been murdered out in India that morning. And as the D.C.'s wife was telling us about it in a hushed voice, and we three were sitting in her shaded living-room, each in his own way feeling the sense of deep personal loss and that this world has indeed gone mad, an Englishman from Abyssinia strode in, was told the news, and said: "Well, I'm damned glad of it! Served him right!" That was my introduction to Moyale.

There are two Moyales, one in Kenya and one in Abyssinia, facing each other across a small depression, once the bed of an old watercourse, about half a mile in width. The Abyssinian Moyale presents tiers of mud-and-wattle huts, some thatched and some tin-roofed, some made of bashed-out paraffin tins (almost certainly its Somali town), with two rather bombastic buildings, the Mayor's office and the Police, standing out in this squalor, plastered and painted and designed to be impressive, put there by the Italians when they thought that Mussolini's Roman Empire had come there to stay. The Abyssinians refuse to use them, I believe, except as latrines.

Kenya's Moyale is little beyond a dirt square on a high mountain ridge, strangely like those you see on the North-West Frontier of India, with one side of it lined by the low, single-storied offices of the District Commissioner and his clerks, also built of sun-baked mud and ant-hill mortar, roofed with mango poles and grass mats, with a very modern police headquarters, plastered and painted white. Its roof is flat, with outside steps leading up to it, and can be used as a lookout. The prison, built by Italian prisoners of war, is unquestionably the finest building in British Moyale.

A tall flag-pole stands in the center of this dirt square, flying the Union Jack. And under the shade of the projecting flat roof covering the D.C.'s office, which, supported by a few slender poles, makes a sort of arcade, were standing all the dignitaries and personages of the territory, the chiefs and headmen, bearded and turbaned: Somalis, Borans, Gabbra. One, a charming old fellow, was a murderer who for twenty years had been given sanctuary on the Kenya side, he having killed his man in a cause adjudged just. One was a grinning Arab from Ethiopia, his beard henna red, a merchant who informed us gratuitously and ingenuously that he would not have had the good luck to be in Moyale when we came had he not been held up by a bad dose of clap—and what did we think best for it? He was wearing a MacLeod tartan wrapped around his thin waist and spindly shanks. Reece had known most of these men for ten or twenty years, ever since he had been a D.C. at Moyale himself, and, as is the unbreakable custom in those parts, he greeted each man individually, asked about his health and affairs, his family's health; and—it was obviously quite genuine—he took a keen interest in their replies. He must have stood out there in the broiling sun for over an hour before he had been brought up to date on local items. Then, with a handshake to the last man, a smile and a nod to the rest, he stepped inside to read the log of the D.C.'s office. This, in such a troublesome district, is as thrilling as a penny dreadful.

The arrival of a motor-car, followed by a towering lorry-load of red-turbaned Dubas, coming into Moyale along the high ridge on the British side, had doubtless been observed in Abyssinia. These two communities watch each other closely. It is said that, through a pair of good glasses, you can even see the distasteful expression on Abyssinian faces as they stare across at, say, a football match played by the black Kenya Police—those admirably smart, and tough, hybrid frontier guards of the N.F.D. And now, as I watched, an American motor truck put out from Abyssinia, descended the low valley, and came up into the dusty square of British Moyale.

A young man stepped out from beside the driver, the District Officer of the other Moyale. An Amhara youth, one of the Abyssinian ruling class, very smart in his immaculate khaki shorts, *safari* shirt, buff golf stockings, with a cock's feather curling from his flat-topped solar topi (adopted, I imagine, from the Italian mountain troops). He had called on Reece to pay the respects of, and make apologies for, Reece's opposite number in Abyssinia—the equivalent of an Ethiopian Provincial Commissioner—by saying that his superior was too ill to come himself. The only answer to that, from Reece, was a sharp twitch of the nose, which even I could see left the young Abyssinian no doubts but that Reece saw, and fully appreciated, the diplomatic illness of his colleague, and was somewhat contemptuous of it. For Reece, as the Abyssinians knew, was paying something more than a visit of inspection this time to the D.C. at Moyale. The young Abyssinian was roast-peanut color, extremely handsome, with a fine, straight nose, noble forehead, and the usual exuberant mop of Amhara hair. His manners were easy and showed that he was a man of good family and breeding. When he had completed the courtesy of apologising for his superior's inability to come across to welcome the British Provincial Commissioner, he stared at Reece—with just the faintest trace of superciliousness on his lips. Reece wiped that off instantly by arising, giving him a quick shake of the hand, and walking with him to the door. The bystanders then saw Reece return to his desk and continue his conversation with the D.C. as if the swaggering young man from Abyssinia had only interrupted them. It was neat. This, the extreme briefness of the interview, was apparent to all the native dignitaries of British Moyale who stood outside. Though no one smiled, you could feel the unspoken amusement and satisfaction in the atmosphere. The young Abyssinian, who would like to have been off-hand, walked, scowling, towards his aide, the truck-driver. He got into the truck and drove off. The Abyssinian attempt to show disrespect to Reece had failed.

Reece had come up there for two things. The first was to inform the District Commissioner that a new frontier line had been established, the final settlement, it was hoped, of the line roughly marked out by an Anglo-Abyssinian boundary commission in 1908. "But *don't* make any song and dance about it!" Reece carefully warned the young D.C. "If you do, the Abyssinians will think that we have 'got' something from them, and then the row will start all over again. Just say, casually, to the people around here, that the line has been agreed upon—here's the map—and *you see that that line is clearly understood*. You'd better go out along it yourself; note everything: we've got some of the wells and high ridges we have been wanting. . . ."

The other was to begin the distribution of the £67,000 which

Reece, after an immense bout of wrangling, worry and delay, both with Nairobi and with Whitehall had (with the last-minute aid of Sir Philip Mitchell) managed to divert from a British payment to Abyssinia in recompense for fancied grievances to a direct payment to the relatives and survivors of a little village just outside Moyale, which the Abyssinians had raided in 1943, murdering forty-four people, mutilating them in the most horrible fashion, and driving off all their cattle. In the final outcome, be it noted, it was the British, the British taxpayer, who paid this money, not the Abyssinians. Of the £2,000 in cash which Reece had brought up, in the back of our car, as the first instalment, Reece told the D.C.:

"Don't give it to them all at once. That would simply smash prices in this district. You must feed it to them gradually. . . . Mnnnnn. . . . Old So-and-So: how is *he* doing these days? Lost two sons, didn't he? Well, begin with him. But don't give him too much. He's an awful old old profligate! . . . He'll want to buy everything in the district. . . ."

Reece, who knew the personal character of nearly every man in the region and almost the whole N.F.D., his failings and strength, vetted the payments which were to be made to several members of that unlucky village. He showed me the photograph taken of one boy lying on the ground naked with his private parts cut off—a horrible sight—and then, as if on second thoughts, he told the D.C. that it would be well to call a *baraza*, at which he and the D.C. would explain the general outline of these payments. "And you *must* keep prices down . . . see that the Abyssinians don't rush every wretched animal they've got across the border in order to cash in on this sudden increase of wealth. Two thousand pounds is a lot of money to put into circulation in this district. It will cause real inflation. It's easy to get prices up, but it's damned hard to bring them down again."

Sitting inside the low office was as good as watching a play. On its whitewashed walls hung two colored lithos of Churchill and Franklin Roosevelt, and a colored photograph, full length, of poor Hugh Grant, in his Highland kilt, who was murdered by the Masai in August 1946. He had once been the D.C. at Moyale. "A brave, hot-tempered Scot!" they told me. "But a very religious chap."

An old Boran chief was brought in who was afraid that he was no longer going to be allowed to be a chief—because he had gone blind. "Reassure him," said Reece to the young D.C. before the chief was brought in. "Don't let the old fellow worry himself to death about that. Put his mind at rest. He's always been a good man." The old white-robed man came in, led and supported by two retainers; and it was beautiful to see the way he relaxed as he heard Reece telling him not to worry. When Reece came across to shake hands and say good-bye to him the old fellow bowed as if he wanted to press his forehead against his protector's hand.

An old Goanese clerk was brought in so that he might talk to me (the man who was writing a book about Kenya). He was now doing a small commission business; previously he had been twenty-six years in the Administration at Moyale. Reece had got him the M.B.E. when he was retired in 1942, and he still had a Portuguese passport, a thing not at all unusual in Kenya. A kindly-looking old man with grey hair, dressed in a worn but neatly kept European brown suit, named da Costa. He was proud that he was being thus displayed; and I, fulfilling the part expected of me, asked him all the leading questions I could think of. Later, encouraged by this interview, he came to me privately with a most interesting account of his present life in Moyale.

The duties of a District Commissioner cover an astonishingly wide range of subjects. Reece, reading the log-book of the station, said:

"About roads. . . . In this part of the world, you know, you should have a drain, a slight camber, so that the water quickly runs off in the rainy season. . . ."

"I'm putting stones in the ditches," said the D.C.

No! That I don't like—the stones in the bottom. As soon as the rains come you have nothing but a bed of boulders in the ditch; then the road falls into it. . . . Now, that stretch of road between here and Buna, that's in bad shape. Been down there lately? Well, if I were you, I'd go out and look it over. I see no reason why the road where it crosses the lava rubble shouldn't go further east—between Buna and— Have you got anybody working on that now? I don't know that I want cuts made just to make the road straight. You give in to the African, and he will make a road that will wander all over the place, of course, like a snake. You've got to go down there *yourself*. . . ."

This way, pushing them out, always pushing them out, Reece tried to keep his D.C.'s on constant *safari* in their districts. Free them as much as he could—even in spite of the objections from their wives—from hanging around the office, and home. He did not see his own wife for months on end, for she, and their two little children, lived in the green mountain paradise of Marsabit. He had his H.Q. in the baking flatlands of Isiolo. But Reece was a man with a burning sense of mission—to bring peace and a good way of life into the N.F.D.—and the sacrifices to duty which he was able to impose on himself, without even thinking of them as such, could not be so easily imposed on others who did not have this divine fire. He regarded the N.F.D. as a trust which had been placed in his safe keeping. He is apparently fond of children and we had a more or less running argument on that philosophical *safari*, tour of investigation as it was, because I said I much preferred cats.

"I know you are fond of animals: I can see that by the interest you take in them, but . . . I can't understand you! Humph—cats!"

"Mnnnn. . . . And that market," he continued to the D.C., "out here—that's a disgraceful sight. Like a rubbish dump. If I were you [it was always put thus] I would put up some shade-shelters for them to sit under, and—ah—provide water for their beasts. Make the market a *pleasant* place, make your people happy. . . .

"You're watching the game-poachers down the *lugga?* H'm? Well, if they've got *rifles*, you know, they might just as easily shoot a human. H'mmmm. . . .

"You're keeping an eye on the township's cattle, aren't you?"

"Yes, sir."

"They've got to be counted. You know that? Traders' cattle—don't take any word from *them*. In any dispute, the local people must have first claim on water. They're *our* people . . . got to look after them. Are you doing any work on the pans? We don't want to spend a lot of money there; they ought to do that themselves. However, you might have a look at *that* on the ground. . . . That's got to be done by an officer. And that bit of road—the repair job between here and Turbi—you can't leave *that* to the natives. Have to see for yourself. You're keeping up your road-book, aren't you? When Hugh Grant was here, he wanted to start a model farm—help 'em to make cheese and so forth. . . .

"What? Of course. A D.C. has to be father and mother and an agricultural pioneer to his people. So far as I know, they never put anything back into the soil. Have you got them to rotate crops here? . . ."

"I don't know, sir."

"Er—*what?* Well . . ."

"Look here, sir. For how many years can they go on planting maize in the same plot?"

Reece gave a dissertation on maize. The young D.C. (he had not been here many months) became, without knowing it, a pupil. Told barely, as I put it, this sounds as if Reece put every one of his D.C.'s through a gruelling cross-examination. And so he did. But, as I have said, a D.C. seldom lasts eighteen months in the N.F.D., whereupon he or his wife begin to show signs of a nervous breakdown, and Reece is continually breaking in new pupils: men that have to learn their job as they are doing it, and leave before they have learned it. This cross-examination was discipline. But slackness never made a "happy ship," either at sea or on land; and Reece, with only eight D.C.'s was administering a territory the size of Britain. But here is the way such a session usually ended: "Why don't you and your wife come over to Marsabit. Do bring Jane. Why not have her stay there for a bit with my wife. Alys would love it. . . . H'm. . . . Now, about these Gabbra around here. You can take it from me, they've been badly treated. I don't want to be sentimental about people . . . not unnecessarily . . . but they *are* our people. What about old Ido and his cattle. . . . Has he got enough water?"

"I don't know, sir. He takes a lot of cattle over into Abyssinia."

"We must be decent to these folk. Help old Ido Mamo if you can. He's always *tried* to be honest . . . anyway. . . ."

Ido Mamo was chief of the Gabbra in those parts, a Mohammedan.

Reece was notorious throughout the N.F.D. for his generosity. On this trip to Moyale he tried to find an old servant of his who had been raided by the Abyssinians and had had all his cattle stolen. "In this case, just because he had been my servant, I think." In the afternoon the servant's brother turned up. After a long and earnest talk with him, Reece gave him some money, and then shook his head as the brother went out of the door. "Lies! Lies! Lies! That man has done nothing but lie ever since he came in here. I don't know what his brother has done—now. Must be something, though. He's afraid to come here. . . ." Reece had his soft under-side; and whenever he came out of the D.C.'s office the old white-bearded Somalis who had known him in his younger days came up to him and stood there respectfully, wanting to talk with him. Occasionally he would make one of them throw back his head and laugh, or pull his beard and chuckle softly. . . . The Arab with the clap was a most engaging creature. In the afternoon he had on a scarlet turban, a primrose silk shirt, but still that MacLeod tartan wrapped round him like a kilt. With a lascivious grin, the old rogue, shifting his tender private parts, intimated that "Boys will be boys!" The murderer followed Reece like his shadow. This amused Reece immensely:

"He's nervous. Nearly twenty years ago, I think, it happened. It was a clean murder, so we let him stay here. But when the people here want to have a joke with him, they just look meaningly towards a tree. . . . Looks as if he had been crucified, doesn't he?" Reece halted and said something to the old man, who grinned—and the whole square shook with laughter. He showed that one great truth: that if you can appeal to the African's sense of humor, he's yours.

There is a little fort on the ridge just outside Moyale. It made me think of the Khyber Pass. It's just a quadrangle of granite boulders, walls about 4 feet high, some 3 feet in breadth: just the right height so that a man can fire a rifle across them. It is manned by a handful of police. The previous night a lion had killed a horse just outside the wall. Within the previous four months they had had two donkeys taken from *inside* the fort by lions which had leapt over the wall and jumped back with the donkeys in their mouths. The wind was blowing; the Union Jack was flapping in the stiff breeze. The fort looked out and over the tumbled mountains along the frontier of Abyssinia, and down into the blue mountains and haze of the scrub country through which Reece and I were going to trek in a few days. It was an inspiring sight . . . those great blue mountains fading, fold upon fold, in the heat haze of the lower plains. . . . The great elephant country of the Tana River lay beyond them: "The finest ivory in all Africa. . . ."

Captain John Lionel Carter, twenty-two years in the Kenya Police, was now in charge of this tiny frontier fort. Leaning over the wall, he showed me where he had had a lot of *shifta* (bandit) trouble. "Sort of a no-man's-land down in there. . . . Won't be, though, now the new line's been decided upon." A few weeks previously, some Somalis, raiding from Abyssinia, had come on two pagan Boran asleep beside their camels and murdered them.

"What did you do?"

"Oh, I moved the people on our side back ten miles."

"Why? Isn't that giving in to the Abyssinians?"

"Oh, Lord, no! If I'd have left our people there, the retaliations would have been a frightful thing. It's not loot that's involved. This sort of *shifta* stuff is almost a religious war—Mohammedan *versus* Pagan. The Boran would have made a counter-raid, and then the whole line along here would be bubbling. We'll find out. . . . I've got some of our police down there now, smelling about. It may take time, but we'll find out who did it. And *then*, if they put their noses on our side of the line again, which they will—"

He stopped himself, and grinned.

Meanwhile, he said, they had officially demanded blood-money from the Abyssinians. The present rate for this was fifty camels for one man killed, the market price for a camel being £3 at that time. That was for a dead Somali. Boran only fetched half the price, and were usually paid for in cattle. One of these murder episodes usually means restrictive measures, in which the police have to move fast, and firmly, to be of any use.

There were sixty Kenya Police, frontier specialists, under Carter. Despite his twenty-two years in the service, he looked hardly more than that age. Fresh-cheeked, clear-eyed, spick and span in his uniform, with his silver insignia shining, he was one of those Englishmen, such as you will find all over the world, who look as if they were just born to keep the peace in the far-off and troubled places. I asked him what it was like when the Italians declared war.

"Er–" He colored. "Don't you know?"

"Know? Know what? I wasn't here."

"*I* was," he said. "I was taking my dog for a walk on the football pitch the night before the war started. And those —— Italians picked me up!"

He had spent the war—and one day—in Italian prison camps.

There are two graves in Moyale which tell its story in themselves—

In Memory of

CHARLES MAYNIER

Who was murdered at Moyale on December 15, 1925.

Requiescat in Pace

Maynier, Officer of the King's African Rifles, did not know that a mutiny was spreading among them. He was shot, by the light of his lamp, as he was reading under a tree just below where we pitched our tents. It is now known as "Maynier's Tree."

The other:

LEYCESTER AYLMER

60th King's Royal Rifles

Killed in action against Abyssinia, 1st May, 1913.

He died doing his duty.

There they are, lying on the top of the ridge, a constant reminder to those who pass by. They are still setting an example. The grass is watered and kept cut around them. Without being sentimental or jingoistic about it, I can say that as I sat there and wrote down these inscriptions and looked up to the blue starlings chattering in the acacia trees above those two graves, my hope was that some of their people might read this. These men—not the followers-on from London City—were the men who knew the full thrill of the British Empire. A moment not without grandeur in the world's history, in the words of unsentimental Somerset Maugham.

We ate breakfast just as the sun rose on our last morning, the Dubas striking their camp and falling-to on our big green tents the minute we stood up. An old secretary bird stalked sedately along the grassy slope below us, his quills erect. "All he needs is a pen behind his ear!" said Reece. The inevitable starlings were chattering in the leaves above us. Brown hawks hunted and circled in the air. Only a few minutes after the sun topped the mountains and began to glare at us, the blue sky became so hot that it became almost white. It hurt to look anywhere near the direction of the sun. It was so hot that after they had struck and packed both our camps and all gear was packed in the top-heavy lorry, the Dubas loosened their white *tobes*, the strips of white cloth they wore as uniform, and sat there in the grass, letting the breeze blow out the cool cloth so that they might air their black bodies. They were a splendid sight, like a gallery of statues. And walking hesitatingly around where they had struck camp was a slender native woman, wearing just the scantiest of rags, leading a little girl by the hand. She was darting at anything that the Dubas might have left, although Reece was adamant about leaving a camping place undefiled: *everything* must be either packed, buried or burned. The woman dived like a hawk on any object . . . then, with the most rueful expression, examined it. She was a scavenger herself, as much as any pinioned hawk wheeling in the sky. When I came near to see what it was that she could possibly find of value, she walked closer to me and gave me a strange smile. . . .

"Most extraordinary creature!" I said to Reece when he came back. "She almost seemed to be flirting with me."

His face fell. "Oh—is *she* here? She's mad. It's the only case of love that I've ever known in native life—true love, between man and woman. Her husband was a Gabbra, a very bad Mohammedan. He discarded her. He went off with another woman into Abyssinia. For years I tried to get him to come back—at any rate, to do the right thing by her. And I saw her—right before my very eyes—go mad from misery. There was no mistake about it: that woman grieved until she went mad. We always give her a little money—tit-bits, to keep her going. There she is . . . wandering about with that poor child. . . . Hell of a thing life is, isn't it? . . ." He walked over, and I saw the woman reach out and take his hand. They stood there like that for a little while, Reece talking gently to her. Then he withdrew his hand, put it into his pocket, and handed her a fistful of money. He returned slowly to me: "Well, let's get going. I'll stop as we go by and say good-bye to the D.C.'s wife. She's still after me to let her have her aeroplane."

The D.C.'s wife, who had farmed herself for years in Kenya, was a pilot and flew her own plane. But "Uncle" Reece would not let her have one in the N.F.D.—"in case she comes down in the lava . . . Dida Galgalla. . . ." And I could see them as I sat in the car, the D.C.'s wife arguing petulantly. Then Mr. da Costa stood by my side.

"Sir," he said, "would you permit me to show you this?"

It was the parchment, the citation of his M.B.E., thanking him for his long and faithful service. "You ought to be very proud to have that," I said.

"I am," he sighed as he rolled it up. "But I find it very lonely here, sir. I have no one to talk to. My wife? Yes, sir. But . . . occasionally one wants to talk to other men. I can't do that, sir. Perhaps it is the 'official consciousness,' sir—the reason why they won't talk to me?"

"Oh, you mean the—the white men here?"

"Yes, sir. I'd very much like to talk with them. Sometimes I get tired of reading. I have had thirty years, all told, in the service of the Government. . . . I—I took up business, my little commission business, because I must have something to do. I *can't* waste my time. . . .

"Well, good-bye, sir," he said, putting out his hand, when he saw that I couldn't give him any answer. I said to Reece, when the old Goan had gone off, that it seemed a pity that the poor old boy didn't have someone to talk to. And I told him about how the ex-Government clerk had asked me to read the citation of his M.B.E. "H'mmmmmmmmmm . . ." said Reece.

If I had not got on to some of Reece's curves by now, I would have thought that it had gone in one ear and out the other. But as Reece leaned out of the car to have a last word with the spruce D.C., he said: "Old da Costa came over and showed Farson his M.B.E. Says he's lonely. Got no one to talk to. Pity, isn't it . . . faithful old chap like that—and nobody here will talk to him? Well, good-bye."

It was as pointed as a knife-thrust.

A last touch of Moyale was the *duka* of the Indian in the bazaar, the man who had sent us some molten pasties. I have never seen such a smile on any Oriental's face as he seized Reece's hand in both his own, and said, "My *dear* Mr. Reece!" Now, the price of Gold Flake cigarettes in Kenya had just been jumped up, by a sales-tax, to make them reach the astronomical British price. I wanted several hundred, and said to the old Indian, "I only wish I had bought them a few days ago, before the price went up."

"But, sir, we have lots here that *we* bought at the old price, and we will sell them to *you* at the old price. How many do you want?" Which, for an Indian shopkeeper, I consider pretty good. He was smiling because he had another gift. By some miracle he had urged, brow-beaten, a mango tree to grow in his garden. Now, in a big grass sack, he seemed to be packing all its precious fruit. "But I can't take them all!" Reece protested. "Oh, yes, sir. You must. Besides, sir, I have plenty left. It is a big tree."

And so we drove out and down into the steaming plains and scrub, to trek through the blue mountains that lay ahead. There is an invisible line here, west of which the Somalis are not supposed to pass. All to the east lay the land of the Somalis. We would hear camel bells from now on all the way to the Tana River. The tinkle of bells under the moon at night . . . and the hoarse cry of thirsty camels.

CHAPTER XXII

The Somalis

THE Somalis are the aristocrats of Kenya's N.F.D., and, in their own opinion, of the entire Horn of Africa. They came from Arabia at some misty date and believe themselves to be the migration of a certain Sherif Ishak ben Ahamed, who crossed from Hadramut in Arabia with forty followers about the thirteenth century. Nobody knows. They are Hamitic, but so interbred with Galla, Arab, Abyssinians and even Bantus (on the Coast) that they range from light brown, even peach-colored, to ebony black. Strangely enough, the blackest among them usually have the most regular features. They are magnificently built. It is always disconcerting to look at one of these men, black as pitch, and realise that he may not have one drop of Negro blood in him. The Somalis have been blackened by desert suns.

Detribalised Somalis have, of course, been penetrating for some years into European Kenya. You will see their settlements, for instance, outside Nakuru, and other townships always composed of rusty huts shingled with bashed-out paraffin tins, with, inside them, silks, satins and finery such as are possessed by not even the Europeans of the district. This hidden luxury is all part of the Somali secretiveness. They are insatiable stock-traders, being the most skilful buyers at any cattle sale; and their women are the most professionally seductive in all Africa. They are disturbingly sex-conscious. The men are very good-natured on the surface, and it is always a pleasure to talk with them, as they measure their sharp wits against yours. They love a joke, especially a manly one. Even their handshake seems a jest, for a Somali shakes hands by first clasping his hand round your thumb, then laughs, lets go, and shakes hands in the conventional fashion. Those up in the N.F.D. know little of the outside world, as I have said; not one in a hundred can read even a sign; and their entire lives are filled with their attention to cattle, camels—and women. It would be a poor Somali who did not have at least two wives. Wherever you find them you will be impressed by their dignity and good manners; and, as many an unfortunate D.C. has found out when too late, a Somali is never so dangerous, or unreliable, as when he is smiling. Perhaps this description of him taken from an old N.F.D. *Handbook* is worth considering:

> The true Somali is an extremely lazy person, for his dignity does not allow him to do any manual work.
>
> He is slightly built, but lithe and wiry and capable of supporting considerable exertion. Treat him with confidence and consideration, he is cheerful, intelligent and willing to learn—though rarely, if ever, trustworthy; but treat him harshly and unjustly, and he becomes sulky, mutinous, obstinate and dangerous. He is an excellent scout, a wonderful and clever trader, and does not lack courage. He never forgets an insult or a wrong and will wait for years to avenge it, while, on the other hand, many instances are on record of his devotion to his employer in times of danger.
>
> [Lord Delamere's life was saved by his Somali boy, Abdulla Ashur, his head gunbearer, who grasped the mane of a wounded lion which was mauling his master, trying to seize its tongue! And although badly mauled himself in the struggle with this prodigiously powerful beast, he did drag it away far enough for Delamere to be able to recover his rifle and kill it. It is perhaps needless to point out that from then on Delamere had an inordinate interest in the Somalis, protecting them, right or wrong.]
>
> As a warrior he is by no means contemptible, being very cunning and experienced in bush fighting, while his extreme mobility makes him almost ubiquitous, so that a column operating against a tribe must be in a continual state of preparedness.
>
> In attack they are very formidable, being able to thread their way through thick bush with wonderful speed. They are very treacherous and will seldom attack, except when greatly superior in numbers.

Intrigue is the breath of life to a Somali, vanity and avarice his outstanding characteristics. But in their paradoxical character they have few vices, and—except for murder—serious crimes are rare among them. In that ethnic confusion of the Horn of Africa, the historical "Land of Punt"—known to the Arabs as Bar Ajam, the "Land of Heat"—the abstemious life which these nomadic desert Somalis are compelled to live has given them a fanatical common consciousness, in their eternal search, and fighting, for grass and water. To come into their life is an emotional experience, one of the most exhilarating rewards of travel.

From the fort on the high ridge of Moyale a blue mountain rising out of the heat haze, some fifty miles away, was pointed out to me as Korondil; and I was told that we should pass around it to get into the real Somali camel country. There were some wells before that, however, at a smaller mountain called Dobel. "And you will probably find some Somalis watering there. Take a good look at it, and just tell me," said one of the police, "if you don't think that's one hell of a place to get ambushed! For that's where the Italian colonial troops caught the West African troops—and did they shoot the hell out of them!" We dropped down from the Abyssinian Escarpment and immediately entered into brush so thick that, literally, I did find it hard to breathe in it. All imagination, of course, but then imagination can do some weirdly real things to you.

And here I noticed something peculiar: Reece was always changing seats in the back. First he would take the right side, then the left. I had to laugh, and feel a little ashamed, when I saw the real reason for it. For that man was taking the side of the blazing sun himself, so that I might have the comparative coolness of some shade. He was angry when I pointed it out by refusing to change sides.

Dobel was, even if I had not heard of the ambush, one of the most depressing mountains I have ever seen. It was just a hump of blood-red bare earth rising out of a miasmic scrub of sickly-green fever thorn, covered with a scabrous growth of leafless *Commiphora* trees. How the Italian colonial troops, the best ones they had, ever found cover on such a bare mountainside was a puzzle to me; and it must have been a terrifying surprise to the West African troops, a large number of whom were slaughtered in this ambush. I believe that an Italian officer distinguished himself in this rout, preventing his men from killing the wounded prisoners. The savageness of the country itself was enough to incite men to do savage things, I should think. The red earth where we sat for lunch under the imaginary shade of an acacia thorn was hot to the touch. There was not a speck of green on this repulsive mountain, and the Boran are quite convinced that it is the home of a giant holy serpent which they worship. It looked like it.

It is in here, in this ghastly scrub country of the N.F.D., that you get a good idea of why D.C.'s and their wives so suddenly go in for nervous breakdowns. For there is nothing beautiful about it. And there is no relief from it, even after the sun goes down. It is always hot and stifling. You do not have the esthetic rewards of glowing sunsets across the lava rubble, or the ecstasy of wandering in the cool green forest of Marsabit; this scrub country of Kenya is about as close as you can get to hell on earth. Oddly enough, as if Nature was trying to make recompense, some of the most beautiful birds in all Africa are found in it.

The lilac-breasted roller is almost too fantastically colored to be believed. A bird about the size of an English blue jay, it has a breast of pure lilac, shining brilliant in such brush, wings of a deep purple, shaded with blue, a mossy-brown head and back, and a long tail with two projecting purple feathers, like a kite. This is a crude description. There are purple rollers and blue rollers and cinnamon rollers. You see them hunched up on a branch as you come down the road; you see them rolling in their peculiar flight from which they get their name; you see them wheeling in the air to catch insects in flight, sparkling like emeralds and amethysts and sapphires above this morose-looking bush. There are carmine bee-eaters and crested hoopoes, and always those doleful old yellow-billed hornbills, black and white, which look as if they are flying backwards. These last seem suitable to the bush, they are so ugly. And then the calls from the impenetrable fastness of the thickets, like a warning—"*Who?*-who-who-who-whooooo?" Until you almost want to answer their question: "Yes, I am here. Come out. I want to have a look at you!" I have heard the anvil bird call in nearly all parts of Equatorial Africa, from the Indian Ocean to the Atlantic, and I have never seen one yet. There is something exasperating about it.

Korondil was a delightful mountain: green forests rising up to grey and scarlet granite rock palisades. They must have been thick with game. It was obviously a volcano with its tip blown off, and from the road you could imagine the crater below its circular, jagged rims. We had seen a few white Somali cattle, unattended in the brush, on the way down to Dobel. At Dobel itself a woman, leading two camels laden with water, cut back into the brush when she saw us and vanished in the scrub. The wells are far back from the road at Dobel. At Korondil we saw several of the gerenuk, giraffe-like buck. Then the earth turned from red to grey. We entered an open scrub country, on the far side of which a blue mountain seemed waiting for us, like some crouching beast; we crossed some miles of absolutely treeless, grassy plain, with the humps of more blue mountains on the skyline, and unattended grey Somali camels grazing—and there, his aeroplane ears rising above the first thicket on the far side, I saw my first reticulated giraffe.

He let me get within 20 feet of him, a huge animal, his sleek coat glistening in the setting sun: a deep red-liver color, with white zigzag stripes. Much bigger and fatter, it seemed to me, than the ordinary giraffe I had seen so many of on the plains of southern Kenya, and far more curious. He could hardly tear himself away from staring at me. Finally, with that rocking-horse gait, he went off into the thorn trees. Whereupon I saw another giraffe which I had not been aware of start off from almost beside me, with two little greyish ones. We went on for a couple of hours in the darkness that night before we again found a space sufficiently open where we could pull off the road and camp. This was by the graves—four stone cairns inside a *boma* of tree trunks—of a big Somali chief and his wives. The stones were laid over the graves so that the hyenas and wild animals could not get at the bodies.

The hyenas howled dolefully on these hot, mournful nights. I don't know why they should have impressed me as being so mournful. But I had a bad bout of my recurrent insomnia about then, and I wrote most of my day's notes sitting up in my camp cot by the light of an inexhaustible electric torch (made in Hong Kong). And it seemed to me that an indescribable sadness hung over all of Africa, as if the land itself resented man's presence there. This impression is reinforced when you see how gruellingly hard it is to live in the bush; the insatiable desire of the Somali to thrust south and westwards is really only his frantic desire to get out of this land of baking heat and scarce water and disappearing grass. They watch the sky in these lands with a dread apprehension; for if the rains do not come it means death for thousands of cattle and sheep and many people. On such nights, notes exhausted, I would snap out the torch and sit there smoking for an hour or so, listening to the sounds in the bush: the night calls of the birds which lived there; the movements of animals. And sitting thus, listening to the brooding stillness, that night by the Somali graves, I heard the tinkle of camel bells.

It was just a dull clunk at first, for these bells are made of wood. Then a camel cried. The moon was shining. And through the bush, about 50 yards from the foot of my cot, I saw a grey, ghostly procession. Tall camels, their snake-like heads bowing to and fro, packed high with the tents of Somali nomads, the cries of men, the cries of children, even the squalls of babies lashed under the camel coverings. They must have seen we were there, but they took no notice of us. I must have watched over a hundred camels stride past me, their bells finally dying out in the suffocation of the dense scrub. They were moving at night, in the coolness, Reece told me in the morning, to reach the wells at Buna. This had been a year of poor rains, and the camels must have been driven half-mad by thirst. "And Buna is where you get the relapsing fever—from the *Spirillum* tick. There's an eighteen-man well at Buna."

The eighteen-man well at Buna was a dog-leg well; with six Somalis, two of them women, standing on the steep, dripping side of the declivity going down to it, and twelve people in the long tunnel, to reach water, underground. They were all singing; that high-pitched Somali "chant of the well" which linked them, with an invisible moving belt, to the synchronisation of black arms and glistening torsos. The Somalis are fanatical Mohammedans, but their women are considered inferior beings and do not wear the veil—not, at any rate, in this grim desert existence, where they do most of the manual work; and how the two half-naked girls on the slippery side of this well stood up to this unbroken passing of the giraffe-hide buckets was beyond comprehension, except that they were all mesmerised by this song.

It was like a macabre ballet, the weirdest part of which was the constant rhythm of song from beneath our feet—far underground—as if some souls were suffering penal labor in the nether world. Again, for my benefit, Reece asked one of the Somalis, "Who dug this well?" and was told that it was a race of giants, now extinct, who were—the six-foot Somali raised his hand 2 feet above his head—"that high!"

They certainly must have been prodigious people, for these holes are cut through solid rock, some as metrically uniform as if bored with a drill.

They were watering cattle, this sunset at Buna, not camels. And the patient, tired animals, with their humps, of the Zebu breed, came in in answer to the call and drank gratefully from the trough as it was filled for them, then wandered back to join the waiting herds. Everything was silent, even the exhausted animals; there was a feeling of dejection. Every drop that man or animal drinks at Buna is handed up out of this well. One woman with a terrible case of elephantiasis was staggering across to an Indian *duka*, tottering under the weight of two 4-gallon paraffin tins filled with water, with legs almost the size of elephants' feet. She was the picture of exhaustion. "She's poor," said Reece. "But when I asked this man why none of them ever gave her a hand to help her up the incline, he replied, 'Oh, she likes doing it!' " It did not seem to me that there was enough of both water and grass at Buna, for the calves among the cattle looked almost paper thin. There was no laughter at Buna.

Relapsing fever is also known as famine fever, and is practically endemic around Buna. It is highly contagious. A minute *spirochaete*, possessed of rotary or twisting movements, gets into the blood stream. It is called after its discoverer, in 1873 (needless to say, a German) Obermeir, *Spirillum Obemeirei*. It is supposed to be an animal parasite. At Wajir, the Medical Officer there said he felt certain that it was carried by a louse. At Moyale they had told me it is a tick fever. It does not kill so frequently as it breaks a human being down with fevers that reach as high as 107° F., and his strength ebbs away, leaving him prostrate. It can lay waste whole districts, and is definitely a deficiency disease. God, in His strange way, always seems to cast afflictions on the under-privileged ones. It is enough to make one angry with life.

Perhaps the sullen sadness that seemed to hang like an invisible mist over the dog-leg well at Buna was not entirely my own imagination. I was glad to get away from there.

Buna was just a sandy waste from which the cattle had eaten every blade of vegetation; the shop of this wretched Indian, who apparently had the fever; and a post of the Kenya Police, which had several bellowing camels inside its barbed wire. The camels were grey, but almost pink in the sunset, and very dirty. The male camel always reverses his procreative organ and urinates backwards between his legs. If he is saddled or carrying a pack, the urine always hits the back strap, and trickles down his legs. As a consequence, the male camel is always filthy. Females are clean and grey. Reece signed the book at this police post and chatted with its black sergeant—always tying them in, his continual linking up of everything in the N.F.D. It was like watching a man weave a pattern, using human beings instead of wool. The black sergeant said there was no water at all in the next wells beyond us. What to do? The pressure of cattle and camels might become too great for the Buna well. What was the correct thing to do if he saw that was happening? Reece, thoughtfully, gave him several alternatives, grading them according to the severity of the drought. I could well understand why the sergeant looked up with unconscious dread at the pitiless sky.

We camped in the stifling bush again. It is on nights like that, when you feel so physically uncomfortable yourself, that you take perhaps the keenest and most honest interest in other lives you see going on around you. In the course of a day one comes across so many tragedies in a country like this. The story of Reece's emaciated 70-pound boy, whose father, dying of consumption brought on by undernourishment, had come to Reece and begged him to take him: "I cannot care for him any more." The old Somali at Buna Police Post who came up and timidly asked could we give him a lift into Wajir. His son had gone mad, he said; he thought he had gone off to Wajir. No; he was not sure his son was there, but he (the father) was going to *start* at Wajir, and then look till he found him. Reece told the Dubas to make room for the old man on the motor-lorry. ("He may be lying—but what's the odds?") I saw him feeding beside the Dubas' campfire that night.

This camp was at the junction of two roads through the bush. And that night hundreds of camels passed us. Everything was going into Wajir. There are seventy wells there. Wajir meant life. It was eighty miles to walk.

All that night I was conscious that camels were passing us. They were being taken through this maze of scrub-brush in complete darkness, except for the moon and the stars of a brilliant Milky Way. I was awake when dawn began to break that morning at exactly 6.15, with the moon directly overhead, looking down on the sinister lifelessness of the scrub-brush country. One bird gave a note or two as the sun rose, and then stopped; as if it was not worth the effort. And a red-hot day was on. Over a hundred camels passed us while Reece and I were at breakfast. I don't know where the men were, unless they had trekked on ahead with the precious female milk camels, which I believe was the case, for the strings of these dirty-legged male camels all seemed led by women, with always a tiny little Somali child of about six or seven walking at the tail end of each family's lot. Some of the little Somali boys were stark naked. They were very businesslike about it. At the age of six a Somali boy is placed in charge of camels as a herd; at the age of eight they are supposed to be able to take camels from one place to another, completely unattended, through the bush. The portable tent folded, with rugs, felt, and wicker frame are all packed in identical fashion—a custom hundreds, perhaps thousands, of years old. Four big red wooden pots, laced with leather, were strapped to each camel's saddle to hold water. There were travelling schools among these camels. Each clan or family group had a camel with long grey boards strapped alongside the load. Each board had a section from the Koran painted in Arabic characters in black. These were the desert school books, all they had; all the "book knowledge," in fact, that the young Somali boy is ever expected to learn. They chant these passages from the Koran over and over until they are indelibly engraved on their memory, although at the younger stage they can have no idea at all of what they mean. When they are older, however, the philosophy of the Koran, that great book, gives them a very good and practical code of life. As a set of rules, especially for the hot, waterless countries where most of the Mohammedans have to live, a full knowledge of the Koran, with its instruction in hygiene, is an education not to be despised. From under the skins on top of some of the towering grey camels little Somali babies stared down at us. Hundreds of bleating white goats came along. They converged at the junction and all went slowly down along the red road to Wajir. Seventy miles still to go.

"This is *all* their home," said Reece when he came back to his cold coffee after talking to one Somali woman. "*All* this bush . . . wherever they go . . . is just home. To you, all this bush around here is just a sort of nameless horror. It has no meaning. Those little *totos* out there, those little Somali kids, they know the name of every bush—and its uses. As they walk, they see things around them that can be used for all sorts of things. This is the tree whose bark you bring Mama when Papa has a headache. . . . That one for the clap. . . . That one makes the camel bell."

Reece, with his infinite curiosity and penetration into the ways of Somali life and every detail of their habitat, had had a list made out of the various trees and bushes of the scrub, and had sent it to each D.C. with the suggestion that he should study it. "It will give him, at least, a little more interest in his work, a better knowledge of the people and their habits and the country he is supposed to be in charge of." He smiled. "I'm afraid that most of them just file it for reference, then forget it. I had a hard job digging up this one for you. You've no idea the stuff that gets lost in our files—the *history* that is lost! I'm starting files now to collect that back history—custom and usage, and agreements we have made with them. That's the only real way we will ever be able to compile a history of the N.F.D."

Somaliland was one of the last bits of Africa to be explored by Europeans. It was supposed to have had an ancient civilisation which the Mohammedan invaders swept away. The European ancients knew it as *Regio Romataica,* from the abundance of aromatic plants it produced. It was the land of frankincense and myrrh and the "balm of Gilead" resin, which have been packed in sheep or goat skins, carried to the coast on camels, and for well over a thousand years have been carried to the mosques and the homes of Arabia on the decks of great dhows, borne on the wings (those romantic craft!) of the hot south-west monsoon. Then the great caravan routes took the spices to Europe, and then over the passes into Germany, etc. I was soon to brush the scented smoke of frankincense to my nostrils on the dhows of Mombasa. This choking scrub no longer had such a horrible meaninglessness to me when I saw that monstrous *Commiphora* tree yielded these fragrant resins.

Reece gave me a list of fifty-two plants or trees, in the district we were in, all of which had a use in one form or another to these Somali nomads. To view the brush with a knowledge of these trees in my mind gave an entirely new meaning to every mile we travelled. He had given both the Boran and the Somali names, but I will use the Somali for brevity. My reference to clap was not factitious: there is a shrub called raidub (*Pentarrhinum insipidum*), whose roots the Somalis boil with meat and then drink the juice as a medicine for gonorrhoea. There are half a dozen gums, mostly acacias, whose gum is chewed or eaten. But there is a tree called baror whose gum is deadly poison—although its fruit may be eaten. A creeper with a red berry had leaves which are boiled and eaten. The boa madow, whose large green leaves, like a fig, are poisonous when green, but are eaten by the camels when they turn whitish. The didin, the myrrh tree, whose wood is used for making head-rests, etc. Dabe, a small thorn tree whose hard wood is used for making spear-shafts and the ribs of the Somali huts. Its fruit is eaten. Burre, a light wood used for making water-pots and stools. Gasangas: the sap is used for soap, and is used as a powerful purge or emetic. The Garas tree holds water in its roots; its fruit can be eaten. Galol, whose bark is used to tan goat skins; also to stop haemorrhage in wounds, and for rope. The bark of the *roots* is used to make vessels watertight. Haye, a hard wood used for wooden shoes, spoons, or for loading camels, i.e. wooden pack-rests. Hagar madow makes plates. Haskul, a variety of aloe used for making rope or fibre mats. Kulan: "The fruit is eaten raw, the juice being a purgative. The nut inside is also boiled and eaten. The wood is used for making writing boards for schools. . . ."

"When you see them passing you now," said Reece, "and think of all of these trees and bushes around us that have gone into what is now being carried on that camel's back—well, it makes all this scrub country come alive, doesn't it?"

Marid roots make the arrow poison. Lebi, a large, gnarled thorn tree, is the wood used for camel bells.

Clunk-clunk . . . these great "ships of the desert" swung to and fro as they stalked majestically past us. On to Wajir, the road to Wajir. . . . There would be over 10,000 camels at the wells by the time we got there.

> 'Sweet to ride forth at evening from the wells,
> When shadows pass gigantic on the sand,
> And softly through the silence beat the bells
> Along the Golden Road to Samarkand.

But there was little of love, of Yasmin's girdle that broke at a lover's touch, along the road to Wajir. A little further on that morning, Reece and I came on a scene that showed all the avarice and brutality of Somali life. This was at a "pan," where some envoys of a Wajir camel-sheik were in camp, demanding money from incoming Somalis before they would let them water their camels there. If they did not pay, it meant that, with sixty miles still to go, and no water whatsoever in between, all the weaker animals, especially the fresh-born goats, would die before they could get to the Wajir wells. Reece, who took in the meaning of the scene even as we came up to it, went livid with rage.

It was one of the most impudent scenes I have ever looked at. For sitting comfortably under the wide shade of a wild fig tree was a knot of Wajir Somalis, with a couple of bearded, ferocious-looking headmen; and in the partial shade of a grove of acacia trees was parked a large herd of camels and goats, with some stupefied, weak Somalis debating what they were going to do about things. From some thick brush beside the wild fig, marabou storks, with their obscene flesh-colored sacs dangling, were rising, and hundreds of doves were darting about —sign of the big pool of water there. I counted over forty grey doves sitting in one tree. Reece, ominously quiet now, stepped from our car and walked up to the aghast Wajir Somalis, who leapt to their feet.

It was worth paying a ticket of admission to see such a set of scoundrels get such a thorough dressing-down. Without raising his voice or even making a gesture, Reece stood there facing the frightened sheiks, and struck them blow after blow of verbal insults. He staggered them, literally. As he took each man in turn, the man fell back from him. In the meantime, at a snapped command, our Rendille Duba had gone across to the waiting camel clan and told them to begin watering. . . .

The camels were standing dejectedly, silent, with their loads taken off them. They were terribly thin and emaciated, dirty from lack of water and even sufficient grazing that would have put them in good heart. They seemed immensely tall as they stood here and there among the acacia bushes; and some obediently sat folded up on the ground, from which their owners now began hastily to unstrap the four deep wooden red waterpots. Now a line of smiling, happy men and women began an instantaneous procession back and forth to the pan. Nobody talked. They wasted no time in gloating over the discomforted Wajir Somalis; they were too anxious to get at the water. Children, naked, were playing about among the crouching camels; tiny white kids, just dropped, were tottering about or being carried in the children's arms; and some of the Somali mothers, especially the younger ones, walked to and fro from the pan with their babies tied to their backs. An uninquisitive passer-by might not have noticed anything unusual in the scene, for, as I have said, the Somali has an immense dignity; and Reece, knowing just how to meet with that, was dignified even in his harangue that was taking the skin off them. He just stood there quietly telling the Somalis who had been trying to hold their brother Somalis up for bribe-money that they were the most mean-hearted, disgusting set of thieves he had ever come across. The strangest part of the whole scene was that there were two armed policemen there who were supposed to guard that pan. Reece put the fear of God into them also.

"There, you see," he said when we drove on again, "is what happens when a D.C. does not go out on *safari* enough in his district. This situation might have gone on for weeks if we had not happened to come along. Why, it's just highway robbery; one of the most impudent cases I've ever come across. And it happened because they know we are not keeping an adequate check on this district."

The happy tribe that had been filling its water-pots at the pan while Reece had been dressing down the other Somalis began to repack their camels. This is always done the same way, each thing going on the camel's back in its proper order. The *kibit,* the fluffy dark mat of chewed bark, which the women always make, goes first. On the caravan it goes under the load, as a padding for the camel's back. Then the stiff mat, interwoven with withes, which makes the hut's sides. Then ordinary plaited grass mats, some decorated. The four big wooden pots, really watertight baskets, are then lashed to the camel's sides. He is sitting obediently on the ground through all this, like a folded-up pen-knife. Then any babies which can't walk are placed on top of the sofa mats, and a stiff hide of some sort makes a cosy tent over them. The camel, groaning its usual complaint about life in general, then raises its rear end, unfolding itself again—and towers above you high in the air with that supercilious look. Our Dubas, after enviously eyeing some of the almond-eyed, pretty young Somali women, walked past the discomforted Wajir sheiks, and were all grinning when they climbed back on their motor-lorry again. The hawk-faced robbers under the tree did not look as we drove off. But the two police saluted with a sharpness that must have stung their hands.

One particularly interesting thing that I noticed here was a cock being carried on some camels in its own wicker cage. Not to be eaten, said Reece, "but to crow at dawn and wake the old men so that they can pray to Allah." At the rate that these camels move, on their weary last trek on the road in to water, they would take four or five more days to reach Wajir.

After leaving this pan, we came into an open, yellow sand country and long stretches where the trees had fallen on the ground from wind erosion, most of them dying during the prolonged drought which hit this country between 1942-5, when immense numbers of the Somalis' animals died, and wild animals as well. Vast stretches where these gnarled-looking *Commiphora* were rotted at the roots and lay stretched on the sand, as if pushed over by elephants, with not one blade of even dead grass. Then there would be the unexpected, almost startling sight of vivid green, where some moisture must still be present under the surface. Here I began to see big numbers of the liver-red reticulated giraffe again. I got out of the car and walked up to six of them, who just stood there staring at me curiously over the flat top of a 20-foot thorn. They shook their ridiculous little heads at me, with their stubs of horns, and then, with a roar of hoofs, made off. There were any number of vultures circling over this scrub. And later on I came on a bevy of them fighting over the red ribs of a lion's kill. From the crushed bones of the buck it could be seen that the hyenas had been there. We came on a Somali boy walking beside a female camel, with the skin of a camel calf that had just died. She would sniff it—and give milk.

In this country of the yellow termite hills, we came on an open plain on which hundreds of female camels were grazing. They were being watched by just a handful of small Somali boys. They came racing towards us when our car stopped on the plain, shouting.

"Do you know what they're yelling at us?" said Reece, with a smile. " 'Give us some water to drink. If you don't, may your father go to hell!' Nice little chaps, aren't they?" Reece sent one boy scampering back to the tree under which they had been sheltering, and had the Dubas fill the big wooden pot that he brought back. The grinning Somali boys took up their refrain again, shouting with great glee: "May your fathers go to hell!"

And then we came in among the wells. There are seventy wells around Wajir. These are not the five- or eighteen-man wells, such as at Marsabit and Buna. They are holes bored down through rock, from which the water is hauled by troupes of Somalis with ropes and goat-skin buckets. They stand on the rim, soaking wet themselves, and the speed with which they throw one bucket down and at the same time start to pull up a full one—all this to the tune of a new type of chant—bordered on the unbelievable. Hundreds and hundreds of camels and goats crouched in great rings under the shade of acacia thorns on this yellow desert, waiting to be called. Three camels water at a time from each trough. Walls of grey camels stood, howling impatiently, as they awaited their turn. The Somalis on the well lips were naked to the waist, their black muscles shining under the brutal sun. . . .

No more romantic setting could have been invented than

Wajir. Hundreds and hundreds of marabou storks stood, with their sacs dangling, before the whitewashed D.C.'s house, like a crowd of petitioners or waiting mourners. They hardly noticed us, just stepping to one side as our car and the big motor lorry drove through them. Thousands of camels, in grey islands, were being watered at the two major wells opposite the D.C.'s house. The air was full of their hoarse cries, the most strident yowling. . . .

"I *hate* camels!" said the D.C.'s young wife. "I loathe them . . . yelling all night!"

Reece did not discuss his D.C.'s with me. Neither shall I discuss them. But I think it can be taken as certain that a *safari* was made by this one, immediately after Reece and I left Wajir. Also that the proper sort of police guard was placed on that pan some sixty miles away. There was a feeling of tension in the air during those few days we were at Wajir, and there was a lot of talk between the P.C. and the D.C. about the activities of the Somali Youth League—the "Sewing Circle"—which was very active in this district.

CHAPTER XXIII

Dance of the Camel

WAJIR was bubbling at that moment with unmistakable signs of native unrest. This was the Somali Youth League. It is impossible to describe the character of this excitable body, except to repeat that it has nothing to do with youth. Its foremost aim is an independent Somaliland, including all the 2,000,000 Somalis that are now in French, Italian, British Somaliland, Ethiopia, as well as those 60,000 Somalis in Kenya's N.F.D. But while its moderate elements might accept a ten-year trusteeship which promised absolute Somali self-rule at the end of that time, its more unruly elements want an independent Somalia now, and, if they could get away with it, would absolutely refuse even a United Nations Trusteeship. When it is considered that 99 per cent of the Somalis are illiterate, one can only wonder what weird ideas of this world and modern times must lie inside their raw and untutored heads. What can they be thinking? A few days before I had started out on this *safari* into the N.F.D., there had been on January 11th a riot at Mogadishu, the capital of former Italian Somaliland, in which the Somalis had killed fifty-two Italians who, so it was said, had brought in pro-Italian tribesmen to make counter-demonstrations against the Somali Youth League. The Nairobi European newspapers ran the story as if it hardly concerned Kenya at all, giving it a bare half-column. Perhaps that was deliberate, for the owners and editors of Kenya's two leading European newspapers are sophisticated men, and it does not seem possible that they could fail to see how the Youth League, getting out of hand in Italian Somaliland, would soon start rioting among the Somalis at Wajir and along their own Tana River, on the border of European Kenya. Perhaps they did not want to arouse the fire-eating Kenya colonels, with their cry of "Tally ho! A-hunting we will go!"—those men with the wooden heads who are always shouting for a strong hand. Although it is also possible, even probable, that these editors did not fully realise the inseparable connections the Somalis in Kenya had with the Somali Youth League outside Kenya, so little do the affairs of the N.F.D. seem to matter in ordinary Kenya life.

All I can say is that I talked with several people of more or less importance about the Mogadishu affair, and not one of them attached any more significance to the Somali Youth League riots than if they had occurred on another planet. It was just "those damned natives"! And as there was even no wireless communication between Wajir and Garissa in the N.F.D. with Mogadishu, or with any other town in the turbulent Somaliland, every bit of news, message or warning of revolt having to go by telegram through the hands of apathetic clerks in the ordinary Post Office at Nairobi, not even Gerald Reece, the Provincial Commissioner of the N.F.D., could know, except by hearsay, chiefly picked up from friendly Somalis, and therefore unreliable, what was the latest development in a situation which affected every Somali in Kenya. All the news that we had by the time we got to Wajir was that a request by the British Military Governor of former Italian Somaliland to ban Italian processions had been turned down by the members of the visiting Four-Power Commission which was at Mogadishu (investigating Somali desires), and that the Somalis, suddenly running amok, had rushed into the houses and knifed fifty-two Italians to death —all done in about forty-five minutes. . . .

There are some 30,000 people living in the District of Wajir, but it covers a vast area, and only a mere handful of people live within the little white-walled town itself, which is hardly more than a mosque, a few shops, and the chalk-white crenellated fort which is so reminiscent of *Beau Geste*, the D.C.'s and the D.O.'s white, Arab-looking homes, the Police Post, and the residence of a P.W.D. officer who was designing new armed police posts along the frontier.

Ten thousand camels were at that moment already watering at the seventy wells around Wajir, and in all, 50,000 camels were converging upon them. But each camel would only stay there one or two days, until it got its chance to drink. Each camel takes 15 gallons in its first long sip, then rests for half an hour, weaving its lips about—those split, tough lips; it then drinks another 5 gallons. When all the camels in each clan's group have had their fill, they are then driven back into the bush again. Some of them are driven for ten days back into the sandy scrub, eating whatever they can find left uneaten, so far is their march between grass and water; then they are turned around and, for ten days, they are driven back. Twenty days in all, away from the wells. But the average time between drinks at Wajir, I was told by the camel sheiks themselves, was fourteen days. They would do this for the next three months, until the Big Rains came—that is, *if* they came. This rather explodes the Biblical myth that a camel can go seven days without water. If a female camel is getting grass to eat, they told me, it can go twenty-one days, and still give milk to a calf, without touching one drop of water. There is no grass around Wajir. The red and yellow deserts around Wajir have been made by over-grazing; even more by the sheer trampling of camels; so great has been the pressure of animals on the limited grass around these precious wells. It is only when you understand what has made these deserts that you begin to get some full comprehension of the extraordinary severity of all Somali life. The crying of the thirsty camel never ceases, day or night.

Their thirst-cry is a long-drawn roar of complaint. Thousands of them, waiting in their grey islands on the red and yellow sand, walls of waving, snake-like heads, will suddenly all wail at once. They are patient, never breaking line as they await their turn, and yet they are almost unbearably miserable. Their cry for water is a sound as if someone was prying up gigantic boards, prying out rusty nails, running a long, rough-toothed saw across a metal drum, or filing the edge of a corrugated iron roof. . . . All night long you hear them passing you in the bush: the incessant clunk-clunk of their camel bells, the high cries of their attendant drivers—"*Hay-ooo! Hay-ooo!*"—under the stars. All around the clock, morning, night and noon, they never stop; the glistening, naked-back Somalis stand on the top of the wells hauling up the water for them. And all night and all day you hear their rhythmic chant, with which, in sets of three, they throw one goat-skin bucket down into the deep well and instantly haul up another full one on the end of dripping ropes. These wells are bored through stone (by that race of eight-foot giants) and sometimes they are dangerous; their lips break and Somalis have been known to fall into them, 50 to 60 feet. With their black woolly heads and muscles glistening in the sun, they have a stirring beauty of strength and suppleness.

From our camp outside Wajir, as I lay under the moon, I heard this song and the camels crying, and realised both the poetry and the physical torture of the truth that if the Somalis live by their camels, they also live for them. And that they have no rest in their nomadic life. Nowhere on the earth have I ever seen such an indispensable partnership of man and animal.

The Somali has even been called the parasite of the camel, for everything in his life is secondary to the welfare of his herds: "without their milk he starves, and lacking their possession he ceases to be a free man."

Among the numerous camel sheiks who had come into Wajir there were two notables: Sheikh Ahamed Liban, of the Degodia, ruling some 2,000 people; Sheikh Abdi Ogle, of the Ogaden, with 1,500 followers. Dressed in their white *tobes*, with silvered daggers in their belts, they were two of the proudest, handsomest men I have ever looked at; both were ebony black. One tribe was grazing north, the other south of Wajir, and, though not supposed to be feeling at all friendly with each other, they more or less kept to their own grazing areas. It is probable that both of them knew of the other Somali robber sheiks—and may even have had a part in it themselves—who were demanding bribe money from incoming Somalis up at the pan sixty miles north of Wajir. If so, they would not have felt the least concerned about it, for that is the Somali way, the survival of the strongest. The Somalis might all join together, for the moment, to get rid of the Europeans and gain their own independence, but after that it would be each Somali tribe for itself, as it had always been. The whole Horn of Africa would be fighting for water. "One good and unanswerable reason," smiled Reece, "why one of the first things we must do before we ever think of handing over power to them is to get these water and grazing rights settled between them. We must, at least, get them used to that much law and order before we ever leave it to them to settle things." But from the quiet and dignified manner of the camel sheiks themselves, as we stood with them among the 10,000 camels at the wells, one could never have guessed that they were all not as gentle as doves together. In fact, though it was known that one or two of these very sheiks before us were prime movers in the Somali Youth League themselves, it was impossible, because of their innate good manners, to know even what they were thinking about us, so gentlemanly were they.

I had been announced beforehand as an important visitor, coming with the Provincial Commissioner, the man who ruled the entire N.F.D., to see and write about the Somalis. Sheikh Ahamed Liban had some presents for me. These were one of the beautiful red water-pots, made of light wood and skilfully bound with red leather, a delightful little light wooden head-rest, made of polished wood, and an exceptionally fine camel-bell, which rang like clear metal, made from the gnarled lebi thorn. Sheikh Abdi Ogle, of the Ogaden Somalis, said that the next evening at sunset (and how he loved it!) his Somalis would dance the Camel Dance. The beautiful little bell was stolen from me somewhere between Nairobi and Nakuru, the water-pot was too big for my limited air baggage, but the memory of that Camel Dance can never be taken from me: it was the wildest, most blood-tingling, frantic, stirring, indigenous ballet that ever came out of Africa.

Reece's indirect way of handling men, the gentle hint, very often more painful than a kick where it hurts most, was never more beautifully in evidence than the dinner he gave out at our camp to the D.C. and D.O. of Wajir that night. The chief difficulty that these overworked and understaffed administrative officers have to face up in the N.F.D. is that, in addition to handling that very specialised type of desert work—the administering of nomadic tribes, most of whose remnants you can hardly find in the bush—they also have to keep up with all the normal developments and professional material that is common to the British Colonial Officer in the normal part of Kenya colony; even with British Colonial Policy overseas, in fact. Otherwise they would make themselves liable for that one thing which is the young D.C.'s nightmare in the N.F.D.: that he will become classed as a "desert specialist" and thus restricted in his line of promotion. It is not therefore just apathy, or lack of awareness, or even the importunate pleading of lonely wives that makes them stick to their office work in the N.F.D. But while we were having some sweet Somali fresh mutton, with the invariable lime-juice, Reece said, with apparent casualness:

"Farson has been most impressed by the way that, from the roads, you never see any of the inhabitants of this country. That the only way to get into touch with them is a gruelling foot-*safari* back into the bush. . . ."

"Of course, sir. A foot-*safari* is the only way."

"Yes, that's it. Foot-*safaris* are an absolute essential. Now—eh—

"You can pick up any amount of information," Reece went on, "out on these foot-*safaris*—gossiping among the people. We've discussed it before. I've told you my own experience. One very often gets the wind of a situation, the essential hint, from talking with even a small boy. . . ."

If I have talked a great deal about the drama of Somali nomadic camel life, the chanting of the five- and twelve-man wells, the weird sensation of hearing singing far out beneath our feet at the eighteen-man dog-leg well at Buna, the sensation of seeing secretive Somalis passing you in the bush at night like grey ghosts under the stars, if I have talked of the dignity and the cruelty and the toughness of Somali life, and of that almost insane self-respect that seems to possess all desert-living Mohammedans, it is not that I have stressed these things because of the mere picturesqueness of Somali life. It is because you get a sense of rhythm from them. Our own lives, those of the Europeans, have lost that sense of rhythm—that you are living in accord with some incorporeal *rightness* of things—even in the free lives which many white men still manage to make for themselves in changing Africa. But the Somalis still have it; and as you witness it, you feel that it is a life that should be perpetuated. The next sunset, in the Camel Dance, I saw how the artistic Somalis loved and paid deference to this rhythm of their life, the genuine poetry of their existence.

During the day I had noticed, in different parts of Wajir, leaning against the white walls of the fort, strolling down the sandy street, entering the mosque, a grotesquely tall and emaciated young Somali, dressed in a blue aertex polo-shirt, with a black-and-red tartan wrapped around his snake-like waist. He had almost a decadently delicate intellectual's face, a fine-line narrow head, such as might have graced any Pharaoh's tomb, and a gollywog mop of woolly black hair more preposterous than that worn by a Fiji Islander. He looked like a Somali pansy, and probably was one. He was obviously the Director of the Ballet, and was accompanied everywhere by a group of similar pansy intellectuals, all looking almost in a swoon from the artistic mood they had thrown themselves in, and all, without a doubt, being the local extreme Left Wing, most dangerous members of the Somali Youth League. They did not have the courtesy of even the mask of good manners, as did the elder Somalis. These youths were uncouth, like all the young left-wing politicians of the present generation. These young men stared at Reece and me with undisguised dislike every time that we came upon them. Yet these were the men who were superintending the building of the sandbag dais on which Reece and the rest of us were to sit—Reece throned like a king—when they did their frenzied dance for us that night. A huge bonfire, made of entire tree trunks, was being piled up. "And yet," I said to Reece, "I have an idea that they are not going to put very much feeling into that dance. They look surly to me."

"They are. But wait till you see them come running at you with their spears. The more they like you—or are caught by the spirit of the dance—the closer they will come to taking your scalp off with their spears. It is a sort of accolade . . . salute. After they have jabbed the spear almost into your eyes, then—as a sign that they like you—they will place the flat blade on your head. You—ah—should show *no* surprise when they poke the spears at you . . . though it's difficult at times."

The red desert was thick with Somalis, several hundred of them. As the sun set the huge bonfire was lighted. One of the young Somalis from the pansy (Youth League) group began blowing on a conch shell. In a little while the Somalis began to sway. A "movement" seemed to be taking shape among them. Then someone shouted, and a screaming Somali came dashing at me with his bright spear.

I prepared myself to register a lordly indifference. But, much to my disgust, the Somali stopped short, just shook his spear at me, grinned, and walked off. He did not lay the flat of the spear-blade on my waiting head. The tall, emaciated pansy, obviously the *maître de ballet*, now rushed at Reece. But his spear just made a swallow's swoop up and over Reece's head. He did not give him the accolade. "Not got any heart in it," I said to Reece.

"Mnnnn. Doesn't look like it." The political hate was still too strong.

But now the blood-red sun had slid down beyond the far horizon, and it was flames from the roaring fire that lighted the dark faces before us. The grunts and groans from the conch-blower became more frantic. He stuffed his hand in and out of the shell with a more fierce insistence. Clusters began to coagulate among the swaying Somalis.

A peculiar bowing and backing began to characterise them. Like the swing of a ship or a marching camel. The *maître de ballet*, with his corps of pansies, began oscillating, looking over his shoulder at the members of his suite. Then, with a peculiar howl, he raised his snake-like arms high over his head, the palms bent down and fingers forward, and–I saw a *camel* begin to parade before me. It was perfect. No totem dance was ever a more complete transformation of man into the animal he was supposed to be representing. Nothing more successful could have been achieved on the stage of the Marinsky Theatre in old St. Petersburg. It was the real, living ballet. The Somalis seemed to go mad. . . . And there they danced–six of them–their long arms, like camels' necks, swaying backwards and forwards. They danced back and forth to the screaming line of the facing Somalis. Then, as if exhausted by the effort, they dropped their arms and broke formation. The thing had caught them, and from a lukewarm counterfeit of the dance they lost themselves in the various interpretations of the camel and its existence. They danced a solemn, slow movement, to the stateliness and grace of the camel. They danced to the female camel, and thanked her for her milk. By this time flames from the roaring fire of dry wood were shooting sparks, like a roaring volcano, into the night sky.

There was no longer any question of *us;* they had forgotten us. One of our Dubas, a Somali, handed his rifle to a brother, and also danced forward, like a camel. And then the old *maestro* of them all appeared. It was the Sheikh Abdi Ogle himself . . . yelling like a fiend after he had finished his own little *danse des chameaux*. He screamed so much that night, during the two hours in which we watched him, and he twisted himself in such amazing antics—for he danced, and deliriously, other dances beside that to the camel—that when I went to say good-bye to him before we drove off the next morning and thank him for this stirring performance, he had lost his voice altogether. He could only whisper to our interpreter.

He must have been made of spring-steel, for he was a spare man, well on in his fifties; and he must have danced, or hopped about, for well on two hours that night—so long that I felt even our courtesy was exhausted. I say hopped, for one of the dances was a game of sorts, in which two opponents, crouched like frogs, threw down their hands with so many fingers outstretched —a sort of odds and evens game, to "match" each other. The loser had to hop one jump nearer a line, whereupon he was captured or lost the bet, as the case may be: precisely the same game that I had seen the primitive Bushmen play over in the Kalahari Desert of unoccupied South-West Africa. The Dance of the Camel had been a thing of grace and beauty; this other dance had been for the sheer gambling devilment of it. It showed that the Somalis loved play, the fun of life. It was a dance of laughter.

As I did not want to leave behind me any feeling that I had favored either one or the other of the two biggest camel sheiks, I asked could they both come into the D.C.'s office, where I could ask them about their camels. This delighted them. This Dance to the Camel was only danced after the Big Rains, they said, as a measure of thanks to their camels, and personal joy. The children learn the dance by watching it. There are always one or two men in every tribe who hand it down. No women dance, of course. The children are taught all about the life of the camel; they have to know that in order to be able to look after camels. The *totos*, four or five years old, are taught to look after the young camels—"under supervision." Six-year-old children can take camels as far off as eight miles away from the next adult person. At eight years old the boys are detailed to take camels off in the bush, completely unattended, for long distances. They are supposed to be able to look after themselves then, and the camels, even in the hyena country. The eight-year-old boys can carry a spear. Imagine the self-assurance and independence thus given a Somali boy. And the manliness he acquires. What is expected of him! (I thought of the little goat-herd boys, who had been speared to death, and mutilated, at Marsabit.)

The camel has three cries, they said. One when giving birth; next, the "Blubble-blubble-blubble" that a male camel gives when he gets lost, or, laughed Sheikh Ahamed, "When he sees a lady camel!"; finally, the thirst-cry, which I have described. A camel will give the "lost cry" when he finds that he has got into a herd of strange camels. It is said that much of the Somali's high-strung nervousness comes because he lives so much on camel's milk, which has only one-fifth the fat content of cow's milk. When I asked them, both these sheiks agreed at once that they loved the female camel best, "although she has much the worst temper!"

They said that a camel could go thirty days without water, if there was plenty of grazing. But when I said to the D.C., "Tell them that I am going to write what they tell me. It would not do for a Somali not to tell the truth about the camel," they quickly corrected that to twenty days, saying that after that, even with grazing, the camel began to weaken, and would, unless it got water, eventually die. The minimum of camels for each family was three for each wife. As the average Somali nomad has two wives, each of whom has her "home," her own tent and grass mats, etc., that meant six camels per man.

When we left Wajir and drove out into the scrub-brush again, it seemed unusually lonely. As if I had suddenly been dropped into the desert after a night at the Opera. Such was the effect of this "civilised" side I had seen of the nomad's life.

I would love to have seen the real Dance of the Camel, out in the bush after the Big Rains, with not a white man within a hundred miles of them!

Incidentally, aside from their *Decameron* vocabulary for every act in the refinement of copulation, the Somalis have fifty words describing exactly the age, coloring and type of camel. Women and camels—the two things that interest them the most in life.

CHAPTER XXIV

Elephants and Jack Bonham

THE Tana River has the biggest concentration of elephants in all Africa. And in my experience it has the most doleful, foreboding atmosphere you will find anywhere on that sad continent. During the dry season, in February, March and April, from 5,000 to 7,000 elephants move in to the river every year from the waterless scrub-desert: elephants; and all the adjacent people, with their camels, cattle, sheep, donkeys and goats. Large numbers of the elephants have to be shot every year, to make the others afraid to come into the river. They ravage the little cultivation patches of the riverine people. But when the rains fail, the elephants simply have to come in. Poor elephants! You see how they have struggled not to. Miles before you come to the river you can easily see the desperate gougings where frightened elephants have been digging with their tusks in search of underground water. For some twenty miles before you get to the Tana, you come in through the dried lumps of elephant droppings. But unless you are deliberately hunting for them, you will seldom see an elephant. They hide by day and come down to drink only in the darkness of night. All through that bush you begin to feel the threat that imperils them.

There are bigger *herds* of elephants over in Uganda and up in the Nile *sudd*. The biggest ivory comes from along the Tana. The record is held by a Dutchman, who shot an elephant there with tusks of 173 and 168 lb. Jack Bonham, the Game Warden of the Coast, who has to shoot about seventy to eighty elephants every year along the Tana, has shot six with tusks of over 160 lb. each. He has shot over 700 elephants up to date, nearly all in thick bush, to whom he usually walks up to within 20 or 30 feet to get the deadly brain-shot. If that is done right, the elephant just sinks to its knees without even a sigh. The Tana also has the best poisoners in Africa; their arrows can make an elephant drop dead within less than half a mile from where he has had one shot into him. Jack Bonham was ambushed by one of these gangs of ivory-poachers; their arrows missed him, but killed one of his gun-bearers.

Getting down to the Tana from Wajir, we were descending all the time, and had to cross some of the worst rivers that I have ever encountered. These were dry rivers, even dead. We always seemed to come to the worst of them during the hours of darkness. There it was . . . a wandering, sandy snake; coming from nowhere, going nowhere. They all had steep banks, down which we had carefully to slide our cars; then soft sands that gripped the tires like a vise. On some of the worst of these river beds, previous travellers had laid corduroy roads of thorn trunks, trying to make a traverse across them, probably just after some rainy season. These trunks, now dry, had broken, splintered. We maneuvered the cars so as to let their headlights illuminate these snakes of sand. Reece, torch in hand, walked back and forth across the sands, trying to find out where any hard places might remain. He guided the truck to them. We invariably stuck. Then, with all the boys straining at what seemed an immovable object, and much shouting, the heavy vehicle was got into motion again. I would not have believed it had I not seen it done.

Everything seemed stunned by the heat and the drought in this lower country. Birds wouldn't even take flight as we came up to them. We came to a place called Habaswein ("Much Dust"), just a few Somali shops and a post for a couple of stupefied Kenya police. A mile or so to the east of it, on a skyline straight as if drawn along a ruler, was a little Somali school, run by a *hadji* who had been to Mecca recently. We found the pupils there, tiny Somali boys, chanting by rote the inscriptions from the Koran they were reading from their camelboards. They probably understood not one word of it, but, when older, would live by the hygiene which that great book lays down. The young *hadji* had great dignity, but a sick and worried expression.

"He is probably finding it difficult to live up to his father's reputation," said Reece, who had known the old *hadji*. "This one, so I am told, has told his followers around here to join the 'Sewing Circle.' Wait a minute, and I'll get it out of him."

They gave us tea and bananas, and discussed the murder of Mahatma Gandhi. "Why," the *hadji* and some of the school's *mullahs* asked us, "should anybody want to murder a man like that? A holy man!" This was strange, from Mohammedans—lamenting the death of a Hindu; and especially after the Englishman we had met at Moyale, who (what a man!) told us that Gandhi "damned well got what he had coming to him!" This made us like these Somali *mullahs*. But then came the other side:

"He's an ingenious little fellow," Reece said to me as we drove away. "Do you know how he explained it? He said that, when the other Somalis had asked his advice about whether or not to join the Youth League, he had to say to them: 'If we don't join it, it may turn out to be a very good thing, and then we lose. If we do join it, then we are all in trouble together. We will probably get into trouble, anyway. So join it. Otherwise, you might miss something good.' Logical," said Reece with a philosophic smile; "but it doesn't help to keep the peace in this neighborhood."

The Mohammedans among our boys and Dubas had all walked up and reverently kissed the young *hadji's* hand. They had been awed by the sight of him. I had never seen them so silent and meditative as when we drove off along the green *vlei* beside which the mud school was located. Hundreds of duck and crane and storks rose from its marshy edges.

We could almost feel the elephants as we came in towards the Tana River the next morning. The thick scrub brush there seemed to reek of their tragedy. Wherever one looked there were these balls of elephant dung, several of them still damp and fresh. But we never saw one elephant. We came on the river where it was flowing around a big bend. The dom palms were weeping along its banks. On a sand bar a light-green crocodile was asleep in the hot sun. There was not a sound: just the river moving along . . . slow, as if suffering, trying to make its way to the sea before the sands exhausted it. It was brown now, barely moving; but when the Big Rains broke it would turn blood red, washing down thousands of tons of good soil from the Kenya highlands. At that time, its color can be seen thirty miles out to sea in the Indian Ocean. And you know, when you see it, that that man was right who said: "Africa is bleeding to death."

Shortly this side of Garissa we came on some low, sandy banks, on which thousands of white goats, sheep and thirsty camels were watering. The camels had just folded up on the edge, and stuck their long snake-like necks out into the river. Somali women and young girls were washing their clothes in the water. Silence and the feeling of an immense relief pervaded the scene. We had made the circuit of the N.F.D., and come back to the greatest treasure it contains—water.

Garissa was just the sun-baked, mud-and-wattle huts of the D.C.'s offices and three flat brick bungalows with wire sleeping cages built on top: the D.C.'s and the D.O.'s, and the house of a "meat buyer"; for it is here that the Somalis sell butcher's meat, cattle and sheep that are trekked to Mombasa. At that moment, because of the trouble seething underground of the Somali Youth League, there were three British officers and a hundred black soldiers of the King's African Rifles camped on the Tana's bank, about a half-mile lower down. There were also three American big-game expeditions, out after elephant, somewhere along the river. A suspension bridge which crosses the river here, was now in the process of repair, having been nearly swept away by the big floods which followed the 1942-5 drought. On the other side of the bridge was "European" Kenya . . . after another two days' drive through the scrub.

It was about the most miserable, depressing habitation I had come on in the entire N.F.D. The D.C. talked as if he also felt like that. In the sweltering interior of the screened brick bungalow he gave Reece the latest "dope" on the "Sewing Circle." One Youth League agitator was in the lock-up, and would be produced when Reece wanted him. He was a particularly "bad hat"; and there was a feeling of tension among the Garissa Somalis because of his imprisonment. Checking up to see what support he might expect if things went wrong, the D.C. had made the uncomfortable discovery that twelve out of his eighteen police were *local* Somalis. "Absolutely useless," said Reece. "Even worse. You can't expect them to fire on their own people.

. . . Not Somalis. . . . What a mess!" This was worse than at Wajir. I don't think that even a wireless transmitter existed at Garissa. (I may be wrong.) Garissa was entirely cut off from any communication except by road with the outer world. That, said Reece angrily, was a thing which must be remedied at once; wireless transmission with Nairobi and Mogadishu, etc., must be established immediately. "This is typical," he said, "of the unpreparedness of our race. We are usually fairly good in a crisis, but we are no good at averting that crisis. Just no blasted *foresight!*"

Our camp here was quite a fair distance away from the river and its mosquitoes, and the Dubas did sentry-go all day and night. There were two Kenya police on guard duty before the D.C.'s and the D.O.'s brick bungalows at night, guarding the stairways that led up to their sleeping cages. While I was dressing the next morning, I saw Reece talking to an ostrich. They were standing face to face, the ostrich, more than naked—all his fine feathers had been pulled out by the K.A.R. soldiery—and Reece, who had been shaving, naked from the waist up. "Tell me," he said as he stood there with the lathered brush; "it's got such an extraordinary expression, this thing, I don't know whether it's normal. Do ostriches *always* look so sad?" The bird's head snapped forward and it swallowed a bar of Lifebuoy soap. "*That* ought to give him a good purge," said Reece.

Later, the too-friendly ostrich strode over to the Dubas' camp, took one peck, and swallowed a "boy's" whole plate of *posho*. At the trial of the agitator, the ostrich threw that highly-strung Somali intellectual into confusion by striding over and sitting down by Reece's chair, listening, with its inimical head-light eyes, to the mass of evasions that this trapped trouble-maker of the Youth League was trying to get Reece to accept.

The Somali was wearing just a snow-white robe, which he wrapped defiantly over the lower part of his face, and he stood like a pillar of salt, staring at Reece with the most challenging hate in his eyes. He had a lean, fanatic's face, very intelligent, such as you will often see bent over the microscope in any research laboratory, or on a religious fanatic. He looked half-starved, yet smouldering with force, as if a volcano was seething inside him. He was black as night, concealed as much as possible within his white sheet—even his folded arms were inside it—answered in monosyllables and looked as if he was trying to give us the knowledge that we could do what we liked with his corporal body, because we had that in our hands, but that we could never, never, never touch what was going on inside him; that was sacred, a thing we could not defile. In a word, he looked like a martyr.

Was he one? At that time the Somali Youth League had not been declared an illegal body at Garissa (it is now), and Reece, in taking evidence, stressed the point time and again that he was *not* punishing this man because he was a member of it. "We must make that clear to him," he said to the listening District Officer. So, step by step, Reece led the Somali's admissions along until they built up this case against him. He had told the natives in the district not to pay the 10*s.* poll tax; he had preached that the D.C. had no authority over them; that all births, marriages, quarrels, etc., must come before the Somali elders themselves for judgment, as it had been before the British came. All this case was written down by Reece in long-hand as he got the Somali's answers to his questions. Then he said to the two Dubas standing either side of the member of the "Sewing Circle": "Take him away."

At this last minute, the Somali turned to try to say something to Reece, to protest; but Reece looked at him as if he was just not there at all. He was placed in the waiting motor-lorry and taken back to jail. Reece then wrote out the order by which this agitator was deported to the wild Turkana district of the N.F.D. "Tell him he can take his wives or anything he wants along with him," he said to the D.C. "He'll probably be there for some time."

But there was no satisfaction about it, not the least feeling that justice had been done. On the contrary, we all knew that a new piece had been added to the East African jigsaw puzzle: that the man before us, acting as a patriot to his people, though perhaps misguided, had got himself enmeshed in the conflicting gears of high policy in London, of colonial policy, of the violently antagonistic views about post-war retrocession of the former Italian colonies, of a British sentimental support of the immediately unobtainable idea of a united Somalia and even with what was best for the Africans themselves. He was no criminal.

The three American big game expeditions along the Tana when I was there had some interesting people among them. One had "one of those startling young American girls!" as she was described to me, who had completely put the wind up the young English Police Inspector. She had turned up on his veranda—in a Mohammedan country—dressed in nothing but the scantiest panties and the ghost of a brassière. He had dashed into his back room and locked the door. "Coward!" enviously declared the other three white men at Garissa as they told me the story.

The District Commissioner at Garissa does not get much conversation; and that afternoon, as he and I went down the silent river in a slender native dug-out, with the unchanging green walls of its jungled banks closing us in, he sang, in a half-mad fashion, some of the limericks that previous and equally desperate D.C.'s had composed about their past. For sheer, excremental obscenity they were the limit. "Pretty awful, aren't they?" he grinned after he sang me the last effort (his own). "Well . . . *that's* what we think of Garissa."

There was nothing on the river at all. We saw one native honey-hunter in his dug-out, paddling up a backwater, a few miserable grass huts, and the vivid green of rice cultivation by the riverine natives in one or two spots; otherwise, just this everlasting wall of jungle; not even a colored flower to break the monotony; one mile after another all the same. It goes on this way, between its walls of jungle, getting narrower and narrower—as most evaporating rivers in East Africa do—until it finally manages to reach the Indian Ocean 200 miles away. In the rainy season, of course, it would be a roaring flood, sweeping banks, even bridges, away. Now it was just like watching someone's blood draining out of him—which it was. Since I was down there, I have heard that there has been a tremendous loss of Somali animals, cattle and sheep in the big drought that I had witnessed starting. Jack Bonham, when he came over for a drink from where he had pitched camp that night, said that he looked forward with dread to the number of elephant he would probably have to shoot this year—to keep them away from the Tana.

I have since had a letter from him:

> I had a pretty grim experience yesterday when I got mixed up with the biggest herd of elephant I have ever seen in the Coast Area. I reckon there were about four hundred of them at least. (I know you get much bigger herds in Uganda, Congo, etc.) I was getting into position for a shot when they *all* started trumpeting, screaming, etc. Never in my life have I heard such a fear-making noise. I have heard four or five cows screaming, but never a bunch like this. My boys were paralysed, and I was as bad, and nobody could call us exactly soft. I did *not* shoot and I was damned glad to get out of it.
>
> Maybe I'm getting "sissy," or perhaps my nerve is going, but I don't want to hear *that* again. . . .

In the same letter he said that "I'm chasing some troublesome elephant and also some poachers. I would *much* prefer to shoot the latter than the former, but King G. doesn't approve of his subjects (*sic*) being treated too roughly." (Jack was alluding either to Indian ivory-buyers or the natives with their poisoned arrows.) "I shot a big bull yesterday and dug no less than six old poisoned arrowheads out of him. He had survived them all right, but they must have cost him a lot of agony. . . ."

So much for Jack Bonham. That night at Garissa, he said to me, "The best poison in Africa is made down the river here," and told me how he had once actually seen two of the riverine natives, such as I had seen once or twice from the dug-out that day, walk up to within 20 feet of an elephant, which only ran 120 yards after they shot their poisoned arrow into him—"and weren't they surprised when I stepped out of the bushes and caught them red-handed!"

He had come up to Garissa in pursuit of poachers; but that last night, as we sat on the roof of the D.C.'s brick-oven of a house, he was more concerned with the gloomy feeling of incipient revolt that one could feel along the river. "What happens on an occasion like this," he said angrily, "is that *nothing* happens—until some wretched officer is murdered out on *safari*. Then the Brass Hats wake up." Bonham's opinion of official far-sightedness was very low; he had been an Intelligence Officer himself. "And if they don't shift *him* [the Somali agitator] out of here tomorrow . . . before the rest of these Somalis can get time to think it over, what they ought to do, then all I can say is: We're just asking for it!"

A footnote can be added to this Somali Youth League. It was originally started by an Englishman, a local "Lawrence," of sorts, who was anxious to help the Somalis along the road to modern civilisation. He had founded what he thought was a cultural organisation. And at that time (1946) the British Foreign Office policy was to work for a united Somalia, under British auspices. British officers, as I have said, become almost sentimental about Somalis, and this Youth League had the enthusiastic support of several individual officers. It was very small at first, having about only 100 members, but it soon got out of hand; and the Somali Youth League now—which is violently opposing the return of any sort of mandate to Italy over former Italian Somaliland—claims to have 93,000 full members and over 300,000 active supporters. In June, 1948, it was declared an illegal organisation at Garissa.

The "Sewing Circle" is now almost as wild as the wind which swept up the Tana River my last night there; a freak wind, occurring about the same number of hours after sunset every evening, owing to the cooling of the desert. A dead, hot silence, in which I was lying under my blanket wondering whether I would have the energy to kick it off or not, and then the whole world seemed flying past me, like the witch's ride on her broomstick. . . . Now I had to hang on to my blanket to see that it was not blown away from me; the tent behind me snapped and flapped with sharp, muffled reports at its guy-ropes; the acacia trees began to whine and bend over. . . . Then everything was hot, still and silent again.

They are like that, they tell me, the mad outbursts of the fanatical Somalis, who, under their "Mad Mullahs," have swept just like that wild wind through the Horn of Africa. The one great difference between them is, of course, that you never know when the Somali tempest will sweep the land.

CHAPTER XXV

Along the Coast

THE 300-mile road from Nairobi to the Coast is an unmitigated horror. The worst comment that could be made about it is that it runs straight beside the camps of two big field units of the Royal Engineers, who tolerate it! Just above Mackinnon Road I found an old friend of mine, his car turned upside down, its top smashed in; his arm in a sling—broken, he thought—while a scared African houseboy and a child's *ayah* stood there dumbly as he, his wife, and their two unharmed children watched an Army motor-cycle dispatch-rider try to patch some exploded tires so that the car, or what was left of it, could get on its way again. The car had hit the chatter-bumps of this grim road, which are like a corrugated iron roof, and just refused to steer any more. "If we slow down to under forty miles an hour on our bikes," growled the sweating dispatch-rider, "we've had it! There's someone busted up along this here — road every day."

Mackinnon Road, fifty to sixty miles west of Mombasa, where thousands of British troops, African laborers and Indian artisans, are clearing the game- and fly-filled bush to make way for the construction of seventy warehouses, each with a floor-space half as big as a football field, will accommodate war materials evacuated from India, North Africa and the Middle East. With Egypt and Palestine gone, Kenya will now become Britain's pivotal position in the imperial scheme of things. Britain's old life-line of the Suez Canal is now highly vulnerable, will be practically useless in another war. Kenya is far enough away from potential areas of conflict to be fairly secure. Yet it is near enough to the Middle East to provide a secondary base for troops, ships, aircraft and supplies. There has been a great deal of talk about this strategic stronghold of Mackinnon Road; it is still just a nightmare of huts in a choking scrub infested with tsetse-fly, in a climate that would stifle a lizard. Nevertheless, when the final settlement is made of the disposition of the former Italian colonies in Africa, it is almost certain that some 70,000 British troops will be stationed at Mackinnon Road. Britain, as has well been said, is in a "power crisis." The broad change in strategic long-term planning, which calls for supplementing her Mediterranean life-line with a new defence belt across the middle of Africa just north of the Equator, means that Kenya will be the easternmost peg of a line which stretches across Africa to the West African colonies, with their valuable reserves of man-power. Nigeria has a population of over 20,000,000 natives. And—a vital reason why England wants (and will almost certainly get) the trusteeship of Cyrenaica, and will postpone as long as possible any withdrawal from the Anglo-Egyptian Sudan—Nairobi will be the hub of a line of aerodromes from London–Malta–El Adam–Wadi Halfa–Khartoum to West and South African aerodromes. These are overwhelming reasons—make no mistake about it!—why Kenya will always remain a White Man's Country.

This fits in perfectly with the United States' increasing interest in the security of the Near and Middle East, particularly in Greece, Turkey and Iran: the determination to support the integrity and independence of these people against Soviet pressure. The British have already made it plain that they would not agree to Libya being returned to Italy. But if Libya or the Sudan or both should pass out of British control, then an alternative air route to Kenya exists in the chain of air bases built by the United States during the war in Africa: Bathurst, Bolama, the British base at Freetown, the big seaplane base at Fisherman's Lake; Accra—then the British air-lifeline from Accra–Maiduguri–Nairobi. As the military base of this strategic web, Mackinnon will soon become the biggest concentration of British war material and troops overseas. And as 1,400 of the 4,000 Italian artisans which the British are now importing into Kenya will be stationed at Mackinnon Road, the Colony can now look forward confidently to soon having a good road from Nairobi to Mombasa.

Mombasa has already been declared a naval base, and will have a cruiser and some smaller warships stationed there. Its harbor, Kilindini, is the finest on the entire east coast of Africa. It is a beautiful and spacious anchorage, three miles long by from three-quarters to two miles wide; smoking today with the stacks of cargo steamers, with deep water quays capable of berthing the *Ile de France*, and with a narrow-mouthed harbor capable of shielding the largest convoys that could put to sea.

But the real glory of Mombasa lies in the Arab life in the dhows of the Old Port, on the other side of the island; as colorful, spicy and virile a life as you will find in all the Seven Seas. Having seen some of the warlike tribes of Africa, I had always wondered how the Arab slave-traders could penetrate hundreds of miles inland and then make a steady business of bringing their native captives out to the coast. I had no idea of the toughness of the seafaring Arab. Mombasa is noted for many things, but for me it will always be the memory of watching the big dhows from Arabia, the Persian Gulf, India, wearing around off English Point at dawn, their immense sails billowing in the rose-red sunrise; then watching them come in directly below the balcony of the Provincial Commissioner's house, in which we were staying; hearing the harsh chanting of their crews, seeing the unbelievable sight of Arab sailors pulling themselves up the rigging, hand over hand, without once using their legs to get a grip on the thick rope. That was a physical toughness I had never seen before. Toughness—and courtesy; for even in this first glimpse I got of the seagoing Arab's fierce physical fitness, I also saw his good manners: as each new dhow came in, all the other dhows at anchor in the Old Port dipped their red flags in salute. As the British Resident himself subsequently told me at Zanzibar: "It is the Arabs who can teach us how to be civil."

There is an air of ease among the races of Mombasa Island that is markedly different from the tenseness one feels in Nairobi and in the townships of the White Highlands. Perhaps it is altitude; tempers are undeniably testier when you live above 5,000 feet. Or it may be just that the British and the Arabs, the Indians and the Africans, have lived together longer at Mombasa than they have anywhere else, and that they have learned how to get on with each other. Anyhow, it is there. Mombasa is one of the pleasantest towns I have found in British Africa. The European homes are out on the cool headland of Old Point, white-walled, among scented frangipani, and flamboyants flaunting every fiery color under the tropic sun. Purple bougainvillaea drape the giant baobab trees. Off to the left, the shoal water of English Point reaches out into the green Indian Ocean, mottled with turquoise and emerald pools, with ragged little native dugouts fishing on the edge of the coral reef. The slow waves break, sending a white surf across the brilliant colors. The narrow streets of the old Arab quarter are stone-paved, with doors of panelled teak and brass studs, some of them centuries old. A desperate, four-foot turtle lies on his back in the fish market, trying to turn himself over with his parrot-like beak; I watched him for three days and saw the increasing agony in his desperate, bloodshot eyes. He epitomised for me the pain, and the scant attention that is paid to it, which lies just under the skin of all African life. The main streets of Mombasa are flanked by modern buildings, so full of Indian shops and signs that you might think yourself in Bombay. Sharp-breasted, saucy little native girls stroll in from the coconut groves on the mainland, dressed in nothing but a kilt of grass. Hundreds of dhows lie off the buff walls of Fort Jesus, and their cargoes of dried shark, salt, rugs, dates, burlap bags of frankincense—the smells, the stinks, the shouting, the sweat pouring from the black skins of half-naked Africans as they trot up and down between warehouse and dhow, the tough, vital Arab seamen strolling about, those from Oman wearing the gilded J-shaped daggers in their belts—all these make a memory that you will never forget. There is Romance in the very smells of Mombasa. In Piggot's Square there is a big grey building whose sign says that it is "Glen's House." It was built by an Arab in memory of his favorite dog. You can dine at night on the tiled terrace of the Mombasa Club, the tall coconut palms standing sentinel, reflecting the glow of your red-shaded table lamp, the women in low-necked dresses and the men in tropic white, and still feel a lingering wisp of the days when Smith, Mackenzie & Co. (which imposing firm still owns this Club) was all that there was of the Kenya that is today—and of even before that; when Burton and Speke set out from their house overlooking the dhows in the Old Port to discover the head waters of the Nile and the great lakes. The dhows have not changed by so much as one rope since their day.

In all this apparent peace I sat all one morning on the cool balcony of the Provincial Commissioner's house listening to A. B. Patel, the one outstanding Indian in Kenya public life who has not allowed his religion to be made his politics. Mr. Patel is a Hindu; for ten years he has represented Mombasa for the Indians on the Kenya Legislative Council, and by a unanimous vote both Hindus and Mohammedans elected him to be their representative on the recently-formed East African Central Assembly of Kenya, Tanganyika and Uganda. Mr. Patel, a moderate, and one of the few Hindus I have met in my life who could put his philosophy in such a way that an Occidental could understand it, described how the conflicting politics of India and Pakistan had crossed the Indian Ocean, and were threatening to make a schism in East African Indian life. The Hindus outnumber the Mohammedans in Kenya, but the Mohammedans of the Aga Khan's sect are far more disciplined, better organised, than the Hindus, backed as they are by all the enormous wealth and political sagacity of that great Indian statesman. The moderates on both the Mohammedan and the Hindu side would like to have the communal difference which had just caused such massacres in India itself kept out of Indian Kenya life, and have the same delegates represent the Indians as a unit in the Kenya legislature. But the bulk of the Mohammedans have been demanding a separate election of Moslem delegates to the Legislative Council: "And the extremists of both sides will prevent the moderates among us from reaching any agreement," sighed Mr. Patel. When I asked him was it true that there had been threats, off stage, of personal violence if the moderates did not support the extremists' views, Mr. Patel looked uncomfortable, and I did not pursue the subject. The one thing that the Indian leaders in East Africa fear most of all is a split between themselves. But as India itself settles down, the Indians in Kenya will also presumably make their peace.

The dhow-builders of the Persian Gulf believe they were sending ships to this anchorage on the African coast over 3,000 years ago. A book, *Periplus of the Erythraean Sea,* written by a

Greek seaman at that time, shows that the Greeks and the Romans were trading with Mombasa in A.D. 80. The Arabs began to build a big city here in the seventh century. A visit to East Africa by Pedro de Covilhão in 1486 led to the Portuguese connection with the coast, and the 264 years' fighting between Portugal and Mombasa, and between Arab and Arab, which ended the Portuguese occupancy in 1750. During this time it can be said that Mombasa held the record for being the most sacked, besieged, burnt, captured and razed of probably any town in the world. The native name for Mombasa is *Mvita,* meaning war; as well it might be. It is also the name of the new cruiser which is going to be stationed there.

Vasco da Gama took Mombasa in 1498; in 1593 the Portuguese began to build Fort Jesus, which is still standing today, now a prison. In 1696 the Arabs began one siege of Mombasa which lasted thirty-three months; they captured Fort Jesus and killed the survivors—just two days before the relief expedition arrived from Portugal, which, upon seeing the Arab flag flying, then withdrew. In 1750 the Imans and Sultans of Oman in Arabia finally drove the Portuguese out, though they are still hanging on at the delightful little island of Mozambique and in Portuguese East Africa to this day. The British first appeared on the Mombasa scene in 1823, when H.M.S. *Barraconta* touched there, under Captain Vidal, and was besought by its besieged inhabitants, then in the midst of an Arab war, to let them fly the British flag against the threat of that great ruler, Seyyid Said, the cynic who asserted, "Mullahs, women and horses can never be called good until they are dead." This first request to come under the British was refused. But the following March, Captain Owen, H.M.S. *Leven,* arrived, found the fort exchanging shots with an investing Arab force, with an improvised Union Jack of its own proudly flying, and then gave them the official right to fly the British flag. The British, H.M.S. sloops *Rifleman* and *Nassau,* had to fire on Fort Jesus in 1875, when a rebellion broke out against the Sultan of Zanzibar. But that was the last time. In 1896 the British began to build the railway inland to reach Lake Victoria; ostensibly to suppress the slave trade, with, as a slight side issue, the intention to give Britain control of the head waters of the Nile; from which date it can be said that

Kenya really started. So recent is the British colonisation that as late as 1901, when the railway reached the great lake, there were only thirteen settlers in what are now known as the White Highlands.

During all these centuries, just as they are doing today—and with practically the same rig—the great dhows with their driving lateen sails were flying on the winds of the north-east monsoon to the coast of Africa, trading there for a few months to pick up their cargo—gold, ivory and slaves, in the old days; mangrove poles, coffee and sugar, in these less romantic times—then sailing back to the ports of Arabia and India on the winds of the south-west monsoon. To be exact: the north-north-east monsoon blows uninterruptedly from December to February; the south-south-west blows from April to September. Mombasa is 1,600 miles from Aden, 2,100 from Muscat, and 2,500 in a straight line from Bombay. So steady and dependable are these trade winds that a dhow may sail from Africa to India without once wearing around. (A dhow does not come about.) In the old days the Arab dhow-masters navigated by the stars; today they use sextant and compass. They are the most skilful sailors of some of the finest ships afloat. The dhows being built at Kuwait on the Persian Gulf today are the last big sailing ships being built anywhere in the world. They average around 130 to 150 tons, but some run up to 200. Dates used to be their main cargo for the westward run, and they are rated in that capacity; a package of dates weighs 180 lb., and a big dhow can easily carry 3,000 of these. These beautiful ships, with practically no mechanical appliances in them, mark the end of the age of the sail at sea, though their day is a long way from being over.

When the dhow season is on, as many as 250 may be anchored in the Old Port of Mombasa at the same time. The bulk will be Somali dhows, coastal trading craft. But the most beautiful and bigger will be ocean-going dhows from Arabia and India. When you see them beached at low tide, as you can at the far end of the inner harbor at Zanzibar, where they do most of their caulking and repairs, you will be astonished by their graceful lines. These abnormally heavy ships, planked with Malabar teak, preserved with a lavish coating of fish oil, have entering and leaving lines that must be as sweet to the water as those of any racing yacht. But once aboard them, and you see the depth from their rail to the heavy deck, masts that are over a yard through at the step, and the unbelievable weight of the heavy spar which raises their immense lateen sail—larger in spread than a tennis court, or so they seem—you are appalled by the amount of sheer muscle that must be exercised in sailing them. A dhow has no machinery except her capstan, though some are now commencing to have engines put in them. You would think it would be beyond human strength to handle these craft; but once you walk the deck of a big dhow and see the figures of its crew, you cease to wonder about that: men who look almost as hard as the teak itself; Negroid many of them, the descendants of former slaves, shaven-headed like the eunuchs in old tales of Arabia; wild-haired Baluchis from the fighting hill tribes of India; men drawn from all that untamed, lost-world bit of coast which fringes the Arabian Sea to Karachi, big-knuckled, seafaring Arabs, who made it a business, setting up towns for that purpose, to castrate Africans for their harems. As fiercely physical a lot of men as ever put to sea.

The dhow-masters, on the other hand, are aristocrats to their slender finger-tips: delicately built men who look as if they have never done a day's manual labor in all their lives, and very likely have not; men with an immense pride and formal dignity. The Liwali, Sheikh Mbarak Ali, who represents the Arabs of the Coast in the Kenya legislature, told my wife and myself that one of the big dhow-masters in the harbor wanted us to come out and have coffee with him. We soon saw that it was going to be an occasion. All morning we saw the long-boats from the two biggest dhows racing each other about the Old Port in preparation for the ceremony, for that was what it was. I had seen the dhow previously, rowing under her stern to admire her beautiful carvings. She was a *baggala,* which means that she had a high-pooped stern that was almost an exact replica of the ships of Vasco da Gama. The Arabs copied these sterns from the world-roving Portuguese, even to the carved scroll-work, ornate false windows and quarter-galleries. These *baggalas* are the most expensive and beautiful dhows. A *boom,* which is sharp at both ends, is the more modern, less decorative craft. I had been on board one of these *booms* with a young Arab official of the Port, and, with him to translate for me, had spent a pleasant hour or two, chatting with these good-natured, witty "Sons of Sinbad," as Commander Alan Villiers (that great seaman) affectionately called them. I had listened politely (but very doubtfully) while the grinning cook assured me that shark-fin, when properly served, is as tasty a dish as I could ever hope to eat: the foredeck was littered with these hard, dried grey shark-fins with a hunk of yellow meat on them. I had met the ship's cat; not quite a thoroughbred Persian pussy, I am afraid. And I had put my hand against the great teak mast and looked up; they lean slightly forward. And the wonder returned how any man could even get a grip on those monstrous shrouds, up which he pulled himself hand over hand. There was one dhow that I did not board! She was a Somali dhow from up the coast, still in quarantine. I was rowed alongside so that I could watch a young English doctor from the port examine the seams of the crew's garments for lice . . . precaution against bubonic plague.

On this occasion I had been rowed about the harbor in a captain's pinnace, which every dhow carries in addition to her long-boat. A hold-boat is a thing of beauty, and holds nineteen men. When a heavy dhow is moved from place to place in the harbor, or, as is frequently the case, she is towed out to the open sea, this is done by the long-boat. Sixteen piratical-looking ruffians are pulling at the oars—these have peculiar little blades shaped like the ace of spades, but painted blue and white or as the owner fancies. They strike the water with a unity that would evoke the envy of a university crew. To cox the stroke, one man sits on the gunwale at the stern, squealing away on a bell-mouthed flute; another beats, howling like a fiend, on an Arab drum. The whole harbor finds its blood whipped up by their savage syncopation. The man with the drum yells until you would think his neck muscles must snap. There is a flag at the bow; and usually the dhow-master's youngest son sits up there, his white turban end flapping in the wind. It is a wild scene. It must, one thinks, be the absolute ultimate of din.

But not a bit of it. When the two dhows' long-boats raced to the landing stairs of the fish-market to take us and our party aboard that afternoon, they let their oars trail when they were some forty yards off the shore, the long-boats coming in on their own momentum, jumped to their seats, and there, jumping from side to side, flinging their hands to right and to left—as they were "throwing the wind away"—clapping their hard hands with a harsh syncopation, they shouted the triumphal chanty of a dhow which has reached its destination. It must have been terrifying for the black slaves who were waiting to be taken aboard as cargo, to be shipped to the cities and harems of Arabia.

This dhow was a 200-tonner and had been thirty-five days from India, carrying tiles from Mangalore. The skipper and his two elder sons received us at the top of the landing stage. They wore spotless white robes and turbans. They took us aft, up to the high poop, covered with its rich Persian rugs and shaded by an awning. They conversed with great ease and sophistication. Black servants bowed from the waist as they held out brass trays bearing the inevitable egg-sized cups of thick coffee. We had a sweet of almonds and a sticky, saffron-colored paste (which gave me gippy tummy) that we scooped up with our fingers. Then perfumed water was poured and a clean towel given to each one of us so that we might wash our hands. Silver-filigree braziers were then held before us so that we might sweep the smoke of the burning incense to our nostrils with our cupped hands. It was all the height of decorum, with my side, I know, feeling anxious that we should not fail to show both good manners and appreciation or that we should appear to be too effusive, which would have been far worse.

A dhow has a small cabin beneath the poop, but it is seldom used, except as a store-room. The crew sleep on deck. The captain and his sons or officers sleep out on their Persian rugs, under the high stars. This strikes me as being about the very essence of the romance of life at sea: to lie at night staring up at the brilliant constellations of the heavens; to watch the dawn rise each day as your great ship—a dhow can easily log twelve knots—leaves her foaming white wake across the Arabian Sea. What a song of sensual delight it must be to sail all your life in ships such as these! The dhow-master stood with uplifted hand to bid us good-bye, and I felt acute envy as I answered his farewell wave. But these were the vessels of the cruellest trade that the world has ever known.

The prosperity of Arab life on the coast of Africa ended

with the slave trade. It has been slowly disintegrating ever since. Once this trip for ten miles inland, from Mombasa to Lamu (still nominally under the rule of the Sultan of Zanzibar, to whom the British pay an annual rent of £10,000), was the granary of Arabia. Its craftsmen excelled in the arts of wood-carving and silver-work. There were orange groves, and cities like Gedi; songs, where today there is only jungle and the monkeys bark. Sheikh Mbarak Ali, a cultured gentleman, mourns this passing, this steady decay of the former Arab arts. He is compiling a history of Mombasa, digging deep into Swahili poetry, where he has found many things that are not yet recorded in history books. He has come on the name of Hercules and mention of the Crusades. He is pursuing clues that he has discovered in *Periplus of the Erythraean Sea.* In some of the old songs, he told me, he has already come on some of the most romantic bits of unrecorded history. He handed me an old yellowed manuscript.

This was the story of Sheikh Mbarak bin Rashid bin Salem al-Mazrui, who rebelled against the rule of the Sultan of Zanzibar in 1871. He had taken to the bush. The Liwali (the Governor) of the Sultan of Zanzibar had laid seige to Mombasa, sealing the city off so that not one of its inhabitants could escape to the mainland to warn Sheikh Mbarak that fresh troops had been brought from the islands of Pemba and Zanzibar to hunt him down. But in Mombasa at that time there happened to be two companies of Arabian dancers, travelling actors, who by tradition, war or no war, were allowed to move about freely. They would, of course, be the bearers of no message; that was their code of honor. They danced every night in Mombasa, and the songs that they sang were *extempore*, as is often the Arab custom, composed on the spot. The present Liwali, Sheikh Mbarak Ali, smiled slyly as he told me:

"Now, it just happened that in Mombasa at that time was Suud bin Said al-Maamiry, the famous and revered Swahili poet. He was a staunch friend of Mbarak Ali. So he made up a song. He suggested that the dancers sing it. It ran like this:

The throngs of the Wizard's followers have donned their beaded cords!
So, wait ye now the coming of their strange-garbed demon hordes!
O Wizard, be prepared for those who leap high on their swords!

The song was a smash hit, said the present Liwali. Written by such a great poet! The Arabian dancers went singing it up the coast. Sheikh Mbarak heard it. He guessed its meaning, Suud's hidden message. For Wizard, he read the Governor; for followers, soldiers; for beaded cords, he read the bandoliers of Sultan Mohammed's soldiery. He fled inland and fortified himself on a hill. He was saved.

"But when my history is finished," sighed the present Liwali as he put on his red fez to walk about the streets of the Arab quarter with me, "I wonder if I can get anyone to publish it? Mombasa is such a long way off from London and New York! And who will be interested . . . when we Arabs of the Coast do not seem to be even interested in ourselves!"

CHAPTER XXVI

Malindi; Fish Goggling

SOME sixty miles north of Mombasa is Malindi, the Melind of Milton's *Paradise Lost*. It is an open roadstead, a green sea caught in a crescent of coral sand, which for several centuries was the anchorage for the first dhows to reach Africa from Arabia. Today two stone penises, looking strangely like blind lighthouses, and the grey ruins of what were once imposing masonry are all that remain of the former life which once thrived there. Modern Malindi is just the D.C.'s office; a couple of excellent hotels, for this is now a bathing resort, to which frayed Kenyans flock at the tail-end of the trying dry season; and, at the lower end of the crescent, as curious a collection of native dugouts as you will find west of Polynesia. These are splinter-like outrigger canoes, so narrow that the buttocks of a European could not pass between their gunwales, with outboards like skis, fixed at the end of arched spars. They look like monster water-spiders when you see them each dawn, putting out for the coral reefs. A couple of miles below where they are customarily beached, on the sea edge of a choking scrub, on a point whose coral sand is as white and soft as talcum powder, where the monsoon sighs through the horse-tails of the leafless casuarina trees, stands the thatched hut of Jack Bonham, Game Warden of the Coast, the man who had shot over 700 elephants by the time we went to "goggle" with him.

Goggling for the fantastic fishes that inhabit the reefs off the Kenya coast is now a sport which has seized that colony by the ears. It has all the excitements of exploring another world. Here in the rock pools of sapphire and clearest emerald, pulling your way down past submarine coral, which grows in plates, mushrooms, cauliflower convolutions and antlers like staghorn, where the grasses on the sea floor become the forests, you come face to face with fishes whose shape and coloring are really impossible to describe. It is literal to say that you do come face to face, for, flitting past these coral heads in the most absurd and grotesque manner, these little fish will swim right up to your face and sit there, seemingly suspended in mid-air, while they satisfy their curiosity. And you can watch schools of these dazzle-striped fish maneuvering in the same pool with you who act as if you were not there. They are a harvest of color and extravagant design.

One fish that I pursued for several days in the pools of Barracuda Reef, about a mile off-shore, seemed different in design and color every time I went down to look at him. And so far as his color was concerned, he very likely was changing. The eight sketches that I made of him, immediately I had to come up for air and swam back to the boat, were all different, and the final one was almost like the first. It was interesting to see how my note-book records my difficulty in describing him. This fish, about 9 inches long, looked like a sole swimming upright. His body was electric blue; his soft dorsal fin, extending from head to tail, was daffodil yellow; his under fin, from head to tail, was snow white; his head was ebony black—and his tail was barred with alternating, arrow-shaped strips of black and white. I don't know whether this one was good to eat or not. I was far more anxious to get him down on paper than into a pan. A large number of these painted beauties of the coral reefs make excellent eating, but others—and you would think that their eerie colors would be sufficient warning—are poisonous. Some have poisonous roes, and an unidentified number are poisonous only at certain times of the year. As the natives are out on these coral reefs all day, it is best to begin by eating only those that they eat. The mainstay—until you get to know the others—can be the trusty old painted wrasse, such as you find off the coast of Britain.

It is quite a sight to get up and see the red dawn over the white, paste-like sand of Casuarina Point, see the splinter-like dugouts sailing out to the reef, and then watch the pools of the inshore coral take on their brilliant emerald in the shallows, darkening to brown over the patches of short seaweed, with the white breakers foaming a mile off-shore out of a cobalt sea. You see the black men standing up in the water, walking along, a good mile out in the Indian Ocean. Some of them have spears and are looking for fish, but most are searching the coral for lobsters and crayfish.

Along the water-edge, as the short waves sparkle inland, scamper thousands of little crabs—sidewise—one arm crooked like a fiddler's elbow, pink and white, their eyes projecting upward on the tips of spikes. The leafless casuarina sigh softly in the faint breeze. And this is the time when you must do your goggling. For about noon the wind gets up, destroying completely the translucent, air-like quality of the pools; and from then to long after midnight you can lie under your thatch of grass mats, listening to the song of the surf. There is nothing else to do. The water is like lukewarm tea. The pools, those miniature worlds of mountains and ravines, are best when they are about two or three fathoms deep. But on the edge of the reef, where it shelves down into dark and unknown depths, you will see schools of large horse-mackerel swimming past, the big grouper, which most people on the reefs fear more than sharks, sharks, and the barracuda, which forms the mainstay—and the stink—in the Arab fish markets.

The Japanese taught the East Coast Africans the use of the goggle. A pair of native goggles cut out of hard wood, with lenses similar to flying goggles, are in my opinion vastly preferable to the 6-inch glass plate with the choking rubber suction cup that you pull over your entire face, such as is used in Mediterranean goggling. For those who have never goggled, it may be well to explain that when you put one of these masks on your face you can see under water for a considerable distance as clearly as in the open air. An ingenious Swede at Malindi, with an ordinary gas-mask and a flexible pipe to a surface float, has made himself able to breathe under water and walk about on the bottom. Jack Bonham, a fanatic goggler, was wandering around this way, some fathoms down, when a big grouper swam up to him with the intention to attack. When it opened its huge mouth to bite, Jack stuck his spring-gun right down into the grouper's mouth. This so startled the big fish that it gave a backward jerk and shoved off. Jack, who usually walked up to within 20 or 30 feet of an elephant in thick bush to get the deadly brain shot, told me: "When I saw that damn big fish staring at me, I was just paralysed with fright!"

And Archie Ritchie, who flew down from Nairobi to goggle with us, described the sensation of watching one monstrous fish "looming up on me . . . getting bigger, and *bigger* . . . and BIGGER! . . . And then I came up!"

Bonham, who doesn't smoke, can stay under water so long that you think he must have drowned. This is where the fanaticism comes in. One of the strangest, most laughable things I saw in my days on the reef, when I was swimming down past some plate coral, was Jack Bonham down there, trying to pull himself under a big overhanging plate, his feet kicking, a stream of bubbles coming up from him, and he and a big fish almost nose to nose. The fish was staring at Bonham, refusing to come out, and Bonham could just not get a shot at him. I could not stay to see the finish. But a couple of minutes later the amphibious Bonham shot up, gasping, a whacking big fish dangling from his lanyard. The long spring-gun, with its perforated barrel, fires a steel harpoon which has a barb capped on its tip; this comes off when a fish is hit, and, as it is attached to its own separate lanyard, you play the fish on that. That day when we were diving on the edge of the reef to watch the horse-mackerel and some big sharks swimming past, Jack put his barb into one fish that he dimly saw, a fish so big that it went off, snapping the strong lanyard as if it were a cobweb. We had no idea what sort of fish it was. Bonham usually got a dozen or so 8- to 9-inch fish for our lunch. It was pathetic to see the way their brilliant colors faded as soon as they were taken out into the open air. For that reason, you can only get their true coloring by observing them in the water; and as they change color almost instantly with that of the bottom or their surroundings, that makes your study so complicated that it is impossible to say what is the normal color of any fish.

There are fish off Malindi with horns on their heads; some have spines that can cut you to the bone with a mere flip of their tail; and there is a fish, called the Moorish idol, with a long streaming dorsal, chocolate, edged with an iridescent

Prussian blue, so bright that it looks almost like color in motion. The dead shape of this fish, just the beauty of its *grotesquerie*, is frequently used in commercial design. All these fish leave you wondering what flight of fancy Nature could have been in when she created them. These colors could not be adaptations for any protective purpose, for I have swum in pools where the schools of fish combined every color in the spectrum; shoals of tiny ones, pearl grey, with vivid little scarlet saddles, that were as bright and flashing as freshly minted coins. Nothing in the coral or the seaweed around them would let them camouflage themselves in that. But I have swum over a ray, lying flat on the sand bottom, the color of sand itself, which did not reveal its presence until I reached down and made a strong swirl in the water over him. It was only about 2½ feet from wing to wing tip, but it had a spiked tail over 4 feet long—a poisonous spike that I might easily have stepped on had I not spotted the ray first as I was drifting along face-down, staring at the bottom. On the coral reefs you wear tennis sneakers (rope-soled shoes are best), so as not to be poisoned by the coral. Some months previously Archie Ritchie cut his leg on this coral and had to be operated on in hospital to let the infection out.

It is now known that the fish's iridescent hues are caused by crystals of a substance called guanin, and appear under the fish's skin as a by-product, because Nature, when she designed the fish, had not, in the words of Brian Curtis, "yet got around to working out a really good waste-disposal system." In his grand book (the most all-embracing book about fish—and life—that I have ever read), *The Life Story of the Fish: His Morals and Manners,* he tells how fish can change colors by an ingenious set of mechanisms known as chromatophores. These contain pigment and are little, sac-like cells, shaped like many-armed stars, which are scattered throughout the skin in great numbers. Each chromatophore contains only one color—red, orange, yellow or black—and it is the amount of color exposed to view, in combination with other colors, which determines the color pattern at any moment. Some fishes are able to stimulate different colors, blues, greens and purples, which, he says, they would never meet under normal conditions. "Fish," he says in his fascinating book (which will catch any fisherman who picks it up), "can boast a brilliance, an iridescence, a variety of pattern, and an ability to change color, unequalled by any other group in the animal world." Copley, in his pamphlet, *Some Fishes of the Coral Reef*, answers the question: Do fish sleep? "It is interesting to know that some of these fish actually sleep—even lie on their sides—on pockets of sand in or about the lumps of coral."

It is another world, like entering a fourth dimension, to swim down into the aquariums of the painted coral. Everything you see is seen so differently. And it is a fantastic world whose beauty defies description. Many of these fish in the East African reefs have not yet been identified. My sapphire-blue-daffodil-yellow upright "sole" that I nearly burst my lungs trying to identify is not given in Copley's work; nor did I see any name or cast made of it in the Coryndon Museum in Nairobi. If my Latin had been up to it, I would have given it my own name, and thus won immortality.

Jack Bonham's hut was mud and wattle, thatched with grass mats made from the dom palms laid over heavy mangrove poles. For companions he had an old dog, dopey and covered with sores that he had contracted from various bush fevers and tsetse-fly bites. But he was still anxious to hunt, as was a little mongoose, Jeep. The old hound slept all day; but little Jeep was almost too companionable. He got his name from the cry he made, "Jeep! Jeep! Jeep!"—a cheery little sound. It was a great sight to see Jeep crack an egg against the wall. He turned around and stood over the egg with his tail to the wall. Then he gave a quick jump, a backward flip of his forelegs, and shot the egg backward against the wall through his hind legs. Given a ping-pong ball, which Jack kept for that purpose, Jeep almost went crazy. He just could not understand why that "egg" shot out and away from him. He would chase it and try again and again. These things help the hot days pass. . . . Introducing himself to me, Jeep shot up the leg of the khaki slacks I was wearing when I came to stay with Jack, and fastened his tiny claws in an open hole in the bone of my leg that I have been carrying about these odd thirty years. I had to dash out of my trousers to get rid of him. But not Jeep! In the torpid afternoon, when the wind was blowing from the sultry sea and I was trying to doze, I heard a faint little "Jeep-jeep-jeep" . . . and there he was, curled up at the small of my back. He was immune to all snubs. He always travels with Jack on his elephant *safaris*, and will chase the big lorry frantically down the road if he thinks he is being left behind.

Our talks out on Casuarina Point, under the tropic moon, were as good as the goggling. And quite as fantastic. We said things that would not bear inspection by daylight. I suppose that Archie Ritchie must have seen as much of wild animals and their habitat as any man living: strange scenes, luring you on to further thoughts, just a little beyond the frontier of the mind. It was discussing these feelings that are beyond the frontier of the explicable that we had our most interesting adventures in those talks. Even in the night we could see the white line of the surf breaking a mile off shore. . . . The life that Archie Ritchie and Jack Bonham and some of the great men among the big game hunters have lived makes mystics out of most before they end up. With the professional hunter, this combination of the artist-adventurer and the killer is not so paradoxical or rare as one might think. They must have had something of the poet in them to make them come to Africa and follow such a life. And it is this sensitivity which enables them to understand the undertones, the nuances of the African scene, and the ways and the whims of the wild animals they are either out to shoot or protect. And so our talks on those moonlit nights were also in another world, beyond the pavement of city streets.

It is a life worth living. Meals eaten in the hot middle day, when the shadows are black upon the sand, and you have only a *sarong* wrapped around you, letting the soft tropic wind feel like velvet on your bare skin, almost drug you with contented laziness. But Jack Bonham knows little rest. His camp on Casuarina Point is the base from which he does his game-warden's work; and there is a jungle of almost impenetrable scrub and desert east and west of the Tana River, almost as large as England, which is hardly controlled at all. It is full of ivory-poachers. Most of these are natives, using poisoned arrows. So it is not only a charging elephant that Jack Bonham might have to contend with. Among the dozen or so black boys in his camp was one slender, smiling youth, now acting as Jack's houseboy, who, only a few years before, had been one of a party which had ambushed Jack Bonham. Their poisoned arrows missed Jack, but one hit his African gun-bearer, who died quickly. Jack and the other Africans caught two of the party; this boy and his sister. Jack kept them for several months as hostages, saying: "When your old man comes in and gives himself up for trying to murder me, I'll let you go." The old native never did show up, of course; and Jack finally turned his captives loose. A year later this boy came into his camp one morning and asked for a job. He got it. Jack shot a bull elephant by moonlight the night after we left him.

CHAPTER XXVII

The Ruins of Gedi; the Sultan of Zanzibar

THIS book ends on the Coast and over in Zanzibar, which is proper; for that is where "it all began." The killing of the big elephant was symbolic. A plantation-owner at Kilifi, a few miles down the coast, had written the D.C. at Malindi that the elephants were ravaging his coconut groves; one had knocked down over fifty trees the previous night. Would Jack Bonham please come along and attend to it? Jack, not altogether pleased with the peremptory tone of the note, and at considerable personal risk, had ambushed the old elephant as it emerged from the thick brush into the moonlight. The plantation-owner would now get more copra. Jack, with some distaste, had done his official job, and a fine old bull elephant which had been roaming this coast long before the British ever thought of settling there was no more. White civilisation was thus further consolidated. And so it will go on, all over Africa; the appearance of the European has made man and the wild animals ecologically incompatible.

A few miles below Malindi, deep in the almost impenetrable tangle of a leafy green jungle, pillared by the grey trunks of monstrous baobab trees, lie the ruins of Gedi. No one yet knows how old the city is, or who built it. No one even knows its real name; Gedi is a name that has been given to it. It is not marked on the maps of Vasco da Gama, who touched this coast at Malindi in 1498. It had been deserted by then. Grey stone columns today tower into a leafy stillness; the grey arms of great trees have crawled through its masonry, tumbling some walls, holding others in position. Most of the Great Mosque has been pushed over by just this growth of trees alone. "Never, anywhere in all the world," said the archaeologist who had come from India to dig at Gedi, "have I ever seen Nature in such a violent mood!" The walls of this dead and forgotten city are about two miles in circumference, and we walked with him around the greater part of his excavations. In passing, he said that he thought it was an Arab city of the eleventh century; he could not be sure. But of one thing he was certain: another entire city lay underneath. Who had built that city, no one could even guess. It was also pure guess-work to say why Gedi had been deserted. One explanation would be that the River Sabaki, which now flows into the sea north of Malindi, is shown on the maps of Vasco da Gama to have once flowed close to Gedi. The river had shifted its course, as rivers often do in Africa, the water table which supplied the wells of Gedi had fallen, and its people had been forced to move away. But then, why was Gedi already deserted when Vasco da Gama arrived at Malindi? The immense well which once supplied the Great Mosque itself is now bone-dry and is rather a frightening aperture. Some 70 feet deep and over 20 feet in diameter, it is a great, open-mouthed dangerous shaft going down into the earth, with its ground-level mouth bisected by the outer wall of the mosque itself. The deduction from that is that the women of the town could fill their water jars without entering the mosque, and in time of war those inside the mosque could get their water supply without having to venture outside its walls. But who lived here? What type of Arab? For Gedi, some six miles from the sea, could never have been a trading post.

Gedi, alone among the early Arab cities built on the coast of Africa, was not built immediately on the sea, but on a high coral outcrop, which originally gave it a commanding view over the country around it. That, and the indication of sumptuousness in the architecture of the Great Mosque, the harems and the huge stone baths, tend to the belief that Gedi was a city where the wealthy Arabs, the Nabobs, came to enjoy their peaceful retirement. Set in the grey walls are still plates of beautiful green celadon. Pottery of Ming blue and white and great Canton jars from China have been found among the rubble; Far Eastern wares from Siam, Annam and perhaps Japan; the green, yellow and blue glazed wares of the Arab world; and a latter debris of unglazed pottery of the local Africans. After the Arabs had departed, perhaps centuries after, superstitious natives came to propitiate the spirits of Gedi. Their recent offerings can still be found in a little shrine, held from falling by the entwining limbs of a grey tree. And at the bottom of the great well two skeletons have been recently found; native hunters, presumably, who had fallen into that 70-foot smooth-walled cylinder of stone before it had been cleared of the surrounding jungle.

The stones and the tree trunks in this green, sun-speckled leafiness are so much the same color that it is hard to tell them apart. This adds to the ghostliness of these ruins, which seem animate with the spirits of the departed. And there are little domestic touches which provoke a plaintive wondering. The steps of the great bath: you wonder what scenes the Sultan had enacted there for his delight. The intimate little touch of a dwelling with its stone larder still intact. There is evidence of great luxury in one group of masonry. Here, on the walls of the harem, you see script in Persian and the scratched sketches, like etchings, which the girls have made. One is the perfect drawing of a dhow, exact in every detail; alike today as it was some 500 or 1,000 years ago. It is a wall that seems to speak. Gedi, in this steaming jungle, is alive with spirits—and not only those of the departed!

The archaeologist said, with, I felt, more literalness in his voice than he cared to admit: "Do you know . . . sometimes when I come in here from the road in the early morning, I feel as if Something had moved away from me! Something that is *waiting*." (I thought of the story of Ambrose Bierce, *The Damned Thing*, which made the footsteps that could be seen running through the field of wheat, yet which was Itself invisible; the Thing that seized his shooting companion and bit through his throat.) The archaeologist smiled, as if apologising: "I really do, you know. It gives me the creepiest feeling sometimes. I feel that if I should turn around quickly—!"

I smiled. "I'd leave that arch alone," I suggested. "If you tamper with that it will get you—that Thing you speak about."

"But I can't do that, you know. I am an archaeologist."

We left it at that. Gedi, standing in its green silence, still refuses to disclose who first cut its graceful stones and set those green plates of celadon in its walls and arches; and who carved the dhow, with such accuracy, on its harem walls? What ship brought her to Africa? For my part, I would like to have these questions remain unanswered. I would like Gedi to be left in peace. But that, of course, is too much to ask for. We will leave nothing alone.

By luck, we missed our places in the big commercial plane to Zanzibar, and were able to get a lift in a little three-seater private plane. Its owner was a young Scot, with the gash from a previous aeroplane crash across his cheek. He and his wife (who was now down with malaria) had been flying about Africa, looking down on it, to see if they could find some place which looked as if it might be an ideal place to live. There was a nice Elizabethan touch in the unconventional boldness of such a survey. He services his own plane, and the minute he settled down at the controls, I saw that he was one—one of that race which for a long time held all the world's speed records, for land, sea and air; the people who produced the Rolls-Royce, the *Queen Mary, Queen Elizabeth;* who built the eight-gunned Spitfire (and that was no accident); who arrived at radar; the people who know not only how to invent and build such things, but, as they have shown in many a war, speed or endurance contest, that they know how to handle them. The handy British!

This inquisitive man flew down low over the coast so that he would not miss having a good look at even this unliveable part of steaming Africa. Occasionally he flew the plane with the joy-stick clasped between his bare knees, while he circled to take a photograph; or when, reaching into a pocket of the instrument board, with its "No smoking" sign, he took out a cigarette and lighted it. It was as casual a craft as one could imagine. From the air the blues and greens along the shore exhibited almost poisonous colors, arsenic greens and sulphate blues. A yellowish road would run miles before it ended in the buildings of a sisal or coconut plantation. Little toadstools of native fishing villages occasionally fringed the shore. And always, ever forming, the emerging coral reefs. Some of them had already become islands, with just the beginning of vegetation on them. And when we saw an immense coral head below the surface out to sea, he would bank, fly out to have a good look at that. The island of Pemba, lying under its pall of grey rain clouds, passed off to port. We circled around three immense fishes we saw gamboling along on the surface: too small for whales, too big for sharks. And then—Zanzibar.

It was not the low, white tropic town I had thought I would see. I had not expected these high buff and grey buildings along its waterfront. But I shall never forget that first sight of it, coming on it from the air: the floating forest made by the dhows' masts, the haphazard splatter of dun-colored buildings, and the immense green cover of coconut palms which clothe the island. I had come to Zanzibar with one major purpose: I wanted to see its Sultan. I had heard so much about His Highness, Seyyid Sir Khalifa bin Harub, G.B.E., K.C.M.G., that in my own mind he had already become a legend. Too good to be true, this wise and kindly old ruler, who seemed to have stepped straight out of *The Arabian Nights*. "Oh, he's a perfect poppet!" had exclaimed the adoring wife of one Provincial Commissioner when I told her my intentions. I was not disappointed. Seyyid Sir Khalifa bin Harub is unquestionably one of the true rewards of travel.

He received us in his audience chamber, an old gentleman, with greying beard, appraising brown eyes, with as witty a turn of talk as ever made an exhaustively hot morning not only bearable, but delightful. Zanzibar's damp heat has killed many a European. That is why its buildings are so high, so that its few European, and the higher strata of its Arab, inhabitants could live, eat and sleep as far up as they could get from the ground. The Sultan placed us so that we could enjoy the faint breath of air that flowed slowly through the top floor of his palace. He raised one delicate hand and smiled: "I am sorry that you should have come to Zanzibar at such a time. Because even I—who live here!—find it hot. I think that this is the hottest day I have known"—he paused—"for thirty years." ("Ah!" I wanted to say, "if only you had been here when our roses were in bloom.") But he saw our smile, and chuckled.

He was dressed in a black robe with only the faintest trace of gold thread along its lapels, his only mark of rank. There were several Arab dignitaries awaiting audience out on the tiled balcony of the palace with far more gold braid. I had come to him with a reputation, kindly enlarged by Sir Vincent Glenday, the British Resident, which led our talk to be almost entirely about boats. The Sultan had been told about how my wife and I had sailed our little 26-foot yawl, in 1925, across Europe from the North to the Black Sea. He is a passionate yachtsman, and still sails his own 30-foot Marconi-rig racer. The half-model of it was on the wall of his audience chamber. He smiled as we returned to our places again, after we had discussed his yacht's fine lines.

"Once, when I was a very, very little boy," he said, again holding up that delicate hand, "my father gave me a boat. A little boat. And I sailed her"—he nodded toward the harbor of Zanzibar—"out there. I was very happy. But some of the older Arabs, they came to my father: 'What are you trying to do?' they asked my father. 'Are you trying to get *rid* of him?' " (The Arab mind is not unused to the idea of forcibly removing a successor.) The Sultan sighed: "And so my father came to me: 'You must give up your boat,' he said. 'You must give it to an Englishman.' 'But why, Father?' 'You must not ask me why. You must give up your boat.' "

The Sultan waited until we had expressed our condolences. Then he nodded solemnly. "One morning," he said, pointing to the window by his side, "my father came to me, and he said: 'Look!' I looked . . . and there was a *big* boat! [I think he said two masts.] 'That is your *new* boat,' said my father."

I smiled. "He didn't want you to sail alone? You had to have a crew with this one, of course?"

He nodded with mock despair. "Yes, yes. . . . I was forced to take a crew." Then, quickly: "But that one"—pointing to the half-model on the wall—"I sail her every day when the breeze is fine. Sometimes to Pemba. . . ."

A black servant in white robe and scarlet sleeveless jacket appeared, and backed out. The Sultan led us into his private apartments to have tea with the Sultana. She was born in Arabia, of a noble family, and the little cakes she had served us were such as those she had eaten as a child in her own country. They had a little tang that somehow tasted of a foreign country. More servants came in in their attractive gold, scarlet and snow-white livery; the tea things were removed, and coffee was brought in. As I have said, it was a sweltering morning; my white drill was sticking to me like a bathing suit. "But this is a special cake!" smiled the old Sultan when he saw me about to refuse. And that too was good. Then silver braziers were brought in, smoking with incense; and the servants backed from the room again. His Highness talked about yachts, and then the great beauty of the Arabian dhow. I wanted nothing better. I had not come to him to talk politics. The British Resident himself had told me how wise were the suggestions of this hereditary Arabian ruler in the councils of state. And Zanzibar, from my brief impressions, was as contented an island as I have ever been on. It is only fifty-four miles in length, with an area of about 640 square miles, holding about a quarter of a million inhabitants. An air of peace pervades it. There is no hotel at Zanzibar. You live on the high top floor of a building provided by the Residency, and eat your meals at the English Club. And when, or if, a hotel is ever built it will be open to people of every color. The Sultan will see to that.

The beauty of Zanzibar comes at sunset. It is the golden-green glow that filters through the tall grey trunks of the coconut palms, gilding the feathery clove trees. These have now been struck by a disease called "sudden death"; some parasite that kills them in a night. A team of British experts is now working to arrest the pest. They hope to find a parasitic insect that will destroy the ant which, they think, is killing the clove tree. Somewhat similar to the way U.S. experts stopped the black citrus fly's first invasion of Cuba by importing a wasp from Malaya whose larvae hatched inside the citrus fly's larvae and devoured them. The scientists had been hoping to do this by placing a parasite, the Magi Moto, or "Hot Water," ant on the Zanzibar clove trees. They then, after some six months, made the startling discovery that the Magi Moto was already there—it was the real culprit. Now what parasite will kill the Magi Moto ant?

Zanzibar's other scene of striking beauty is the harbor on a still sunset. If you stand by the Fish Market, rich with the smells of dried shark and the reeking barracuda, dripping their yellow oil into the stone gutters that run with waste, you will see at the far end of the placid harbor, dhows beached on the yellow sands before the house in which David Livingstone lived.

Someone had the unfortunate idea of building an annex to it. But look westward. . . .

The masts and hulls of hundreds of dhows will meet your eye. Arab captains who have been ashore shopping, their henna-red beards crimsoned by the sun, are being rowed back to their ships in little pinnaces. You hear the sound of caulking-mallets. Black men, glistening with sweat and the oil of fish that they have been carrying on their heads, trot past you with another load. The sky is a pale robin's-egg blue with a few rose-colored clouds floating lightly. Where have you seen that sky before? A scene in Venice? Yes, this is a Canaletto.

The Kenya Government, with its invariable generosity, chartered a special plane to fly us from Zanzibar to Mombasa, so that we might catch our Viking plane back to England. This was another little three-seater, which came in with a cloudburst. There is no tarmac or cement airstrip on the 'drome at Zanzibar. We stood there, gloomily, while the rain and wind bent the coconut palms.

"Ready?" said its youngish pilot.

"In *this?*"

He grinned. "If we don't get off now we may have to wait here for days. This 'drome will be unusable in a couple of minutes."

We got in.

I have known one or two scaring take-offs, but this one was quite scary enough for me. He warmed her up, tested the switches, and opened her out. The rain blinded us completely. I knew her tail was up and we were thudding along. Then the thuds ceased: we were airborne. A coconut tree zipped beneath us. We climbed through the clouds, and Zanzibar had vanished beneath their pall. It was just as if it had never been there. Clutching the joy-stick with his bare knees, the pilot took a packet of cigarettes from the pocket of the instrument board, marked "No smoking," and handed me one. We lit up. We headed out to sea and across to the coast of Africa, the Englishman at the controls.

He, too, was symbolic. His self-reliant usefulness. I thought as I sat beside him, looking down on that sultry coast, that if more young men like him would come to Africa, love Africa—

and become interested, not just in their own lives, but in making a co-operative life with the African and the Indian—that some wonderful things might lie ahead. But, as I have shown, it is not the young men who are coming out any more. There will be a further handful of settlers on new farms in Kenya and Tanganyika; a big influx, undoubtedly, into the mines of Tanganyika and the two Rhodesias, and into the steel mills. But the *land* development of East Africa from now on, I think, will be by such big planned economies as the vast sisal and tea estates (run by paid managers), and by such Government-sponsored enterprises as the Overseas Food Corporation. On this, the Tanganyika figures are highly interesting. The total area of the Territory is some 342,706 square miles, of which the area alienated for non-native settlement is only 2,885 square miles. That gives no true picture of the European settlement, however, for the greater part of Tanganyika is unproductive. In terms of the present productive area of the Territory, there are at present some 6,334,000 acres under cultivation by both indigenous and non-indigenous inhabitants, of which non-native cultivation covers only 1,846,278 acres. This gives some idea of the considerable importance of native African holdings. But now a further 2,555,000 acres—of relatively unproductive land—has been set aside for the Overseas Food Corporation. In other words, the land area about to be developed by the Groundnut Scheme far exceeds all the present European cultivation in Tanganyika. This is an immense project, with immense risks, which began very badly; but in the long run it may turn out to be the very school in which some of the most important lessons of modern Africa will be learned. It cannot succeed unless it learns these lessons; and if it applies them, as it is beginning to do—to announce that most of its food products must first go to the native African, for one example—then it could be said that a gigantic laboratory has been established to work out an equable, co-operative partnership of black and white man.

Kenya, with its high proportion of farmer-settlers, most of them keenly aware that the problems of Kenya must be solved inside Kenya—and on the land—is another laboratory. In its intellectual capacity to solve the social problems, it is unquestionably the most important of the two. If these two territories, with their immense native populations, 7,000,000 and 5,000,000, cannot find some answers to the problems caused by the African's inexorably increasing birth-rate, who can? South Africa, with the high proportion of over 2,372,000 whites to 7,805,000 black men, is already facing a color crisis of alarming proportions; although few will admit it. Segregation, if correctly defined, is just a desperate attempt to quarantine the black man. This will mean an eruption some day.

It is my opinion that in these two territories, Kenya and Tanganyika, lies the last chance in Africa for the working out of a truly representative civilisation in which the black man and the white man can live on terms of peace, co-operation, and something like equality of opportunity. The Indians in East Africa need no one to look after them.